MASS MEDIA IN
SUB-SAHARAN AFRICA

AFRICA

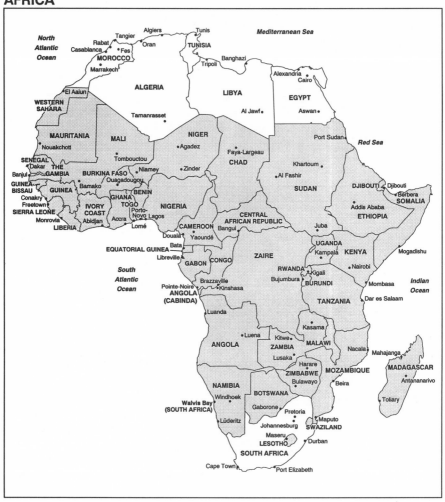

MASS MEDIA IN SUB-SAHARAN AFRICA

Louise M. Bourgault

Indiana University Press

Bloomington and Indianapolis

The paper used in this publication meets the minimum require-
ments of American National Standard for Information Sciences—
Permanence of Paper for Printed Library Materials, ANSI
Z39.48-1984.

Manufactured in the United States of America

Library of Congress Cataloging-in-Publication Data

Bourgault, Louise Manon.
    Mass media in sub-Saharan Africa / Louise M. Bourgault.
        p.   cm.
    Includes bibliographical references and index.
    ISBN 0-253-31250-7. — ISBN 0-253-20938-2 (pbk.)
    1. Mass media—Africa, Sub-Saharan.   I. Title.
P92.A46B68   1995
302.23'0967—dc20   94-27829

1 2 3 4 5 00 99 98 97 96 95

for Neil

Contents

Acknowledgments

I WISH TO thank all of the persons with whom I have worked in the mass media in sub-Saharan Africa, persons who shared their frustrations and their pain, their humanity and their optimism, their time and their insights. I wish them well. It is my fondest hope that the perspectives and suggestions provided by this outsider may land on fertile soils in the new and changing African media scene.

I am grateful to Jasmer Singh Narag of Media Development Consultants, Kano, Nigeria, and James Murray of American Mediaworks, Athens, Ohio. Over the years, both of these individuals have been particularly supportive of my efforts and have shared with me their keen penchant for social analysis.

I also wish to thank Northern Michigan University for granting me the sabbatical leave needed to prepare this manuscript. This work has also been supported in part by a Faculty Research Grant and a Peter White Scholar's Award, both from NMU. For these, I am also grateful.

I am indebted to Perrin Fenske, director of NMU's Office of Research Development, for his consistent encouragement with this project, and for his office's assistance, including that of Carol Etton, in the production of the final manuscript. Veronica Varney was also helpful in typing portions of the work.

Jacqueline Greising, Michael Strahan, and Judith Myler of NMU's Olsen Library deserve mention for their dogged help in locating particularly obscure reference material. Student assistants Travis Ashbrook and Alison Crockett were also helpful in tracking down some of the sources used in this volume.

Finally, I acknowledge the many contributions of my spouse, Neil Cumberlidge, to this volume. During the last 18 months he has edited many drafts of this manuscript, offered much editorial advice and support, served as my in-house computer expert, and generally endured my obsession with this project. To him I am especially grateful.

It is perhaps fitting to mention at this juncture that the course of rapid change in sub-Saharan Africa, however sometimes beneficial to the citizenry of the continent, has often worked to undermine my best efforts to keep this book current. In the final phase of preparation, I have made a concerted effort to incorporate the latest changes in media and politics on the continent. But given the pace of unfolding political drama in Africa, this has not been easy. I have done my best. Nevertheless, I take full responsibility for the inevitable oversights.

Marquette, Michigan
May 1994

Introduction

As an american graduate student of mass communication in the 1970s, I was initially inspired by the works of Wilbur Schramm, Daniel Lerner, Everett Rogers, et al., on the power mass media could have for promoting positive change in the developing world. I was spellbound by the promise mass media appeared to offer for the advancement of both development and democracy.

Intrigued by these prospects, I volunteered in 1973 with the United Nations Volunteers to work in the now renowned Educational Television Project (*Projet Télé-Scolaire*) of Côte d'Ivoire. That experience turned out for me to be both exhilarating and disappointing. It was exciting because the project seemed to offer so much potential for promoting education in Africa. Ivorian children were indeed learning more and performing better in school as a result of televised education. But the project was equally disappointing because it seemed to generate so much cynicism. Naively perhaps, I had expected the staff, composed roughly of 250 Ivorians and 250 expatriates during the time of my stay (1973–75), to be as fired up about development as were the theorists I had read in graduate school. Sadly, I discovered, the project staff were not. For most of them, it seemed, working in the *Projet Télé-Scolaire* was just another job, a post in the civil service for the Ivorians, an assignment in *la Coopération Française* for the expatriates. I wondered why the day-to-day reality of this and other similar projects so rarely appeared in the works of those who wrote so optimistically about mass communication in developing nations.

At the end of my two year stay in Côte d'Ivoire, I still believed in the power of media for positive change, but I was convinced there was something amiss with the way media were being harnessed to carry out this good work in the developing world. I determined I needed to learn more about the media and its application to African problems. Thus began for me a 20-year odyssey into the study of African societies and the role of media in their development.

My odyssey took me through a doctoral program in Mass Communication and African Studies at Ohio University, and to Kano, Nigeria, where I taught Mass Communication at Bayero University. Later I worked as a private consultant training Nigerian media personnel to develop skills in print, radio, and television operations. Throughout my four-year stay in that West African country, from 1980 to 1984, I continued to observe the media, to consume it, and to work on the training of prospective and active media operatives.

Some years later, I was invited to work again in the developing world with the United States Information Agency (USIA), first in Tunisia, and then in Haiti in 1986. Later with the USIA, I traveled on assignment as a visiting media specialist to a host of Black African nations: to Madagascar, Rwanda, Tanzania, and Chad in 1987; to Zaire, the Central African Republic, and Uganda in 1990; and to the Republics of Benin and Nigeria in 1992.

With the United States Agency for International Development (USAID), I worked in Swaziland in 1987; in Liberia in 1988–89; and in Rwanda in 1992. And in 1993, I served as an election monitor in the Congo's second round of legislative elections. In between work and study, I have traveled informally to some twenty other nations on the African continent since 1973.

Off and on over the last twenty years, I have been perplexed by the product that I have found in African newspapers and on African radio and television. And I have often been surprised by the behavior of African media professionals. I have often wondered what unseen forces mold their motives and actions. I have always made observations, checked them with African colleagues, and continually tried to refine my thinking about the way the media are organized in Black Africa, about the nature of the media's work, and about the persons who carry it out. Each time I have returned from an assignment connected with the mass media in sub-Saharan Africa, I have come away with fresh insights and new questions regarding the problems besetting the African media and the people who work to put the media out for the public. After each trip, I have pursued new angles of inquiry attempting to fit together the many pieces of the puzzle which would explain the particular configurations of the Black African media. And each time I have interacted with the African media, I have noticed, along with differences, many similarities as I travel from country to country. But every time I have traveled to the continent, I have come away concerned with the lack of accounts in the literature of day-to-day or *lived reality* of the mass media in sub-Saharan Africa.

My academic background combines training as a social scientist in mass communications with anthropology and African studies. It has sensitized me to the broader social, political, and cultural contexts within which media institutions and systems operate, and the way these factors color both the content and the organization of the media in sub-Saharan Africa. Long-term subventions within sub-Saharan media organizations, together with my academic training, have clarified for me the imponderable complexity of forces shaping the African media. It is this mix of difficulties which I have sought to unravel in this volume.

I have long pondered over how best to convey the immediate reality of sub-Saharan media organization, production, and consumption. It is these accounts of "lived reality" which have seemed problematic, for their appearance is unusual in the traditional literature in the field of international mass communication. But I have found the impetus needed to provide such accounts within some of the recent debates in anthropology over the place of experience, both that of the subject of study and that of the anthropologist.

Edward M. Bruner writes that the conceptual apparatus for interpreting field data has for too long encouraged anthropologists to filter out their own experiences in the production of scholarly monographs. But he adds that good ethnographers now increasingly return the experiential component of their work with "illustrative snatches of personal narratives, bits of biography, or vivid passages from their fieldnotes" (1986, p. 5). In this work I have done some of the same.

Mass Media in Sub-Saharan Africa represents the results of my efforts to marry the direct experiences I have had, in and with the mass media in sub-Saharan Africa, with the literature already available on the subject. It combines my desire to provide both a scholarly update on the current state of the media in the sub-Saharan region and an account of insights I have gained through the roles I have played. These roles have included, along with that of researcher/ scholar, those of volunteer, professor, media trainer, project proposer, and project director.

It is axiomatic that an update on the sub-Saharan media will be out of date as soon as it is printed. This volume has already undergone numerous revisions in an effort to keep up with the rapid pace of events unfolding on the media scene in sub-Saharan Africa in the 1990s. It also goes without saying that the book is tainted by my own biases: those of a Western academic, steeped in libertarian and egalitarian notions, predispositions nurtured perhaps by my own relatively privileged position. The work undoubtedly also bears the mark of my own training in (what was once) a positivistic social science, one now in the process of reconstituting itself.

Because *Mass Media in Sub-Saharan Africa* derives both from my experiences and from the available literature, I have focused mainly on media institutions and issues in major francophone and anglophone African countries. This effort, however, has left some parts of the continent less well covered in the work. Lusophone Africa, the Horn of Africa, Southern Africa (with the exception of Zimbabwe), and Island Africa are regions scantily treated in the available literature. Moreover, these are regions where I have spent little time. The enormity and complexity of sub-Saharan Africa makes detailed accounts of every country impossible in a work of this size. Clearly, more systematic attention to the media of these subregions is warranted in future works of this kind. Nevertheless, the model I use in this volume is an original synthesis derived from social, political, and cultural theory. As such it is generalizable across a range of countries in the region. This model argues that mass media in sub-Saharan Africa have all been affected to varying degrees by three factors: the precolonial legacy of the oral tradition, the presence of an alienated managerial class, and the domination of modern African societies by systems of political patronage. To the extent that these conditions have been operative throughout much of Black Africa, the generalizations I put forth will be appropriate for all of the region. Only the degree to which these factors operate and the local variations of these conditions will change from one country to the next.

It has not been easy to put down on paper the many thoughts and feelings I have about the media in sub-Saharan Africa. I have hesitated for years to make observations which appear critical in any way to the continent which has taught me so much and which has been such an important part of my life. In this regard, I have fallen into the dilemma which besets most Africanists of Western origin: how to critically evaluate social situations under study without at times waxing critical. Africans have been much maligned by earlier writings, and they have been understandably sensitive to comment, however well intentioned, from outsiders.

Nevertheless, major changes are set to befall the African media as governments restructure their political organization to allow for multiparty democracy. Increased press freedom is in the offing, and there are efforts underway to create private print and electronic media outlets which will compete with government-operated media systems. New technologies, especially satellite communications, interactive computer networks, and so-called small media, such as fax machines, portable video camera/recorders, and low-power television and radio services, are set to affect the media of sub-Saharan Africa in multiple ways. As the African media steer toward a new course, it seems a splendid time to take stock of past practices and propose changes where necessary.

Mass Media in Sub-Saharan Africa is written with the view of examining the past three decades of media practice, warts and all. I believe a review of past media practices is an important undertaking. It is necessary because mistakes have clearly been made in African mass media. It would be naive to imagine that systems of such complexity could have been introduced problem free. Media institutions have been created, and sometimes less than optimal modes of operation have been practiced. Institutions, behaviors, and norms, moreover, have a way of outliving their value. And this could well occur in the sub-Saharan African media. But if these media are to be responsive to the changes shaking the continent, they will have to take stock of their situation and make some adjustments in the way they conduct their affairs. Other aspects of mass media in Black Africa, creative trends, especially those most closely tied to the African oral tradition, are generally healthy and offer considerable promise for audiences. These practices must be examined, developed, and encouraged.

In this book I explore the historical, political, social, economic, and cultural factors which influence how managers of the media lead and how subordinates in the media follow. I also examine how these factors contribute to the way media are created. I also review the role the international community has played in bringing the African media to the point at which they now find themselves. This role has often been counterproductive for the Black African media. Indeed, I attempt to show that the African mass media content and practice represent a coalescing of factors generated by both internal and external conditions.

Where possible, I make suggestions aimed at altering some of the practices I have observed. These suggestions derive largely from my experiences as a trainer of mass media professionals. I do not assume these proposed solutions to be all inclusive, because the work of improving the mass media of any region is a collaborative effort. I alone do not pretend to have all the answers.

The first two chapters of *Mass Media in Sub-Saharan Africa* present the theoretical framework which underlies the arguments made throughout the book. The next seven chapters apply the framework to the aspects of the African mass media under consideration. Chapter 1 presents the precolonial legacy, examining social, political, and value orientations and communication styles of traditional oral societies. Chapter 2 details the legacy of African elite alienation and the systems of political patronage which have been the inheritance of the African media since their inception.

Chapter 3 treats the organization of electronic media, the systems of management which operate them, and the *modus operandi* of senior, middle, and junior media operatives. Chapter 4 looks at the practice of radio broadcasting in sub-Saharan Africa, the modes of production, and the product of the creative staff. It examines news and information broadcasting, entertainment programs, cultural and educational broadcasts, and radio services targeted to rural populations over a range of countries. Chapter 5 looks at the practice of television production in sub-Saharan Africa, the modes of production, and the product of the creative staff. It examines in some detail the television systems in five nations of sub-Saharan Africa: Côte d'Ivoire, Gabon, Kenya, Niger, and Nigeria.

Chapter 6 reviews the history of the press in sub-Saharan Africa from its initial establishment in the nineteenth century through to the 1990s. Chapter 7 analyzes the discourse style of the African press, exploring its relationship to the precolonial oral tradition. Chapter 8 examines the conditions surrounding the development of multiparty politics and the interaction of the press in this process. In so doing, it examines more closely political and press developments in the 1990s in the nation of Zambia.

Finally, chapter 9 explores the evolution of the role of the media in the process of development, considers questions of social change in the light of radical postmodern theory, and proposes a reorientation of the African mass media toward more decentralized programming, suitable for rural audiences of the twenty-first century.

MASS MEDIA IN
SUB-SAHARAN AFRICA

1 | The Precolonial Legacy

IN THE 1990s, the winds of change are once again blowing through the continent of Africa. The Cold War has ended and for the first time in thirty years, Africa may be spared of polarizing superpower politics. The twin processes of government decentralization and multiparty elections are beginning to shake the foundations of centralized national power and iron-clad rule. The media which have been so much a part of the African status quo from the 1960s through the 1980s will undergo profound shifts in this decade and in the next century.

To better assist in this transformation, it is useful to explore how the mass media in Africa have performed over the last thirty years. It is instructive to examine how the unique combination of historical, political, social, economic, and cultural factors have conspired to produce media in Black Africa as we found them in the early 1990s.

This book will look at the cultural foundations of the African peoples upon which the media were overlaid in sub-Saharan Africa. It will examine the people who have built these institutions, both expatriate civil servants and their successors, the African elites. It will review the political and social forces which have shaped these media in the past few decades.

This book focuses specifically on the media of sub-Saharan Africa with the exception of South Africa. The 48 or so countries and island nations that make up sub-Saharan Africa (or Black Africa) are highly diverse.[1] Geographically they stretch from the fringes of the Sahara through the rain forests of Central Africa to the southern edge of the Kalahari Desert. Linguistically they encompass 2,000 or so languages and dialects and as many ethnic groups, each with its own unique culture.

Despite their diversity, the nations of Black Africa and their media share some common traits, which justify their discussion in a volume of this kind. With the exceptions of Ethiopia and Liberia, the nations of Black Africa share a common history of colonialism. They were all colonized by one of the great imperial powers of Great Britain or France, or one of the lesser powers: Portugal, Belgium, Germany, Italy, or Spain.[2]

Partly because of their colonial experience, these nations suffer from similar economic conditions: extraverted economies with weak agricultural and manufacturing sectors. All experienced artificial border creations, and most became independent during the 1960s. On perhaps no other continent has the impact of the external world been so great. On no other continent have the social changes of the last 100 years been so dramatic.

The media in Black Africa are unique. In no other region of the world have the media been forced to endure change so rapidly. No other peoples have so quickly shifted from face-to-face communication to electronic communication without first passing through a stage of writing and literacy. When development theorists first noted this condition, they felt that the media offered great promise for Black Africa. But they did not seriously take the preexisting cultural and social conditions into account, underestimating the difficulty of the venture. And these theorists underestimated the degree to which the forms of modern communication they were imposing were alien.

This chapter will explore the precolonial legacy of Africa, examining the historical, political, social, and cultural conditions in Africa when the imperial powers took over. I will try to show how the precolonial legacy, especially the legacy of the oral tradition, has been very much a part of the Black African media. Because most systems of mass media were introduced during the colonial period, analyses of these systems, historical or otherwise, tend to reflect only what has happened during this century. Communication scholars, like other social scientists, have tended to treat Africa at the onset of colonialism as a *tabula rasa*. Nothing could be further from the truth. Rubin and Weinstein, analysts of politics in Africa, remind us that although governments change, this does not mean that older forms disappear (1974, p. 10). The same could be said for all forms of communication—the technological forms change, but the preexisting styles of interaction may not. Precolonial Africa was peopled by a range of societies whose modes of political and social organization and whose cultural styles profoundly influenced the institutions thrust upon it. Any study of modern mass communications in Africa must necessarily explore the political configurations, the communal organization patterns and styles, and the discourse systems into which these mass media were born.

Precolonial Political and Social Organization

There is a great paucity of literature examining the relationship between traditional political organization and modern mass media in Black Africa. This is hardly surprising, as few scholars of political science have attempted to study the link between modern and traditional authority patterns in Black Africa. Some scholars contend that early denial of political organization in Black Africa helped to justify the imposition of colonial rule on that continent (Rodney, 1972, p. 242).

Fortes and Evans-Pritchard, anthropologists who studied traditional government in Africa, concluded that there were two styles of African political systems: one with government and one without (1940, pp. 5–6). Political systems or states without formal government included most of the Bantu-speaking groups of the West and Central African rain forest and the pastoralists of East Africa. These societies were arranged according to kin or lineage groupings. People tended to live in small villages or nomadic groups, nominally under the headship of a clan or lineage head. Traditionally clan or lineage heads had corporate rights and duties. They might oversee marriages, and they regulated access to property or land on behalf of the group. They assumed corporate liability if one of the members of the group was harmed. In redistributive systems, they might recycle wealth for the group through the sponsoring of communal feasts or celebrations.

Lineage members were required by tradition and custom to carry out certain work on behalf of the entire group. This work might involve the maintenance of roads or bridges, the construction of communal meeting places, or the performance of certain rituals—funeral rites, naming ceremonies, circumcision rites, and seasonal rituals involved with agricultural cycles. The roles and obligations of all persons were tightly inscribed through their social positions. These positions were defined through kinship relationships, birth order, membership in societies of age-graders, gender, and rules governing marriage.

Although the kin/lineage model remained the dominant form of social organization up until the colonial period, there were many social groups in Africa who had evolved or were in the process of evolving into larger and more complex social polities. The medieval empires of the Saharan fringe, the Ghana, the Mali, and the Songhai empires, for example, each united persons of different lineage or ethnic groups under a single central authority. At the time of European contact, the Yoruba and the Ashanti kingdoms, the Hausa city states, the Baganda in Central and East Africa, and the Zulu in southern Africa all had central authorities and systems of administration of peoples which permitted them to govern and administer multiethnic kingdoms. These systems of government had evolved competitive mechanisms for the transfer of power upon the death of a ruler.

As precolonial polities continued to develop, their organizational structures naturally became more complex. Occupational specialization occurred, and some of the kingdoms, such as the Buganda of the Central African highlands, and some empires, such as the Songhai and the Mandinkas, developed caste systems as a means to regulate the division of labor and impose a centralizing power. In some parts of Africa, a landed aristocracy developed, one which wielded considerable control over access to farmland.

Despite vast differences in the style and scope of leadership in the peoples of precolonial Africa, at least one generalization seems to have held true for all.

Fortes and Evans-Pritchard noted that the African ruler was not to his people merely a person who could enforce his will upon them: "He [was] the axis of their political relations, the symbol of their unity and exclusiveness and the embodiment of their essential values" (1940, p. 17; quoted in Arens and Karp, 1989, p. xvii). Precolonial authority figures, in either the precolonial kingdoms or states without government, were extratemporal. Arens and Karp remind us that Africans believe that power resides in the interaction among the material world, the supernatural, and the social (1989, p. xvii).

The African oral tradition corroborates the views of the African ruler as a spiritual symbol of a people. Shaka, the greatest warrior-king of Zulus, is presented in oral poetry as the "paradigm of the greatness and the regenerative vitality of ancestral values" (Ogundele, 1992, p. 13). And Sunjata, the founder of the thirteenth-century Empire of Mali, appears in the *Epic of Old Mali* as the "insuperable champion of a just cause and the architect of an eternal imperial glory" (Okpewho, 1992, p. 296).

Precolonial Religion

African social life was bound up in its relationship to the cosmological system of the group. Mbiti (1971) informs us that most Africans recognized the existence of a single creator god or force who remained distant from the affairs of men together with a host of lesser deities who were actively involved in human affairs and whose relationship to human beings could be traced through myth or stories of kinship. In some of the kingdoms, the Ashanti and the Yoruba among them, ancestors were deified, and complex cosmologies emerged.

Tradition dictated the system of reciprocity through which humans could negotiate their relationship to the deities, who could be offended or pleased and appeased depending on the manner and frequency with which certain rites were performed. A violation of tradition could bring down the wrath of gods causing ill fortune, illness, and death to a member or members of the group, these latter eventualities necessitating further recourse to rituals of supplication or cure.

Precolonial Values

Social values engendered in African systems of social organization strongly stressed group orientation, continuity, harmony, and balance (a point we will return to later in a discussion of the oral tradition). As Bonnie Wright points out, the question "Who are you?" was meaningless without the additional query "Of where and of whom are you born?" (1989, p. 54). The locus of individual identification was with the larger social grouping. An individual without a group was a contradiction in terms. Placide Tempels, author of *La Philosophie Bantoue* (1959), wrote that "a key feature of the conception of human nature [for the African] is that the person is not an entity separate from others, but rather participates in other beings (including persons) and is in part constituted by other beings" (cited in Riesman, 1986, p. 74). The obverse of group orientation was an underdeveloped sense of individualism.

Some authors have described group orientation as the value of plurality. Chernoff argues that the locus of individual identity depends upon important attachments to the group. The existential dilemma of the African, where it occurs, derives from an inability to establish group ties, that is, to find meaning within social networks (1979, pp. 153–72). The contrast between the traditional African sensibility and that of the highly individualistic Westerner is marked. Existential angst of the latter, by opposition, defines itself ultimately in questions of personal self-definition and self-worth.

Corresponding to the pluralistic life world of the traditional African was the highly valued sense of social harmony, one which required the individual to negotiate personal needs into the framework of the group. Indeed, pluralism engenders a world view in which forces must continually be balanced. The African in traditional society lived his or her life juggling forces and demands of kinsmen, age-graders, ancestors, and gods. Happiness and success were defined as the ability to juggle forces. Smitherman observes:

> Though the universe [was] hierarchical, all modes of existence were necessary for the sustenance of its balance and rhythm. Harmony in nature and the universe [was] provided by the complementarity, interdependent, synergistic interaction between the spiritual and the material. Thus we have a paradigm for the way in which opposites function. (1977, p. 75)

The balancing of forces is a theme which repeatedly manifests itself in African art forms. John Chernoff's analysis of Akan music styles in Ghana argues that contrapuntal styles of drumming express in a profound artistic way the need for social balance and the achievement of harmony.

Strong group orientation sustained the importance of continuity. This value stressed the need for the African to regularly reify his or her membership in the group through the continued performance of rituals whose form was maintained through tradition. As members of the senior age-grader groups passed from life to death, their influence remained. And the need for harmony made requisite for the African the appeasement and placation of oppositional forces among both the dead and the living so as to retain smooth group relations. Proper treatment of the dead was carefully inscribed in tradition as was the treatment of the living.

As these societies became more differentiated, the maintenance of balance and harmony between peoples and their gods also became more complex.

Rules governing these relations emerged and were encoded in the myths of the people. These myths were passed on through the oral tradition, the dominant discourse style of precolonial Black Africa. The groups along the Saharan fringe and the Swahili along the East African coast acquired writing from the Arabs. The extent to which writing was diffused within the populations differed, but it is fair to say that Africans, in general, did not achieve a high degree of literacy, for education in Africa took another form.

Precolonial Education

Literacy never was an active component in children's education, which was conducted in and through the oral tradition through a number of techniques. First, there was informal education. Children learned civility by observing their elders in the community. They were expected to internalize the rules of their society by quiet absorption of the behaviors of others and rapt attention to the symbolic quality of their civil and religious rituals.

Second, children learned the requirements of adulthood through segregation and training in age-grader classes conducted by same-sex elders. These classes, which included survival lore for the boys and domestic skills for the girls, were in some cases followed by ordeals designed to test strength, fearlessness, oblivion to pain, and group loyalty. Third, children learned survival skills through observation, imitation, and play. Young girls would help their mothers with child care, household tasks, and farming. Young boys would assist their fathers in herding and agriculture, or watch their fathers during a hunt, sometimes organizing their own hunting games to take small animals.

Fourth, children learned the rules of their societies and their duties to the elders and the ancestors through oral lore. Elders meted out moral lessons through the use of riddles, proverbs, and moral tales. They also told the histories of their people through foundation myths and stories of great ancestors who had come before them.

The incursions of literacy in some parts of Africa date as far back as the ninth century after Christ. Arabs brought literacy to the trading classes of the Saharan fringe and the Swahili coasts, and Arab literacy eventually trickled up to the ruling elite who used it in the administration of their empires and trickled down through the religious training of Muslim boys. But the training in literacy never permeated the popular consciousness. Functional literacy remained limited to a small elite group, the wider masses having learned only enough Arabic to recite the Holy Quran and to copy passages from it (Goody, 1968, p. 216). Rather, it was the informal, nonspecialized, and oral nature of African education which had a deterministic effect on popular precolonial consciousness.

The Oral Tradition

The importance of the oral culture, or the oral tradition as it is sometimes known, and the effect of this discourse style on the thoughts, governance styles, and organizational patterns of precolonial Africa have been understudied. Technological determinists take the view that the dominant mode of communication employed by a society has a profound effect on the thought patterns of its people and the cultural style they acquire. These cultural patterns in turn influence reflexively the cosmology, the mode of governance, the rule of law, the mode of social behavior, the source and ethical value orientation of these societies, and the perception of the self. Technological determinists, such as Walter Ong, use as a model or basis of analysis the narration of the oral tale by a bard, as the filter through which to explain the world view of oral societies. Such scholars maintain that from a study of the performance style and setting, it is possible to derive a set of descriptors or psychodynamics of oral societies.

The Western world has been deeply influenced by the Gutenberg revolution, which ushered in the age of print. Printing brought about linear thinking, the use of logical syllogisms, and the paramountcy of logically derived principles in the acquisition of knowledge. Printing has also distanced readers, the users of information, from the source of information, thereby engendering the critical spirit which has been a hallmark of Western scholarship and, by diffusion, Western thinking since the Age of Reason. When considering the organization of oral culture information, the reader should be alert to differences between the oral world view and that of the world of print.[3]

In explaining oral culture or orality, Ong invites us to consider a world in which "no one is ever able to look anything up" (1982, p. 31). Here, he argues, knowledge must be stored in easy-to-recall formulary expressions, expressions with rhythmic patterns, whose utterance triggers the recall of additional bits of information. Ong informs us that in oral societies the word also had great power because it made things come into being. He refers to the Book of Genesis (whose origins lie deep in oral prehistory), which opens with "In the Beginning there was the word." Words indeed did in the Bible have generative power, for "And the Word was made flesh" continues the story of creation. Likewise in Africa, and indeed in other oral cultures, words were used to make things come into being. Words were used to declare the unity of a people. Words were used to declare a state of war. Words were used in powerful incantations and in healing rites. This explains the power of the curse and the power of insult in traditional African societies. Words were not so much discursive symbols indicative of concrete entities, but rather generative powers creating a separate subjunctive reality all their own. As Ong notes, words or facts have no visual metaphors. They are not symbols, but "they are occurrences, events" (1982, p. 31). He adds that oral peoples commonly and probably "universally consider words" to have great power, "even magical potency" (p. 32).

In the West, words are symbols which stand for referents. They are not sacred or sacrilegious, but rather functional tools. They may be used to explain an idea in a printed text and then edited or changed when a better turn of phrase comes to mind. The initial awkward phrasing is edited out, disappears, and fails to form part of the tapestry of official ideas. How then does the operation of orality as the primary mode of communication color social discourse? And what is the relation between this social discourse and the way people think?

As noted above, knowledge in the oral world could not be looked up. There were no libraries and no computer banks. Knowledge was memorized by bards who specialized in the storage and transmission of information. They used heavily rhythmic patterns, repetitions and antitheses, alliterations, assonances, and a host of formulaic expressions as the tools of their trade. Knowledge and wisdom were said to reside in those persons able to transmit information with artistic flourish through accepted stylistic conventions.

Ong's many works on the oral tradition represent a comprehensive integration of the works of many literary scholars, anthropologists, psychologists, and linguists who have studied preliterate societies. In his synthesizing work, *Orality and Literacy* (1982), Ong sets out to explain the profound differences which separate primary oral cultures from those deeply affected by the use of writing. These differences emerge as powerful explanatory tools, aiding us to understand the precolonial social world of Africa and its modern popular discourse style today.

Ong isolates qualities which he calls the psychodynamics of orality. These qualities are important to this study because, as much social theory argues, reality is created in a social context. And the way reality was constructed and presented in the oral narrative was then the way people experienced existentially the events and persons depicted in stories. It is worth repeating that bards, storytellers, and village historians used stories to recount the genealogies of people, to tell of their histories and their struggles, to recount stories of the gods, and to impart moral lessons. But their role was to entertain as much as to impart information. Thus, performers were always anxious to "please the ears of their audiences" (Okpewho, 1992, p. 70).

Additive Rather Than Subordinative Thought

Ong argues that oral discourse has a tendency to be additive rather than subordinative. The additive characteristic refers to the way events were created by the bard in the telling of the tale. The artist would use fixed stylistic conventions to call up events in the narrative to mind. Events were recounted one after the other, and the more the oral bard told, the more he would remember. A crowd of listeners would actively participate in the telling, shouting out important phrases or historical elements the narrator might be inclined to forget. In this way events or elements or personages important to the entire group would simply be added on in the narrative, creating a powerful piece of group recreated history, the ultimate exercise in groupthink.

A literate version of a story might read something like this: While the blacksmiths shod his horses, the king readied his troops. When all were prepared, he called for his sword. But the oral version of this text might be "sounded": "The blacksmiths shod the horses, and the king readied his troops. And he called for his sword." The first example emphasizes syntax, the logical and chronological order of the story. It stresses a clear order of narration and a preordained plan as to how the story will flow. It suggests that the end point of the story is known in advance by the writer or by a narrator influenced by literacy. The second version is focused outward on the sound it will make and the rhythm it will create. If the pacing is sufficiently stimulating, the bard or the audience will add additional details, embellishing descriptions, or adding more action as the crowd follows on. So the bard might add to the second version: "And the groom fed the horses, and the valet polished the shield. The king mounted his horse, and he called for his sword." Additional details in the literate version must be planned in advance and would not be added on unless they advance the storyline.

The additive quality of oral-tradition narration renders unimportant the need for time markers. If it inhibits narrative flow, the chronological order of events is dispensed with. Subordinatives and statements of causality are likewise subservient to flow needs and group participation in this public narrative event. Thus, the events in the story seem to occur mysteriously in some far-off time in history, grounded only loosely in the real world. This explains in part why such stories seem to have a magical quality.

This style of discourse is readily apparent to anthropologists who have worked with native informants. Time markers play a much less prominent role in their accounts, hence linear sequencing is often absent from their talk. Critical anthropology has of late just begun to struggle with the intellectual difficulty (and possible academic dishonesty) of piecing together for written scholarly analysis the stream of talk gathered from informants in the field (see Clifford and Marcus 1986). Also missing from the stream of talk gathered up by field-workers in anthropology are accounts bereft, or nearly bereft, of causal markers. Informants seem merely to list things which have occurred, while giving little clue to the interconnection of events. When the field-worker asks why something has occurred, he or she, likely as not, will be greeted with a second stream of elements from the informant. The simple cause-and-effect constructions so common in the Western mode of discourse simply do not emerge with great frequency (Bourgault 1988–89).

This type of discourse also occurs in social situations far removed from fieldwork. I recall from my days as a professor in Nigeria the fascinating stories university students would use to explain why assignments were not turned in on time. I recreate one such conversation to illustrate the point:

Student: I was standing in the motor park. Many people were there. I gave my money to the lorry drivers. Some bad men came. They roughed the turn boy. We called the police. The police beat some people. But the thief-men seized many bags from the vehicle. My assignment was inside.

Professor: But your assignment was due before break, before you were to go to the lorry park.

Student: My father was not feeling fine. He called for me. The thief-men were so bad! They abused many women in the park. They were badly dressed and very rude.

Professor: But why did you not turn in your assignment before leaving?

Student: They took all my money. Now I will have to leave the university, for I have no money and my father says I must work on the farm.

Professor: If you are leaving the university anyway, why does your grade on this assignment matter?

Student: My father is so ill. The family is very worried. Please I beg you, let me do this assignment again.

Thus the conversation would continue as the student "informant" scanned my face intently for encouragement, signs of pity, softening, agreement, or disagreement. When I had had enough of this story, i.e., when I had been thoroughly rhetorically beaten, the conversation would end.

What is important about this small example from modern social life is the way the two discourse styles, mine and that of my student, were at odds. I was looking for logic, consistency, and sensitivity to elements of time. He was looking for dramatic effect, empathy, and a break. Like the oral tales observed by A. B. Lord (1960), this text was not created for a performance, but rather *in* performance (cited in Okpewho, 1992, p. 33).

Aggregative Rather Than Analytic Thought

Ong argues that traditional people tend to think in clusters, and in antithetical phrases and clauses. They prefer to speak not just of monkeys, but of clever monkeys; not just of foxes, but of wily foxes; not just of soldiers, but of brave soldiers; not just of masses, but of downtrodden masses.

The propensity to think in clusters comes from the need to recall and to create stock characters and stock sequences in a narrative. This derives directly from the need to delight audiences with vivid images, to hold their attention, and to promote their active participation. Okpewho illustrates this example in the Sunjata story narrated by Bamba Suso (Innes 1974). Sunjata calls on his four allies: Kama Fofana, Sankarang Madiba Konte, Fass Koli, and Tira Makhang. Bamba goes through the response of each of the four, noting how *each one* answers Sunjata's call with 1,444 bowmen. Okpewho remarks that Sunjata did not call for a specific number of bowmen, so there is little chance each ally would have supplied the same number. Rather, the alliterative number is a stylistic device: "the formula of 1,444 bowmen repeated over and over rings like a sweet refrain" (1992, p. 77). Clearly accuracy in the discourse was subordinated in the oral world to the need to delight the imagination with both vivid and memorable images and a repetition of verses designed to move the narrative forward through group participation.

Redundant and Copious Thought

Orally based discourse is redundant and copious for several reasons. First of all, the oral narrative, unlike the written work, does not permit the listener to "back-loop" if he or she has missed anything. Moreover, the listening situation in an African village tended to be very fluid with persons joining the story circle late, much after the event had already started. Therefore, it was imperative for the oral bard to continue to repeat certain major points lest any audience members be left out of the story.

Communication was intended to pass on information to the audience, but also to delight the ear in the process with the sound of the words, with the virtuosity of the speaker. Repetition was also used as a delay mechanism, giving the teller a few moments to recall a detail he might have forgotten. Thus speakers would often repeat phrases, adding emphases and altering the cadence of the repetition, making for tonal variety and dramatic effect. Tonal semantics were heavily employed and sometimes involved using words which had little meaning but sounded effective (Smitherman, 1977, pp. 94, 134–37).

Okpewho illustrates repetitious oral elements in a war song of the Kipsigis of Kenya:

Child's mother *oo wo ho*
Child's mother *oo wo ho*
Put the pot on the fire *oo wo ho*
Put one which can hold a head *oo wo ho*
The army is going to war *oo wo ho*
The army is going to war *oo wo ho*
You don't know where *oo wo ho*
The army is going to war *oo wo ho*

The army is going to war *oo wo ho*
To Mangorori *oo wo ho*
Oye leiro oo wo ho
Oye leiro oo wo ho. (Okpewho, 1985, p. 137)

The nonsense syllables *oo wo ho* facilitate the rhythmic marching of soldiers' feet as they sing the song.

Conservative and Traditional Thought

According to Ong, knowledge in oral societies is difficult to acquire because it must come through experience and its retention must be carefully inscribed in formulary expressions and mnemonic devices. The exigencies of
memorization of knowledge engenders a traditional mind-set. Oral societies
were not societies which delighted in novelty, because novelty represented a
possible overload of the human memory circuits. If today, computers have
speeded up information gain to the point where it can be said a fact is no
longer a fact because it is always subject to the latest nuances imposed by
additional data, the opposite was certainly true in oral societies. Tried and
trusted knowledge—the wisdom of the gods and the ancestors passed down
through tradition—was sacred. As Balandier notes, "What we find [in traditional Africa] is not so much a body of thought progressing by way of contradiction and controversy as one preserved and transmitted on behalf of the entire community" (1966, p. x). Thus, new ways of solving old problems were
frequently ignored. Novelty in such societies came in the form of new illustrations to support old rationales and cosmologies, such as building new shrines
to ancestors when exhortation before old ones had failed. And novelty came
in the form of new stories or subjects treated with old stylistic formulae.

Thought Which Is Close to the Human Lifeworld

Ong points out that persons from oral cultures find it difficult to separate
events from their activators (persons or social forces) and to parcel out underlying principles from concrete events. Thus, in rural Africa, if an event occurs
in nature or in history, humans or spiritual agents operating with them are said
to cause it. Thus, some babies are said to die because they have been bewitched
by jealous co-wives. Some politicians are believed to maintain power because
of their recourse to and manipulation of benevolent or malevolent spiritual
forces.

The scientific revolution introduced into Western society a host of abstract
causative agents with which to explain phenomena. These abstractions have
permeated popular consciousness. An invasion of the body by bacteria combined with the body's low level of resistance causes disease. A condition of
poverty, combined with easy access to and high profits for drugs, plus lack of

strong male role models, has led to high crime rates in North American ghettos. This sort of analysis could not exist in oral societies because the dominant communication tool did not supply it. Analytical categories which would permit such a style of thinking were nonexistent.

For similar reasons, self-analytical tools were equally missing among much of the populace. Self-analysis requires the individual to stand back from his or her thoughts and feelings (as well as from the group) and to examine his or her life with the same powers of analysis abstractions make possible in other (literate) situations. This is not possible. The work of Soviet psychologist A. R. Luria has emphasized the role of literacy in the acquisition of tools for self-analysis (1976, pp. 15, 55, 150). Indeed, psychology tells us that in group-oriented societies, development of an individually differentiated ego and superego is not a goal, for the collective ego and superego subsume its functions. Through the mechanisms of projection, introjection, and undoing, individuals subsume their identity into that of the group (Riesman, 1986, pp. 77–78).

Sublimation of individual identity into group identity gives life a serendipitous character and an individual the sense that he or she is in the hands of fate. Forward planning becomes difficult if not impossible for the individual whose behavior is closely tied to a group whose actions he or she cannot easily predict. Moreover, planning requires individuals to stand back, to take stock of their strengths and weaknesses, to analyze their present social, economic, or political situation, and to then formulate a concrete plan for future action. Again, in oral societies such analytical tools are nonexistent, or they are conjured up with great difficulty because it is not possible to think in the future tense. Indeed, Isaac Obeng-Quaidoo, drawing from Mbiti (1971), notes that the African conception of time recognizes a long past, an immediate present, and a distant and indeterminate future (Obeng-Quaidoo, 1985b, p. 112). Conjuring is in fact an apt descriptor for the way traditional Africans dealt with the future, i.e., through the use of oaths, incantation, supplications of the spirit, or magic.

Agonistically Toned Thought

Ong notes that persons in oral cultures have a propensity to engage with others in verbal and intellectual combat. The oral world sees life in polarized terms. The world is full of villains, vice, and evil—all needing vilification. The world is full of heroes, virtues, and good—each demanding exhortation. Orality situates knowledge in the human life world where human beings struggle.

Anyone familiar with African-American verbal games, including the numbers, where young men trade insults about their mothers or games of signification ("signifyin"), where youths engage in verbal put-downs, will quickly recognize this pattern (Smitherman, 1977, p. 82). Smitherman provides an example of a street corner "signifyin" rap between two African-American men taken from Richard Wright's autobiography, *Black Boy* (1966):

"You eat yet?" (Casually trying to make conversation)
"Yeh man, I done fed my face" (Casually)
"I had cabbage and potatoes" (Confidently)
"I had buttermilk and black-eyed peas"
(Meekly informational)
"Hell, I ain't gonna stand near you, nigger"
(Pronouncement)
"How come?" (Feigned Innocence)
"Cause you're gonna smell up the air in a minute"
(A shouted accusation) (Laughter runs through the crowd)
"Nigger, your mind's in a ditch." (Amusingly moralistic)
"Ditch, nothing, nigger, you're gonna break wind any minute now"
(Triumphant pronouncement creating suspense)
"Yeh, when them black-eyed peas tell that buttermilk to move over that buttermilk ain't gonna wanna move and there's gonna be a war in your guts, and your stomach's gonna swell up and bust!" (Climax)
(Crowd laughs long and hard)
"Man, them white folks oughta catch you and send you to the zoo and keep you for the next war!"
(Throwing the subject into a wider field)
"Then when the fighting starts, they oughta feed you on buttermilk and black-eyed peas and let you break wind!"
(The subject is extended and accepted)
"You win the war with a new kind of poison gas!"
(A shouted climax)
(There is a high laugh that simmers down slowly and the subject switches to white folks). (Smitherman, 1977, pp. 80–81)

On these matters, Smitherman notes that speakers may not act out the implications of their works. And listeners, moreover, do not necessarily expect any action to follow. If the rap is good enough, no action need follow. The game has been won. The goal of the game was to top one opponent with a better insult.

In a world where symbols are taken to be as powerful as their discursive referents, this kind of verbal combat made sense. It was combat not with the immediacy of the indicative mood, but combat in the realm of possibility, of suspended disbelief, combat in a kind of subjunctive mood.

Okpewho describes group festivals in Urhoboland (Nigeria), where contestants engaged in a "battle of songs," "designed to attack verbally either a rival community or a specific member of that community." He notes that the contest was "an exercise in poetic exaggeration" and that "a community attacked in one festival would wait for the next festival to reply accordingly" (1992, pp. 31–32). Ritualized combat was an important element in these games of insult.

Oral narratives also contained a high level of physical violence because enemies who were "close to the human life world" or spirits or witches operating for enemies were thought to be sources of evil. It followed that these evil doers needed to be slain, hacked, or bludgeoned. The very lack of interiority of these oral narratives demanded that their storylines develop into some kind of action, some kind of physical contest. Their very structure and style of presentation did likewise, for the sound of insults, whacks, punches, or swords slashing engendered its own form of onomatopoeic excitement and kept the group following and participating. Anyone who has attended a cheaply made Kung-Fu movie shown to the masses in Black Africa will have some idea of audience verbal engagement and delight which accompanies these agonistic pieces.

The opposite of vilification is high-blown expression of praise of one's patrons, one's deities, one's ancestors, or even oneself. Formulary praise songs form an important part of the African oral tradition and can be studied at length through consulting with Finnegan (1970), Okpewho (1992), Jones, Palmer, and Jones (1992), and others.

Okpewho provides an example of self-praise poetry taken from the Bahima of Uganda.

> I Who Give Courage to My Companions!
> I who Am Not Reluctant In Battle made a vow!
> I Who Am Not Reluctant In Battle made a vow at the time of the preventing
> of the Elephants and with me was The Tamer of Recruits;
> I Who Am Not Loved By the Foe was full of anger when the enemy were
> reported.
> I Who Am Vigilant called up the men at speed together with the Pain
> Bringer;
> I found the Giver of Courage in secret conference.
> I Whose Decisions Are Wise, at me they took their aim and with me was
> Rwamisooro;
> I Who Overthrow the Foe returned the fight as they attacked us.
> I Who Am Nimble withstood the bullets together with The Lover of Battle;
> I Who Am Invincible appeared with The Infallible One.
> . . . .
> I Whose Aid Is Sought was assailed by bullets which left me unscathed and
> with me was The Fortunate One.
> I Who Stand Firm In Battle defeated them utterly and so did The One Who
> Needs No Protection. (Morris, 1964, pp. 52–54; cited in Okpewho, 1992, p.
> 143)

Okpewho notes that songs of self-praise were often performed by a warrior or by a young boy at circumcision, circumstances where the poet was eager to demonstrate his manhood. In these cases, all the poet's hyperbolic skill was mustered in an effort to convince listeners of his worthiness.

Okpewho also notes that praise poetry and praise songs were used typically for the benefit of patrons who engaged the oral entertainer. The praise language was usually lofty and exaggerated. The high-blown language would serve to sustain attention from audiences and encourage remuneration from patrons. Thus, the subjects of praise songs were commonly given attributes impossible within the laws of nature or at least greatly exaggerated. Far from encouraging lying, these poetic traditions simply cultivated group pride through the most elevated idiom possible; listeners knew the feats described were exaggerations (Okpewho, 1992, 143–44).

Empathetic and Participatory Thought

Walter Ong writes that for an oral culture, "learning or knowing means achieving close, empathetic, communal identification with the known" (1982, p. 45). The chronicler is bound up in a communal whole with the hero of an oral tale, and also with his audience. This can sometimes mean that the bard himself, in the telling of the tale, may assume the persona of the hero. The above noted group orientation present in traditional African societies, together with the communal ego and superego, makes it easy for a bard, with the rapt attention of his audience, to slip into the role of hero. Okpewho shows in his work how a bard, tired from the long recitation of the Mwindo Epic of the Banyanga of Zaire, uses his own performance fatigue to illustrate dramatically the travails of his hero.

In a song accompanying the tale, the hero is denouncing the evil schemes of his father.

> My little father threw me into palavers.
> Substitute, replace me now!
> My father believed that I would faint away.
> He threw me into palavers. (Biebuyck and Mateene, 1969, p. 140)

The real quarrel ("palavers") between Mwindo and his father started when the latter, unwilling to have a male child succeed him on the throne, threw the newborn Mwindo into a drum, sealed it up, and threw it into a river so that the child would be choked to death. But the child was aided by supernatural forces and survived to overcome his father. We can see the immediate connection between the narrator and the child at this point: *just as the child, in the course of his struggle with his father, is in danger of "fainting away" (especially in the air-tight drum), so is the narrator, in the course of his struggle with this rather long story, in danger of fainting. The second line, in which the narrator calls on one of his accompanists to take over the perform-*

*ance from him and save him from losing his breath, applies just as much to
the struggling hero as to the narrator. Here in this song, the narrator shows
his brilliant creative imagination by associating his plight with that of the
main character of his story.* [Emphasis mine] (Okpewho, 1992, p. 87)

This empathetic style clearly makes the narrative even more compelling.
And as participation heightens among the audience, the story truly becomes a
celebration of the oneness of the group.

Situational Rather Than Abstract Thought

The opposite of empathetic and participatory discourse is discourse which
is objective and distanced. Objectivity in discourse requires the manipulation
of an abstract set of principles and the application of these critical principles
upon an event, a social situation, a group of persons or an individual. The
research of Luria and others shows that the development of abstract principles
is engendered in the acquisition of literacy. Here students master rules governing the discursive relationship between words and ideas. They also learn that
the ordering of words and their presentation are governed more by internal
rules of logic and meaning than by the affective, performative, and social demands of their use in an edifying presentation. The printed word does not depend upon context. It creates its own contexts and has an independent existence outside the day-to-day world of lived reality.

Neither the abstractions nor the necessary distancing were available to the
bard. His performance was always subordinate to its social context. Since
narratives were not composed so much in public *but for and with the public*,
words, phrases, and even story segments were used as much for their sound
and their participation value as for their discursive meaning. Moreover, a bard
who offended an individual patron or a section of the audience could not expect much in the way of a reward. Thus, the stories were designed to be inclusive, i.e., to incorporate the sentiments of entire audiences. Even bards who
engaged in social criticism did so only if the weight of community values and
traditions was solidly behind the message.

This group orientation fostered a set of values which emphasized plurality
and harmony and the balance of social forces. Clearly, group identity in traditional Africa could be seen like a pebble thrown into a pool of water where the
initial ripples represented the family, the immediate source of group values and
group consciousness. The ripples became increasingly wider but more diluted
and tranquil as the circle widened. These larger circles could represent more
distant relations of clan or ethnic group. In the traditional African states, they
might, at their outer edge represent the boundaries of the state, that which had
the least hold over group consciousness. It is important to realize that the purpose of group identity was to help people to distinguish insiders from outsid-

ers. But group consciousness was contextual, i.e., situational. A person might be an outsider as regards his eligibility for marriage within a certain group, but he might be an insider when it came to trade relations or other economic endeavors.

Sensitive to social context, bards would vary the content of a given tale depending upon the composition of the audience. Outside ethnic groups lampooned as the enemy in one tale told to a small ethnically pure village might miraculously be transformed into allies by the same bard telling the same tale to a multiethnic audience. Okpewho writes of a tale which mentions the betrayal by a Jokadu messenger, Hajii Darbo, of the nineteenth-century Mandinka warlord Kelefa Saane. When Gambian griot Sherif Jabate was asked to perform the tale on Radio Gambia, he left out the name of the messenger so as not to cause offense to the people of Jokadu who also might be listening. When questioned on the omission, Sherif Jabate replied: "I know the name of the man who was sent, but I have not mentioned it. *The past and the present are not the same*" [emphasis mine] (1992, p. 58). Clearly, Jabate was demonstrating his sensitivity to a wider national audience. Indeed, this constant desire to balance social forces and to achieve harmony in social relations is very much a part of the oral tradition and clearly accounts for a preference for situational sensitivity over the abstraction of accuracy.

The study of African art, religious styles, and other expressive forms shows that African culture exhibits remarkable plasticity and has an ability to syncretize a diversity of cultural forms and styles absorbing these and making them their own. Waterman's study of juju music, with its call and response, its complex harmonies, its talking drum, shows these are all expressive of the value demand for harmony and synthesis of diverse elements (Waterman, 1990, p. 38). Analysis of traditional plastic art forms consistently express the same theme (Sieber and Walker 1987; d'Azevedo 1975).

The propensity to synthesize and incorporate diverse elements into a new whole derives from the same inclusive tendencies of oral art forms described above. West African Highlife music, for example, is said to have derived from older Yoruba ojala, combined with palm wine guitar of the early twentieth century, military marching band styles, and European ballroom dance styles popular between the two World Wars (Waterman, 1990, pp. 27–54). How does this marked tendency toward syncretism square with what Walter Ong has called the homeostatic tendency of oral societies?

Homeostatic Thought

Ong's explication of the homeostatic tendency is rendered thus. Oral societies have a profound need to keep in social balance. Because reality is socially, in fact verbally, constructed for a consuming public (rather than hidden away in archives or in ancient texts), words which have lost their meaning, or names, places, or persons which are no longer relevant simply drop out of present accounts. Indeed, as T. O. Beidelman, Edmund Leach, and Claude Lévi-Strauss have noted, oral traditions reflect a society's current preoccupations rather than an idle curiosity about the past (cited in Ong, 1982, p. 48). Thus, as new people move into towns and others move away, histories of villages or towns must continually be updated, and the memories of former residents no longer participating must be sloughed off. The oral world presents a view of itself which is apparently seamless, where old contentious issues are ignored and new accounts are created. Because of this apparent lack of historicity, societies appear to be homeostatic. One has a sense from listening to tales or from talking to people in villages that life has gone on unchanged for generations. Goody and Watt have called this view of history "structural amnesia" (1968, p. 33). Their work provides a striking example of it.

Early-twentieth-century British records derived from the foundation myth of the people of Gonja (in present-day northern Ghana) reported the existence of the original founder of Gonja State and his seven sons. These seven sons were said to have started the seven clans of the Gonja. Sixty years later, when the myth was again recorded, only five clans were mentioned in the tale. Gonja bards were adamant that there had never been any more than five original sons. What had happened to the two other clans? Through a political division resulting from colonialism, one had in fact disappeared. The second had at some point merged with one of the remaining five. Since two of the groups had lost their relevance, the myths had simply been changed (Goody and Watt, 1968, p. 33).

Homeostasis as a characteristic of African culture has a Janus head. It can be dysfunctional, insulating African cultures and rendering them resistant to new and useful cultural additions. It can ossify village life and make it static. Homeostasis can also be positive, protecting cultures from too much rapid change and allowing people to absorb new information in their own idiom. It can help folks to make sense out of a world which seems to shift too quickly. Both of these aspects of homeostasis have been observed at one time or another in African traditional culture. In any case, the oral art forms have helped Africans throughout history to negotiate and make sense of their world. Unfortunately, oral culture and the art forms which supported them were relegated to the background of history when the colonial powers took over the continent of Africa.

Ayittey argues that colonial powers held indigenous African institutions and cultures in contempt and that the elites who replaced them at independence were no better. Both groups considered traditional Africa as backward and primitive, and both sought to replace the cultural forms and social structures of old Africa with alien systems (1992, p. 10). But as we have seen, cultural forms often persist and outlast the structures which originally gave rise to them. This is the principle known as "cultural lag." The oral tradition, the discourse style it fostered, and the value systems it nurtured disappeared neither with colonialism nor with the independence which followed it. African traditional culture simply became intermixed with the alien forms thrust upon it. African traditional forms are, *prima facie*, forms for communication, and they are suffused in and through both the practices and the content of the mass media of Black Africa.

2 | The Colonial Legacy

Into the world of traditional oral societies and oral culture came the colonialists. Thoroughly imbued with the values of modernity, a belief superiority of
the modern industrial state, they created a new political, social and economic
order in Africa.—Sbert, 1992, p. 194; Amin, 1990, pp. 133, 33, 71

It is well known, of course, that the African colonies themselves were artificial political entities created largely in 1885. In this fateful year, European
powers met in conference in Berlin to sign formal agreements detailing how
African territories would be carved and how African lands would be expropriated. The borders worked out through European negotiation bore no relation to ethnic divisions, common history, or other factors on which polities
have been built. Preexisting African nation-states and cohesive ethnic groups
were divided arbitrarily by feats of negotiation. Thus, the Hausa of the Sahelian fringe in West Africa, for example, came to occupy what would become
two different countries, Niger and Nigeria. The first was administered by the
French during the colonial period; the latter, in that same period by the British.
Neighboring ethnic groups with a history of acrimonious relations equally
came to be grouped together in the same nation by the same feat of European
negotiation. Thus, the Abomey in what was then the colony of Dahomey (now
Benin) became amalgamated with ethnic groups upon which the former had
preyed during the days of slavery. In the Sudan, Islamicized urban dwellers of
the dry north of the country came to be grouped together in a single nation
with the pagan Dinka of the Sudd.

Elite Alienation

The legacy of this arbitrary creation of African nations has been the bane
of most African nation-states since independence. Modern states have been left
a legacy of disparate ethnic and religious groupings with little or no cultural
cohesiveness and little shared history save their common colonial experience.
The oddities of this colonial legacy have imposed upon postcolonial governments the monumental task of forging national consciousness and national
identity among disparate groups of peoples. It is significant that the single

most important task of mass media, particularly government-owned African media, has been the nurturing of these new national identities (Hachten, 1971, p. 39; Wilcox, 1975, pp. 22–28).

During the 50- to 100-year period of colonial reign on the continent, the European powers introduced to Africa a new world together with a new way of doing things. This new way was tied largely to the new economic order brought to the colonies. Despite lofty British claims regarding "white man's burden" in Africa and French references to a "civilizing mission," European investment was the driving force behind imperialist incursions into Africa.

In Africa, European capitalists established extractive industries: gold and diamonds in Southern Africa, copper in the Northern Rhodesian and Congo copperbelts, iron ore and bauxite in West Africa, and so on. They developed plantations throughout the continent and enjoined African subsistence farmers through a variety of methods to produce agricultural products for export to Europe: groundnuts and cotton in Senegal; wheat in Mali; pineapples, coffee, and cocoa in Côte d'Ivoire; coffee and cocoa in Ghana; tea in Kenya, and rubber in Cameroon. Africans were paid in cash or in kind to work on the production of cash crops.

The colonial regimes levied taxes against African households or villages and thus insured the availability of a work force in need of cash while they introduced Africa to a monied economy. The exigencies of cash-crop production had a deleterious effect on subsistence farming as able-bodied men left the family or communal farm to participate in European-dominated agro-business. The legacy of colonial export-based monoculture has had a further negative effect on African economies, leaving them vulnerable to price fluctuations on the world market.

In conjunction with the spread of the money economy, trading posts flourished, making European manufactured goods, fabrics, tools, building materials, and manufactured trinkets (heretofore scarce in Africa) available for purchase. Africa's dependency on Western imports began in earnest at this juncture.

Banking was introduced in the colonies to manage local activity and to secure the transfer of capital out of the colonies and into the metropoles. The colonial governments also established large bureaucratic structures to manage the new territories and to keep the new economic activities under their control. Government offices were installed in order to interpret and disseminate colonial policy. Taxation bureaucracies were created to levy and collect tax. Army and police were trained to maintain peace and stability. Civil engineering services were established to construct and maintain roads, bridges, and railroads. Communication infrastructures such as post, telegraph, and telephone were installed to link parts of the colonies to their capitals and to the metropoles. Educational services were created to provide natives with basic skills in numeracy and European literacy so that they might take up some of the routine tasks in the colonial administrative apparatus. Finally, the colonial regimes introduced, rather late in the game, mass media, chiefly radio, used largely to serve the interests of the expatriates who operated the colonies on behalf of the metropole. Typically, and significantly, these radio services were positioned almost exclusively in the capital cities of the colonies, as were most newspapers; the latter introduced in the main, by both colonial governments and enterprising expatriate entrepreneurs.

In short, the colonial powers introduced an entirely new framework of operation and a new world into their colonies. It was a framework which oriented Africa outward toward the metropole rather than one which fostered integration between and within African colonies and peoples. And it was a framework which imposed the demands of international capitalism on social orders which had been heretofore communalistic, inward-looking, and self-sufficient.

The colonial institutions arrested the social, political, and technological development of the existing precolonial polities and made them irrelevant. The gradual social processes leading to greater integration of African peoples, which might have occurred in the absence of colonialism, were thwarted. Indigenous political and social institutions and the lifestyles they supported were robbed of their meaning and purpose. African village life began an inexorable decline, one from which it has never recovered (Sbert, 1992, p. 197).

As the diverse forces of colonialism imposed themselves on Africa, they created a new sector of the populace who would tie the continent to the rest of the globe and who would become the conduit through which the rest of the world could come to Africa. This new social sector created by colonialism has been called the "modern elites" (Rubin and Weinstein, 1974, pp. 42–46). And they are important here for our purposes because they run the African civil service, including, historically, the government-operated mass media.

The Modern Elites

Some sociologists have used self-designation as the determining factor for membership in elite status (Smythe and Smythe, 1960, p. 4; Scarrit, 1971, p. 31). Bretton points out that attempting to classify African elites into neat categories may be an empty exercise. He maintains that too many forces are at work shifting and obliterating neat categories as soon as they have been recorded. He argues that the African elite is by definition someone who depends on outside sources of capital for his or her livelihood, and who as such participates in a "broader international class" (1973, p. 169). It is far easier to describe the elites who are plainly visible in Africa (and easily recognized by their compatriots) than it is to classify them.

The modern elites are the products of Western education. In the early colonial period, most Western education was conducted by missionaries and aimed mainly at the primary school level. By about 1920, colonial governments were taking seriously the need to develop a small cadre of educated Africans who would eventually be able to run the colonies. The colonial powers expanded thereafter government-sponsored education at the primary and secondary level and began offering university scholarships to eligible candidates. There developed eventually, between the wars, a small group of educated indigenes. These individuals became politically conscious and featured in independence movements which began to spring up in the 1930s and 1940s.

By the 1950s, educated individuals were somewhat more numerous and more vocal. An indigenous elite class had developed around the capital cities where colonial powers had established their governments. In the shifting political and economic tides engendered by these developments and by World War II, it became clear that colonies would soon be independent. In the independence struggle which ensued, African elites presented their own class-based concerns as those of the nation (Davidson, 1992, p. 157).

In fairness to the elites, it should be noted that as a group they were not entirely disingenuous. Davidson notes that they were deceived by a central maxim that "Once sovereignty [had been] realized by Africans no matter what the conditions, the road to freedom and development would be theirs to follow" (1992, p. 162). By this time, they had been thoroughly suffused with a sense of their nation's "underdevelopment," a term first used by Truman in 1949 to describe all traditional societies. Many believed they had only to follow the lead of the developed West, and the riches and benefits of the industrialized world would be rained upon them. For indeed, this had happened in their own lives. It was thus natural to expect their example could be a model for their own nations.

The elites represented groups whose livelihoods depended on the modern Western sector of the economy. They worked in commercial sectors, in import-export businesses, marketing cloths, dry goods, foodstuffs, building materials, and other products from Europe to which the Africans had become accustomed. Or they worked in the collection, packaging, transport, or shipping of cash crops grown at low cost by the nonliterate Africans of the interior. Significantly, some of the elites were journalists, especially in West Africa.

Civil Servants

Many elites worked in government, serving as clerks, messengers, or teachers for the alien governments. Most of these civil service positions were low in rank, the colonialists having reserved the best positions for their own military or civilian expatriate class. When independence became a foregone conclusion, colonial administrations did begin training some of the native personnel to assume high-level managerial posts. And the colonial powers generally increased their efforts to provide more education for the native population. But most analysts agree that the civil service and higher education training made available for Africans by colonial governments was too little and too late. Historians are divided as to where to place the blame for this condition. Apologists for the colonialists argue that independence movements in Africa picked up pace more quickly than colonial policy had anticipated. Other more critical authors such as Rodney maintain that colonial powers never planned very seriously for their eventual departure (1972, pp. 261–309). Whatever the case, the fact remains that by the time independence did come, the available African administrative force was woefully inadequate for the task.

At independence, Zaire had fewer than ten college graduates (Ungar, 1987, p. 63). Upper Volta (now Burkina Faso) had one. And the whole of British East Africa together with Northern and Southern Rhodesia (now Zambia and Zimbabwe respectively) had fewer than ten secondary school graduates (Andreski, 1968, p. 153). Africa was to pay a high price for its undertrained civil service.

At independence, native civil servants, some in training courses and others occupying relatively low-level seats, took over high-level positions left vacant by departing colonialists. They acquired most of the bureaucratic strictures and systems which accompanied these posts. Bretton notes that these undertrained and undereducated bureaucrats were no match for the new cadre of European bankers, investors, and givers of aid who descended upon Africa in the postcolonial era (1973, pp. 187–91). Compounding this inadequacy was the fact that the new African civil servant class had inherited the sense of privilege, superiority, and high expectations their European predecessors has bequeathed them.

Colonial administrations had developed elaborate personnel procedures to assure that colonialists serving European governments out in the colonies lived apart from the people they ruled, both socially and economically. Colonial administrators lived in separate quarters (called GRAs, Government Reserve Areas, in the British colonies) in comfortable (and often lavish) employer-supplied homes. Besides their high salaries, they enjoyed numerous perks, such as free medical care, car loans, lengthy paid holidays to Europe, subsidies for children's education, and retirement fund contributions.

The separateness and arrogance of the new civil servant class combined with their relative lack of training was a disaster waiting to happen. It ultimately gave rise to four sets of behaviors which have been a further detriment to the continent. First, there was the need of the African civil servants to strengthen existing barriers between themselves and the masses so as to prevent the latter from attempting to share too equally in the national cake. Second, there was the need to perpetuate arcane and Byzantine operating procedures to shroud incompetence and diffuse responsibility for the errors they would inevitably make. Third, there was the need to depend excessively upon foreign advisors and assistants and those few trained African bureaucrats who did possess a high level of skill and expertise. And fourth, and most significantly, there was the need to depend upon the continued inflow of capital from the outside necessary to maintain the modern economy and the participation of the African elite in it. Thus, since independence, the civil servant class in Africa (particularly the upper echelons) remains a group set apart from two other groups in their societies: the urban proletariat and the rural masses.[1]

It is most important to recognize that in establishing the colonial administration, the colonial powers did not set up a mere bureaucracy. They also created a social class and with it a model of how that class should live. It was elitist to the core. This model has come to dominate the lifestyles and the thinking of the modern ruling classes in Africa ever since independence.

The civil service has operated broadcasting in independent Africa, just as the European civil service did before the colonies were on their own. This means that for better or for worse, broadcasting in Africa is deeply influenced by its colonial past and especially by its legacy of elite African civil service management (see chapter 3). And though the history of newspapers, many of them in private hands, is much more complex and more varied, it too is deeply imbued at the top levels with a sense of participation in the elite circles (see chapters 6 and 7).

Education of the Elites

The elites are literate, representing the most Western-educated elements in African society. The first generation of nationalists believed it was "the heritage of the articulate and literary minority" and not the rural multitudes "who could seize and hold control of the nation about to be born" (Davidson, 1992, p. 145). In many places the elites sought the destruction of the indigenous institutions and lifestyles, believing them regressive and shameful (Ayittey, 1992, p. 10). These attitudes toward traditional Africa came largely from the educational experience of the elites.

In the British colonies, the earliest educational efforts had been undertaken by missionaries. Mission schools have had two aims: schooling children in the basic arts of numeracy and literacy and winning converts to Christianity. Both of these aims strongly undermined traditional African values and lifestyles. The acquisition of literacy offered quiet introspective and independent paths to the acquisition of knowledge. Conversion to Christianity implied the rejection of an African polytheistic world view and its concomitant attachment to the extended African family system. Thus, schooling at the outset offered the African child of the colonial period the promise of undermining his or her values. Compounding this was the fact that most of the early mission schools were boarding schools. Children who attended them were sent away to distant outposts to learn the ways of the "white man." This process further cut children from the ongoing learning processes through which they would acquire the skills for rural agrarian life. By the 1930s, more secular forms of education had been introduced in the British colonies, but the earlier model had been set.

French colonial policy had provided considerably less access to education. Because of the Gallic suspicion of the Church, missionary activity was much less pronounced in the French colonies. But when government education was finally introduced (in the late 1920s), it followed the broad lines of French assimilationist colonial policy. Here the aim of education was clear: to educate Africans to become Frenchmen (Bretton, 1973, pp. 43–46).

Thus, Western education has required many an African child to choose, at a very tender age, between a traditional rural lifestyle and a more urban, Western one. The trauma faced by many a child departing for school has been well described by many an African writer who has no doubt borne a similar pain (Saitoti 1986; Kane 1969).[2] These books equally describe the estrangement felt by these children when they return home for school vacations. In some cases these children have been cut off from important (and often secret) rituals, rites designed to incorporate traditionally schooled children into full social participation in village life as adults. For many a child started on the path of Western education, there could be no turning back. Cut off from his or her rural roots, s/he could only go forward. To this day, this accounts for some of the pressure put upon African governments for places in secondary schools. It also accounts for the particular disaffection of primary-school leavers in Africa caught in the nether world between village orality and the more full-blown literacy of the elite classes (Obeichina, 1975, pp. 188–96).

Secondary school for the African child has meant even more geographical and psychological distancing as secondary schools have always been fewer in number and likely to be located only in the larger cities and towns. University education marks the final educational step in separating the African from his or her past. This is particularly true when the students have been sent abroad for an advanced degree. Individuals considered most fortunate by the elites are those among them who possess the most coveted educational prize of them all: advanced Western degrees. The pattern which began during the colonial period is still alive and well today. In most African nations, the possession of a British, French, or American university degree, until quite recently, almost guaranteed access to a well-paid position in the civil service.

Schools in Africa have alienated African children in two major ways: by taking them from their communal existence, and by barraging them with foreign content. For reasons of expediency, much formal education (including primary) has been and continues to be conducted in the Western language introduced to former colonies by the colonial masters. As Africans master the skills of language arts, they typically do so not in their mother tongue but in a foreign language. African schools have long depended on foreign textbooks, the most irrelevant of these replete with references to "Our ancestors, the Gauls," snow, Christmas trees, and the "heroism of Cecil B. Rhodes." Thus, the content of formal education has looked outward toward the rest of the world rather than inward toward Africa. And with few teachers, many of them underqualified, African schools have tended to reuse worn-out colonial educational practices with emphasis on strict discipline, rote learning, and a marked lack of emphasis on problem solving (Rodney, 1974, p. 271).

Thus, students who have been most proficient at mastering the rules and the disciplines of an alien lifestyle have been rewarded by the educational system. This may explain why African students seem to delight in the demonstration of arcane pieces of erudition. The use of highly stilted Victorian English in student essays is one common example. The extravagant use of Latin phrasings in letters, student papers, and scholarly works is another. These extreme demonstrations of Western erudition undoubtedly must appear to the user to compensate in some way for the lack of fluidity in native oral lore expected of senior oral folks.

Western education has meant, in some cases, that modern elites lack linguistic ease in their native tongues. Although most elites still speak the language of their parents and grandparents, they have lost much of the nuance and subtlety of the multireferential vocabularies without day-to-day practice (Rodney, 1972, p. 282). Elites and other urban dwellers often pepper their vernacular speech with foreign words or phrases. And having lost vocabularies associated with complex kin terms, urban-dwelling elites often fail to learn how they are related to their rural extended families.

Even the most carefully adapted and best planned schools would create some dissonance between an African child and his or her rural past. This is because inherent in the acquisition of literacy is the absorption of linear thinking patterns over globalistic styles of thought.[3] We have already seen that orally based thought is contextual and situational. Other causes aside, schooling introduces a child to a style of thinking and reacting which is markedly different from that which operates in the rural African villages.

Literacy also fosters individuality. A child masters the words on a printed page in solitude. S/he learns to depend upon the manipulation of abstract symbols and content to acquire information. This is very different from the traditional learning context which obtains in African villages where the lessons of life are taught by observation and imitation.

Elite Marriage

If schooling outside one's native village takes people away from their roots, marriage choices keep them from returning. Marriage in Africa has undergone profound changes in the twentieth century. Though marrying within one's lineage or ethnic groups is still preferred (at least by a youth's parents), interethnic marriages are now quite common. Young elites often meet in secondary school or university and are likely to prefer a love marriage to an arranged one. In point of fact, some arrangement, allowing for limited choice on the part of youth and some input from extended families, is still the norm. But here too, elite (or would-be elite) families may be concerned with factors other than kin or lineage.

The modern sector has opened up vast and tempting possibilities for "marrying up," which may mean marrying across ethnic lines. When this occurs, the couple is further estranged from their separate rural origins. In such cases, often as not, the language of the household is English, French, or Portuguese. The children of this marriage are often better schooled in the Western language of the home than in the African languages of their parents.

Elite Family Relations

Much has been made of the strength and resiliency of the African family, of the importance of kinship ties, and of their persistence within city life. Yet, this is an area fraught with considerable difficulty for the elites involved.

In rural areas, African social relations have been organized along lines of kinship or lineage groupings. The lineage grouping is an established social matrix. Lineages have been bound together by networks of social and economic obligations, overseen by a lineage head or a group of elders. Lineage heads offered protection for group members, and lineage members were bound to work on their behalf for the group, performing agricultural labor, maintaining communal facilities such as roads, bridges, meeting houses, and markets. Economic and social rules governed who married whom, who could aspire to political power, and who performed rituals on behalf of the group. Rituals dramatically enacted the relationship between the lineage members and their departed ancestors who were believed to participate actively in the affairs of the society. Although there was considerable variation in how these systems operated, they maintained life as a rather seamless web in the villages because the rights and duties of all lineage members were circumscribed by traditional religion and ritual (Obeichina, 1975, p. 228).

All elites have rural origins. As Obeichina notes, even persons "influenced by literary culture never completely lose touch with their oral culture" (1975, p. 27). It is probably because of the religious overtones bound up in the duty to their ancestors that lineage relations hold such emotional and psychic power over modern elites and generate so much psychological conflict and ambivalence.

The modern elite is expected to return to the village to enact rituals key to the survival of the group. But visits to the villages of origin present their own special difficulties. Creature comforts to which urban folks have become ac-customed are lacking in most African villages, making the trip to grandfather's village an uncomfortable prospect. Air conditioners will certainly be lacking, and standing or ceiling fans will be a rarity at best. Refrigerators, pipe-borne water, and indeed electricity may be nonexistent. Young elites may find life in rural African villages slow paced, lacking in the diversions of the electronic age: TVs, VCRs, radios, and cassette recorders.

Elites may even be expected to supply these and other expensive gifts to poor village relatives who live partly outside the moneyed economy. Elites are rarely able to meet all the material and financial expectations of their less fortunate family members. To avoid this form of social embarrassment, most elites visit less often than their families would like, and somewhat less often than they feel they should.

When an elite moves to the city, his/her lineage obligations follow him/her. An elite is also expected to share in the spoils of his or her position. Urban elites often provide semipermanent lodging for rural relatives who move to urban areas in search of employment or to further their education. Often the country relatives remain in the elite home, and act as semiservants, all the while pressuring the more prosperous relative to use his or her connections to secure paid employment for the poorer ones (Mytton, 1983, p. 88). These situations generate an undercurrent of family tension, much of which is borne in relative silence in deference to the extended family system.

As elites become more estranged from their rural past, all of these conflicts tend to compound themselves. Elites begin to lose track of their rural families: who has given birth, who has married whom, which child's entry into secon-dary school in the capital is imminent, etc. These lapses lead to misunderstand-ings which create more alienation and further tension. Rare is the elite who does not fear that he has slighted one or another kinsman or kinswoman in some way. There is always the possibility that an offended kinsman will resort to witchcraft against the elite whose transgression has gone too far. There is also always the fear that the ancestors will punish in some catastrophic way an erring elite who has been remiss in fulfilling his/her family responsibilities. The obligations are as numerous as the extended family is large, and they often clash with competing demands of the struggle for survival in the African urban setting.

African Urban Life

It has been said that the colonialists did not create cities so much as they created administrative centers. Early on in the colonial period the need for cash and the attractions of the nascent economy brought many unskilled Africans into the urban areas to serve as day laborers and household servants. The pattern continues today at an ever-worsening rate. The present urban growth rates for Africa are between five and nine percent per annum (Amin, 1990, p. 8).

Because of imbalances in African economies, and because of the hesitancy of foreign investors to put much capital into Africa, the much vaunted plans for industrialization of the 1960s and 1970s did not materialize. In all but a few places, a comfortable working class has not emerged. A sizable indigenous business class is equally absent. Colonial policy favored the development of an Asian shopkeeper class, which was dominated by peoples from the Indian subcontinent in East and Southern Africa, and by Lebanese or Syrians in West Africa (Rodney, 1972, p. 236). As noted below, the trend has not been reversed since independence. The general absence of an African merchant class has not been healthy for African urban development. The result of these conditions is that African cities contain two parts: relatively clean, well-off neighborhoods (the former GRAs or their equivalents) and the shantytowns. In the first live the higher-level African civil servants and the expatriates, in the second live the urban proletariat.

As economic conditions for the masses have worsened in the 1970s and 1980s, crime has increased as the "have nots" continue to encroach more and more aggressively on the "haves." Once pleasant African neighborhoods of the 1950s today more resemble armed camps, where elites live behind high walls inset with jagged pieces of glass or barbed wire, deterrents to would-be thieves attempting to gain entry into elite compounds. Indeed, African elites today feel compelled to avail themselves of numerous antitheft arrangements including fierce guard dogs, armed human sentinels, car and house burglar alarms, etc. In some of the more dangerous cities such as Lagos and Kinshasa, defensive arsenals often include firearms. The children of the elites are driven through the shantytowns to separate private schools whose cost places heavy burdens on the typically large (even among elites) African family.

Urban life is not only dangerous, it is expensive. The presence of a few well-heeled foreign investors and the operatives of aid agencies tends to have two effects. First, it drives up the prices of middle-class rental properties, i.e., those constructed of durable materials and fitted with such conveniences as running water, modern plumbing, electricity, and air conditioners. Second, expatriate housing tends to set a very high standard for African elites as to what constitutes an acceptable dwelling for a well-placed African family. Since the symbolic dimension of events and objects is as important as the substantive ones, the need to appear prosperous plays an extremely prominent role in the elite psyche (Mbembe, 1992, pp. 27–28). And the relative insecurity and serendipity of civil service postings makes even more requisite the external demonstration of the badges of elite status.

Prices for foodstuffs in urban areas are high. Monocultural agricultural policies have seriously weakened the agricultural sectors of African economies.

Most African nations now have to import more than 50 percent of the food consumed within their nations. Elites with foreign-trained palates are particularly dependent upon foreign food imports. Processed Western foods typically sell at three to four times their price in their countries of origin.

In short, the material conditions of all urban dwellers, including the elites, is very precarious indeed. And their numbers have swelled as their many children grow up educated and aspire to the same or better opportunities enjoyed by their parents. Simultaneously as African economies have contracted in the 1970s and 1980s, these elites or would-be elites encounter an ever-greater struggle for comfortable survival. It follows naturally that their efforts have been more and more concentrated on shoring up their buying power.

Underdeveloped private sectors have meant elites must clamor for jobs in the civil service. Many African governments have succumbed to elite pressure by multiplying the number of positions in state bureaucracies while incurring additional foreign debt to pay salaries and other administrative costs. This has been a temporary political remedy at best (and one which the structural adjustment loan conditions of the World Bank are designed to redress) and has only served to further distort and render more parasitic the administrative class.

As the major source of capital, civil service postings are further used as a base to accumulate capital to engage in other occupations. Thus, we find African civil service officers running lucrative fleets of taxis, engaging in "gentleman farming," operating transport businesses, etc. All of these take away from the civil servants' time at the office and lead to high absenteeism and shoddy performance (Theobald, 1990, p. 99).

African elites live in a world which is profoundly alienating. Cut off from their past, they must find new social relationships and make new friends in the cities. But these potential friendships are likely as not to be with elite peers, potential rivals for the same posts. In an atmosphere pervaded by plots and day-to-day shifts in loyalties, an element of mistrust tends to enter relationships with folks outside the kin network.

The System of Patronage

Throughout the 1960s, the new governments who had inherited power from the colonialists struggled with their new nations. The history of Africa's first decade of independence is fraught with conflict and bitter disappointment. New leaders, emboldened by their own anticolonial rhetoric, had begun to believe in the magic of their own words. They were not, however, as free of the yoke of the colonial system as they had imagined. Though colonial governments had been dismantled, the economic conditions they had introduced were still very much intact. Africans found themselves where Africa had always been, firmly positioned at the periphery of the world's capitalistic system

(Amin, 1990, p. 70). This meant they did not very much control the purse strings of their economies.

The economic position of Africa put its leaders in a double bind and generated the need for a good deal of double-talk. One style of discourse was needed for the world political and investment community; another style was needed for home consumption. As Bretton notes, one set of messages was needed to assure investors that their interests were secure; a second was needed to keep the indigenous people united under the banner of the preindependence period, i.e., anticolonialist sentiment (1973, pp. 170–71).

In many cases, the doublespeak failed and the precarious ruling coalitions unraveled. One after another, radical African leaders of the 1960s were overthrown: Patrice Lumumba of Zaire in 1961; Kwame N'Krumah of Ghana in 1966; Modibo Keita of Mali in 1968. In all three cases, the increasingly socialist rhetoric of these leaders and/or their growing coziness with Moscow/Peking were important factors in their demise (Ungar, 1987, pp. 63–64; Amin, 1990, p. 44). Other leaders, such as Sylvanus Olympio of Togo and Milton Obote of Uganda, simply fell as they failed to manage the contradictions of their new states.

In time, the military general Mobutu Sese Seko was given power to oversee, on behalf of the capitalist order, the vast and lucrative land which had been the Congo (now Zaire). N'Krumah was replaced by a series of inept leaders who lacked N'Krumah's vision but who were, ostensibly and intermittently, more friendly to Western interests (Davidson, 1992, p. 232). Keita was replaced by military strongman Moussa Traoré. Olympio and Obote were ultimately replaced respectively by General Gnassingbe Eyadema and "Field Marshall" Idi Amin.

To be sure, there was an abundance of disgruntled locals available to assist foreign adventurism by the major powers in the ex-colonies. The new states faced intractable problems generated by administrative and political vacuums, disparate and disunited ethnic groups, and weak economies. One after another, their regimes fell to military coups. These regimes were replaced by military men more professionally and psychologically attuned to the use of authoritarianism, patronage, and brute force as means of containing or at least managing the contradictions and the distortions of the modern African state.

Nonmilitary leaders who achieved longevity in office, such as Félix Houphouët-Boigny of Côte d'Ivoire, Kenneth Kaunda of Zambia, Leopold Senghor of Senegal, Julius Nyerere of Tanzania, Hastings Banda of Malawi, and Jomo Kenyatta of Kenya, all learned to balance the contradictions of their states. They learned to please foreign investors and quell the fears of international bankers. They learned to neutralize potential opposition through the awarding of lucrative appointments to the civil service or the granting of material favors: logging concessions, land grants, or import-export licenses. They learned to balance the wishes of competing religious voices and to keep their military satisfied with its share of the national cake. In the process most of them crippled their national legislatures, packed their judiciaries, and replaced elected local government officials with federally appointed ones. While they went about the business of shoring up their power, they silenced their opposition, created a personality cult, and muffled the press. In short, nearly all of the African regimes of the 1970s or 1980s engaged in a leadership style known as patronage.

Internal Patronage

Systems of patronage function in societies where the real owners of power, the owners of capital resources, are uninterested in competing locally for power. They are uninterested in who holds power or how it is wielded, providing they are able to continue to accumulate wealth. Into the vacuum come the "Big Men" who form cozy partnerships with the outside and who fashion internally a machine able to manipulate the access of diversified and desperate local groups to money.

The regimes left by the colonial powers were not proper nation-states. Nominally, they were independent, but functionally, they were not. They had little shared history except the common colonial experience. They had little common cultural/linguistic glue to hold them together. In fact, they represented quite different groups of people, often with competing interests and differing allegiances to the outside world (Bretton, 1973, pp. 24–28).

Africa's Big Men politicians have played off these conflicts and these competing interests by rewarding some and punishing others. Where necessary, Big Men have tried to achieve an ethnic balance in the distribution of spoils. And because the rewards of Big Men are based on loyalty rather than competence, patrimonial regimes are characterized by high levels of incompetence, insecurity, and corruption.

The most common form of patronage in Africa comes through the appointment of elites to the executive branch of government or to the civil service. Since there is little or no separation of power in these regimes, top-level positions in either the civil service or the cabinet tend to be difficult to distinguish from one another. In these systems, civil servant and cabinet shuffles are common. Cabinet reshuffles have material, social, and symbolic dimensions. Some ministerial assignments are less lucrative than others because they are less well paid or because they offer less opportunity to collect the graft for which systems of patronage are notorious. The Ministry of Post and Telecommunication may offer far better opportunities for collecting bribes from foreign corporations installing communication links than the Ministry of Education. The latter must content itself with creaming off salaries of rural teachers or collecting bribes from potential students hoping to be nominated for scholarships abroad. Cabinet reshuffles are also used as a means of curbing the development of factions, the inevitable trickle-down networks of patron-client relationships. A minister who moves loses many of the camp followers he (or in rare cases, she) has favored and rewarded within his (or her) own ministry.

These reshuffles also send veiled messages to appointees. When a president removes one of his previously trusted followers from a position of high visibility to one far removed from the capital, chances are he is using the assignment to convey displeasure over some public action or statement made to the press by the subordinate. The move itself is likely to generate much public rumor and speculation, activities which abound in social situations characterized by a scarcity of accurate information (Nkanga, 1992, p. 4). The move is in fact intended partly for this purpose, for Big Men know full well that their people are highly attuned to the use of nuance, understatement, and symbolic behavior. And the generation of rumors about the thoughts and feelings of the Big Man, easily altered and spread through the oral networks of the masses, only contributes further to the mystification which symbolically upholds the Big Men cults. Meanwhile, the civil servant, whose fate is the subject of public speculation, has been given a terminal case of nerves. The lesson will not be overlooked by others in the bureaucracy.

Systems of patronage, it seems, provide their own peculiar forms of insecurity. Beholden to the head of state for his livelihood, the minister or the civil servant must constantly keep a sharp ear for the continuous changes in the political winds. Does the president favor an American aid package presented by the U.S. ambassador this week? If so, then the civil servant must be cautious in offering public comments about American foreign policy. Did the president initiate the new directive taken by the minister of youth and sport? If so, the civil servant in question will take care to praise the aforesaid minister as well.

Theobald characterizes the climate of one-party states as replete with alliance making and breaking, character assassination, and victimization (1990, p. 128). Such a political climate leaves little incentive for the development of professional expertise and independent professional judgment. Why seek to become skilled in the management of the Ministry of Rural Development when, likely as not, one may be transferred to the Bureau of Internal Revenue? Nor does this system engender professional collegiality: openness in sharing professional problems may lead to the perception of weakness to one's coworkers. Such apparent vulnerability may later be used against a civil servant by other ambitious colleagues in their own ongoing scrambles for favorable treatment and lucrative assignments.

The media, of course, are bound up in the same web of patronage which envelops the rest of the civil service. And top media management is equally at the mercy of executive power, and their positions are equally insecure. If this instability were not bad enough, media managers must bear a double yoke. Because their work and their organizations are particularly and peculiarly public, managers must be extra cautious in the way they conduct business. One ill-timed comment by a junior reporter may cost both the newsperson and the station manager their jobs.

The system of patron-client relations in Africa, according to Bretton and Theobald, hearkens back to precolonial modes of social and political organization. It had always been part of the African tradition not to insist on the separation of powers. On the subject of corruption, Bretton adds that "the susceptibility of traditional rulers to mild forms of bribery conditioned them to be receptive to more remunerative approaches in the modern setting" (1973, p. 125). Traditional respect for the ruler is deeply embedded in the African psyche. Thus, it has not been very difficult for skillful Big Men to bend the public will to their own. Theobald adds that elites themselves are "slaves to the cult of the big man" and so must collect bribes "to display their wealth ostentatiously as well as meet the escalating demands of large followings on their generosity" (1990, p. 81).

African economies developed during the colonial era were oriented firmly toward Europe. Little effort was made on the part of the colonial powers to assist in the development of an internal private sector. Rodney shows that loan policies in colonial banks generally kept indigenous Africans from acquiring the capital needed to launch new businesses. Instead, what encouragement was given for the development of an internal entrepreneurial class was directed to Asians (1972, p. 236). These entrepreneurs, of course, clustered primarily around the administrative centers where the buying power was always the greatest.

Asian business communities have always been a target of bitter resentment by the African masses. The harnessing of local ill will toward Asians, combined with the expropriation of Indian businesses and properties in Uganda under Idi Amin, sent shock waves through Asian business communities in Africa. Amin's demonstration of power reminded Asians of their vulnerability on the continent and their need to cooperate fully in the system of patronage of their adopted homelands.

Not surprisingly, one-party states have been less than encouraging of would-be African entrepreneurs. A powerful indigenous African business class has clearly not been in the interest of the Big Men. Rulers such as Mobutu of Zaire have much preferred to hold on firmly to all the internal levers of power, making the task of distributing favors far easier to control. The creation of parastatal organizations whose chief executive officers are appointed by the head of state has been a favorite tactic of the Big Men, one which serves to deceive the masses with nationalist rhetoric. And this accounts largely for the fact that so much African business has remained, until the 1990s, in the hands of parastatal organizations whose CEOs are appointed by the head of state.

External Patronage

If African elites are beholden to their local patrons within the political system, the patrons themselves are bound into the demands of the international capitalistic system. The African middle-class elites depend for their existence on the modern world economy to which they are tied. Meanwhile, the rural masses are left to their own devices in their struggle for survival. Tied to the world monetary system, the very existence of the elite class depends upon the availability of foreign exchange, generated through cash crops and underpaid urban labor. In the weak condition of African economics, foreign exchange availability means playing an economic game in which the foreigners inevitably hold most if not all of the cards. Africa's economic climate has steadily worsened since the 1970s, causing more hardship for all and further exploitation of the rural masses and urban poor. Annual GNPs for a number of Black African countries actually declined in the 1980s (Clough, 1992, p. 78). A number of factors have contributed to this state of affairs, most of them related to Africa's vulnerability to outside economic forces and the immense and widening gap between rich and poor in the North-South axis (Kuhne, 1993, p. 16).

Foreign influence over African economic activities has taken several forms. There have been the foreign owners or managers of outside capital who have participated directly in the African economies (Bretton, 1973, p. 75). Foreign investors have been aided and abetted by their own governments, whose diplomatic staffs are positioned, in part, to protect and promote the economic interests of their nationals. Of these, extractive industries, whose influence has been the most pervasive, have created special opportunities for direct participatory control. They have dictated or manipulated production, volume, distribution, marketing, and royalty payments (Bretton, 1973, p. 76). A growing cadre of educated elites has worked locally with extractive industries over the last thirty years and has collaborated with the efforts of the outsiders.

To lessen the apparent power of these interests, many African nations resorted, especially during the 1970s, to the nationalization of important industrial or extractive sectors of their economies. But nationalized industries always remained dependent upon foreign experts and consultants, outside capital, and external markets. So nationalization merely added a layer of elite African state bureaucracy to industry and commerce. Apparent attempts to diversify African economies have historically come in the form of foreign aid packages. But aid, even if well intended, has often been difficult to separate from trade.

The collusion of interests between givers of foreign aid and capitalist designs was always especially apparent in the former French colonies. As Bretton notes, "French aid and trade are conducted through elaborate subsidy arrangements that virtually tie the African economy to French capitalization, consumer practices, and policies" (1973, p. 7). (See also chapters 4 and 5.) Even where the benefits accruing to foreign patrons have been less evident, the fact is that foreign aid is a direct extension of the national domestic/foreign policies of donor nations. At the very least, foreign aid grants or loans usually stipulate that equipment purchased through the loan must come from the donor country.

More often than not, aid given is far more conditional. The restrictions which accompany grants or loans, be they access to military bases, trade concessions, investment opportunities, export outlets, or diplomatic support at international forums, are what is referred to by disgruntled aid critics as "tied aid." Indeed, the charge is well placed. As Rubin and Weinstein note, governments with cash to spare do so to serve their own interests (1974, p. 292). The United States' record of aid contributions is particularly dismal in this regard. Over half of its aid to its principal African clients—Ethiopia, Kenya, Liberia, Somalia, Sudan, and Zaire—between 1962 and 1988 went directly to the leaders of these countries (Clough, 1992, p. 78), ostensibly to shore up their support against the Soviet Union.

To avoid the pitfall of so-called tied aid, many African nations turned to multilateral banking agencies such as the International Monetary Fund or the World Bank. Indeed, these agencies took over much of the task of providing financial capital to Africa's beleaguered economies in the 1970s and 1980s. Ordinary commercial association with Africa had less and less to offer entrepreneurs from the developed world as former colonial ties attenuated (Economou, Gittelman, Wubneh, 1993, pp. 100–101). And bilateral aid to Africa declined during the 1970s as traditional givers of aid found their own economies contracting after the oil shocks of 1974 and 1979 (Reed, 1992, pp. 7–8). Aid did increase to sub-Saharan Africa during the 1980s, but a proportionally larger share of it came in the form of multilateral aid (Riddell, 1993, p. 140). Such multilateral assistance projects were conducted with technical help supplied by organizations of the United Nations, such as UNESCO, UNICEF, the FAO, the WHO, and the ILO. But critics of these projects have always been easy to find among the African elites, who charge that these projects too represent the long arm of imperialist power and excessive control by American-dominated interests (Bretton, 1973, p. 83). The charge has been difficult to refute particularly during the 1980s as World Bank loans have been tied increasingly to structural adjustment programs with their heavy commitment to African foreign debt servicing and their concomitant focus on export production increase (Reed, 1992, p. 16).

If the criticisms are valid, the spirit in which much of them are lodged is less so, for it is from these aid programs that so many of the elites now gain their livelihood. It is also a well-known fact of life in the aid business that elites benefit disproportionately from aid packages and that much aid given winds up in foreign bank accounts of the elites (Kuhne, 1993, p. 20; Rahnema, 1992, p. 166).

Inevitably, the headquarters of aid-giving organizations are located in the capital cities (the administrative centers). These aid bureaucracies provide a burgeoning source of employment to African elites who participate in the erstwhile development of their nations. To be fair, it must be said that elite hypocrisy is equally matched by that of the external donors who have squandered aid money on arms and gaudy "white elephant" projects (Kouassi and White, 1993, p. 37; Ayittey, 1992, p. 282).

To a degree, African elites recognize the relative weakness of their positions *vis-à-vis* the wealthier nations giving aid, and they are fully cognizant of the disparity between their own salaries and those of foreign advisors working alongside them in the aid-giving project. Salary/perk differentials are a source of frequent irritation among them. Frustrated and angry, elites in these projects sometimes work to undermine the goals of even good projects. And internal squabbling among elites and their expatriate counterparts sometimes creates costly delays in project schedules (McLellan, 1986, p. 59).

Again, the inevitable condition of alienation among the elites emerges here for consideration. Here is a class fully cognizant that the international economic deck is stacked against them. Here is a group of people, many of whom possess foreign degrees and should, they feel, were it not for the accident of the geography of their birth, be in a position to enjoy in perpetuity, the perks, privileges, and comfort of a middle-class Western lifestyle. And here is a group of people forced to work alongside foreign experts, tangible human symbols of the international capitalist order, the perceived (and sometimes real) source of their exploitation and that of their nation. The anger and alienation of these elites has hardened them to the plight of peasants in their own societies and to the outrageous disparities between their lifestyles and those of the poor. Ayittey provides some shocking examples. Angolans with cars can fill their tanks for less than one dollar; they can fly from Luanda to Paris and back for the cost of two cases of beer! Zairian elites in 1982 earned $5,000-$9,000 a month while their peasant counterparts earned no more than $50 at best (1992, p. 118).

Amin is critical of the elites and the intelligentsia for their failure to devise alternative cultural and social models for the enrichment of their lives and those of the masses. He blames the extraverted character of their education, their disinterest in the study of their own condition, together with their alienation and sloth for this shortcoming. And he implies that their social positions are too comfortable to encourage them to think of alternatives to the present system (1990, p. 99). Ayittey is equally dismayed with African elites, but he also feels they may be burdened with a sense of inferiority which leads them to believe they cannot find the solutions to their own problems (1992, p. 208). This notion forms part of the well-known characterization of the African, described by Valentine Mudimbe, as "the Other" (1988).

Under these conditions, it is no wonder that elites often serve as a break on the few well-intended and well-planned aid projects (see chapters 3, 4, and 9). Nor do elites seem to have much interest in devising projects of their own, for such activity implies the unpleasant prospect of elite relocation to some rural backwater that such development activity would entail. Relocation to rural areas, apart from the sheer discomfort and inconvenience involved, generally detracts from the ability of elites to engage in the struggles and squabbles for power, the jockeying for position characteristic of patronage systems. Most of these battles take place within sighting range of the executive palace or mansion and the government buildings of the capital. To be out of town is to be out of touch. The last thing a modern elite wants is a "bush posting."

Summary

African elites live in a world which is profoundly alienating. Cut off from their past, they must find new social relationships and make new friends in the cities. But potential friendships are, likely as not, to be with elite peers, potential rivals for the same posts. In an atmosphere pervaded by plots and day-to-day shifts in loyalties, engendered by a system of political patronage, an element of mistrust tends to pervade relationships with folks outside the elite's kin network.

Cut off from their ancestral religion, African elites have made faith in progress their new religion. Cut off from rural social support systems, they must find individually the means of survival in the modern world. Detached from the sanctioning power of group-based ethics, they have replaced communitarian sharing with individualism, greed, and arrogance.

We have seen that life in the cities is harsh and alienating, full of crime, high prices, embattled neighborhoods, competitive work relations, endless demands of rural kin, and demoralizing comparisons with well-heeled expatriates. Finally, we have seen that African elites occupy the position of the "Other." In their particular case, it has an ironic double sense. It implies that they are neither fully participants in the rural life of the villages nor fully incorporated into the Western world.

All of this is to say that African elites as a group are not very comfortable in their skins. Frantz Fanon described this class in a book about them called

Black Skin, White Masks (1967). As Bretton notes, Africa's modern elites have had to break with the traditional past because they did not play a part in it (Bretton, 1973, pp. 170, 191). This rupture has serious repercussions through all facets of African social life and symbolizes what is wrong with Africa. Its effects have resounded loudly through the mass media.

3 | Broadcast Management

BROADCASTING IN BLACK Africa was largely created by the colonial powers, chiefly for their own purposes. And broadcasting on the continent has always been chiefly state-controlled, heavily government-subsidized, and urban-based, usually emanating from capital cities.

The peculiar effect of the colonial legacy on the broadcast enterprises of Black Africa can be appreciated through an examination of the social nature of managers, their style of management, and the effects of management practices on managees. This chapter will look at African media management through three analytical lenses: political patronage, elite alienation, and orally based value systems. These frames of reference will provide a comprehensive picture of broadcast management in Black Africa as it has been practiced up until the last decade of the twentieth century.

In the 1990s, the African media are poised on the brink of change. Much government-controlled African broadcasting may soon decentralize as multiparty democracy gives way to greater freedom and creates a demand for more accountable institutions. Meanwhile, private broadcasting is beginning to emerge as African economies have been forced to bend to the pressures of the international marketplace. In the light of ongoing reorganization, it is useful to review past practices, to highlight the healthy and productive trends in management, and to point out dysfunctional and unproductive patterns. In this way, positive activity may be promoted, and negative practices may be abandoned.

Douglas McGregor, in his landmark work *The Human Side of Enterprise* (1960), summarized most of the theories of management of the previous decades by describing two predominant schools of managerial thought and practice as falling under Theory X and Theory Y. He described Theory X as a style of management which focused on the ability to manage people in earlier times through physical force or coercion and more recently through monetary reward or appeals to moral precepts. Theory Y, he noted, focused not on authority, but on the needs of subordinates for growth, autonomy, knowledge, self-respect, and the recognition of others. These needs were taken from the top of the Maslow hierarchy under the assumption that the more basic needs (physiological needs, safety and security needs, social needs for affiliation, love, and friendship) would otherwise be met (Quaal and Brown, 1976, pp. 16–17).

Theory Y is clearly an improvement over Theory X because it stresses the need for flexibility and selective adaptation in discovering ways to tap potential commitment and achievement motivation of the human resources of an organization. A possible weakness of Theory Y is that in the emphasis on the human potential of an organization, the role of directive behavior by management has sometimes been underplayed by its adherents.

In their summative work *Broadcast Management* (1976), Ward L. Quaal and James A. Brown offer Theory V, a management theory which is more inclusive than either X or Y. Theory V stresses the *dynamic* of management processes involving both directive behavior on the part of management and the creation of a work environment fostering human growth. Quaal and Brown provide their Theory V definition of management:

> Managing is a process involving persons relating to one another through directives. It is this dynamic interrelationship of person to person through directives and their being actualized through execution which constitutes the essence of management. (Quaal and Brown, 1976, p. 18)

Management is thus a triad which can be investigated through any one of its three components—managers, managing, and managees. Broadcast management in most Black African nations has almost always resembled Theory X, sometimes Theory Y, but almost never Theory V.

Implicit in Theory V is the issue of intentionality of the organization, i.e., its purpose. It assumes that broadcast organizations must have a dominant focus, a key purpose around which management operates. There has been a built-in central weakness in African broadcast organizations, a weakness caused by a confusion of purpose. In theory, broadcasting is a *mass* medium, enjoined by definition to disseminate information, news, and entertainment to the entire populace, or at least to those portions of it reached by radio or television signals. In practice, broadcasting in Black Africa has often been "narrowcasting," targeted by intent or by omission chiefly at the urban sections of the populace, particularly the more educated. This fuzziness of purpose has plagued broadcasting in Black Africa and contributed to its lackluster performance.

Senior Managers

Senior management includes the managing director or the director general, often the titular heads of broadcast organizations, the general manager, the head of day-to-day operations, the manager of news and public information, the manager of programs production, the comptroller of finance and administration, and the technical manager or chief engineer.

Assignments to senior management have come largely through two routes. The first is by direct appointment through political patronage; the second is by advancement through the civil service. Politically sensitive management positions, especially the managing director, the general manager, and the manager of news and public information are very often appointed directly by the head of state or his deputy, an information minister. The more technical specialties in finance, engineering, and broadcast production are more likely to come through the ranks of the civil service.

Many countries with a British colonial legacy inherited at independence organizations modeled along the lines of the British Broadcasting Corporation. Designed to provide some autonomy from central government organization and pressure, most corporations have been abolished since independence and placed directly under government information ministries.

In the former French, Portuguese, and Belgian colonies, government broadcasting was always firmly tied to the central administrative structures, and it remained so well into the late 1980s. It has only been since the wave of privatization of the media and other government structures, coupled with the dual cries for multiparty democracy and more press freedom in the 1990s, that the close ties of broadcasting with government are beginning to loosen throughout the African continent. (See chapters 4, 5, and 8.)

The colonial legacy left strict rules governing the civil service structure. Access to civil service posts is obtained through the attainment of acceptable levels on civil service examinations combined with the presentation of certificates of appropriate levels of formal education. Neither civil service standards nor the criteria used by patrons are reliable guarantees of creativity or of the managerial skill needed to administer a broadcast organization.

Lateral transfers have also been common within the African civil service. Thus, a person who has worked in the Education Ministry, in Social Affairs, or even in the Internal Revenue Service may be called upon to manage some aspect of a broadcast organization. Such persons are likely to have little understanding for the particular nature of broadcasting or the special demands placed upon broadcast professionals.

Occasionally, broadcasters have been promoted within the organization. Thus, a person who was once an effective on-air talent or a qualified TV or radio producer finds that he (or more rarely, she) can no longer broadcast. He (or she) must now supervise and administer. Whatever the personal loss for the individuals involved and the concomitant loss of the broadcast product, these persons tend to make the best managers. Unlike the patronage-based appointments or the lateral transferees, the "in-house advancers" have a feel for the processes and exigencies of broadcasting. They have been tested in the fire of reporting, audio production, or television directing. They are also able to give instruction to subordinates in the running of broadcast equipment and in the maintenance of production schedules. They tend to be sensitive to equipment needs.

Senior Managers and Patronage

Whether a person has obtained an appointment by direct nomination of the executive branch of government or whether s/he has moved through the ranks of the civil service, the maintenance of such an individual's rank has usually depended upon the pleasure of the patron. Ould Daddah, an African scholar of public administration, remarks on this situation: "In these conditions, it is impossible to talk about meritocracy, rationality, efficiency or any of the other concepts of Weber's [administrative] formulations" (1988, p. 113). Indeed, the dependency such a system fosters creates a built-in insecurity, one which permeates through the organization.

High-level managers avoid sharing problems with one another, for this could be perceived as a sign of weakness. As one well-placed Liberian broadcast middle manager noted, "Chiefs do not talk to one another, because each is afraid one may topple the next." Rather, such officers tend to communicate by terse memoranda. This slows down communication and decision making and renders broadcast organizations inflexible and unresponsive to problems.

An atmosphere of blame and suspicion often permeates media organizations as restless bureaucrats attempt to quell the formation of factions and alliances of junior staff vying for power and/or recognition from their superiors. Senior management meetings take on a false character wherein managers play at coorientation and engage in a kind of administrative doublespeak. Each one plays his or her assigned role of feigning interest in the organization, making a pretense of public service while privately seeking to minimize broadcast activity with a potential for conflict, all the while deflecting blame from above for inevitable errors committed in the cut and thrust of daily operation. As one Liberian broadcast manager allowed, "Of course African media is boring and repetitious, but we'd prefer to be bored than to lose our jobs!"

The quixotic nature of governments and the governments' dependence on the winds of politics and international patronage rooted to events outside Africa make for frequent meetings with ministries. Heads of broadcast services are often called to the Ministry of Information (or its equivalent) to attempt to decide on policy. A good deal of confusion abounds in and from these meetings as well as from the directives obtained therein.

Squeezed between the need to satisfy multiple, conflicting sets of patrons, media managers are often paralyzed into inactivity. Does a news item featuring the head of state with the U.S. ambassador make the head of state look small?

Was the ambassador's sound-bite longer than the president's? Will a new drama program on family planning offend the Islamic community? Will a new music program be accused of unduly copying the West? Will a development project shot in Village X offend with its poverty the minister of information whose mother happens to reside there? Or alternately, will the airing of the aforementioned segment generate accusations that the minister of information is funneling excessive aid to his kinsmen? Will a critical editorial on American foreign policy jeopardize a prospective aid package?

The resolution of these questions demands time and energy, often taking up a disproportionate share of management work hours. They can keep managers from tending to the day-to-day operations of the station. In large countries like Nigeria, managers are frequently absent for periods as long as eight days, ostensibly for management meetings held in Abuja or Lagos.

Senior Managers and Alienation

Senior managerial positions are typically occupied by persons who hold at least a university education, a degree often obtained overseas. This and other social reasons puts managers well into the elite category as regards social status. Senior managers have access to a considerable number of valuable employment perks: usually a government-supplied home in an upscale neighborhood, a government-supplied vehicle (or access to a station vehicle), a government retirement pension, free or subsidized medical benefits, etc.

Senior managers make numerous work-related journeys: trips to the capital cities (for those managers posted at regional stations) for meetings with high-ranking officials in government; trips to neighboring countries to attend seminars on media-related issues sponsored by the United Nations or bilateral aid agencies; and trips to the First World sponsored under the auspices of the United States Information Service, the Deutsche Welle or other German media aid foundations, and the specialized agencies of the United Nations.

Managers spend a good deal of time in communion with central authorities, focusing on their problems and their policy concerns. This emphasis affords senior management less time and less ability to concentrate on two important groups below them: their staff and their audiences. Socially, management is quite separate from staff. The former live in better neighborhoods, are better traveled and more educated, and are far better paid.

As noted, managers who have climbed the professional ladder within broadcasting are most able to empathize with staff problems and concerns and are the most attuned to the demands of the work environment. These professionals are rare. And the social separation of management from staff is often reinforced by the physical layout of the electronic media organizations. In Nigeria, NTA management wings are often separated from the production wings by several floors. Sometimes these functions are housed in separate buildings. This physical layout reifies the already prevalent notion that Big Men do not operate equipment, lift heavy objects, or otherwise soil their hands.

A frequent complaint heard from staff is that their managers do not understand them and that they fail to appreciate the work-related or personal problems of subordinates. In Nigeria, during training courses I conducted during the early 1980s, I heard numerous complaints, many of which seemed justified. Managers would assign trainees to courses without first consulting candidates regarding their individual or collective training needs or availabilities. As a consequence the training courses often contained students with mixed abilities and interests. It seemed that management did not know their personnel very well. Often trainees were scheduled for broadcast duty and training courses occurring at the same time! Or managers would assign trainees to attend classes even though said trainees had already worked or were about to work an eight-hour shift on the same day. Some of the trainees were on holiday when they were summarily summoned to attend sessions. When I pointed out these difficulties to senior management, they would often simply reply that the staff needed to "make sacrifices for the good of the station," and that "it was not possible to consult 'these boys' on matters of station policy." The trainees, treated like children, behaved as such: arriving late, leaving early, and devising excuses for numerous absences. The moralistic and paternalistic tone of admonitions from senior management typifies attitudes found in management systems operating under Theory X.

Managerial alienation from audiences is a different but somewhat related problem. Because funds are in very short supply, most broadcast organizations do not have functioning research departments. They depend upon feedback from letter writers in order to know audience reactions to programs. Mytton shows how urban letter writers in Tanzania tended to outweigh those from rural areas and, hence, tended to reinforce the already predominant urban biases of broadcasting in that country (1983, p. 113). Cruise-O'Brien's account of research at Radio Senegal notes the same tendency (1985, p. 190).

Indeed, there has been considerable ambivalence among broadcasters regarding the danger (read democratizing potential) of mass media. Merrill argued in 1971 that early in the developmental process, national leadership in Africa did not want a truly mass media system. He argued that reaching the masses did not really matter to governments in transitional stages, that truly *mass* media was irrelevant, and that "only elite lines of communication really mattered" (quoted in Head, 1974, p. 334). Because of the worsening economy in the 1970s and 1980s, this attitude still held true throughout those decades. In the 1990s, however, the African masses have at last begun to clamor for information rights.

Mytton provided an analysis in 1983 similar to Merrill's earlier judgment:

> It should not be assumed—though in the literature on the subject, it often is—that political elites necessarily desire an effective means of mass communication or have any clear policy on how to use it. They may want to control the media capable of reaching large sections of the population, yet at the same time be suspicious of the power these media possess: power which is ultimately beyond their control. (Mytton, 1983, p. 94)

This ambivalence toward the media is one reason for the institutional confusion over its role and purpose. Faced with this lack of clarity, broadcasting throughout the continent has devoted a lion's share of airtime to the coverage of political speeches. Mytton's discussion shows how much broadcasting in the early 1970s in Zambia was devoted to lessons on Kenneth Kaunda's philosophy of humanism. Research showed these broadcasts to be among the least popular radio programs, with popular music shows, advice for the lovelorn, development programs, and stories from traditional culture winning out handsomely (1983, p. 91). As Mytton notes, "The radio cannot demand that we listen to it. Although most professional broadcasters know this, governments tend to ignore the point" (1983, p. 94).

Tanzania also ignored the point. Mytton's case study of Tanzanian media details early parliamentary debates over the amount of news covered on Radio Tanzania. Responding to a criticism from a Tanzanian parliamentary backbencher that the Voice of Kenya carried more news than his own nation's radio service, the Tanzanian minister of information replied with satisfaction: "All important speeches by the President, Ministers, Parliamentary Secretaries, Regional Commissioners and other TANU and Afro-Shirazi leaders [are] considered first, before news from neighboring countries, and from Africa as a whole, and all other important news" (1983, p. 99). The information minister's definition of news was clearly apparent in his response.

Mytton concedes with fairness that it was probably important to broadcast the speeches of these modern politicians in the early days of independence. And he notes that Nyerere's policy was designed to counter the effects of excessive Western influence in broadcasting. But he adds quite perceptively that no one in Parliament was concerned with how audiences felt about the length or the quantity of speeches to which they were being subjected (1983, p. 100).

Indeed, the exigency of nation-building has been used throughout the continent to foist upon broadcast audiences talking voices or heads and endless rounds of redundant footage of arriving dignitaries paying courtesy calls on the head of state or other important officials. These talking voices/heads undoubtedly have symbolic, status conferral value for the masses. Perhaps this is enough, for it is quite clear that the masses pay little attention to the content of these broadcasts. I have frequently seen viewers turn down the sound at such points in a television broadcast, assured no doubt that little information can be gained from them. Still, the idea that the African masses should be made to listen to long windy speeches in a language they may understand poorly suggests either a fundamental disregard for the mass audience or at least a basic failure to understand or empathize with them.

Management attitudes toward their rural countrymen are often very paternalistic. After a research presentation showing that development broadcasts aired in Liberia had not significantly changed behavior, one senior manager remarked with annoyance that broadcasters would now be forced to "go out to the villages to find out why the people don't do *what we tell them.*" The alienation of these elite broadcasters from their audience, especially the proletariat, undoubtedly contributes to some of the problems. One middle manager in the Liberian Rural Communications Network[1] commented on the subject:

> Most of our elites [at LRCN] don't know much about the country people. They grew up in Monrovia. When they talk about going to their villages, they will be embarrassed. They do not know how to perform the rituals and the greetings. (March 1989. Interview with author [name omitted]

George Ayittey, a Ghanaian professor of economics, echoes these comments with stronger words: "They [elites of Africa] depreciated the indigenous as 'backward' and 'primitive' " (1992, p. 10). And Cameroonian communications scholar Jerry Domatob remarks on the subject that the "views, activities, trials and triumphs of the vast majority who are peasants, laborers, farmers, shepherds, and market traders are usually excluded from the media" (1991, p. 32). Women journalists in Lagos themselves told me that as they advanced and became middle class they became "selfish and uninterested" in the problems of their unsophisticated sisters, the city market women and their rural counterparts (USIA, American Partners Lecture Tour, March 1992. Lagos).

Senior Managers and the Oral Tradition

Undoubtedly, the oral tradition has contributed importantly to the emphasis on speeches and pronouncements in the African media. In traditional African societies, respected elders, particularly males, were expected to mete out kernels of wisdom liberally peppered with formulary sayings or proverbs. The delivery of speeches, carefully inscribed in the philosophy of the national leader, be it Kaunda's African Humanism in Zambia, Senghor's Negritude in Senegal, or Nyerere's African Socialism in Tanzania, is the modern equivalent of a much older tradition. And tradition explains why these speeches are heavily didactic and moralistic.

Balinagwe Mwambungu, a sub-editor with the government-owned *Daily*

News in Tanzania, noted that leaders love to be praised in the press (cited in Ayittey, 1992, p. 212). The use of the visual media as a showpiece for the glad-handing of African leaders, it appears, is a form of video praise poetry. It seems curious, at first glance, that the masses have complained so little about this style of news coverage. It was not until the late 1980s that audience acceptance of this style of broadcasting began to erode. At that time Africans came to learn of the disintegration of Eastern Europe and belatedly began to clamor for more information. The changes in Eastern Europe occurred, not coincidentally, with the arrival in Africa and elsewhere of satellite television services, finally giving at least to elite viewers access to comparatively free visual media. And trickle down of international satellite-borne news to the masses has come through their association with wealthier employers or relatives or from watching satellite feeds on large display television screens through electronics shop windows in major African cities. Until that time, the vast majority of Africans seemed locked into believing that singing the praises of government officials was the most that could be expected from the electronic media.

When I taught television production at a university in northern Nigeria, I was consistently surprised at the TV programs students made. After several practice runs with training scripts devised to force studio action and movement, students were assigned to create their own programs. Unfailingly, they sought out the most long-winded and unanimated guests (faculty members were particularly well suited to this task), put these guests face-to-face with a student interviewer, and launched into the subject of the day. The guests, experts in such engaging topics as "scientific socialism" or the "state creation movement" (ever a popular topic in multiethnic Nigeria), would pontificate without interruption. One afternoon during one of these productions, the student interviewer himself fell asleep (on camera) along with several of his classmates who were acting in the role of audience. When I pointed out that falling asleep at the microphone did not constitute good interviewing technique, there was much mirth in the studio classroom. Apparently, none of the students had expected the guest to be engaging. Only his presence was required.

One had to look no further than the broadcasts of the Nigerian Television Authority to determine whence these students had acquired their models. Nigerian television is replete with this sort of symbolic interview. Nor was sleeping on camera restricted to students.

In a training course I conducted at an NTA regional station, during a panel discussion (a forum for talking heads and speech-making), guests regularly nodded off while others made pronouncements. An informal prohibition against airing reaction shots of sleeping panelists only perpetuated the charade that these broadcasts were designed to inform and interest the wider public! Clearly the oral tradition has been distorted from its original intent by this style of patronage-ridden broadcasting.

Managing

Managing and Patronage

It has been a theme of this work that systems of patronage foster a climate of fear and insecurity. There is little "bottom-up" communication in broadcast organizations because they tend to reflect the ethics of the one-party state. This is the exact opposite of the ego-strengthening, growth-fostering management style advocated in Theory Y.

While it is certain that some broadcast managers would defend their management styles with arguments alleging that authoritarian structures represent the "African way," the evidence of traditional styles of chieftancy ruling through consensus does not corroborate this assertion (Ayittey, 1992, pp. 37–77).

In the absence of standards of professional behavior based upon competent performance, there develops instead confusion over appropriate behavior. The less powerful soon learn the rules of the informal reward structure. They develop a poisonous tendency to create factions aligning themselves behind the more powerful chiefs or managers vying for power within the organization.

Authoritarian structures are "blame" structures. They place a premium on "loyalty and obedience and sensitivity to the demands of those in authority [while] undermining the values of excellence, independence, originality, and goal orientation" (LeVine, 1971, p. 78). Middle managers, such as production supervisors and news editors (sub-editors in the ex-British colonies), may re-create the authoritarian models of the organization within their spheres of influence.

Inevitably what gets lost in the shuffle of arguments over "disobedience and insubordination" is the product. With so many disputes centered on issues of power and protocol, practitioners tend to forget, as do their superiors, what their original purpose and goals ostensibly are: the production of broadcast programs. It is, of course, no surprise that they forget. Rewards, alleged to be granted for a job well done, are often not granted on the basis of excellence. They tend to be given to the most sycophantic or the most obedient.

In conditions of scarcity which characterize most broadcast organizations in Africa, rewards can be items other than salary. They may equally refer to access to training programs at home or overseas, preferred assignments, work schedules, or sometimes even access to the tools necessary to complete routine assignments—vehicles, audio or video recorders, lights, etc. Again, more serious attention to product and the delinking of professional tools from personal relationships would go a long way toward improving these organizations.

Robert Nwanko noted that the coordination of complex institutions including broadcast organizations is one of the most difficult feats to achieve in Third World nations. Logistics, of course, are the primary cause of these problems. Productions are frequently delayed because of electrical power outages, missing spare parts for broadcast production or transmission equipment, shortages of trained repair personnel, faulty communication links, poor transportation, etc. The lists of technical difficulties are endless and the delays they cause are demoralizing. They sap the strength of the most dedicated of operatives (1974, p. 308).

Sometimes, the technical shortfalls have been created by senior management. The diversion of service vehicles for personal use in African broadcasting is so common that it is an assumed perk of the big bosses. But let a subordinate attempt to divert a station driver to pick up his child at school and he will surely be disciplined. Some of the personal use of service vehicles is in fact big business. I recall frequent delays in shooting schedules in the *Télé-Scolaire* project in Côte d'Ivoire when the "patron" was using project vans to transport pineapples from his large plantation to market at harvest time. A different patron commandeered project generators and electrified his village. And a third patron sold an entire transmitter to evangelists operating a religious broadcasting station in neighboring Liberia!

Replacement of parts has often not been a particular concern of management. One engineer of Harris Broadcasting of Illinois, a company supplying production and transmission equipment to NTA, averred that spare parts and training for technical operatives were the first components of telecommunication/broadcasting equipment packages to be bargained out of commercial agreements. Funds were very often siphoned away from these needs so as to make way for the "gratuities" of well-placed Information or Communication bureaucrats.

Patron-client relationships not only foster an attitude of arrogance toward subordinates and toward the organization, they also can foster a profound indifference. I recall one senior manager at headquarters in Liberia railing against upcountry staff: "They are just going to have to learn that we here at 'Central' have other things to do besides solving their problems." As he said this, he forgot, of course, why the central headquarters existed in the first place: to manage the network for the subsidiary stations! (See chapter 4.) This particular chief was in fact so busy with other activities that he rarely spent more than a few hours on the job per day. Such attitudes are diametrically opposed to the notion espoused in Theory Y that an "employee" become "prompted to look to the job as an integral part of his personal daily living" (Quaal and Brown, 1976, p. 17). In fact, the opposite is more likely to occur. The employee looks at daily living as part of his job. One general manager with whom I requested a meeting told me not to come to the station until after 11:00 A.M. because, "I read my papers at 10:00 and that is when they [station messengers] bring me my breakfast."

The economy of time is an issue which must also be examined not only with patrons and clients but also in terms of kin and lineage relations. Because station personnel have so many family responsibilities, they are often called away for long periods. One very competent and dedicated Nigerian television authority general manager with whom I worked once gave me a running account of a nine-day absence from his station. He had spent four days officiating at a turbanning ceremony receiving a traditional title; three days arranging for medical care for an ailing relative; and two days registering his child for elementary school. (His wife was under Islamic seclusion, Purdah, and did not go out publicly during daytime hours.) The deleterious effects such a lengthy absence would have in a Western broadcast organization would be considerable. In Africa, where the organizations are hierarchical and authoritarian, the absence of the chief executive for nine days is stultifying!

Ghanaian Communications scholar Isaac Obeng-Quaidoo argues that Africans have little commitment to work in the modern sector because work is a necessity for survival only but remains unconnected, as in the Protestant Ethic, to one's eternal reward (1985b, p. 113). This argument merely presents one more reason for the establishment in sub-Saharan Africa of alternative "earth-based" rewards for quality performance advocated in Theory Y.

Managing and Alienation

Mention has been repeatedly made in this text of the alienation of senior management. It has been said that this group belongs to a class which inherited the perks and privileges of colonialism. In Liberia, which lacks a colonial history, the Americo-Liberians (together with a small group of educated indigenes) acquired a similar privileged position before the civil war begun by Charles Taylor broke out in 1989. In all cases, it is these groups who must mediate between the "haves" and the "have nots." The elite class is the embodiment of the contradictions of their societies, and it is this class which must somehow make the contradictions palatable for the masses. They do this by giving these contradictions an acceptable public face. Thus, they often appear to champion the cause of the masses. This accounts for the strident articles in the local press, which rail against the status quo, the privileged expatriate class, the enemies of the people and so on (Domatob, 1991, p. 32). This criticism of outsiders, though often well deserved, tends to camouflage the cooptation of the elites into the present economically distorted system. Ayittey also notes with chagrin that many African intellectuals living outside of Africa have assumed a similar role in justifying the status quo of the past thirty years in the world press (1992, pp. xvii-xix).

Another way elites have coped with their alienation is by presenting an acceptable face of the media to outsiders. In the many lectures I have given to African media professionals, I have often been struck by the desire of audiences to obfuscate the reality of their positions. The case of Rwanda is telling. In 1987, I lectured to journalists during a time in that country's history when there was almost no press freedom. During one of my lectures, I presented a tape called "Assignment Africa" (1986), produced by David Royle, narrated by Hodding Carter, and originally aired on U.S. Public Television. The tape presents a critical view of U.S. journalistic coverage of Africa. It accepts that the American media have been highly negligent, and it blames a host of U.S.-based factors for this. These include the expense of covering the African continent; the Western focus on "crisis journalism"; the disinterest in Africa by the African-American community; and even the inherent racism of American network news management. In the interest of balance, however, the tape reviews some of the problems foreign reporters have in gaining access to stories. A major issue elucidated in the production involves the difficulties reporters have in obtaining visas and official permissions needed for their work and the delays reporters experience in interviewing officials.

My Rwandan audience fully agreed with all points critical of the U.S. position but denied any of the criticisms pertaining to African governments, including their own. I repeated the same lecture using the same video program in Madagascar and got a very similar response. After the lecture one of the participants confided privately to me that the Malagasy journalists were fully aware of the delay tactics of their government's Information Ministry, but they would never admit them to an outsider (USIA, American Partners Lecture Tour, Kigali and Antananarivo, February–March 1987).

When I returned to Rwanda in 1992, the press climate had changed dramatically. President Habyarimana had agreed to hold multiparty elections, and he had loosened many restrictions on the press. In the new spirit which emerged, all press persons whom I met on the later visit, including those who worked for the government, complained about the previous excesses of government media control. When I revealed to them what their colleagues had told me five years earlier, they merely laughed. Clearly, they were amused by the doublespeak of their colleagues (USAID, Democratic Initiatives Project Paper Preparation, Kigali, July 1992).

This doublespeak comes from a kind of a double bind. Because of the extraverted character of media education (in which I have admittedly played a role), media personnel are all too aware of the expectations outsiders have about the mass media. It has become their job to mediate between what they may believe should obtain within their organizations and what in fact has obtained in the last twenty to thirty years.

In Nigeria, in the early 1980s, I was always struck by the ability of managers to talk in rational and logical terms about the role of management. Displaying frayed administrative charts, they would explain orderly chains of command, neatly typed program schedules, and clearly written programming policy. They could freely quote broadcasting history and policy guidelines. Yet somehow, the day-to-day operations of these stations (not to mention the tales of the junior staff) revealed an alternative management style. Managers would receive telephone calls from powerful outsiders and suddenly issue new policy directives or reverse old ones. Persons occupying key positions in flow charts would be bypassed in important decisions affecting personnel or operations within their apparent jurisdiction. Programs scheduled for broadcast would fail to air! It was clear to me that the structures laid out rarely matched the reality of the organization. I never knew if it was clear to the managers. What is evident, however, is that these professionals had acquired the ability to describe in seemingly lucid and glowing terms processes which were much more random and serendipitous within their organizations.

One production middle manager proudly informed me he attended public television viewing centers to gather feedback for his productions. When I suggested we go together, he looked sheepish but agreed to take me along. Though he knew the city intimately, he had a great deal of difficulty that evening locating his "regular" feedback site!

The issue of media training for junior staff often revealed considerable confusion on the part of management regarding the work of broadcasting. I was hired to conduct training for studio operatives, and I always pressed for access to studios because the training, as I had explained, was practical. Inevitably my role was described as that of a "lecturer," and my access to studios was given heavy restrictions. One general manager agreed that I be allowed to use the studio for training courses in TV production, but he mandated that the course be disallowed from moving sets or lighting from their existing positions!

Managing and the Oral Tradition

The oral tradition offers some useful modes of operation, techniques which can be used with profit in solving group problems. The workings of the oral tradition can be clearly seen at senior management meetings. Though these meetings tend to be long and windy affairs, they are functional. Each manager is expected to speak in turn stating his position on a given problem or project. Redundancies are tolerated, even welcome. Where managers exercise comparative political freedom, such as in Nigeria, there is value to these exchanges. As Elliott and Golding remark, managers "mediate the inevitable into the desirable" (1979, p. 71).

To a great extent, the purpose of management meetings, as in the West, is problem solving. But the focus tends to be on the human aspect of a problem at hand rather than on a technical solution. If Studio A becomes inoperative, for example, the problem discussed will, in all likelihood, be defined as how to coax the staff of Production Studio B to allow access to Studio A's operatives. Comparatively less attention will be given to the repair of inoperative equipment. Ong would consider this focus as one which is "Close to the Human Lifeworld" (1982, pp. 42–43).

This style of problem solving is reminiscent of justice seeking behavior described by James Fernandez in his study of the traditional court proceedings of the Fang peoples of Gabon. Fernandez describes the roles of the *ntia mezdo*, the chief debaters who put forward arguments for the plaintiff and the defendant in a case. The *nkik mesang*, the chief justice, listens to both sides. But his role is not to establish the truth of the case but to reconcile the two opposing parties into a new way of doing things (Fernandez, 1975, pp. 206–209).

Anthropologist Alma Gottlieb made similar observations after participating in a trial among the Beng in Côte d'Ivoire:

> As elders conversed among themselves, I realized their model for this trial must have been very different from my own: rather than announcing a victor and a loser, their aim was for both sides to come out satisfied. . . . The point of the trial could only be to mend, not wound. (1993, p. 194)

So too, when there are conflicts between people at the stations, oftentimes, all sides will be heard. The role of the general manager will be to act as the *nkik mesang*, hearing all sides and attempting to make a wise decision, one which will re-establish harmony at the station. The substantive issue may be lost in the discussion or relegated to the background in the need of harmony and consensus.

With this sort of attachment to harmony needs, management spends a great deal of time discussing who said what to whom, who has breached protocol, who has spoken harshly, etc. These issues are undoubtedly of extreme cultural importance and must be handled judiciously by a wise general manager. The drawback of this focus on human interaction is that it leaves comparatively less time and energy for the substantive issues of broadcasting: equipment repairs, program scheduling, production quality, and audience feedback.

Where general managers are less than wise, or where the pressures of patronage are too strong, even the time-tested traditions of orally based harmony seeking behavior become warped and double edged. Management becomes strongly hierarchical and dialogue suffers.

One high-level manager in Liberian broadcasting told me that he was loathe to disagree with the project manager, the operation's chief executive, because to do so would cause her to lose face. Rather than do this, he said, he would speak to her privately after the meeting. While such behavior may respond to social rules of politeness, it strongly contradicts the apparent purpose of a meeting. Moreover, the practice of engaging in postmeeting discussions on a subject apparently resolved in a meeting causes confusion among other participants who have assumed a decision is final. If pronouncements made and agreements reached are undermined afterwards, the staff soon becomes disinclined to follow any directive emanating from management.

Because social rules are in flux in modern African societies, this sort of confusion over the rules of etiquette is prevalent. The traditional value of face saving or reverence for authority (incidentally not confirmed; see Ayittey, 1992, pp. 37–78) may in fact exist in stark contradiction to the structural demands of a modern multitask organization. Some individuals may cling to the older rules of conduct, while others may gravitate to new models of behavior. I recall my own difficulties with questions of etiquette as I sought discussion time with Nigerian management authorities. Sometimes secretaries encouraged me to interrupt managers in meetings with others, and sometimes they requested that I wait until an earlier visitor had finished business. Sometimes others would interrupt *my* meetings with managers, and other times *they* would wait. I was well aware that the Western propensity to treat one piece of business with one client at a time was certainly not the norm.[2] But what exactly was the norm, I could not fathom. Puzzled, I inquired on this point among junior staff. There was no consensus among them as to the appropriate protocol governing this situation. Clearly, some rules were needed to remedy the confusion. This is why I believe self-examination among managers in these modern broadcast settings is so important, and why station policies governing private meeting behavior, access to superiors, and other protocol must necessarily be established.

Another traditional behavior which has some bearing on the modern organization is the habit of governance through secrecy. Beryl Bellman's book *The Language of Secrecy* provides an extensive analysis of secret keeping in the Poro Complex, the traditional village politico-spiritual governance structure in parts of West Africa. Bellman argues that the content of secrets is far less important than the "doing of secrets." James Fernandez comments upon this point in the Foreword to Bellman's work:

> The conveying and withholding [of information] is not only a way of maintaining privilege in the social order; it is more fundamentally, a way of establishing its very domains and categories of interaction. (1984, p. viii)

Modern media organizations in Black Africa also engage in the process of "doing secrets." Here management engages in controlled discourse, discourse with a "sub-text" which limits what will and what will not be discussed.

I recall a case in Liberia where the cultural value of open versus closed discourse became readily apparent. It had long been the policy of the network management to maintain considerable control over upcountry operations. USAID's policy was to strive to promote network decentralization (see chapter

4.) One day, central management at the Liberian Rural Communications Network was engaged in a debate about an organizational problem in one of its upcountry stations. Their meeting proceeded as various section managers discussed the issue, meting out blame for the wrongdoers. Both I and another expatriate technical assistant who worked "upcountry" were in attendance.

When my colleague, not noted for his subtlety, could stand the discussion no longer, he finally blurted out a diatribe which went something like this:

> The reason this problem has occurred is because the upcountry broadcasters are frustrated. They feel they have no support from headquarters. You have most of the money and supplies. They have to beg for their share. You do not help them. You are wasting everyone's time here at the Central Administration! You should all be working upcountry where the real work is going on instead of sitting around doing nothing and holding meetings.

The project director was aghast. The other senior managers sat in angry surprised silence. The project director finally blurted out: "Dr.—, you cannot just tell us that we must decentralize and go upcountry when we are having a meeting about another matter!" He retorted, "I can't, huh, well, I just did!"

Many lessons could be learned from this example, and volumes might be written about the ambivalent role of expatriate technical advisors and their frequent lack of cultural sensitivity. But the point highlighted here is a different one, one which deals with the question of discourse framing. The issues raised in the discussion by the Liberian central managers regarding an upcountry station were carefully circumscribed. And the tenor of the discussion centering on distant regional staff was a highly moralistic one, one which treated the upcountry station personnel as lacking seriousness and dedication to the project. The comments of central management clearly derived from a Theory X style of management. They showed little concern for the autonomy needs of the upcountry staff or for promoting the self-worth of regional subordinates advocated in Theory Y.

My colleague's perhaps ill-timed remark was meant to puncture this frame and to shift the discourse to the level of organizational analysis, a level which made mention of a subject participants were loathe to discuss: the role top-heavy, Monrovia-based managers played in exacerbating upcountry problems and the complicity of this elite group in the maintenance of centralized power. By speaking aloud, this technical advisor broke the group's code of silence. The managers were not pleased. But they also had very little comeback. He had broken such a powerful discourse taboo that he all but left the group speechless. Arens and Karp remind us that an ethnography of power norms teaches how norms allow the powerful who are few to dominate over the many (1989, p. xv).

Managees

Managees and Patronage

In the absence of effective leadership, "rank and file" broadcasters have been left to their own devices. They must sort out for themselves the rules of the operation, as these are rarely provided from above. This can often lead to too much autonomy, a failure to link management directives with the actions of staff. This de facto policy of laissez-faire might be viewed by some as an excess of Theory Y.

Production teams generally recreate the authoritarian models they derive from their superiors. It was not uncommon during the early 1980s at NTA stations in Nigeria to find studio crew teams who resisted taking orders from TV directors. "Who is he to tell me what to do?" was a frequent complaint. "Does he think he is in his father's house when he is here at the studio?" some crew members would ask about television directors attempting to produce and broadcast live programs. Hierarchical thinking abounded, making it difficult or impossible to conduct running team efforts. Intransigent crew personnel would refuse to carry out certain tasks because of the real or imagined low status of the director. Others would refuse to carry out certain tasks because of the perceived low status attached to them. Such assignments included, for example, cue card "pulling," flat moving, or floor managing.

Inattention of management to studio details created other problems. Incorrect operating procedures, for example, became routine in the presence of faulty equipment. The job of floor manager in television production disappeared after floor managers' headsets long remained inoperative.[3] By the time the headsets were repaired, the role of the floor manager had been eliminated. The same happened with voltmeters which no longer worked. New audio operators were trained in sound recording without ever learning their purpose and function. After a while audio teams stopped requesting the VU meters be repaired.[4]

Managees and Alienation

Alienation poses a problem among low-level personnel. The dominance of Western models of education seem to paralyze thinking, giving junior staff the appearance of lacking common sense.

I recall a group of journalists whom I addressed in Tanzania. They railed against their superiors and the government for failing to provide the training they needed to produce good development journalism. (Most of these journalists had the equivalent of high school degrees.) I responded that the alert reporter finds ways of cultivating sources of information and uses these sources to help make up for the deficit in formal education. I suggested these journalists could consult, for "backgrounders," the numerous experts who lived in and around Dar es Salaam and who worked in development projects. The journalists apparently found this idea so novel that they reported it in the next day's press. What was most surprising to me about the interchange was that these reporters had apparently not thought of this themselves, even though they frequently subjected these experts to formal interviews, and even though reporters and experts regularly retired to the same "watering holes" around Tanzania's capital in their off hours (USIA, American Partners Lecture Tour, Dar es Salaam, March 1987).

Alienation engenders a strange kind of inflexibility in thinking as well as a bifurcation in the thinker's mental set. Highly skilled at solving problems in the home context, low-level media personnel seem to forget these skills when they come to work. It is as if there were no connection between their home lives and their work lives.

I recall producers in Nigeria determined to make certain preparations during their off hours for productions they were making at work. Gathering set properties and contacting talent for productions were two prime examples. Time and time again these producers would fail to accomplish the tasks which they'd set out at the end of the workday to complete. While Obeng-Quaidoo might argue that this occurred because Africans have no commitment to work in the modern sector (1985a, p. 113), I thought otherwise. Broadcasting is, after all, a "people-oriented profession" and is quite unlike industrial wage labor to which Obeng-Quaidoo refers. And broadcasters do receive recognition from community members for a job well done. I believe that broadcasters often forget their commitments to the job because their home lives are too separate from their work lives to allow for any integration of the two. Home lives simply provide no cues to remind broadcasters of their professional tasks. This psychic bifurcation is thus closely related to the alienated quality of the broadcast service itself, one which has only poorly served the wider public.

The above described "psychic bifurcation" is perhaps also related to the operation of group norms at home and individual norms at work. When the individual broadcaster arrives in his/her compound in the evening, his/her ego merges somewhat with that of the family. Kin-based activities and problems come to dominate the broadcaster's concerns, leaving little room for job-related goals and agendas. This situation is a far cry from the exigencies of Theory Y which prompt employees to look at the job as an integral part of their daily living. Mindful of these facts, management needs to take additional steps to help with the integration process, demanding that broadcasting better relate to the people and the neighborhoods in which their operatives abide. Management should also work to promote team spirit in stations (instead of divisive competitive structures based on patronage), the same kind of spirit which operates in villages and neighborhoods working communally to solve local problems.

In a class on research design with Swazi broadcasters, I conducted a number of exercises designed to help broadcasters identify the motivations of rural listeners. Time and time again, I found the broadcasters unable or unwilling to empathize with rural populations though all of them had relatives who lived in the homesteads of rural Swaziland. On the subject of rural listeners and development, these trainees would simply offer, "We can tell the homesteaders (rural Swazis) what to do, but they will not do it." Besides a lack of empathy, this statement illustrates the didactic social position in which these broadcasters placed themselves vis-à-vis their rural audiences (USAID, Training Course in Research Methods for Development Broadcasters, Mbabane, July–August 1987).

In the same course, I attempted to teach the organization of focus group meetings as a research technique to assist broadcasters in better understanding rural audiences. Despite all my best efforts (in explaining motivations, hierarchies of need, fears, superstitions, traditional pride, etc.), I could not convince these broadcasters that focus groups were not didactic meetings designed to instruct rural Swazis in modern behavior but rather were tools designed to *solicit information from homesteaders*. The idea of seeking information from illiterate peasants was completely alien to this group. And when these broadcasters conducted their own focus groups they assumed the "top-down" styles of communication they had absorbed from school and from their highly stratified society, reverted to their original ways of thinking, and produced authoritarian and directive communication for the homesteaders. They too were operating according to the authoritarian Theory X management model.

If communicating to groups of lesser social status is a problem for many African broadcasters, so is communication with those of a higher status. Swazi broadcasters assigned to conduct in-depth interviews with development professionals so as to gain information for programs found themselves paralyzed before doctors, health professionals, social workers, and even agricultural experts—all fairly sympathetic groups of persons inclined to help broadcasters accomplish development goals. A parallel situation occurs among reporters assigned to interview politicians. This group is likely to wish to intimidate young and inexperienced journalists.[5]

In the above situations, the gulf is so wide between social classes (and between "school-based" discourse and informal social intercourse) that the standard rhetorical devices Africans use in day-to-day conversation, devices used to give and to seek information, become ossified, and broadcasters appear to lack "common sense" in these modern situations.

Managees and the Oral Tradition

Many of the above examples described under the subheading "alienation" can equally be analyzed from the perspective of "situational thinking" or "situational behavior." And Obeichina reminds us that oral thinking styles are still very common in Africa even among educated urbanites because African life is still very much tied to the oral world (1975, pp. 26–28).

Managees are the members of the broadcast organization most affected by oral thinking styles because they tend to be among the least formally educated in the organizations. Camera operators, sound operators, television studio crews, and production assistants in many African countries are likely to hold no more than secondary school educations.

It should be recalled that situational thinking permits a person to behave appropriately in concrete situations but fails to foster in the individual a response repertoire needed for decontextualized advanced planning. This aids in explaining why well-meaning and well-intentioned producers often fail, outside the confines of the broadcast organization, to accomplish the work which they have set for themselves. Situational thinking applied to daily activity also fosters the ritualization of life. Thus, certain practices judged appropriate in any social context are quickly adopted and ritualized while other more individualistic behavior styles are quickly abandoned (Chernoff, 1979, pp. 160–61).

The ritualization habit explains another behavior I initially found curious among Nigerian broadcasters. I noted these staff members had a strong propensity to routinize apparently random occurrences and to incorporate them into regular practice. A great deal of studio training in Nigeria occurs on the job, particularly for lower-level production personnel. Since relatively little status or importance was attached to these positions, training was done in a very informal manner, often by persons with little more skill than that of the trainee. When I was conducting training at the stations of the Nigerian Television Authority, I often met with resistance when attempting to institute new studio procedures (such as proper camera focusing). The resistance did not surprise me nearly so much as the explanations junior studio operatives often gave for their way of working. Attempting to validate a particular (and often incorrect) procedure, young cameramen with as little as two to three months on the job would explain: "This is the way we always do it!" as if the lessons of an eight-week seconding with another (only slightly more experienced) team member were somehow immutable.

Production personnel were equally reticent to engage in crew rotational schemes used typically in American television production classes to teach the entire production process to students. Sound technicians had to be coaxed to assume camera positions in crew training sessions, and camera operators would assume the role of audio operator only under intensive prodding. Each seemed to feel that he/she had only one job to do and could not see the relevance of becoming proficient in more than one assigned task. This seemed particularly odd, as there was a great deal of job mobility in the country owing to the "oil boom." It may be that they were loathe to acquire too many skills for fear of being assigned too many different tasks. I would argue, however, that another factor was operating, a factor attached to oral tradition. The acquisition of knowledge for its own sake is not a value fostered in oral cultures. Knowledge in such societies is valued if it is directly tied to tangible outcomes. Learning a skill associated with a task other than the technician's immediate assignment must have seemed irrelevant. It threatened to clutter his/her mind with too many facts and too many details which he/she could not put to immediate use.

Chernoff argues that externalized (ritualized) institutional procedures and roles are important to Africans because they "provide a framework and help them to know what is happening and get into it" (1979, p. 161). In other words, the ritualizations and conventions are the means through which the African connects to the larger social world.

Limited abstractive abilities of lower-level personnel, thinking which is situational rather than objectively distanced, also make imagining the audience difficult. Sometimes it seems broadcasters in sub-Saharan Africa have forgotten the listeners and viewers to whom their programs are addressed. The media have acquired a kind of coded language whose understanding is limited only to certain (chiefly urban) groups. Buzz words and jargon have prevailed. Journalists have tended to address their stories only to small sections of the population. Their work has been exclusive rather than inclusive. It has had a tendency to reflect the urban realities and the concerns of station personnel rather than the mass audience. This tendency of course has been identified among Western broadcasters as well. The BBC for years produced plays only about middle-class subjects. And American networks hardly showed working-class families until "All in the Family" was broadcast in the early 1970s. But the tendency has seemed more glaring in Africa than elsewhere because there is so little integration between the rural masses and the urban groups, and because the rural lifestyle and level of comprehension is at so much variance with broadcast content.

The issue of audience targeting raises once again the "intentionality" issue in African broadcasting. As noted above, mass media managers have long seemed uneasy with the notion of truly targeting the masses whose potential reactions could not be forecast. It is no wonder that junior-level operatives have had difficulty focusing on an audience living in distant locations, an audience whose parameters have been blurred through lack of research.

Related to the question of audience analysis among African broadcasters is the issue of self-analysis. On this note, I have often been surprised by the limited degree to which media professionals (at various levels) identify with the calling. Elliott and Golding made similar observations in their study of Nigerian newsmen (1979, pp. 173–84). Katz and Wedell, citing James Scotton (1974), remind us that recruitment of broadcasters in many Third World countries, most of Africa included, is conducted through routine civil service procedure which places little emphasis on the potential candidate's aptitude, interest, or creativity (1977, p. 231). Broadcasters are defined from the outset as members of the civil service rather than as a specialized group of talented communicators. Hence, to quote Scotton, "it matters little whether they work in broadcasting or in the Ministry of Public Works" (1974, p. 282). This view is corroborated by Rita Cruise-O'Brien in her study of Radio Senegal (1985, p. 193).

Civil service careers have slightly less attraction in comparatively wealthy countries such as Nigeria, where careers in the private sector can sometimes be more lucrative. Because of this, it seems, many Nigerian broadcasters I trained expressed dissatisfaction with their jobs. It came as no surprise that such practical attractions as higher salaries or easier opportunities for promotion elsewhere could and did attract individuals to their sectors. What did, however, give me pause, was the imagined (or perhaps unimagined) ease with which many employees expected to transfer professional competencies. When questioned on these matters, many revealed only the vaguest abilities at self-analysis or job skill analysis in the abstract. Though many Nigerian broadcasters were dissatisfied with their present positions, only those with concrete practical reasons (low pay or no foreign scholarships, for example) could articulate the source of their dissatisfaction. Equally noteworthy was the fact that many of these individuals would also create elaborate fantasies projecting themselves into, what appeared to me, professions for which they were profoundly unsuited. Painfully shy and retiring chaps, for example, would imagine future success as African curio merchants, an occupation which requires verbal abilities and presentational styles roughly analogous to those of used-automobile salesmen in the West. Contrasting with these were other individuals, equally unsuited to their present media occupation, who seemed content and happy with their performance. Rewards from management, elsewhere for a job well done, moreover, seemed more based on patronage criteria than on performance. Thus, managerial behavior created confusion about professional roles rather than fostering a sense of professional identification. It is little wonder then that broadcasters failed to internalize their roles and carry their assignments home with them!

The above points might seem to suggest that media organizations and their employees are unaware of talented broadcasters operating in their midsts. But this is not the case. African broadcasters are very alert to their immediate surroundings. An individual who displays talent either on or off screen is eagerly sought out by producers in the organization. But such a person tends to be regarded more as a fortuitous discovery whose talent should be harnessed in the immediate than someone whose skills should be used as a model for emulation. This is again illustrative of situational thinking which I believe pervades the media in Black Africa.

Summary and Suggestions

This chapter has highlighted some of the difficulties over the last thirty years in mass media organizations in Black Africa, difficulties which derive from an alien management style onto which patronage structures were grafted. Station operation has been conducted by managers who belong to an alienated class of elites. I have tried to show how a system riddled with political patronage and alienation, intermixed with the values, behaviors, and psychodynamics of the oral tradition, has generated a particular set of qualities characterizing electronic media organizations of Black Africa.

Patronage systems are by definition authoritarian and thus engender management styles described by Theory X. Alienated managers, distanced from their subordinates and their audiences, have all too often substituted moralizing rhetoric for functionally based operational norms and procedures. This too is a practice incorporated in Theory X. The oral tradition, with its emphasis on consensus building and its concern for group harmony, has fostered a style of management more akin to that advocated by Theory Y. Elements of both styles of management have thus been found in the broadcast organizations of Black Africa, but the two styles have rarely been integrated.

A comprehensive overhaul of the management system, one substituting professional managerial behavior for alienated patronage structures and one incorporating the potential of the oral tradition into its procedural norms, is needed. These changes will help to marry the existing X and Y management styles into a healthy operation based upon Theory V. What is needed are well-trained senior managers concerned with serving as well as leading their staff, interested in providing a broadcast service responsive to all sectors of society. To do this, African managers must draw unashamedly from their rural roots. Meanwhile, other structural changes in African broadcasting are necessary.

Unless immediate structural changes occur in the political arena, broadcast management will continue to be based on systems of patronage, and obedience and loyalty rather than excellence and innovation will remain criteria for success within the organization. If concomitant sociostructural changes do not occur, broadcast managers will continue to be alienated. Alienation will persist as long as education continues to be extraverted, rural folkways are undervalued, and Western lifestyles tend to be held up as cultural models for Africa.

The movement toward decentralized broadcasting seems to offer exciting possibilities for making broadcasting more responsive to the masses and for incorporating the rural world view into the media. In anticipation of political and social shifts ushered in by the wake of democratic and pluralistic trends, a program of comprehensive retraining for management and staff should begin. Training in management techniques must proceed at full speed. Africans respond especially well to strong leadership advocated in Theory V, so the investment in management training will be well worth the effort.

Management training must be practical as well as theoretical. It should be aimed at fostering problem solving skills. African business people with successful enterprises might be enjoined to participate with management in these exercises. Case studies examining the operations of model enterprises, especially media organizations, could be used with a view to show how success has been achieved through performance. And role playing exercises which force managers to assume the positions of subordinates are recommended to decrease manager-staff distancing and build empathy with personnel at all levels. Management training must also incorporate routine elements of production. Managers simply cannot manage if they are not reasonably conversant with equipment and production processes.

Related to this issue is the need to teach managers job skill analysis and to train managers in the task of matching aptitudes and personalities of staff with positions and assignments. These efforts will support clamors for the delinking of broadcasting from the civil service appointment and promotion scale and to increased rewards for quality job performance.

To elevate the value of African rural roots, management must be resensitized to the realities of African village life. Ideally, this should be done through subventions of managers to villages in rural areas. Such subventions could also help build empathy with audience members. This approach is viewed as a means to help embed village administrative approaches, especially the tradition of group orientation, to the problems of the modern civil service (Daddah, 1988, p. 108).

Managers must be initiated in ways to integrate rural and urban lifestyles in a changing Africa. African popular musicians, storytellers, and carvers are able to keep up with changing social trends while integrating opposing rural and urban world views in their work. More training for broadcast managers should include sensitivity sessions with African contemporary artists—sessions where artists discuss their creative work and the means through which they derive their inspiration and generate new ideas. The collective and pluralistic aspect of traditional art forms provides a powerful working model for media production, one which must necessarily be more fully utilized in broadcasting.

That training for studio operatives and reporters must include practical sessions in the use of equipment and the basic techniques of the trade is evident. Less immediately obvious but equally important is training in critical thinking skills. Problem solving exercises are needed to show operatives they can use their own immediate environment to come up with solutions to work-related difficulties. The exercises used in basic study skill classes taught at U.S. universities could be locally adapted by sensitive trainers and used for this purpose. Many of these techniques can be taught, but they have not been tried in African media contexts.

With regard to imparting sensitivity to the oral world, many of the same suggestions which apply to senior managers are equally applicable to middle- and junior-level staff. Raising up local artists and asking them to present to broadcasters will be instructive and should serve to help equalize the status of the former to the latter. Inviting artists to discuss how they go about their work may also help broadcasters to better see the value of local artists and to incorporate the approaches of the latter into the procedures and productions of the stations.

Where possible, it may even be useful to include the services of nonalienated academic specialists—folklorists, ethnomusicologists, theater arts professors, and so on, who can work collaboratively with producers and artists to alert broadcasters to the importance of the oral tradition and to its adaptation potential for the mass media. Many of these academics have become disenfranchised from civic life over the years. Some would surely welcome an opportunity to participate in exciting practical applications of their academic disciplines in newer and more open media.

4 | Radio Broadcasting

THIS CHAPTER LOOKS at the establishment of radio during Black Africa's colonial era and reviews the evolution of radio during the postcolonial era. It
traces the means through which radio evolved into a mouthpiece of political
leaders and explores the contributions of the oral tradition to this progression.
It also reviews radio programming in sub-Saharan Africa over the last thirty
years, exploring both the efforts radio has made to satisfy urban tastes and the
initiatives, however tentative, the medium has undertaken to provide a public
service suitable to the needs of rural populations.

The chapter also provides a case study of an innovative rural radio project
in West Africa, the Liberian Rural Communications Network (LRCN). This
case study serves as a cautionary tale for policy makers in development radio.
It highlights the contradictions inherent in development broadcasting projects
wedded (unfortunately) to the aims of international political patronage and a
complicit class of local elites. But this case study also illustrates the day-to-day
operation of an effective radio network, broadcasting to rural populations. It
exhibits what can be done if governments/donors/investors really take to heart
the task of rural enlightenment through media.

The chapter ends with a brief review of recent developments in sub-Saharan
radio broadcasting: the emergence of private radio stations and the movement
toward partial privatization and/or decentralization of government broadcasting services. I suggest these developments could be healthy because they highlight trends toward increased social pluralism and because they hint at broader
guarantees of freedom of expression. In spite of liberalizing trends, there are
ominous clouds on the horizon. Privatization could well lead to increased
domination of Africa's airwaves by foreign services and to greater opportunities for elite profiteering from scarce financial resources available around capital cities. Privatization must therefore be coupled with guarantees (from gov-
ernments/investors/aid-givers) to serve rural populations both as a means to
provide rural folks with information services and to help guarantee their integration into newly emerging pluralistic polities. As of mid-1994, the movement toward decentralized broadcasting in sub-Saharan Africa was tentative
at best. And in most cases, where such moves were afoot, governance arrange-

ments for newly decentralized structures were yet to be clearly elaborated. It was therefore too early to assess the social contribution of the new broadcasting services.

The Colonial Period

Radio was introduced to Africa during the colonial period and served initially to provide links for expatriates to the metropoles. In 1927, the British East Africa Company began a BBC relay service for settlers, broadcasting from Nairobi, Kenya. This was, in fact, the second radio service on the African continent, for radio broadcasting had already begun in 1920 in independent South Africa.

In 1932, the British established the Empire Service, designed to serve their colonies and dominions in Canada, Australia, India, and anglophone Africa. This service relayed the BBC from Salisbury, Southern Rhodesia (now Harare, Zimbabwe), in Southern Africa and from Lagos, Nigeria, in West Africa.

French efforts in broadcasting began with a small-scale effort in Madagascar in 1931. The station broadcast 13 hours of music and information per week in French and Malagasy. Besides serving resident French citizens, this service also hoped to underscore the value of colonial rule among Malagasy elites. But French broadcasting seems to have begun in earnest in Senegal with the establishment of Radio Dakar in 1939. Its mission was to promote coverage for the francophone countries in the region (Gibbons, 1974, p. 113).

In the Belgian Congo (now Zaire), Jesuit priests at Albert College in Leopoldville (now Kinshasa) established in 1937 a small-scale radio operation broadcasting in French two hours a week on Sundays and holidays. Two years later, a radio engineer, J. Hourdebise, began a private station called *Congolia* which provided daily services in French but also in Lingala, Swahili, Kikongo, and Chiluba. Thus began the Belgian colonial pattern of leaving to private individuals or religious groups some public services which were more fully organized elsewhere by the colonial governments. The pattern was mirrored in education.

In both the French and the British colonies, radio was seen as an arm of colonial policies. But as colonial policies differed, so did radio output. Interested in building an African audience, the British promoted the use of African vernaculars very early in the process. The Nairobi service broadcast in the Kikamba and Kikuyu languages. By the mid-1930s, a radio service was begun in Accra, Gold Coast (now Ghana), and relays were soon added in the colony to Sekondi, Kumasi, and Korofidua. African personnel were introduced to the service in 1936–37. Indigenous languages were added in 1939 with broadcasts in Eve, Twi, and Hausa; two additional languages were added during the 1940s.

As a complement to the service for expatriates in Salisbury, Southern Rhodesia (now Zimbabwe), the British helped establish a Central African broadcasting station in Lusaka, Northern Rhodesia (now Zambia) in the late 1940s. It was described by Fraenkel as the first "fully fledged station broadcasting exclusively to Africans" (1959, p. 17). This service broadcast in six different languages. Early broadcasting in the anglophone countries thus had begun a path toward decentralization. In this way, British broadcasting policy mirrored educational policy and the policy of indirect rule (1983, p. 34).[1] In anglophone West Africa, efforts to indigenize broadcasting proceeded very rapidly during the 1950s. The BBC began training African broadcasters at the BBC staff training department in 1951. By 1956, there were 163 African managers of Ghana radio, and 445 technicians. These figures had increased from the 1949 figure of 13 indigenous managers and 46 local technicians (Tudesq, 1983, p. 23).

Radio in anglophone Africa was designed to provide something of a public service to its native peoples, even though this was resisted somewhat by settler populations in East and Southern Africa (Tudesq, 1983, p. 19). By 1949, broadcasting in Nigeria was flourishing and was inaugurated into that government under the Nigerian Broadcasting System (Kolade, 1974, p. 87). Nigerian broadcasting offered stations at Lagos, Abeokuta, Ijebu-Ode, Port-Harcourt, Enugu, Kano, and Zaria. The Nigerian Broadcasting System also had rediffusion stations at Calabar, Kaduna, Jos, Warri, Katsina, Sokoto, Onitsha, Maiduguri, and Ilorin. Local language broadcasts began that year.

In most of their colonies, the British eventually established, before independence, broadcasting services designed along the Public Corporation model of the BBC. Some of the early broadcasters were among those who clamored for independence. This was true in Sudan, in Kenya, and in Nigeria (Tudesq, 1983, p. 29). Perhaps it was inevitable that such services would eventually be dismantled as semiautonomous bodies and absorbed into the more controlling government structures which would emerge after independence. Today there are seven countries with a so-called public corporation status. These include Ghana, Malawi, Mauritius, Nigeria, South Africa, Zambia, and Zimbabwe (Martin, 1991, p. 183). But as Mytton reminds us, having this nominal status guarantees little in the way of autonomy (1983, p. 78).

The French colonial policy of direct rule was mirrored in broadcasting. Thus, radio was viewed in the French colonies as a useful and inexpensive means of countering "the discussions of educated Africans turning rapidly to subversive and anti-governmental ideas" (Tudesq, 1983, p. 15).

In accordance with the French colonial assimilationist policies,[2] radio programming in the French colonies was initially French in orientation and language of delivery, designed to help turn listeners into *évolués* or Black Frenchmen. Efforts to indigenize broadcasting in francophone Africa finally did begin during the late colonial period. But French efforts were designed in part to prepare the way for independence, an independence which would incorporate francophone Africa into a broader economic and political unit under the French Constitution of the Fifth Republic of 1958.[3]

As the French colonies prepared for independence, the French government established a variety of agencies which tied broadcasting in French Africa to France. In 1956, for example, the French government created the *Société de Rediffusion de la France d'Outremer* (SORAFOM). This was a French parastatal set up to build and manage radio stations in Africa, to purchase programming materials and technical equipment, and to train staff (Gibbons, 1974, pp. 110–11).

The French began, under SORAFOM, an ambitious training program at the Studio Ecole in Paris in the mid-1950s. By the late 1950s many of the station managers were Africans, including the directors-general of Radio Abidjan (Côte d'Ivoire) and Radio Brazzaville (Congo). Around this time, the French government began to find it useful to provide indigenous language broadcasts to Africans to disseminate its own point of view and to counter the effects of indigenized services available to their subject populations from neighboring British colonial services. Interestingly, the training of management personnel in Paris had its desired effect. Francophone African radio participated little in the struggle for independence but rather served to retain ties of the people to France by enfranchising top broadcast management among the elites. The French had learned how to manage decolonization currents from their experience in Algeria and from the lessons of greater autonomy in the British colonies.

Still, by 1960, there were only two stations in francophone Africa broadcasting entirely in French: Radio Brazzaville and Radio Gabon (Tudesq, 1983, p. 34). Nevertheless, the remaining stations broadcast less than 40 percent of the time in indigenous languages (Tudesq, 1983, p. 34). They were also unlike the anglophone stations which were in spirit somewhat separate from the British government. In areas of editorial and policy control, the French stations revealed the Gallic penchant for centralization. Later, SORAFOM was transformed into the *Office de Coopération Radiophonique* (OCORA) and became involved in the establishment of French-language television.

In 1969, OCORA was replaced by the *Organisation de la Radio et la Télévision Française* (ORTF), which represented the ultimate in French centralization, because it combined domestic broadcasting in France with overseas functions. Indeed, broadcasting in French Africa retained very strong ties with France even after independence of the French colonies, and this is still true in many states today (Nyamnjoh 1988). Nowhere is this more evident than in the language policy. Reports from the early 1980s showed that Côte d'Ivoire was producing 89 percent of its broadcasts in French. Similar statistics for the

Congo and for Gabon were at 80 and 100 percent respectively (Tudesq, 1983, p. 144).

At independence, the vast majority of anglophone countries had broadcasting systems based upon the BBC's model of public corporations and public service broadcasting. Most of the French colonies had radio services heavily influenced in style and substance and in political tenor by the French model.

The Belgians had a mixed system which included the participation of the government of the Belgian Congo, the Catholic Church, and private industry. The government service, begun in 1940, included locally trained indigenous broadcasters, who produced a variety of indigenous language programs destined for rural audiences (Tudesq, 1983, p. 35).

Postindependence: The Consolidation of National Power

During the 1960s, the genesis of certain patterns of broadcasting emerged in Black Africa. First and foremost, the first generation of anglophone politicians of the independence period recognized the power of radio. Many already had training or practical experience as journalists. These included Jomo Kenyatta of Kenya, Kwame N'Krumah of Ghana, Nmamdi Azikiwe of Nigeria, and Hastings Banda of Malawi. They were cognizant of its value as a tool in consolidating the nation. N'Krumah dismantled the regional station at Kumasi, and Nigeria eliminated the public corporation status of the NBC in 1961 (Tudesq, 1983, p. 36), a status it later recreated in the 1970s. Tanzania put its semiautonomous radio under the Ministry of Information and Tourism in 1965.

Other anglophone countries retained the official designation of broadcasting as a public corporation but tightened the reigns of control nonetheless. By the 1970s, most of the anglophone countries had placed their radio broadcasting systems firmly in control of their governments.

From the early days of independence, leaders in the francophone countries were well aware of the power of radio as a political instrument. They had witnessed its use during the war when Radio Brazzaville had served as a propaganda instrument for the Voice of Free France. And they had seen its effective use by the Gaulist government in the early days of the Fifth Republic. President Fulbert Youlou used radio to quell demonstrations against his regime in the Congo in 1960. Maurice Yameogo of Upper Volta (now Burkina Faso) used it in 1959 to attempt to unite his people against divisive elements coming through the airwaves of Radio Mali and Radio Sudan (Tudesq, 1983, p. 36).

Indeed, the development of external services began very early in the independence period. Gamel Abdul Nasser had been among the first heads of state to use external broadcasting signals in the 1950s beamed south of the Sahara to promote anti-imperialist struggles. N'Krumah of Ghana used the Voice of Africa to disseminate his message of pan-Africanism to the rest of the region in 1959. Tanzania installed a powerful transmitter in 1966 with the intention of broadcasting liberation news to the Southern African region. Many other countries have since established external services including Senegal, Côte d'Ivoire, and Nigeria. External services are a means by which governments can counter propaganda of rival neighbors who may be reaching their own populations through indigenous services. Radio Tripoli of Libya today demonstrates this regularly, much to the chagrin of its neighbors to the south. External service broadcasts are also a means through which governments communicate with one another (Tudesq, 1983, pp. 240–41).

Cognizant of the important role of radio in consolidating the new nations, a number of countries launched ambitious plans during the postindependence period to distribute cheap radio sets. These included Madagascar, Niger, and Upper Volta (Tudesq, pp. 39–40). Togo, Mali, Zaire, Niger, Ghana, and other countries established radio clubs. Both efforts were designed to bring about awareness among rural peasants of their new governments. A French phrase often used to describe this function is *"la sensibilisation politique."*

Early five and ten year development plans from the 1960s show a marked and near universal intention to expand broadcasting, at least radio, to rural areas. Where TV existed, it too was slated for expansion. Where it did not yet exist, plans were quickly drawn up for its establishment.

In this regard, the United Nations Educational Scientific and Cultural Organization (UNESCO) was instrumental. Inspired by technocrats charmed with the model of the nation-state (discussed in chapter 2), UNESCO promoted the expansion of broadcasting services in Africa. A cornerstone of UNESCO's thinking was Wilbur Schramm's *Mass Media and National Development* (1964). Schramm drew extensively from the work of an earlier scholar, Daniel Lerner, who had devised a model for socioeconomic development that underscored the importance of mass media in promoting this process. The model advocated that a given level of urbanization, about 25 percent, was needed before an acceptable level of literacy could be achieved. With appropriate levels of literacy, the mass media, it was argued, should be introduced. Mass media would then act as a "mobility multiplier," leading people to seek new opportunities for economic growth and advancement. The media would also foster the creation of "empathetic personalities," capable of envisioning themselves in different social and economic positions (Lerner 1958). UNESCO was also instrumental in establishing a number of projects in school broadcasting during this period.

UNESCO used the logic of modernization as a basis for promoting acceptable baseline levels of media penetration. It advocated following minimum target saturation standards: for every 100 persons in the population, there should be ten daily newspapers, five radio receivers, two cinema seats, and two television receivers (UNESCO 1961).

The use of mass media for development was a highly salable idea, one which appealed to the new elites in the recently independent states. Radio permitted elites and governments to talk directly to villagers, thereby reorienting existing (precolonial) village hierarchies toward the central government (Tudesq, 1983, p. 69).

Partly enamored perhaps by the development rhetoric of UNESCO, educational radio was launched seriously in the 1960s. Rural education projects were promoted in Ghana (where they had been introduced by the British in 1956) and in Niger. School broadcasting projects were begun in Nigeria, in Togo, in Burkina Faso, and in the Congo, among others. And teacher education programs were initiated in Sierra Leone, Uganda, Kenya, and Rwanda.

These efforts were not without their elements of propaganda, for the governments involved had always seen development in terms of the politics of "nation building," i.e., the need to integrate populations into the new statist structures which were the legacy of the colonial period. As noted above, many of these broadcasting projects had been established to "politically sensitize" the rural populations.

Eventually, these projects fell on hard times as proponents and targets became disenchanted with them. Tudesq notes that as more and more Africans acquired radios by the end of the 1960s, their interest in group listening began to wane. Also, the novelty of the broadcasts wore off. Some projects failed because of poor conceptualization or poor implementation. Some adult literacy programs were ill-received by adult audiences, some of whom objected to literacy lessons originally designed for school children (1983, p. 91). Finally, most of the early rural radio projects were insufficiently integrated into the existing national broadcasting services. This is a plague which has continued to affect most externally funded developmental radio efforts.

Posthoc analyses have also argued that in their rush to acquire these tools of modernity, new governments focused far more on the hardware of communication technology than on the software. Looking back on the period, some analysts have maintained that proponents of the new media systems genuinely, if erroneously, believed that the simple acquisition of modern communication technology would lead to changes in economic performance by target groups. Yet if observers examine the period more closely, they may discern that a certain amount of bad faith or disingenuousness clearly marked the push to mediate these societies. Tunstall points out, for instance, that though UNESCO was promoting *rural development* through media, national leaders in Africa had other aims in mind, chiefly, the consolidation of their new nation-states. And Tunstall adds, quite perceptively, that when Western-trained elites imagined mass media for their countries, they dreamed of the Western-style media to which they had become addicted (Tunstall, 1977, p. 213).

Suppliers of hardware, eager to sell their wares, found the advocacy of rapid media mobilization a handy rationale and found UNESCO to be a so-

phisticated marketing organ. Not surprisingly, given the enthusiasm and prestige of media proponents, the number of transmitters increased handily during
the postcolonial period. In 1960, there were 252 broadcasting transmitters on
the continent. In 1975, there were 458. The number of radio receivers grew as
well. In 1965, there were 32 radios per 1,000 on the continent. In 1975, there
were 69 per 1,000. By 1984, there were 164 per 1,000 (Martin, 1991, p. 185).

As radio broadcasting expanded in the postcolonial era, governments
found they needed to increase the size of their staff and expand training opportunities accordingly. To fill the need, UNESCO, the International Press Institute, and other training bodies quickly established short courses in radio
broadcasting. These organizations supplemented the already considerable
training efforts of the BBC in London and the Studio Ecole in Paris. But the
numbers of professionals trained have never been sufficient to meet demand.
Potential broadcast trainees have always outstripped the supply of available
training schemes. Part of the crying need for broadcast training in Africa has
come, of course, from the low level of technological development on the continent. But another source of continual broadcast training demand has arisen
from the way broadcasters have historically been appointed. Positions in
broadcasting (as in other branches of the civil service) have often been allo-
cated as rewards to political patrons. Frequent staff additions and transfers
have thus exacerbated the dearth of technologically skilled personnel.

Telecommunications extension proved costly in the postindependence period, especially considering the desire of governments to introduce television.
Governments for whom commercialism had been philosophically an anathema
found it the only way to support the growing expansion of electronic media.

Despite competition from TV, radio coverage did expand considerably in
the 1960s, though ambitious plans for rural services with considerable rural
autonomy tended to be abandoned (Tunstall, 1977, p. 213). By the late 1960s,
political pressures had mounted as regimes began to note the disappointment
of their populations with the unfulfilled promises of the precolonial era. Regimes thus began to find various means to curb media access (Boafo, 1991, p.
105). And preference was given to telecommunication investment designed to
consolidate central power, i.e., repeater stations disseminating messages from
the capital cities where broadcasting could be more carefully monitored and
controlled by insecure national governments.

This pattern has continued into the 1990s. Until this decade, the vast majority of countries have maintained an average of one to four national services,
usually beaming from the capital, often using repeater stations to extend the
signals to rural areas. Only a handful of countries have offered regional stations with a modicum of local programming. Where available, these regional
stations have used only limited personnel, serving chiefly to relay news bulletins and other programs from their capitals throughout the day. And very few

countries have dared to establish regional stations with considerable autonomy. Here, the case of Nigeria with its three-tiered system of broadcasting, which includes federal, regional, and state services, must be cited as a special case (Kinner, 1988, p. 226).

Mytton's analysis of Tanzanian radio history shows a pattern of benign neglect of rural radio services. Tanzania's 1964–69 Five Year Plan included specific and clear aims for broadcasting to rural populations, notably the building of satellite stations for rural areas and the establishment of community reception centers. But at the end of the five years, only the government's plan for a new medium wave transmitter to service Dar es Salaam had been implemented (Mytton, 1983, p. 99). Interestingly, this was a commercial service, one whose brochure boasted that it was East Africa's most powerful advertising medium (Mytton, 1983, p. 99).

Mytton writes of the contradictions the Tanzanian government's actions implied as it ignored its own plans:

> It sometimes seemed that the government was less interested in broadcasting from the point of view of fulfilling the three aims mentioned in the Plan than in what it could do to publicize its own policies and activities. The commercial service publicized the government and brought in much needed revenue: a combination which pleased both politicians and treasure officials. (1983, p. 99)

Radio News

Personal Address Systems of Presidents

Africa, according to A. J. Tudesq, inherited a double heritage. On the one hand it acquired European styles of governance, complete with political parties and constitutions; on the other it acquired a penchant for secrecy necessitated either by clandestine activities launched against the colonists or against potential rivals for national power in the new states. This double heritage forced new African governments to subjugate information policies to the political exigencies of the nation-state (Tudesq, 1983, p. 92).

Until the 1990s, most of the Black African nations have been one-party states.[4] Contrary to widespread belief, some did tolerate dissent and promote or at least allow dialogue among competing interests within the structures of periodic "closed-door" party conferences. Here disagreements were ironed out and compromises were achieved among competing elites. But once the deals had been made and the spoils had been distributed, represented players were expected to speak with a unified national voice to the masses. And the national media were charged with disseminating this message of unity and with promoting the appearance of national consensus. To achieve these ends, African governments have kept broadcasting under tight control.

It is not generally known that the attitude of many heads of state toward information had its genesis in the Communist Party to which many owed allegiance in the early preindependence period. Houphouët-Boigny was one example (although he quickly distanced himself from the Communists after 1949); Sekou Touré of Guinea was another (Tudesq, 1983, pp. 95–96).

In order to weld disparate groups into a nation and to stave off threats to the established order, leaders felt a need to create new national symbols. In a world where the written press hardly penetrates, the electronic media were called in to do the task. In the 1960s, there were few potent and tangible symbols of the abstraction of the nation-state. And the few which did exist (government buildings, flags, etc.) could not easily be transported to the rural areas. Radio was available and offered a handy, if imperfect, solution.

Electronic media function well in the communication of personalities. Moreover, oral thinking is close to the "human lifeworld." In other words, it defines events in very personal or human terms. The first African leaders were unusually charismatic figures, making the creation of personality cults on radio somewhat natural and self-apparent. The characteristics of the media fused with the orality of the audience and produced a solution for the political needs at hand. Herein lies the genesis of the seemingly sycophantic media which has characterized so much of African broadcasting. Herein also lies the reason that so much airtime has been filled with the words, deeds, smallest movements, and activities of presidents.

There were instances, of course, when the use of the personality cult backfired on the head of state, making him the target of reprisals for all of the ills which befell the country. Thus, an excess of personality cultism led to the demise of François Toumbalbaye of Chad, Sylvanus Olympio of Togo, Kwame N'Krumah of Ghana, Idi Amin of Uganda, Francisco Macias of Equatorial Guinea, and Jean Bedel Bokassa of Central African Republic. More gifted politicians, those with far more staying power, have been able to skillfully use a more moderate form of the personality cult, together with systems of patronage, to shore up their regimes. These include Félix Houphouët-Boigny of Côte d'Ivoire (1960–93), Amadu Ahijo of Cameroon (1960–82), Jomo Kenyatta of Kenya (1963–78), Julius Nyerere of Tanzania (1961–85), Leopold Senghor of Senegal (1960–80), and to a lesser extent, Mathieu Kérékou of Benin (1972–90) and Omar Bongo of Gabon (1967-9-), who was reelected under dubious circumstances in December 1993 (*Africa Report*, January–February 1994, pp. 8–9).

These skilled politicians have been adept at publicly condemning corruption which indirectly or directly supports their regimes. The need to mask the "irregularity" of public officers and public institutions has long accounted for the jealousy with which regimes have withheld information from their publics. In some states, information control has been a central preoccupation of the head of state. For many years, Gabon's president, El Haj Omar Bongo, for example, headed seven different government ministries himself, including the Gabonese Ministry of Information. And in Malawi, for a very long time there was no Ministry of Information; Malawi's long-serving head of state, Hastings Banda (1964–94) was himself director general of the radio (Tudesq, 1983, p. 105).

The statist character of broadcasting in Black Africa has long been evidenced in the fact that directors-general of radio are more often politicians (or military men, since in Africa these two careers can often be interchangeable) or career civil servants rather than professional broadcasters. The situation in Nigeria is the exception. There, Chris Kolade and Georges Bako were two former broadcasters who later served as directors general of federal radio.

Directors general of radio have tended not to stay very long in their posts. If they pleased the head of state, they were likely to be appointed minister of information or become directly attached to the presidential press corps. When broadcast managers incurred the president's displeasure, they were likely to be demoted. The constant power shifts of men at the top have caused havoc in broadcast organizations riddled with patronage, for with each new appointment, staff members have needed to form new alliances. One student of Beninese broadcasting described the situation in Benin in the early 1970s as one bordering on anarchy (Tudesq, 1983, p. 119).

News: Dreary Broadcasting

The presence of a heavy state structure, loyal to the head of state and responsive to the rapacious demands of the personality cult has led to confusion and inertia in African broadcast organizations. Henri Bandolo, who studied broadcasting in Cameroon in the late 1970s, described the professional paralysis plaguing Radio Cameroon. He said station indirection and lethargy were the inevitable results of contradictory directives received from a host of politically connected officers: the provincial governor, the provincial delegate for information, the minister of information, the director general of radio, and the station manager (Tudesq, 1983, pp. 113–14).

Professional sycophants or their cousins have found themselves with jobs in broadcasting, rewards, no doubt, for some favor or other to the ruling group. Broadcasting sectors have become bloated with personnel, untrained and unspecialized, the spoils of patronage systems. And budgets have been eaten up for salaries of these hangers-on. Personnel figures from 1980 are quite astonishing. The combined number of employees for radio and television in Benin was 246. In Cameroon, the figure was 400. In the Congo, there were

390 staffers in broadcasting. In radio alone in Côte d'Ivoire, there were 270, and in Zaire, there were 1,800! Radio employed 600 persons in Tanzania, 160 in Burkina Faso, 150 in Niger, 80 in Rwanda, 546 in Senegal, and 160 in Togo (Tudesq, 1983, p. 119). With all these paid positions, it is no wonder that funds have been rarely available to pay artists, musicians, or actors for their more valuable contributions or for the performance rights to their music or spoken tales.

Paralyzed and confused by the constant to-and-fro of directors and presidential "yes men," broadcasters have seemed to mentally disengage from their work, attending to it chiefly for purposes of self-censorship. Wooden figures have stood at microphones reading dreary news bulletins recounting the comings and goings of the head of state or those of his ministers. To these, newspersons have added "actualities" consisting of long, barely edited speeches made during official events by ministers, other officials, or the head of state.[5] Broadcasters, moreover, have opted for the safe course of reading directly from their national wire services or an international news service, the latter often poorly adapted to the level of comprehension of their audiences. Few reporters have bothered (or dared) to produce news reports gathered from their own initiative, for these have been judged as risky and potentially offensive to any number of persons better placed in the hierarchical pecking order. And editorial comments, where made, have largely been used by reporters to reaffirm their loyalty to the power of the state.

Mytton's analysis of the 1960s shows the gradual decline in the quality of news in Tanzania, born, he writes, of the need to establish the existence of the nation in a symbolic sense. He notes that by 1964, radio news had begun to cover "less and less of any kind of Tanzanian news other than the speeches and activities of the President, Ministers, Commissioners, and so on" (Mytton, 1983, p. 100). Debates in the Tanzanian parliament actually focused on whose speeches would be covered! One MP asked that reporters follow parliamentary members around on constituency visits, arguing that people were "crying out" for news of their activities (1983, p. 102).

Mytton adds that a new policy was instituted in 1967, designed to cover the activities of ordinary people. He explains: "The idea was to move away from an elitist and centralist view of things, yet it was to be a long time before such changes were implemented, and it might well be argued that they have not progressed very far to this day" (Mytton, 1983, p. 102; see also Amupala, 1989, p. 44).

Western observers have often been surprised at the degree to which African media serve as mouthpieces of the government. They are astounded at the apparent tolerance of broadcast producers and audiences for the redundant talking heads and talking voices on African broadcasting. It is useful to examine whence these qualities have come.

Bilateral development aid to Africa declined during the 1970s. Broadcasting organizations in the former British colonies were by then completely indigenized, and French staff were at a minimum. Already under the control of insecure governments in the 1960s, the media came under military control in the 1970s. Concurrently, the African media became more fully incorporated into the civil service structures. With this change, broadcast content came to focus more and more on news. News has tended to be defined as government announcements and politically oriented speeches, and the pattern was repeated in television broadcasting.

At least three important factors led to the regression of broadcasting into a kind of political megaphone. The first was the function of the civil servant and his or her lack of specific qualifications and talents for broadcasting. The second was the practice of censorship, and the third was the emphasis on high-level political appointments in the area of information dissemination. Tunstall describes it admirably:

> One consequence of this Ministry of Information pattern of control is that all broadcast producers, and at least some journalists are civil servants. Usually, they are on ordinary civil service salary grades and subject to promotion by seniority. Radio scripts are civil servant wise, vetted in advance by higher authority. *This does not favor scintillating journalism or riveting radio broadcasts* [emphasis mine]. The Government senior public relations personnel are superior civil servants within the same Ministry as the journalists and producers. The senior public relations jobs are thus the journalistic jobs which have not only the highest pay and status, but also the greatest potential for independence and initiative. It is commonly said that in Africa, all the best journalists and producers are in PR. (Tunstall, 1977, p. 114)

Thus, we have seen that by the late 1960s, a pattern had clearly emerged in African broadcasting, one which favored direct government control of broadcasting, the use of broadcasting, both internally and externally, to disseminate government propaganda. This was supported by commercialism where necessary.

Commercialization had its own consequences. It led to an emphasis on urban-oriented broadcasting and to programs targeted to cities where consumers with money could be located. These consumers, in any case, were the persons best equipped to understand the government propaganda. The role of foreign investors who installed the equipment in Africa could not be discounted in this process. Nwanko argued that they helped to promote commercialism in African media because this would help insure timely repayment of their commercial investments (1974, p. 300).

A countercurrent had nevertheless been established with the aid of UNESCO and the efforts of bilateral aid groups. It was a trend which leaned toward extending services to the rural populations, providing them with some modicum of programming useful to their needs, intermixed albeit with messages designed to increase awareness of modern political elites and their governments. UNESCO and other aid organizations have continued their work in Africa with mixed results, contributing to the varied texture of radio in Africa.

Growth of Vernacular Language Services

Only a few countries in Black Africa are in a linguistically comfortable position regarding the language medium of radio broadcasting. Rwanda needs only to broadcast in Kinyarwanda (which it uses for 70 percent of its transmissions) to be understood by most of its listeners. And Burundi needs only to transmit in Kirundi (which it also uses for 70 percent of its transmissions) to be widely understood. The Gambia can use mainly Wolof and be understood by the vast majority of its listeners. The use of Arabic can easily service majority populations in Mauritania, Sudan, and Somalia. In ethnically homogeneous Swaziland, the vast majority of listeners understand Siswati, heavily used in broadcasting along with English. And Tanzania benefits from a major African *lingua franca*, Swahili, in which most of its broadcasts are transmitted. Other than these few exceptions, most African media must use a range of vernaculars if they are to be well understood by their audiences.

In 1969, UNESCO launched an all-out effort to increase the numbers of vernacular languages in which broadcasting was offered on the African continent. Not surprisingly, there was considerable resistance to this effort from the African elites, the decision makers who have traditionally run broadcasting. Such policy makers had to be coaxed into providing a service more comprehensible to the masses. Nevertheless, efforts to increase the number of language services available did come as the number of transmitters grew during the 1970s and 1980s.

Radio broadcasting continued to expand, albeit slowly in the 1970s, because it was too important a tool to be ignored. In 1960, for example, there were 252 transmitters on the continent. In 1964 there were 370. In 1976, only 58 more had been added. But by 1987, the number of transmitters had increased to 1,059 (Martin, 1991, p. 185). These figures correspond roughly to investment patterns we have seen, investment which declined in the 1970s and began to rise again in the 1980s. The rather astounding growth in radio transmitters in the 1980s can be attributed, at least partly, to the development of FM services (Yeboah-Afari, 1988, p. 1284). In some cases, governments (Nigeria, Zimbabwe, Swaziland, Lesotho, for example) moved to FM services as part of an effort to modernize broadcasting or to satisfy constituencies. In other cases, FM transmitters were provided by UNESCO (in Kenya) or by bilateral aid projects (in Ghana) designed to promote rural-based community education (Mills and Kangawa, 1983, p. 20; Amakyi, 1988, pp. 16–17; Boafo, 1991, p. 119).

By the end of the 1970s, meanwhile, a number of states had achieved complete coverage of their territories. These included Gabon, Kenya, Côte d'Ivoire, Sudan, and Nigeria. Alas, for many states, complete radio coverage was competing and continues to compete with two other types of communication services: external radio services and television.

With the growth of radio has come a steady increase in the number of broadcast hours. Tudesq estimated that the number of broadcast hours doubled during the 1970s (1983, pp. 139–42). Tied to the general expansion of government-owned radio in the 1970s and 1980s was an increase in the number of broadcasts destined for rural areas. This development, however, was tied to the multiplication of translated news broadcasts.

Most of the vernacular language services have been provided from the capital cities. Governments have been hesitant to create regional stations with too much autonomy. Such regional stations, it has been feared, might serve as focal points for regional or ethnic loyalties rivaling national ones. Moreover, regional stations have been seen to present security risks, necessitating the deployment of militia to guard broadcast installations. The easiest way to provide more service to rural areas was to multiply the number of languages in which news was broadcast.

News bulletins produced originally in a European language in the capital were increasingly translated into more rural languages. In the late 1970s, news on the Ghana Broadcasting Corporation, for example, equaled 17 and a half hours per week. It was translated in six local languages, the transmission of which used another 21 hours (Ansah, 1979, p. 9). Thus, for many years, news has represented between 25 and 50 percent of the broadcasting on radio in Africa (Tudesq, 1983, pp. 138–47). And oftentimes, the urban broadcasters transmitting these vernacular news bulletins have lacked facility in the language of transmission. Such a mode of operation could hardly pass for a rural service.

UNESCO's schema for categorizing programs must be taken with caution. Program classifications provided by UNESCO are those supplied by governments themselves. Sometimes programs reported as cultural or educational are, in fact, news or propaganda programs (Tudesq, 1983, p. 146). Furthermore, according to Ruijter, 90 percent of what is termed news on African media is political news (1989, p. 64).

Satisfying the Elites: Urban Entertainment Programming

Critics of the urban and elite bias of African broadcasting abound. (See Tunstall 1977; Katz and Wedell 1977; Nwosu 1985; and Martin 1991.) Boafo summarized the paucity of broadcasting service to wider populations in sub-Saharan Africa and its preoccupation with elite issues and concerns:

> The utilization of communication technology in Black African societies also seems to be oriented generally to purposes other than genuine national development and societal change. . . . what is typical and outstanding in Black African societies is the use and management of communication technology, especially the dominant mass communication systems, to establish what Tehranian (1980) terms cognitive tyranny by the ruling groups, "to propagate the views and values and to perpetuate the interests and positions of the political leadership of the elites." . . . The content of mass communication in Black Africa countries abounds in propaganda, demagogy, cheap entertainment, empty promises, and farfetched ideologies of dubious significance or relevance to individual or societal development. (1991, p. 109)

Boafo's gloomy picture nevertheless seems somewhat exaggerated. African broadcasting has made some useful advances and developed some novel programming, albeit most of it for urban audiences.

UNESCO regularly collects statistics which quantify in terms of hours various categories of broadcast programming. These include the following classifications: informational (news), educational, cultural, religious, advertisements, entertainment, and other. UNESCO's figures clearly indicate that the vast majority of broadcasting hours fall in the categories of informational (largely news) and entertainment.

As is evident from the UNESCO statistical data, entertainment occupies a good 50 percent of many African broadcasting services. One very popular type of program is the request program, in which listeners write or call in asking for dedications of a favorite song, usually to a loved one. Listening to the BBC World Service's "A Jolly Good Show," hosted by Dave Lee Travers, gives some idea of the flavor of these programs and some of the enthusiasm with which they are received by African listeners.

In Rwanda in 1977, these *"Disques de l'auditeur"* (Listeners' Records) programs were broadcast twice a day. In Gabon, *"Dites-le avec les disques"* (Say It with Records) was aired three times weekly during the same period. And in Côte d'Ivoire, a similar program was running daily in 1982. Unfortunately much of the music played on these programs or other entertainment shows is very Western-oriented. Survey after survey show a pattern of neglect in the airing of traditional music, local popular music, or African music generally.

Real found in 1976 that 67 percent of the music played in Liberia had North American origins, and only 33 percent had African origins (1985, pp. 96–97). In a content analysis of Radio Nigeria 2 FM Lagos, an all-music station, Luke Uka Uche found in 1983 that only 26 percent of the records played were Nigerian, and only 4.5 percent of the selections came from other African countries. Uche noted that a "whopping number," 69.5 percent, came from foreign musicians outside Africa (1986, p. 74). A big surprise to outsiders is the widespread airplay and the inordinate popularity of American country music on African radio signals! More astonishing perhaps is the broad appeal of French-style popular music, particularly romantic "crooner" ballads popularized by Charles Aznavour, Johnny Hallyday, and Julio Iglesias in the francophone countries!

Obeng-Quaidoo reported in 1985 that 80 percent of music on Ghana Broadcasting 2, a commercial shortwave service, was popular Western music. The author feared that the emphasis on Western music was having a homogenizing effect on Ghanaian youth (Obeng-Quaidoo, 1985a, pp. 238–48).

There have been some showcases for modern African music, often a fusion of electrified instruments with traditional instruments, sounds, and themes. *"La Musique du Niger"* (The Music of Niger) brought the sounds of Salif Keita, Bazoumana Sissoko, and Siramory Diabaté to audiences of this Sahelian country. Congolese pop stars have gained recognition since 1976 through *"Chantons et dansons congolais"* (Singing and Dancing Congolese Style), a broadcast of Radio Congo. In 1971, Côte d'Ivoire created *"Discotheque Ivoirienne"* (Ivorian Discotheque) and "Top Ivoire Hit Parade," two forums for playing modern Ivorian music. And modern Cameroon music has been a regular feature of Radio Cameroon (Tudesq, 1983, pp. 198–99). Despite these advances, foreign music still dominates the airwaves, and with the proliferation of commercial FM services begun in the 1980s, the domination seems likely to continue. The emergence of private radio in the 1990s is further likely to bolster this trend.

Availability and marketing are undoubtedly reasons why Western music is featured so prominently in African radio. UNESCO has gathered statistics on the dollar value of imported and exported sound recordings, tapes, and discs by region of the world. The results show that inter-African trade in sound materials is dwarfed by trade in non-African materials. In the late 1980s, Côte d'Ivoire, for example, imported only $2,000 worth of sound material from other African countries, while it imported $1,314,000 worth of such material from elsewhere, including $94,000 worth from North America. In the same period, Côte d'Ivoire sold no sound material to other African countries, whereas it exported $48,000 worth to Europe, and $46,000 worth to the United States. Madagascar imported no sound material from the rest of Africa, $205,000 worth from Europe, and $46,000 worth of tapes, etc., from North America. And Madagascar exported $1,600 worth to the rest of Africa, $56,000 worth to Europe, and $28,000 worth to North America (UNESCO, *World Communication Report*, 1989, pp. 515–17).

Within African countries, recording and copyright problems sometimes inhibit the distribution of local popular music. Local groups may wish to be paid large sums before allowing their music to be aired on national broadcasting. Because Africa's contributions to popular music are so substantial, the low priority it gives to its own material raises some disquiet. Obeng-Quaidoo, for example, expressed concern with producers he interviewed from Ghana Broadcasting 2, who claimed to play predominantly Western music because they felt it reflected youth preferences (1985a, p. 238). In an age when African groups are becoming increasingly popular in North America and Europe, it seems unfortunate that African broadcasters are not making more of an effort to promote their own cultural products. This comment is especially pertinent to Nigeria where there were 24 recording companies as early as 1971 (Real, 1985, p. 97). Music from Southern Nigeria's prolific and well-known pop industry is hard to come by in Northern Nigeria, either on radio or in the kiosks where tapes are sold. It could well be that the orientation of radio producers and distributors is too elitist and too extraverted. Or perhaps the near absence on Northern Nigerian airwaves of Fela Ransome-Kuti, Ebenezer Obey, I. K. Dario, and other Southern Nigerian pop stars is evidence of deep-seated regional rivalries and cultural differences of Nigeria.

Besides music, other entertainment programs include sports broadcasts, which may include play-by-play coverage of important sporting events held at home or in neighboring countries. Major events such as world cup coverage and the All Africa Games are brought in by satellite with transmission rights purchased by the country where necessary. Sports play a very important role in African popular culture, because Africans first obtained a place on the world stage in the area of sports.

Entertainment programs play a less important role in the more Islamic countries, Mali and Mauritania, for example. Those countries especially open to outside influences, Côte d'Ivoire, Nigeria, and Gabon among them, spend a good deal of broadcast time on entertainment.

Cultural Programs

Cultural programs generally refer to those programs which broadcast traditional African festivals and other folklore. UNESCO's figures show that this type of programming typically represents less than 15 percent of broadcasting in Africa. Boafo laments the fact that more airtime has not been devoted to recording and preserving these traditional cultural practices (1991, p. 117). Tunstall argues that a lot of traditional culture is too violent and too undemocratic to be of much use in the modern setting (1977, p. 115). This is yet to be documented by research. Moreover, there is some evidence that the inherent plasticity and adaptability of traditional culture could be more fully explored and used on the radio.

I believe the resistance to traditional cultural broadcasts comes more from the historically elitist and centrist nature of radio. Elites, who operate broadcasting, are largely unfamiliar with traditional culture, and the extraverted character of their education has given them little reason to value it. Broadcasting, furthermore, based as it is in large cities, has provided relatively few opportunities to collect cultural materials. In many cases, too, the importance of forging a new "twentieth-century" man or woman allied to the goals and symbols of the nation-state, has overlaid traditional cultures. Land's analysis of media in the Côte d'Ivoire, for example, shows that government information policy has clearly placed traditional culture and its preservation as secondary to the formation of a "new Ivorian man" (Land, 1991, p. 19). The late President Houphouët-Boigny (1960–93) of Côte d'Ivoire, of course, proved to be extremely open to the Western capitalist world, so his policies in this regard should not be seen necessarily as representative.

Julius Nyerere of Tanzania, in contrast, always believed in the importance of traditional culture. In an early speech, he decried the ignorance of the modern elites in Tanzania who did not know their own tradition or culture (Mytton, 1983, p. 111). And he enunciated policies for broadcasting designed to rectify these lacunae. But the centripetal forces of the modern nation-state prevented these policies from full implementation. The Tanzanian RTD (Radio-Television Department) built up a collection of traditional music (as had Zambia at Radio Lusaka) in cooperation with musical groups organized by the Tanzanian African National Union (TANU) youth league, the police, and the National Service. It also promoted new music, which was an amalgam of traditional styles. Mytton notes that, nevertheless, Radio Tanzania never really fulfilled its mandate to preserve traditional culture. Broadcasting retained its urban focus, making commercially recorded music (along with news) the most readily available Tanzanian radio fare (Mytton, 1983, pp. 112–13). The logical contradiction between the desire to promote rural culture for a primarily urban audience and the pressures to serve the interests of the nation-state detracted from traditional cultural promotion in Tanzania, as they have in most other states.

In this regard, Radio Gambia, the broadcasting service of the West African microstate of the Gambia, seems to represent some kind of bright spot. Radio Gambia has made a policy of broadcasting a heavy dose of cultural programs, including oral history programs. Among the most popular contributors to Radio Gambia are the griots. Here as in much of the Western Sahelian region (including Senegal, some of Guinea, and Mali), the griots are a professional caste of traditional entertainers who specialize in oral history much like the troubadours of the European middle ages. The griots' craft is particularly well suited to radio broadcasting, since these bards have cultivated their skill in oral delivery to a high degree. They are able to adjust traditional stories to modern times, a shift which denotes their adaptation to a new set of national patrons, patrons who superseded the Big Chiefs and traders for whom griots sang in earlier times.

Griots have been used by Radio Gambia not only in purely cultural programming but also in development broadcasts where they have fashioned their narrations to promote national unity, public health, and new agricultural methods (Conateh, 1974, p. 101). They have also been used by Radio Mali and Radio Senegal. The latter produced *"Regards sur le Sénégal d'autrefois"* (A Look at the Senegal of the Past), narrated by Cherif Fall. The program dealt with oral history accounts from the pre-nineteenth-century period. Radio Senegal also promoted the ancient art of storytelling through the work of griot el Hadji Djibi Thiam Coki, who broadcast for ten years *"Le meilleur diseur"* (The Best Storyteller) in French and in Wolof.

Similar types of vernacular programs have included *"Sous l'arbre à palabre"* (Under the Palaver Tree) and *"La Soirée en mooré"* (The Evening in Moore), both broadcasts of Radio Upper Volta (now Burkina Faso) in the 1970s. These programs extolled traditional values (respect for authority including traditional chiefs, elders, and husbands) through the use of traditional music and tales. In Zambia, Julius Chongo told stories in the Nyanja language every week during the 1970s in the program *"Pocheza N'madzulo."* Similar broadcasts have also appeared periodically within the vernacular services of Togo and Ghana (Tudesq, 1983, p. 196).

Other broadcast services have provided over the years more sophisticated programs of a historical nature. These have included, for example, *"Histoires et légendes du Congo et de l'Afrique"* (Stories and Legends of the Congo and of Africa), broadcast by Radio Zaire and appreciated mainly by educated urban males. Radio Gabon has produced over time *"Une date dans l'histoire"* (A Date in History), *"La Tribune de l'histoire"* (The Tribune of History), and *"Culture de notre temps"* (Culture in Our Times). Côte d'Ivoire has produced *"L'Histoire de La Côte d'Ivoire"* (History of Côte d'Ivoire) and *"Connais-tu mon beau pays?"* (Do You Know My Beautiful Country?). And Senegal produced *"La tribune de l'histoire"* (The Tribune of History), *"La tradition d'hier à demain"* (Tradition of Yesterday to Today), and *"Afrique Histoire"* (Tudesq, 1983, p. 189).

Educational Programs

Educational programs occupy about 20 percent of the broadcast fare on radio in selected countries surveyed by UNESCO (*World Communication Report*, 1989, pp. 404–408). Of course, what is defined as educational is often difficult to determine. Some of the programs classified as "educational" might just as easily have been grouped in either the cultural or the informational categories.

UNESCO has been involved periodically in a number of educational pilot projects. In fact, in the 1980s, UNESCO favored the promotion of decentralized rural-based community communication services operating on low-power FM transmitters.

An example from that period was the Homa Bay Community broadcasting station in Kenya's Nyanza province. The project was designed to provide a community-based rural service, one which served local needs in news and development. Such efforts have been fairly common over the years. Unfortunately, the project was actively discouraged by the Kenya government for political reasons (Heath, 1986, pp. 10–14). Katz and Wedell had noted in 1977 that such UNESCO efforts were rarely integrated into ongoing government policy. They further observed that government broadcast organizations in Africa cooperated only superficially with development efforts, embracing them half-heartedly, for the real interests of broadcast policy makers lay elsewhere (1977, p. 185). Boafo echoed this sentiment a decade or so later (Boafo, 1991, p. 119).

Tunstall noted that educational broadcasting in Africa is fraught with difficulties because it generates turf wars between other ministries involved, that is, the Ministry of Rural Development, the Ministry of Finance, the Ministry of Economic Planning, etc. (1977, p. 114). It is important to remember that the extraverted and nonindependent character of most African nations has made them subject to cross-pressures from outside. Aid packages with broadcast components proposed by an outside agency to one ministry, let us say the Ministry of Rural Development, have often conflicted with the activities of a second government office, say the Ministry of Information. This accounts, in part, for the fractious behavior of aid recipients termed by Sydney Head as "defective reciprocation" (Head, 1974, pp. 364–65).

"Defective reciprocation" seems to have been operating in Kenya where the Moi government initially accepted the Homa Bay Rural Radio Project in 1981 because he had a policy of cooperating with UNESCO, then scheduled to open a regional office in Nairobi, the first in the Third World, in 1984. When Moi had consolidated his power and no longer felt in the shadow of Kenyatta, some two and a half years later, Moi reversed his decision and had the installed Homa Bay equipment dismantled and brought to Nairobi. Moi provided not a shred of explanation for the actions of his ministry officials (Heath, 1986, pp. 10–14).

It is unfortunate that more serious attention is not devoted to education, for in survey after survey listeners report their interest in such programming (Mytton, 1983, pp. 81–86).

Religious Programming

Religious broadcasting tends to average less than five percent of broadcast schedules in UNESCO's selected countries. Religious broadcasts by national services lean heavily toward the transmission of services of major Christian or Muslim groups. Animistic religious practices have not been regarded by African broadcasting organizations as falling into this category. Where broadcasts of this kind are offered, they are classified as "cultural" (Tudesq, 1983, pp. 85–86).

In Christian nations/regions, radio stations may well do remote broadcasts from the nation's major churches or cathedrals on major religious holidays. In areas dominated by Islam, radio presents verses of the Quran, and also announces the Islamic calls to prayer. More extensive religious broadcasts are held on Islamic holidays. A number of religious organizations provide programming free to African stations. This has been especially true in recent years of evangelical Christian groups.

It should be noted that religious broadcasting is available extensively in Africa through the efforts of various groups who operate their own religious broadcasting stations. These include Radio Vatican, which broadcasts on shortwave to Africa, and ELWA, a powerful evangelical station based in Liberia which broadcasts on shortwave throughout West Africa. And Oslo-based Trans World Radio also operates a powerful transmitter from Manzini in Swaziland.

Advertising

Advertisements are carried on a number of services in order to help stem budget deficits. Though most radio services at least initially eschewed advertising, very few were able to resist the temptation of supplementing their budgets with commercial revenues. By the late 1980s, at least 29 of the 49 countries under review in this volume were airing commercial advertisements on their mostly government-controlled stations (Martin, 1991, p. 184). Advertisements, where available, take up on average less than two percent of broadcast time, though this percentage is highly variable (UNESCO, *World Communication Report*, 1989, p. 404).

Other Types of Programs

That radio is the paramount aural medium is a truism which bears repeating. Programs that have done particularly well are those which use the medium in a personal and direct way. Some of these might properly be classified as entertainment; others might be considered informational or educational.

Tudesq describes a program which appeared early on Radio Dakar. Created by broadcaster Ibrahim M'Bengue, *"Makhouredia Gueye, chauffeur de taxi"* (Makhouredia Gueye, Taxi Driver) featured a fictitious taxi man, newly arrived from the countryside, who drove around Dakar encountering and surviving numerous scrapes with urban life (1983, p. 35). The theme of coping with the new urban environment has been an important one in Africa's popular electronic media and has also frequently appeared in popular literature.

Mytton reports on the success of advice programs in Zambia in the early 1970s. Listeners would write in with questions on how to handle work-related problems, misunderstandings with relatives, and most especially, the travails of their love lives. Mytton argues that in the Zambian climate of rapid social change, these programs were helping viewers to build relationships and find their way in the new environment. In this way, the Zambian Radio "Abby" or "Ann Landers" was providing a needed service. Mytton felt that radio was replacing "wise old men of the village" in an urban context (1983, pp. 85–86).

Other popular programs well suited to the radio medium include summaries taken from the local newspapers. The idea, taken from the BBC, provides nonliterates a means of access to their nation's print journalism. Variously termed "Newspaper on Air" or "Pick of the Dailies," these programs are commonplace on radio in anglophone Africa.

International Shortwave Radio Broadcasting

No account of radio in sub-Saharan Africa would be complete without mention of international shortwave services. Audiences for shortwave broadcasts emanating from outside the countries where they are received are higher for the African continent than for any other region of the world (Vittin, 1991, p. 49).

Controlled information from local media and a dissatisfaction with local programming are the chief reasons Africans tune in to shortwave services. Shortwave services, particularly those from Europe and the United States have prestige value and are generally considered more credible than available local fare (Vittin, 1991, p. 52).

Overall, in Africa, Radio France Internationale and the Voice of America are the two external services with the highest listenership (Vittin, 1991, p. 50). The British Broadcasting Corporation is still the preferred favorite in the former British colonies, though it faces considerable competition from the Voice of America and Radio South Africa. And in the 1980s, Radio France Internationale began to vie for audiences with a new player on the international broadcasting scene, Africa No. 1.

Established in Libreville in 1981, Africa No. 1 represents the partial fulfillment of Gabonese President Omar Bongo's dream to make the Central African nation of Gabon a center for the transmission of Bantu culture on the African continent. Broadcasting from five shortwave transmitters of 500 kilowatts, the station can be received throughout most of Black Africa.

Africa No. 1 is known for its up-beat, fast-paced broadcasting style. It features a high concentration of popular music, 75 percent of it African in origin, rapidly paced, youth-oriented features, news flashes, games, and contests. The station broadcasts primarily in French, though it does offer some limited programming in English and other African languages (Head, 1985, p. 372). Africa No. 1 also relays broadcasts from Radio France Internationale, Radio Japan, and Swiss Radio Internationale.

The station has been highly successful in capturing the attention of regular shortwave listeners. Surveys show that audiences tend to locate Africa No. 1 among the three or four most preferred external services. These vary according to the country. A survey conducted in Dakar in 1987, for example, found Africa No. 1 was the third most popular foreign station after Radio France Internationale and the Voice of America (Vittin, 1991, p. 51). A survey in Abidjan, Côte d'Ivoire, in 1985 placed it first! Africa No. 1's popularity there was followed by Radio France Internationale and the Voice of America. In Ghana, a BBC survey conducted in 1987 found Africa No. 1 ranked third after the BBC and the VOA (Vittin 1991, p. 51).

Africa No. 1 is a commercial station which boasts 20 million listeners in 15 countries (Vittin, 1991, p. 46). In 1988, the station's gross revenues were 58.5 million francs (about $9.4 million), up 16 percent from the previous year (Fortner, 1993, p. 238). Forty percent of the stock of Africa No. 1 is owned by SOFIRAD, the French government's *Société financière de Radiodiffusion*; most of the balance is owned directly or indirectly by the family of President Bongo. SOFIRAD's participation in this venture permits France to enjoy an indirect presence in African radio.

Perhaps in contrast to movements toward globalization of radio services in Africa, there continues to be another radio potential in Africa, one which is vying to pull African broadcasting in the opposite direction, toward the establishment of small-scale, community-based services. The impetus to establish such services exists in the minds of scholars, the United Nations, especially UNESCO, non-governmental organizations, and other visionaries, even if it has often been absent among financiers and politicians.

Community-Based Radio

Kwame Boafo decries the fact that so little effort has gone into community-based radio in Africa. He notes that only Burundi, Burkina Faso, Ghana, and Liberia appear to have taken some steps to expand community access to the electronic media with the establishment of local community radio stations (1991, p. 109).

Burkina Faso's efforts in this area have been considerable. Rural radio efforts began in 1961 with the *"sensibilisation"* campaigns previously noted. In the mid 1970s, rural radio was reorganized under an autonomous service in conjunction with the establishment of a center for the training of rural radio personnel, the *Centre inter-africain d'études en radio rurale* (CIERRO),[6] organized under the *Union des radios et télévisions nationales d'Afrique* (URTNA),[7] with the assistance of the Deutsche Welle of the Federal Republic of Germany. Rural radio increased its broadcasts from 15 hours and thirty minutes in 1974 to 51 hours in 1980. The broadcasts included magazine programs, contests and games, and development programs heard in 700 rural listening centers. Producers regularly recorded discussions between peasants, extension agents, and radio club discussion leaders. The importance of rural radio in Burkina Faso was demonstrated by the fact that the director of Rural Radio was later appointed to the post of director general of the National Service (Tudesq, 1983, p. 185).

In 1979, Burundi launched a project in rural radio also designed to give listeners access to the microphones. Peasants were encouraged to share problems of their daily lives with one another (Tudesq, 1983, p. 185). And Burundi has used innovative radio soap operas to systematically treat such themes as rural exodus, spouse abuse, adolescent delinquency, and civil corruption (Ngabirano, 1993, p. 9).

The Liberian Rural Communications Network (LRCN) Project

Liberia's experiment in rural radio, though nearly defunct in 1993 due to the civil war,[8] is instructive because it shows what can be done in African radio when some of the stultifying strictures of excessive elitism and dependence upon civil service structures are removed. For this reason, it bears examination in some detail.

In 1979, the United States Agency for International Development (USAID), in cooperation with the government of Liberia, signed an agreement to create community-based, indigenous-language radio in Liberia. This led to the creation of three upcountry stations in areas not previously served by government broadcasting services.[9]

In the early 1980s, three 10-kilowatt stations were constructed. These stations reached 55 percent of the nation's rural areas and 70 percent of its rural population. The project, known as the Liberian Rural Communications Network (LRCN), was designed to disseminate nonpolitical development communication messages with both national and regional/local appeal. The network planned to offer programs in twelve Liberian languages as well as English.

Unique in the conception of a project of this scale and size was the emphasis on localism in areas of recruitment, participation, and planning. Each station was served by six or seven producers. During the initial training phase, which took place during the early 1980s, producers were chosen through an extensive screening process designed to identify candidates sensitive to the needs of rural populations and fully conversant with one or more of the local languages in which they would broadcast. Once selected, these individuals were trained in radio production techniques, development message design, basic evaluation techniques, and radio journalism. Their formal training lasted two years and included an internship in the station where they would eventually be assigned.

Because the LRCN was designed to work alongside ministries and organizations involved in the development process, it invited staff members from other ministries to share in its training activities. These Development Agency Producers or DAPS came from Health, Education, and Family Planning, for example, and were trained at the LRCN in simple audio production techniques, message design, and development communication theory. After broadcast communication training, these DAPS returned to their ministries and later came back intermittently to the network to work with LRCN's producers as their ministries' campaigns evolved. They were thus able to serve rural audiences in a double capacity, as content experts in specific ministry-related fields and as radio message design specialists. The inclusion of personnel from other ministries went a long way in decreasing the interministerial rivalry which has been the bane of so many earlier developmental broadcasting efforts.

Each of the stations was assisted by a small cadre of volunteers monetarily rewarded with small honoraria. The volunteers made it possible for the stations to fill otherwise unmet broadcast needs of the community, including, in some cases, extra language service and broadcasts by and for women.[10] The presence of volunteers serving as producers was particularly encouraging to local listeners, as it further anchored the station to the local areas.

Although policy making and much fiscal control were handled for the stations through the central production unit in Monrovia, the stations were still very much a part of their communities, and each had its own local personality and programming agenda. Locally, the three stations were advised and overseen by Public Advisory Committees (PACs), made up of important political and religious personalities from the areas served. The advisory committees met frequently throughout the life of the project to advise local management on local programming needs and matters of policy. They also carefully monitored the broadcasts to insure adherence to local cultural mores and linguistic purity of the vernaculars used.[11]

Local participation was consistently encouraged through local fund-raising efforts. The local stations frequently held parades, rallies, beauty queen contests, and open houses—all of which were designed to bring in funds from the local areas and to dispel the notion that operating funds must necessarily all come from Monrovia or from the United States.[12]

The stations also opened up the airwaves to local personal announcements sponsored by ordinary citizens who might pay to publicize a birth or a death in a family or to call distant relatives to attend some type of family gathering.[13] This service was greatly appreciated by listeners who otherwise would have had to travel to Monrovia in order to make use of the Liberian Broadcasting Service's (LBS) paid announcement service. The stations also encouraged local businesses to advertise on the stations, for it was hoped that the local stations would help to stimulate the local economies. To this end, the stations regularly conducted remote broadcasts from the local marketplaces and other public venues where passersby were interviewed and even encouraged to come to the microphones to try out their skills as disc jockeys.

A key component in the project was the Department of Development Services. This department was responsible for the organization of training activities in the early stages and in the design of retraining/refresher courses after the stations began broadcasting in 1986. The Department of Development Services gathered a great deal of baseline data from the listening areas which would eventually be serviced. This information was printed in handbooks for each district serviced by the three radio stations. The ten area handbooks each contained locality maps; names of clan and town chiefs and other local notables; history and current information profiles of every town served, including lists of such amenities as schools, clinics, churches, mosques, markets, and market days. Finally, the handbooks provided important demographic data, much of it gathered systematically for the first time.

Area handbooks were housed in the libraries of each of the stations and were readily available to broadcast producers and other staff members. Field assistants were among those staff members who made the most consistent use of these manuals.

Each station employed one field assistant, attached administratively to the Department of Development Services. Field assistants were intended to play a key role in linking audiences with producers. Thus, the initial selection of field assistants was based typically on the ability of the candidate to demonstrate rapport with rural populations. The best ones were those who had previous experience in rural areas, having served as extension agents with other ministries or as census takers (Bourgault, 1989, pp. 82, 90).

Field assistants were specifically trained to use the area handbooks to identify key rural informants able to aid these field assistants in better serving their village audiences. They were also shown how to gather feedback on the development messages and programs for use by producers and by the research wing of the project. Where possible, field assistants organized at least two listening groups for each language area served. Field assistants would encourage town or quarter chiefs to meet in village listening groups with the people in the village square and listen on a radio to the rural broadcasts spoken in their language.

Designated language producers and field assistants would then regularly visit the villages on their project-supplied Suzuki motorbikes. Armed with boom-boxes and cassette tapes of potential programs, they would try out upcoming shows, solicit feedback, and generally gather ideas for further program development.

Toward the end of the project, the field assistants were also trained in formal pretesting methods and in the use of focus-group research techniques for gaining additional insight into knotty areas of development.[14] Field assistants considered this training to be particularly useful and quickly adapted some of these classroom-taught techniques to their village-based activities.

In any given development campaign, there was often an LRCN producer, a Development Agency Producer (DAP), and an LRCN field assistant working on the creation and transmission of a project-related development message. By visiting the villages and gathering feedback, field assistants quickly determined those messages which were comprehensible through the audio channel alone and those which required transmission through more than one sensory channel to be effective. One very problematic area uncovered by field assistants was in the conveyance of the Oral Rehydration Therapy (ORT) formula.[15] Testing the radio message detailing the ORT mixing formula showed that respondents could remember only one or two of the four ingredients used in making the solution and few or none of the prescribed proportions. So one field assistant collaborated with several health workers to design posters showing the ingredients in measured quantities and to conduct live sessions demonstrating how to mix ORT solution. These village-based demonstrations were very popular and widely attended.

The Liberian Rural Communications Network also recognized that development communication was more than the creation of action-oriented development spots or radio dramas. Development communication was seen more broadly as a service which helps to anchor people socially through the preservation and sustenance of local tradition. To this end, LRCN planners recognized, early on, the importance of recording, preserving, and broadcasting local village histories. Histories were collected on audiotape by producers, often with the help of field assistants, who would prearrange meetings with village elders, bards, and other important village informants. These recordings were retained at the station and broadcast from time to time. In a similar way, traditional music was recorded and archived for later use.

One innovative project carried out by the LRCN in conjunction with the United States Educational and Cultural Foundation was the sponsoring of a seminar on the preservation of Liberian culture and history. To this end, resident Liberian historians, folklorists, ethnomusicologists, and nine LRCN producers and field assistants joined together in a three-day workshop to share ideas on how best to maintain and preserve Liberia's traditional heritage.

Toward the end of the project, producers began experimenting with the creation of village-based dramas. The problem explored here was how to engage villagers in discussions surrounding particular development issues, and then how to involve them in the creation of a drama expressing the problems bound up in the adoption of a given development strategy.

The use of popular or street theater in the service of development is not new to Africa. Its presence has been described in the development literature since the 1970s. And the use of broadcast drama was not new to the LRCN. Since the beginning of transmission in 1986, LRCN's producers had been creating effective studio-based development dramas and short dramatized development messages. What was innovative here was the production and recording of dramas produced in the villages and the subsequent broadcast of these plays over regional development radio stations. Although these exercises were of considerable technical complexity, the productions were aesthetically pleasing. They had a village freshness and authenticity, enhanced by vocalized sound effects and songs by local singing groups. Most significant, however, was the ability of village-based drama to generate genuine "grass roots" enthusiasm and excitement and sometimes nearly universal participation in role-playing possible solutions to the people's own development problems.[16]

Of course, the LRCN project represented a considerable capital investment of about $11 million in U.S. funds and about $5 million in Liberian counterpart monies. This sum would have to be scaled down considerably to make it applicable for adoption by countries not benefiting from such extensive external aid. A rural broadcasting service similar to that of the LRCN could be achieved at a much reduced cost through the following means: use of solar-powered transmitters which do not require continuous sources of electrical power; elimination of overseas training for management; a decrease (perhaps by half) in the amount of training offered local personnel; and a reduction in the amount of foreign (expensive) technical assistance.

The project showed that people responded very well to a service designed especially to cater to their development needs. Audiences were thrilled with the localism of the broadcasts. Research conducted by the project demonstrated significant gains in knowledge and awareness of development issues and problems and an overall growth in the use of radio.[17] Public advisory committees worked with enthusiasm to improve the station by raising money and by offering counsel to producers of programs. Also, producers chosen for their creativity and oral ability in their native languages proved to be effective and committed broadcasters.

The use of field assistants who provided feedback worked to improve broadcasts. The ability of field assistants to devise creative solutions to development problems and to enjoin others to participate speaks to the initiative media professionals in Africa can have given appropriate leeway within the organizational structure. This is not to say the LRCN was not plagued by strictures of patronage and elitism. In fact, centralized control was a major weakness and source of difficulty throughout the life of the project. There was a tendency for the staff based in Monrovia to multiply. The Monrovia production staff, for example, produced in one week just slightly more than a single day's output of an upcountry team.

Some of the upper-level management began to atrophy on the job as the project moved forward. Development and research personnel could hardly be enjoined to leave their air-conditioned offices in Monrovia. And supervisory personnel in program production were equally reticent to leave the capital even though rural signals from upcountry stations did not reach Monrovia.

The Central Production Unit had been designed as a training center. After training was complete in the early phases of the project, the CPU remained as a home to central management, and, as such, a kind of albatross, a magnet for personnel and resources. The final report of the consultancy team expresses deep regret at the original siting of the Central Production Unit in Monrovia. It argues that the rural focus of the project would have been better served, had the original location for the CPU been placed upcountry at one of the regional stations (Institute for International Research, 1989, p. 71).

Eventually the CPU staff did what underengaged bureaucracies do elsewhere. They made work by creating endless rounds of meetings and issuing redundant formal memoranda. Alienation stemming from underutilization of the staff caused a great deal of bickering. Senior staff squabbles were largely concerned with power struggles: who was answering to whom, who was creating alliances with whom within and outside the network, i.e., with the director of the Liberian Broadcasting Service or with the Ministry of Information.

Senior staff squabbles, at least in the latter stages of the project, were rarely about questions of policy or substance. Systems of patronage are not concerned, after all, with public accountability but with personal loyalties. In such systems, it is not what one accomplishes which is important, but whom one pleases. It was clear toward the end of the project that a power struggle was emerging between senior staff with differing degrees of alliance and connections to the Doe administration. Indeed local patronage problems were never far below the surface at the LRCN.

Unfortunately, the matter of LRCN's statutory relationship with the Liberian Broadcasting System (the national service) had never been resolved. The Doe administration had allowed the development stations to operate under conditions of partial autonomy so long as the network remained in the project phase. But as the U.S. involvement wound down after 1987, the demands of patronage began to rear their ugly heads. A well-placed member of the Doe administration began to demand costly favors in exchange for his cooperation with the project. This eventuality is characteristic of so many projects funded from the outside. Such projects respond to goals held by outsiders, goals of development and decentralization, but they often fly in the face of the centralizing tendencies which have been so much a part of the political backbone of one-party states and the elites who support them.

Patronage has a Janus head. Liberia has always been a client state of the United States, and although the LRCN was a model project in development communications, not all of the U.S.'s aid was so exemplary. Sixty-six percent of the $600 million in aid the United States gave to Liberia between 1962 and 1988 went directly to the head of state (Clough, 1992, p. 78), and a disproportionate amount, $500 million, went to the Doe administration in the 1980s (Harden, 1990, p. 238).

Doe's support of the LRCN lasted just as long as the project. Afterward, it seemed that Doe would ultimately have absorbed the development network into the Liberian Broadcasting System, a service which played a major role in his propaganda efforts. As the USAID technical team prepared its final report in the spring of 1989, there were clear signs that the project was headed in this direction. But events in Liberia moved too fast for Doe. By December 1989, Charles Taylor's forces were moving into Nimba county from positions in Côte d'Ivoire. By the spring of 1990, they had moved on to Monrovia. By the end of that summer, Samuel Doe had died as bloody a death as the one he and his soldier colleagues had inflicted on William Tolbert ten years earlier. Today, rebel leader Charles Taylor of the National Patriotic Front of Liberia (NPFL) controls all three upcountry stations of the former LRCN project, using them to broadcast his own political views and objectives.

Two factors provide some dim hope amid all of the chaos which has characterized this story and Liberia's recent history: first, that in the wake of the decline of superpower polarities, Western nations seem to feel it no longer behooves them to support the Sam Does of this world; and second, that the lessons of "mega projects" run in cooperation with centralized states seem headed for reconfiguration. Clough and others have recognized that with the strategic decline in the importance of Africa, African nations may actually be better off. Foreign governments will be less inclined to give aid. This does not mean that aid will cease but rather that private voluntary groups will begin to spearhead more and more projects. Western governments, less concerned about the political implications of aid, will be free to funnel funds through voluntary groups with the most promising projects.

As the LRCN example has shown, the combination of inputs in training and active encouragement of decentralized services can considerably improve the output of a nation's radio service. A project less tied to a government, particularly a government like Samuel Doe's, could go a long way in improving radio service for the people.[18]

In the 1990s, radio in Africa still remains a potential rather than an actual benefit to the masses of rural Africans who make up 70 percent of that continent's population. Populations with access to radio range from 40 percent to 100 percent depending on the country, with a median of 75 percent. Land area covered ranges from 35 percent in some countries, 100 percent in others, with a median of 60 percent. As of 1992, there were 123 radios per 1,000 persons in the African population, a figure which shows that radio receiving-sets are not keeping pace with population growth in this decade (Taylor, 1992, p. 4). The number of sets per thousand also contrasts rather dismally with the figure of 1,008 radios per 1,000 in the industrialized nations. This is hardly surprising when considered against the pattern of military expenditures in Black Africa. Military investment in sub-Saharan Africa represents 108 percent of the total expenditures on health and education (UNDP, *Human Development Report*, 1992, pp. 133–85). Radios in Africa, moreover, are still disproportionately in the hands of urbanites.

Winds of Change

In the 1990s, African radio is caught up in the wider political changes sweeping the continent. Political developments since the collapse of the Soviet Union have led many governments to allow (or fail to prohibit) the establishment of private radio stations. And related to this trend is a parallel move to consider decentralization of national radio services. In most countries, decentralization is still in the stage of contemplation, part of a larger debate on political pluralism and public access to the means of communication.

Much of the impetus for restructuring broadcasting has come out of national conferences held in the early 1990s, where the hue and cry for private access to the airwaves has arisen in a wholesale public revolt against existing governments together with their apparatus of controlled media. (See chapter 8.) The economic impetus for private broadcasting has come from the general liberalization of African economies, most of which are the result of structural adjustment programs initiated in the 1980s.

A variety of trends are affecting the radio scene in Africa. In some cases, "pluralism" has meant more access by foreign owners to African audiences. In Benin in 1991, FM 90 went on the air in Cotonou. This commercial station is a joint partnership between Radio France Internationale and the *Office de Rediffusion et de Télévision du Benin* (OTB) (USIA, 1992, p. 1). As of 1991, Senegal was allowing Radio France Internationale to broadcast 18 hours a day on Dakar FM. Meanwhile, Africa No. 1 had obtained broadcast rights for round-the-clock service on another FM frequency in Senegal.

In other countries, foreign license applicants compete with locals for frequencies. In 1992, for example, the government of Côte d'Ivoire allowed 17 contestants to compete for private FM broadcasting licenses in the country. Of these, only five were accepted: Radio France Internationale, the British Broadcasting Corporation, Africa No. 1, Radio Nostalgie (a private French service), and Jeune Afrique Musique (JAM). Only the fifth was a local contestant (Laké, 1993, p. 4). In April 1994, the BBC launched BBC Afrique on 94.3 FM in Abidjan (Davies, 1994, pp. 679–80). Besides these, a Catholic station, Radio Espoir, was created on FM in Abidjan, a concession demanded by the Vatican for the Pope's recognition of the expensive Catholic basilica commissioned by the late President Houphouët-Boigny in Yamoussoukro.

In 1992, a Zambian government privatization subcommittee was considering new laws for the governing of anticipated private radio media. The government had already received inquiries from potential investors, the majority of them foreign, interested in operating urban-based FM services (Wunsch, Bratton, and Kareithi, 1992, p. 26).

Uganda had plans in 1994 to launch its first private radio station, Radio Kampala. It was to be owned by two foreign nationals and a group of Ugandans. It planned to broadcast light music, entertainment, educational programs, and news bulletins (*Africa Communications*, May–June 1993, p. 8).

Burkina Faso actually had the first radio station in francophone West Africa not controlled by the Ministry of Information. *"Entrez et Parlez"* (Come in and Chat) was set up in February 1987, during the revolutionary regime of Thomas Sankara. *"Entrez et Parlez,"* though not commercial, provided for the people of Ouagadougou, the Burkina capital, the opportunity to criticize the government. The station was short lived. Sankara was killed in October of that year, and the new president, Blaise Compaoré, silenced the service. But the taste for private media had been awakened in Burkina Faso. Three years later, Compaoré authorized the creation of Horizon FM (Laké, 1993, p. 8). Soon, a number of other stations began to broadcast. Most of these have not survived, owing to technical and financial problems; they lack the financial resource of the French and British governments. Radio France Internationale now broadcasts on an FM frequency in Burkina Faso, and the BBC has applied to the Burkinabe government for broadcasting rights (Bejot, 1993, p. 91).

Mali and Burkina Faso present somewhat more diverse pictures of potential broadcast pluralism. As of mid-1993, there were 12 private radio stations operating in Mali. The first of these, Rural Radio of Kayes, founded in 1988, is considered to be the first "private" radio station in francophone West Africa (Laké, 1993, p. 6). There are three other commercial stations in Mali: Radio Liberté and Radio Kledu in Bamako, and Radio Kenedougou in the Sikasso region. Five other Malian radio stations belong to associations. These include Radio Kayira, Fréquence 3, and Radio Tabale in Bamako; Radio Foko in Segou; and Radio Kuyirime in Kouchala (Laké, 1993, pp. 6–8). French interest in broadcasting on the African continent remains keen. As of March 1993, Radio France Internationale and Africa No. 1 had been authorized to broadcast on FM in Mali.

As of 1994, many governments in Africa allowed tentative liberalization of the airwaves as they studied the situation. Many were working on regulatory mechanisms which would govern new private broadcasting services. They were considering ways to decentralize existing government services. Burkina Faso, for example, intended to establish a superior council for communication, which would govern the new private media. The Burkinabe government reaffirmed its intention to protect journalistic freedoms and to end the monopoly of the state in broadcasting (Bejot, 1993, p. 91). In early 1994, the Gambian government announced plans to place Radio Gambia under the control of GAMTEL, the Gambian telecommunications parastatal, a move which was likely to make the radio service more responsive to market exigencies (White-Halbert, 1994, p. 43).

In Nigeria, federal and state government services have moved toward privatization since the late 1980s. In 1988, the federal government established, through Decree No. 25, a technical committee on privatization and commercialization. The body was charged with devising plans for partial commercialization of the Federal Radio Corporation of Nigeria (FRCN), along with other government media. This move led the stations to increase their advertising efforts and to charge for news coverage of events or items featuring nongovernment personalities (Mbachu, 1992, p. 29).

In September 1992, the then head of state, General Ibrahim Babangida, announced that a national audiovisual board would be established to examine applications for private media licenses and to otherwise oversee the operations of private broadcasting (Bourgault 1995, forthcoming). To this end, the National Broadcasting Commission (NBC) was created. In May 1993, the commission announced that it had issued private television broadcasting licenses to 14 companies and that the licensing of a number of private radio stations was soon to follow (*Africa Communications*, September–October 1993, p. 26). Yet to be agreed on in Nigeria and elsewhere are an array of issues governing the nature of these private or decentralized services each will have toward their audiences. In Nigeria, the government has now established the Nigerian Communications Commission which is charged with establishing a regulatory code for private broadcasters (*Africa Communications*, September–October 1993, p. 27).

It is yet too soon to forecast the fate of these structural changes in radio broadcasting in Africa. What does seem guaranteed is that powerful international broadcasting entities will make new inroads into the domestic African media scene. Their presence could help to safeguard freedom of expression about domestic issues. But ominously, international radio stations could serve only to "crowd out" domestic political views by offering their own slick programming or by creating a near monopoly over the available airwaves.

Meanwhile, the domestic services will no doubt continue to battle against an entrenched penchant for suppressing controversial views. This occurred in Mali, for example, just two months after the 1992 law authorizing private broadcasting was passed. Radio Kayira, founded by filmmaker Oumar Sissoko, was accused by the minister of communications of "irresponsibility." A few months later the station was afflicted with "a series of sudden power cuts," explained by the Malian Ministry of Energy as the work of bats who must have gnawed through the station's power lines. Meanwhile, government-owned Radio Mali was unaffected (Jaumain and Tamboura, 1992, p. 39).

Political wranglings notwithstanding, it is clear that African governments in the 1990s will continue to restructure broadcasting. Some will no doubt leave a good deal of it primarily to private investors; others are likely to join in partnerships with private or foreign government interests. And some, no doubt, will retain chiefly government control over the airwaves. As René Laké of the Panos Institute notes, "Radio pluralism seems to be coming very slowly and carefully . . . radio continues to be under state monopoly, either by law or de facto" (1993, p. 1).

The move toward political pluralism, which occupies much of the current discourse on democratization in Africa, has begun to show the need to incorporate the continent's rural masses. Rather than viewing pluralism as a cause of political fragmentation, African leaders and scholars have begun to see pluralism as a panacea for ethnic and cultural heterogeneity (Wiseman, 1991, pp. 7–13). These sentiments are yet to spill over in meaningful ways into the debates on broadcasting for the rural masses. The current spate of enthusiasm over newly burgeoning radio services in Africa seems preoccupied with urban entertainment services and middle-class political concerns over media access. Meanwhile would-be private media owners are concerned very much with potential profits. Unfortunately, little attention or energy has as yet been devoted to providing genuinely rural-based or "rural-friendly" broadcasting services to the media-starved regions of the hinterlands.

5 | Television Broadcasting

THE MEDIUM OF television in sub-Saharan Africa tends to be an elite and an urban phenomenon. This chapter will describe the manner in which television has been used to promote the political aims of the controllers of power, particularly the heads of state. To this end, information of a general nature on African television will be provided together with more focused studies, the latter examining the nature of television in five different countries. These detailed studies will be used to illustrate both the diversity apparent in Black African television broadcasting and the convergence toward increased dependence on commercial interests outside the continent.

The studies of the systems operating in Côte d'Ivoire, Gabon, and Kenya, for example, show that a collusion of forces is pushing these systems toward the greater use of entertainment, together with a growing dependence on external sources of programming. These trends became especially evident in the 1980s, aided and abetted by the availability of Western satellite transmissions, the worldwide move toward privatization of telecommunications industries and services, together with the growth of home market competition for audiences from videocassette recordings.

The less representative nation of Niger has made a concerted effort to provide rural television programming at community reception centers, programming which is largely developmental in nature. The case of the television service of Niger, Télé-Sahel, will be explored in this context.

Finally, the case of Nigeria will be discussed. Nigeria is Black Africa's giant, and as such it is often considered a bellwether or a harbinger of things to come in Africa. Nigeria's complex television situation exhibits two seemingly contradictory trends. On the one hand it is responding to elite pressure to privatize, pressure designed to aid Nigeria to jump on the telecommunications bandwagon and capitalize on the huge supply of existing sophisticated services available through satellite program suppliers. Meanwhile the public and state television services are making a concerted effort to produce popular entertainment programming for the masses. Such efforts are possible because Nigeria's comparative wealth and vast market potential make these local productions attractive to advertisers.

Nigerian initiatives in local programming provide an excellent opportunity to examine the operation of oral psychodynamics in the production process and the thorny issues surrounding the development of an African television aesthetic.

Elite Service with Elite Control

History

The television age began in Africa with the inauguration of WNTV in Ibadan, Nigeria, in 1959. A second station soon followed at Enugu, Nigeria. Thus, Nigeria had two television stations before independence from Great Britain in October 1960. Television was also introduced before independence in Kenya, Northern Rhodesia (now Zimbabwe), and Southern Rhodesia (now Zambia), where it served mainly the expatriate community.

In most of the other countries, TV was established just after independence in the early to mid-1960s. These included Sierra Leone, Burkina Faso, Sudan, Gabon, Côte d'Ivoire, Congo, Niger, Senegal, Madagascar, Ghana, Djibouti, Equatorial Guinea, and Zaire. TV also began at this time in Ethiopia and Liberia, two countries which were never colonized.

In some countries financial constraints or political considerations delayed the inauguration of TV broadcasting services until the 1970s: Benin in 1972; Central African Republic and Togo in 1973; Uganda in 1975; Guinea in 1977; Swaziland in 1978. The former Portuguese colonies were also late in obtaining TV service. Angola's television, opened in 1976, was the first in lusophone Africa. São Tomé and Príncipe, which has only a very limited service available to a few on closed circuit, began in 1982. Cape Verde began its service in 1984; Mozambique in 1990; and Guinea Bissau reopened its TV service in 1990 after a brief experiment with television service in the early 1970s.

A few countries resisted TV for a long time. Namibia (then Southwest Africa) obtained a television service in 1981. Mali, the Seychelles, and Somalia created their services in 1983. Burundi and Mauritania did not have TV until 1984. Cameroon delayed television service until 1986. Chad waited until 1987; Lesotho until 1988; and Botswana until 1989. Tanzania still cannot boast a service, except that of the commercial Television Zanzibar, begun in 1974, a station whose signals do not reach the Tanzanian mainland. Finally, a few small nations in Africa are still without TV at this time. These include Gambia (which nevertheless receives a television signal from neighboring Senegal), Rwanda, and Malawi. To date, Rwanda's plans to introduce a television service in the near future have been interrupted by a ghastly civil war. Today, geographical TV coverage on the continent ranges from 1 percent to 90 percent with a median land coverage of 30 percent. And population coverage varies from 10 to 100 percent with 40 percent being the median value (Taylor, 1992, p. 4).

The big rush to televise came for most countries just after independence. Television, like a national airline, was seen as a symbol of national status. And though more attention has been paid to television hardware than software, the television signals in most countries have never gotten very far beyond the capital city.

There is some evidence that, historically, telecommunications investment which was to have gone into radio was sacrificed for the new and more prestigious medium. In the initial stages of television, some countries put as much as 95 percent of their information budgets into this new medium (Bagilishya, 1988, p. 70). Most of the television services inaugurated in the 1960s or 1970s were in black and white and were subsequently colorized within eight to fifteen years. Conversion to color TV broadcasting occurred despite the absence of full territorial coverage by radio signals of most of the countries involved. Even today, with the availability of solar-powered FM technology, a community radio station could be set up in every town of 10,000 people for what it costs to build and operate a national television station (McLellan, 1986, p. 151). The fact that more efforts have not proceeded in the direction of rural radio indicates that government priorities still lie other than with serving the vast mass of people living in the rural areas. Indeed, these factors show unmistakable evidence of the elite aims of television.

General Information

Although most African nations have TV, Africa is the continent most poorly served by transmitters. In 1988, there were 160 television transmitters as compared to 500 in Oceania and 21,800 in Europe. Africa is also the continent having the fewest number of receiving sets. There were 3.7 million receiving sets for 365 million inhabitants in 1988 (Bagilishya, 1988, p. 70). In contrast, Oceania had 6.7 million sets for a population of 23 million! The number of television receivers in the nations of Africa has expanded from 600,000 in 1965 to 15,000,000, and the number of TV sets per 1,000 people has gone from 1.9 to 28.2. Yet overall only 1.1 percent of the African public own TV sets.

One reason for the low penetration of television in Africa is the absence of electricity in rural areas. Another is the high cost of television sets. A small black and white set can cost between $300 and $500, a figure higher than the average annual income for most African peasants and workers.

As in the case of radio, African governments used the promise of education via TV as the carrot needed to justify the launch of such an expensive service. Attracted as they had been to radio, UNESCO and bilateral organizations rushed into Africa, often in partnership with private financing ventures for technical development, to help African nations to set up television.

Early educational TV services generated mixed results, suffering from high cost, over-ambitious planning, and insufficient coordination between donors and recipients. Inevitably, the projects were closed down after costly experimental phases. Today, most bilateral aid organizations and United Nation agencies eschew the use of national television systems in development projects. Television has proved a sink for massive amounts of capital with little of its effects reaching the grass-roots level (McLellan, 1986, p. 139). And because of its high investment costs, television in Africa quickly became commercialized. As Sig Migelson, Time-Life's vice president, explained in 1966: "The various underdeveloped countries are having to permit commercials because they can't afford a television system otherwise" (Schiller, 1992, p. 151).

By the 1970s, TV broadcasting in Black Africa, where operative, tended to have two functions. It was serving as the president's personal address system (or that of the party in power), and it was providing cheap entertainment. Admittedly, there were some exceptions as shall be described below. The situation in radio has always been more complex and more varied.

The move toward TV as an entertainment medium gained new impetus in the 1980s. In that decade, a number of countries increased their hours of transmission and found they needed to fill more airtime. At the same time many countries experienced economic shortages and were forced to comply with International Monetary Fund and World Bank structural adjustment programs. These funding organizations mandated a decrease in the number of public servants on federal payrolls and the institution of businesses more responsive to market forces (Tudesq, 1992, p. 108). This has led to increasing commercialization of existing services and the creation of privately owned commercial stations. The drive toward TV as entertainment has also been furthered by competition for audiences from home video recorders and satellite-to-home reception services.

Increased programming of entertainment fare tends to go hand-in-hand with an increase of program imports, mostly from Europe and the United States. Comparisons between the 1970s and the 1980s show trends toward increased program importation. Zimbabwe went from broadcasting 52 percent foreign fare in 1984 to 61 percent in 1987. Zaire went from 25 percent imported programming in 1974 to 70 percent in 1989 (Tudesq, 1992, pp. 147–48). A 1984 survey showed that Uganda was importing 83 percent of its broadcasting, and Kenya, 52 percent (Varis, 1985). Today, in many African countries imported fare consists of over 50 to 70 percent of the programming. These include Angola, Gabon, Mozambique, Senegal, Togo, Zimbabwe, and Zaire (UNESCO, 1989, p. 148; and *Télérama*, 1988, pp. 370–429). In some countries the proportion of imports is even higher: Djibouti, 90 percent; Cape Verde, almost 100 percent.

Imported programming comes from a variety of sources. American commercial program distributors such as MCA, Time-Life Television, Paramount, Viacom, and Lorimar do a brisk business, supplying programs to Africa on a sliding cost scale largely determined by what their markets can bear. Episodes of "Dallas" can sell for as little as around $260 per hour-long installment in Africa, a cost which would be 10 times higher in Europe or elsewhere.

It is well known that African TV screens are regularly filled with reruns of U.S. serials: "Dallas," "Dynasty," "Ironside," "I Love Lucy," "The Virginian," "Hawaii 5-0," "Good Times," "The Jeffersons," "Championship Wrestling," "The Six-Million-Dollar Man," "Magnum P.I.," "Mannix," etc. There is evidence that audiences prefer locally produced fare, but little of that is offered.

Since 1987, the United States Information Agency (USIA) has added Afnet to its Worldnet transmissions, making free public affairs programming available to African TV stations by way of U.S. embassies or American cultural centers. This service is available to the countries in which the United States has the most interest: Gabon, Côte d'Ivoire, Nigeria, Liberia, Kenya, and Zimbabwe.

France has a long history of providing cultural programming to its former colonies and the francophone countries of the former Belgian colonies. More recently it has been extending its services to lusophone Africa as well. Canal France Internationale, a French satellite service, provides four hours of free programming, including news items monitored from French television by the *Agence International de télévision* (AITV) and cultural programs formerly supplied on cassette by *France Media Internationale* (FMI). These services are available to 24 different national television organizations but not to private ones. Reception dishes, satellite charges, and down link costs are also provided by the French government. The countries are free to use these services directly, to record them for a delayed transmission, and/or to integrate them in their own broadcasts (Tudesq, 1992, p. 149). There is some evidence that the ratio of imported programs to locally produced fare has increased in those countries where the services of Canal France Internationale have recently become available (Tudesq, 1992, p. 150).

Private French interests are also marketing their services in Africa. Canal Plus (a French pay television service) and La Cinq (a commercial station created by Havas Media in 1984) are marketing their programming to private television interests in Gabon and Senegal. Through an ingenious partnership which includes some French government participation, they are working with private interests in Senegal, Gabon, and Tunisia in the development of Canal

Plus Afrique which will provide some modicum of African programming to be shared between participants and European viewers.

The Federal Republic of Germany makes cultural programs available through its organization, Transtel, which supplied 12,000 hours of programming in five languages to Africa in 1988. These include documentaries, sports programs, and musicals, all of which are free or very nearly free, being heavily subsidized (Bagilishya, 1988, p. 73). In September 1992, Germany's Deutsche Welle TV service began providing two hours of current affairs broadcasts on satellite to national and regional networks in Africa (*Africa Communications*, May–June 1993, p. 20).

The government of Great Britain supplies programming through the British Council and BBC Enterprises, the world's largest program exporter. In April 1992, BBC World Service Television began providing an encrypted service which will be available to national subscribers and individuals with the appropriate technology (*Africa Communications*, July–August 1992, p. 21). Private British production products, the works of the ITN license holders and others, are marketed through International Television Enterprises.

With the growth of satellite services and the availability of (and competition from) video cassettes, local production in Black Africa is in decline, and imported programming is increasing. Interestingly, Nigeria, the biggest producer of local programming in Africa, is also the biggest importer (Tudesq, 1992, p. 147). Simultaneously, educational and information programs are decreasing, while entertainment programming is on the rise (Tudesq, 1992, p. 137). Countries with communal receiving sets, such as Niger and Ghana, seem to have made the most concerted attempts at resisting the wave of entertainment television sweeping Africa. Tudesq reports that 24 percent of the broadcasts in Niger were of an educational nature, and 23 percent were cultural in 1989 (Tudesq, 1992, p. 137). During the same time period, Ghana was devoting 22.1 percent of its schedule to educational programs. Niger's attempts at rural broadcasting have unfortunately been dashed by economic crisis in the 1990s. Ghana meanwhile appears to be holding its own through a concerted effort to show development programs imported from other African countries (Aoulou, 1988, p. 390).

Video is rapidly gaining a competitive edge over local broadcast services in Africa. An African communication expert describes the situation:

> The young television in Africa faces stiff competition, and is even trapped by video because the local elites, used to its quality, encourage the government power structures to extend television where it does not already exist and demand programs comparable to those to which the video has habituated them. [Translation mine] (Quoted in Bagilishya, 1988, p. 74)

Such persons take their frame of reference from the programs shown on video and tend to scoff at their country's local production efforts. These attitudes have been exacerbated by the recent introduction of international satellite programming available to elites with satellite reception dishes.

As these trends continue, Africa's peasants (70 percent of the continent's population) become further marginalized by TV broadcasts programmed for the elites. Such shows contain rapid pacing and are replete with scenes which have little resonance with peasant reality and its value systems and which offer incomprehensible foreign dialogue.

Most television in Africa begins at about 5:00 or 6:00 in the evening and continues until 11:00 or midnight. Many countries are poorly equipped, having only one or two modest sized TV studios, supplied with three cameras which function sometimes sporadically. Few stations have a suitable share of sets, props, costumers, and makeup people. Only a few countries such as Zaire, Gabon, Nigeria, and Zimbabwe have film laboratories. Local fare typically consists of news, public affairs, children's programs, women's programs, cultural programs, and quiz programs.

Women's programming tends to be particularly dismal. The woman's role in modern African society tends to be defined as a strictly domestic one, and women's programs are given over to cooking programs, housecleaning shows, and broadcasts on child care. Where women are given a more important voice than this, it is in the broadcast of programming to elite women. These are likely to feature the "talking heads" of successful elite women with important positions in government (such as women in the Ministry of Women's Affairs). Alternatively, broadcasts for elite women may center on clothing, hairstyles, or other frivolous issues. There is little evidence on African television that women produce almost half of the food consumed in Africa (Peebles, 1984, p. 9) and contribute the lion's share of the productive work on that continent. As McLellan notes, "the few women seen on African television tend to be portrayed as subservient and dependent to men, young sexual objects—relegated to second class citizenship" (1986, p. 86). Not surprisingly, the controllers of media, like those in society at large tend to be men. They lack as much empathy for women in general as they do for their rural audiences. Consequently, rural women are doubly ignored. Children's programs are rare, relegated to the few women producers who work at the stations. By and large, they tend to be haphazardly conceived and provided with few resources.

Television News and Information: The Jewel of African TV

According to A. J. Tudesq, television was established in Africa at the behest of the head of state. The respective heads of state were able to establish a monopolistic control over the television system even more easily than in radio (1992, p. 73). The relationship between television and the head of state is very apparent as television services, or their new colorized versions, have often been inaugurated on the birthday of the head of state or on the anniversary of his accession to power.

Information is seen by African television as the "jewel" of the service. On this subject Tudesq writes:

> Information is not seen as a presentation of novelties, a search for the sensational, but as a military act, an explanation of governmental decisions and a means of orienting opinions. [Translation mine] (1992, p. 111)

As Ivorian broadcaster George Benson has stated, "news, in our countries [is designed to] transmit to our mostly illiterate populations, the directives and the orders of our party and of our government" (quoted in Tudesq, 1992, p. 113). Some nations are even more open about the role of propaganda in the news. Congolese Prime Minister Sylvain Goma announced at a seminar on news in 1980, "The role of our media is to struggle against imperialist propaganda" [translations mine] (cited in Tudesq, 1992, p. 112).

News is typically scheduled around 8:00 P.M., the time when the maximum number of viewers are watching television. And much of the programming schedules are filled with national news, particularly in those countries whose budgets are insufficient even to provide cheap imported fare.

In Central African Republic in 1990, out of four hours of daily broadcasting, one hour was reserved for news. In Uganda, news represented 35 percent of the broadcast schedule in 1984. In Burkina Faso, that figure was as high as 53 percent in 1985 (Tudesq, 1992, p. 111).

News broadcasts typically begin with the latest activities of the head of state. In Côte d'Ivoire, during the long presidency of Félix Houphouët-Boigny (1960–93), the evening news always began with a slide on which were written the president's thoughts of the day. This was typically followed by news of the activities of government ministers, sometimes supplied with footage produced by the station. It was often followed by some international news, typically news of Africa with visual material produced by one of the international agencies, World Net (of the USIA), Visnews (television news service of Reuters of Great Britain), or Canal France Internationale. Accounts of other events having occurred within the capital together with news items supplied by the local news services were read by anchorpersons. Editorials, always supporting the government's point of view, were freely intermixed with the news and were rarely identified as opinion. This pattern has been common throughout the continent on the largely predominant government services, though many poorer countries are less well served by external news services.

Newscasters generally read the news from typed scripts, as TelePrompTers, if ever available, are almost always inoperative. Apart from what has been supplied through the international agencies mentioned above, there have been few visuals, with the exception of slides depicting the head of state. These have been used liberally throughout the broadcasts. Video footage, where available, has tended to document the speeches or meetings of the head of state or his ministers.

Bagilishya notes that about two-thirds of what is described as local production emanating from African stations is in fact news which details "the smallest accomplishments and gestures of the head of state or of his ministers of government." Such news is often reedited into larger news/information programs, suitably titled "special editions or reports" (1988, p. 73). Daniel Arap Moi appears constantly on the Kenya Broadcasting Corporation. When he is out of the country, Kenyan television broadcasts old news reports in which his activities feature prominently (Tudesq, 1992, p. 112). And Radio-Télévision Ivoirienne (RTI) regularly preempted scheduled programs to bring special news features about the latest activities of former President Houphouët-Boigny (Land, 1991, p. 29). The Nigerian Television Authority requires its stations to break scheduled programs for events or announcements deemed important by the network authorities (Aliyu, 1982, p. 15). These are usually presidential specials or addresses.

News of presidents and other important government officials tends (even more than in radio) to feature the speeches of important politicians. Describing the news in Zambia, Mytton remarked on the propensity of reporters to cover speeches. He tactfully attributed this habit on the part of reporters to their lack of training:

> For coverage of local news, both suffered from a shortage of trained reporters. One consequence of this was that many stories were not really about events, but merely reports of speeches made by leading politicians at events. The content of the event, and the event itself often went unreported, simply because the journalist assigned to the story covered only the opening speech. At such opening ceremonies and speeches, all the paraphernalia of the mass media would be present: movie cameras, floodlights, still cameras, and tape recorders. Typically, as soon as the minister or other speech maker had finished on each occasion, the media would leave, and the following day all that was reported was an edited version of the speech. This was generally true of much news reporting in Zambia, not just in the press, but on radio and television as well, journalists followed the President, ministers, and district governors around. Few stories about their activities went beyond the editing down of a long speech, expect, perhaps, to relate that the occasion was attended by leading party and government officials. (Mytton, 1983, pp. 75–76)

The propensity to cover news in this way may indeed come from lack of training. Training problems noted in regard to radio are even more apparent in television where the constant assignment of political cronies to jobs in the civil service has been equally if not more apparent. As Tudesq notes, those journalists who have had professional training have a greater sense of professional liberty than those recruited for "extra-professional reasons" (1992, p. 108). Lack of training certainly contributes to the tendency of African news persons to hang on to the pronouncements of government officials. The system of political patronage certainly is another. Not to be discounted, however, is the more sinister trend of charging newsmakers (or would-be newsmakers) for coverage.

Because of the paucity of production budgets, it has been noted that up-country ministers and government representatives often cannot obtain coverage for their activities unless they pay for it out of their own operating funds. Tudesq calls this *"publi-reportage"* or a sort of public relations reporting. In the absence of other criteria, this need for payment for journalism has set up a dangerous precedent, one which fails to create a distinction between journalism and advertising. This "journalism for a fee" is widely, if clandestinely, used, sometimes to pay a single reporter, sometimes to pay an electronic media team. To what extent the funds are returned to administrative coffers remains an open question.[1]

In their roles as civil servants, those journalists who move up the professional ladder in the news media are those who have pleased the president with their coverage. It should come as no surprise then that journalists find themselves in a contradictory position. On the one hand, they are the persons whose job is considered the most important by authorities. Yet they are the persons who have the least liberty to exercise independent professional judgment. In some countries, news production is so closely supervised that the content of news broadcasts may even be determined by someone higher than a national television staff member. In the Congo, for example, daily news content is determined by one of the eight presidential counselors (Tudesq, 1992, p. 118). Although journalists do not embrace their curious role with great enthusiasm, they often display a surprisingly odd tolerance of it.

Mytton has shown that journalists have often seen themselves as part of the government (1983, p. 79). It is perhaps partly for this reason that they have been able to participate in sycophantic media activities, activities which do not appear to engender the kind of outrage Westerners, schooled in a different news tradition, tend to expect. Besides the coercive role of government in promoting the reporter as praise singer, besides the role limited budgets play in encouraging such behavior, and besides the civil service structure which fosters it, I think it is important to consider the role of oral culture as an additional element which has contributed to this process.

My own experiences conducting training workshops for television news reporters in Nigeria shed some light on the subject.[2] In these workshops, discussions about the coverage of speeches frequently emerged. This is because these were highly practical sessions, and I attempted to use the work the reporters were already doing as the basis for class exercises. Thus, each training session with TV reporters would review the previous week's TV news bulletins, critique them, and edit them. In the course of this work, we discovered that over one half of the local evening news on NTA affiliates was typically devoted to speeches of local personages.

As soon as we'd begun to edit such stories, the journalists would begin to giggle and scoff, remarking that politicians and traditional rulers would no doubt complain about the edited versions I was promoting. Interestingly, many of the speeches being covered were not major policy speeches by important politicians. Many represented speeches no more significant than courtesy calls of traditional rulers to modern politicians or the exhortations of various traditional rulers delivering prize-giving (graduation) addresses to secondary school students. Not unlike the reports documented by Mytton in Zambia, the occasions had generated the presence of the full regalia of the media. Thus, a local chief, calling upon students of the government girls' secondary school to "work hard, remain virtuous, and uphold the values of the nation," was duly recorded on videotape. As soon as the speaker had stopped his oration, the crew had dutifully turned off the cameras and departed. No summaries of these events were provided by NTA reporters, who focused little or not at all on the real victors in the story, the graduates themselves. Only the tedious and highly excessive speechifying had seemed important to journalists. And redundancy was clearly the order of the day, for during graduation season, numerous speeches, all with analogous messages, were given airplay often on the same day.

Many of the reporters seemed surprised and amused at the notion of editing these pieces. Remarkable to me was the fact that many of these journalists claimed to have been locally trained, at least through short courses provided by the Nigerian Institute of Journalism (in Lagos) or the NTA College in Jos. When I inquired about these courses, I learned that students had been "lectured to" and that very little time had been spent in these training sessions on practical exercises. I began to question some of the methods of this journalism training.

NTA Kaduna reporters also indicated that to edit the pieces to the extent I advocated (limiting them to about four minutes, i.e., cutting them about in half) would undoubtedly bring complaints to management from the "slighted" speaker (Bourgault, 1987, p. 221).

The practice of attending to speeches in this way has often been interpreted by foreign analysts as an example of a politically controlled media. But this seems a simplistic interpretation of a more complex cultural phenomenon. Indeed, many of the speakers covered in the newscasts described above had no official claims to coverage. Traditional chiefs had been stripped of their political power in the constitution of Nigeria's Second Republic. Nigerian television journalists were apparently giving airplay to their speeches because an important cultural value was attached to them.

I would argue that these reporters were exhibiting a relish for the spoken word (a major preoccupation of oral cultures) in the coverage of these graduation speeches, courtesy calls, and other ceremonious occasions. This sort of behavior must certainly be deeply engrained, for it occurs over and over again throughout the African media in systems and in countries with very divergent histories and backgrounds. (See chapter 7.) Surely there is a relationship between this kind of rapt attention to the pronouncements of authority figures and precolonial attitudes toward such personages. On this subject, the analysis of Fortes and Evans-Pritchard on precolonial African political systems is pertinent:

> An African ruler is to his people not merely a person who can enforce his will on them. He is the axis of political relations, the symbol of their unity and their exclusiveness, and the embodiment of their essential values. (P. 17, quoted in Arens and Karp, 1989, xvii)

Clearly, the users of the mass media as instruments in the development of a personality cult are fully cognizant of their ability to tap into people's deeply held notions about political authority. That the reporters should respond to corrections with giggles is indicative of the contradictions they must see in their positions, contradictions which they must face daily. They take it on the chin laughing in a kind of half self-mockery.[3]

Surprisingly, the creation of personality cults through the mass media has been little examined by British and American media scholars. Michael Schatzberg's analysis of the metaphors of power used by Mobutu of Zaire provides a useful and very dramatic example of this sort of activity, fully implicating the Zairian media in the process.

Schatzberg shows that over the years Mobutu carefully cultivated an image of the Father of the Nation. This metaphor has been particularly potent because it creates bonds of dependency among the populace. Schatzberg argues that the strength of this image tends to be all-encompassing, crowding out other more modern symbols of a modern polity. He argues that the media have covered all the acts of Mobutu as gifts—for example, when a new wing of a hospital was opened, or when a road was commissioned, it was because the father was giving a generous gift (1988, p. 77). Similarly, when civil servants were paid (on time or otherwise), it was because Mobutu was a generous father, giving food to his subjects. All of these symbols have made it difficult for the people to see how life in the nation of Zaire might otherwise be organized. The metaphor is ominous because it suggests that just as a gift is given freely, it can also be taken away. Schatzberg adds that "the media fatuously portrays the notion that all comes from Mobutu's magnanimous hands. It is as if no national budget existed at all!" (1988, pp. 79–80).

Equally important is Schatzberg's analysis of the historical origins of Mobutu's metaphor. Quoting from Vansina, he argues that Mobutu's style of rule "derives from the pre-colonial big man who tied clients to himself by favors and expectations of favors, and dropped them whenever their stature or their power bases acquired features that seemed to give them some independence to maneuver" (Vansina, 1982, p. 67; quoted in Schatzberg, 1988, p. 80).

What is important in Schatzberg's analysis is his recognition and identification of precolonial cultural norms. He writes succinctly on this point:

Through clever manipulation of the image of a generous father, Mobutu has created a system in which all he receives is but a demonstration of a culturally imbedded concept of mutual exchange: no theft, no corruption, no exploitation, only grateful children repaying their generous father. (1988, p. 81)

Throughout his discussion, Schatzberg emphasizes that the media have actively and consciously played a role in Mobutu's metaphor making.

Mobutu is not the only African leader who has used the media in this way, although he has been among the most outrageous and the most successful. Houphouët-Boigny of Côte d'Ivoire cultivated a similar if more benign persona. Television's primary role in Côte d'Ivoire has been identified as political: "To speak for the ruling party, personified in the Ivorian Head of State, legitimizing both party and President on a continuing basis" (Land, 1991, p. 19).

Cameroonian scholar Achille Mbembe argues on this point that "officialdom and the people share many references in common, the least of which is the conception of the aesthetics and stylistics of power" (1992, p. 13). This explains to some extent how and why the public has remained so tolerant of the kind of news broadcasts to which they have been subject, at least until the 1990s.

Mbembe points out further that the postcolony is an "intimate tyranny" which links the rulers to the ruled. He says that subjects internalize authoritarian epistemology to the point where they reproduce it themselves in their daily lives (1992, p. 23). This may explain the pompous behavior of civil servants and flagrant demonstrations of wealth which seem to preoccupy Africa's elite classes, popularly known in East Africa as the *Wa-Benzi's*, the "People of the Mercedes-Benz."

Arguing that African societies are characterized by scarcity, Mbembe notes that people have an opposite desire for the depiction of affluence and majesty. All this is fed by demonstrations of pomp of African leaders. This explains the curious propensity of the masses to adulate outrageous displays of wealth by rulers and sometimes embrace white elephant projects, such as the marble basilica built by Houphouët-Boigny in Côte d'Ivoire in the late 1980s.[4] In this way African popular tastes can be likened to those of American movie-goers in the depression era who particularly relished the wealthy fantasy world of Hollywood in the 1930s.

Interestingly, Mbembe notes that the postcolonial African is fragmented in his or her identity. This is why his or her loyalties can change overnight. Because the people living in the modern sector are so weakly grounded in their identities, they can easily shift allegiances. This may explain why journalists who adamantly defended the one-party system one year in Rwanda were clamoring for multiparty democracy the next. This is why media managers seem to contradict themselves. (See chapter 3.) Such persons constantly live surrounded by contradictions of the extraverted modern African nation-state. On a cultural level, this schizophrenia is facilitated by the consciousness of the oral world which is situationally and contextually determined.

Case Studies of Television in Black Africa

The following case studies provide a sense of what TV is like in the nations of Côte d'Ivoire, Gabon, Kenya, Niger, and Nigeria. They are designed to provide contrasting glimpses of African TV operating under different conditions. They also give an idea of the kind of assistance TV has received from external sources, the kind of training television personnel have acquired, the nature and source of programs they import, and the kinds of local programming they produce. Finally, they show patterns and sources of growth which have been apparent in recent years.

Côte d'Ivoire

The development of television in Côte d'Ivoire has been the most rapid of all of francophone Africa. The country established a black and white TV system in 1963, and went to color in 1973. The development was fueled by an ambitious Educational Television project which began in 1968. Based in Bouaké, the second largest city of the country, the *Programme d'éducation télévisuelle* (PETV) or *Projet Télé-Scolaire* embarked on this effort to try to make up deficits in its educational system. Like most other African countries, Côte d'Ivoire suffered from a low literacy rate and a lack of trained teachers, particularly in rural areas. The PETV project was designed to rectify this situation.

In 1971, the project began its first broadcasts to primary schools, starting with grade one. With each subsequent year, it added an additional grade for educational broadcasts and expanded to new schools. In nonelectrified rural areas, school television sets were equipped with batteries designed to last two years.

The project was widely promoted as a revolution in education by its proponents—the World Bank, which financed the equipment installation; UNESCO, which assisted in training teachers to use the new medium; the French Ministry of Cooperation, which provided personnel for program production and local producer training; and the Canadian government, which supplied printed texts designed to accompany the educational broadcasts. The project led to an increase in the number of pupils able to obtain a primary education. The percentage of children in school increased from 54 percent in 1970 to 65 percent in 1976–77. By the early 1980s, televised education was reaching 75 to 85 percent of the school pupils (Lenglet, 1985, p. 157). And much of the feedback showed better results in national examinations on such subjects as reading and writing.[5]

But the project was never without its critics. Rural parents were leery of this educational medium which they perceived as entertainment. Many felt it drained precious funds away from other worthy efforts in the national education budget. Another more serious problem was the fact that the PETV was producing too many primary school graduates in proportion to the available number of secondary school places. The project was finally abandoned in 1981.

During the 1970s, Côte d'Ivoire also experimented with rural educational broadcasts. Capitalizing on the infrastructural investment made in the interest of the PETV, an Out-of-School television component (*Extra-Scolaire*) was introduced in 1973. The OSTV wing of the project was based in Abidjan so that it could collaborate closely with ministries and parastatal organizations.

Lenglet's analysis of the OSTV described a number of problems. These included confusion over the target audience of the program, the project's high cost, the unworkability of schoolteachers as "animateurs" (postbroadcast discussion group leaders), the lack of clear objectives, and difficulties involved with collaboration with other development agencies (1985, pp. 161–62).

After the termination of the PETV, the *Extra-Scolaire* component of the project continued, but efforts to organize communal listening centers and gather feedback from the field were abandoned. Georges Keita, the head of RTI's rural broadcasting, aptly describes the problem producers without feedback must face: "The problem is developing the right material and knowing how to penetrate the rural psyche, which isn't easy, considering the gap between country and city" (quoted in McLellan, 1986, p. 105). To this comment McLellan perceptively adds, "The majority of producers and directors do not have the know-how, willingness, or resources to penetrate the rural psyche" (1986, p. 105).

By 1986, *Télé Pour Tous*, the *Extra-Scolaire* broadcasts had, according to

McLellan, become a "mainstay of Wednesday night programming." But few of the 20,000 schools which once possessed TV sets were open for rural listeners. The responsibility for resurrecting them had been passed on to the Ministry of Rural Development. Some of the more ambitious villagers were using car batteries to power the government-owned TV receivers, sitting idle in the classrooms (McLellan, 1986, p. 16). More of them were watching in their homes or in the homes of wealthier neighbors, for private ownership of TV sets has increased substantially in Côte d'Ivoire since the 1970s.

Côte d'Ivoire has held a cultural policy which has always been very open to the West. It is not surprising that Côte d'Ivoire should be the country which launched with UNESCO and French aid perhaps the most ambitious educational television project in the world. The role of television in Côte d'Ivoire has been clearly defined as promoting first, the unity of the nation, and second, the development of the *modern* Ivorian individual (Land, 1991, p. 19). To this end, President Houphouët-Boigny, who died in December 1993, put his faith in a service which would bring development to his people. The political failures of his ambitious plans in educational television did not deter the overall development of television. But today, television is moving in other directions. Rural viewers are expected to watch television from privately owned sets.

Côte d'Ivoire has two government-operated channels, the first of which covers at least 85 percent of the country's land surface. The second channel, begun in 1985, is for the moment experimental and can be received only in and around the capital, Abidjan. Both of the channels are commercial, showing on the average about five ads per hour, each about 40 seconds in length.[6]

Côte d'Ivoire is one of the wealthier countries in sub-Saharan Africa, with a per capita income of $790. As a result, advertising in Côte d'Ivoire is more developed than elsewhere in Africa. The advertising industry bears the indelible mark of multinational activity. Eighty percent of the advertisements on Ivorian television are foreign (Tudesq, 1992, p. 90). Havas Media International (which buys time on African media for foreign advertisers) opened its first bureau in Africa in Abidjan in 1973 under the name Havas Côte d'Ivoire. Subsidiaries of major advertising agencies also operate in Côte d'Ivoire. Lintas Worldwide produces advertisements for Unilever for such products as Belivoire (soap) and Omo (laundry detergent), and Filiane, affiliated with EP Conseil, produces commercials for Maggi (bouillon) cubes and local beer. Advertisements are produced and broadcast in French, but also in Dioula, Beté, Sénoufo, and Baoulé.

After the experiences of the 1970s, television in Côte d'Ivoire moved very clearly toward the provision of an entertainment service. In 1985, Channel 1 devoted 41 percent of broadcast time to information, and 35.6 percent of its time to entertainment, while Channel 2 devoted 17.3 percent of its time to information and 77.8 percent to entertainment. Clearly, the purpose of the new government service was to provide additional entertainment.

The RTI has experienced of late an increase in the number of program imports, a typical pattern for TV in the 1980s. In 1985, Côte d'Ivoire devoted 130 million CFA (about $500,000) to the purchase of foreign programming, but only 40 million CFA (about $170,000) for local production (Tudesq, 1992, p. 187). About 85 percent of the second channel's fare consisted of imported programming.

Much of the programming aired in Côte d'Ivoire is today supplied by Canal France Internationale. CFI is a satellite service for which the time, downlinks, and programming rights have been provided by the French government. Côte d'Ivoire uses 60–65 percent of its feeds (Tudesq, 1992, p. 150). Indeed, with the availability of CFI, Côte d'Ivoire is showing more imported programming than ever (Tudesq, 1992, p.151). Côte d'Ivoire also makes use of Afnet provided by the USIA. In one of its more intriguing partnerships, an Ivorian newscaster is able to interview, live from Washington, American political personalities, compliments of the Department of State. Côte d'Ivoire also purchases liberally from international program suppliers such as Time-Life, Lorimar productions (who supply "Dallas"), Viacom, CBS, and so on.

Côte d'Ivoire has been making some tentative attempts at program export. It participates in *Images Sud-Nord*, a group established by M. Hervé Bourges of the SOFIRAD, a French parastatal which finances projects in telecommunication.[7] The purpose of *Images Sud-Nord* is to extend African television to industrialized countries. In 1992, Ivory Coast had provided four programs for the service, about average for francophone countries. Côte d'Ivoire has been producing one of the most important historical series in Black Africa, *"Le Passé au Présent"* (The Past to the Present). One program devoted to the history of Benin cost 3,000,000 CFA an hour (about $12,500) to produce (Tudesq, 1992, p. 179).

Côte d'Ivoire also produces variety programs distributed to the francophone African subregion. Geared at modern youth culture, these programs present popular African musical groups. "Podium" features competitions between pop singers or bands. Another, *"Afrique-Etoiles"* ("Africa-Stars"), features Junior and Mary Domingo, dressed in evening clothes, sipping champagne, and chatting with their regional pop star guests. Sponsored by Air Afrique, *"Afrique-Etoiles"* was inspired by the French broadcast *"Champs-Elysées."*

With 54 sets per 1,000 persons, Côte d'Ivoire is the Black African country best equipped with television receivers. And although TV reaches the rural areas, which are for the most part electrified, TV remains an urban and upscale phenomenon. A 1987 survey showed that 78 percent of the urban population had access to television (82 percent in Abidjan, the Ivorian capital), but only 22 percent of the villagers were similarly served (Tudesq, 1992, p. 227). Among the latter, the survey further showed that 60 percent of the rurals with at least a secondary education watched television every day, while 59 percent of the illiterates never watched at all (Tudesq, 1992, p. 246).

Côte d'Ivoire has embarked on a thorough attempt to extend TV to the entire country. By the late 1980s, Côte d'Ivoire could boast having a TV signal which reached 90 percent of the population. This was accomplished technically through 13 transmitting centers, 24 relay stations, and seven delayed broadcasting centers (Land, 1991, p. 18). Côte d'Ivoire is also a member of INTELSAT, the International Telecommunication Satellite Organization. In 1992, Abidjan, the country's capital, was designated the seat of RASCOM, the Regional African Satellite Communication Project, which pools space segments of 17 different African countries who operate domestic satellite services (Unoma, 1993, p. 12).

TV's primary role in Côte d'Ivoire has been to serve as an integrating social force for a primarily national culture, a service designed to "provide a window on the world, showing the new Ivorian man the way to modernization." Ivorian television's secondary role, according to Land, is to provide a "mirror of Ivorian culture, primarily in the *singular* [emphasis mine], and one that reflects its image in the light of the dominant political party" (Land, 1991, p. 19). Houphouët-Boigny's successor, the former Speaker of the National Assembly, Henri Conan Bedie, was groomed for the office of the presidency by Houphouët-Boigny. A member of the same ruling party, the *Parti Démocratique* of Côte d'Ivoire, Bedie is likely to continue the policies of his predecessor and mentor.

UNESCO consultant Bernard Faivre d'Arcier commented that Côte d'Ivoire was experiencing in the 1970s a unique form of culture shock. Excessively open to outside influences, it was attempting "to gamble on rapid evolution, open to the exterior, one that would foster a kind of natural selection in the play of values between the old and the new" (d'Arcier, 1978, p. 25).

It is clear that this cultural policy represented almost a sinister neglect of Côte d'Ivoire's traditional cultures. In a speech before the Eighth Congress of the International Union of Journalists and the French Language Press, the president warned against clinging to past traditions and failing to adapt to the modern world:

> . . . it would be . . . vain to want to make of tradition one's only refuge and of the past one's only reference under the pretext of preserving our eminently respectable values from the permanent upheaval of our times. . . . These values will not maintain their reasons for existing and will not truly be prolonged unless confronted with the realities of the world that enrich, evolve, and sometimes humanize them through contact. (Houphouët-Boigny, (excerpts from speeches), 1980; quoted in Land, 1991, pp. 35–36)

With this sort of extraverted cultural policy, enunciated by the head of state, it is no wonder that the *Extra-Scolaire* project, with its program *"Télé Pour Tous,"* the longest running and most successful rural broadcast in Africa, was relegated to the service's background. Indeed, as Mitchell Land notes, "The Ivorian state's emphasis on openness to cultural influences from the preferred Western models delegitimizes traditional values of the ethnic cultures" (1991, pp. 14–15). The embrace of Western cultural models and values diverts attention and interest of decision makers from the less glamorous and more arduous task of promoting development among recalcitrant groups in the interior.

Indeed, Boafo comments that such developmental efforts tend to come from the outside, from UNESCO or from other foreign donors. Because these projects are not integrated into long-term strategies and programs, they do not last (1991, p. 110). It bears repeating that these projects have never been a primary concern of elites or planners. They have been tolerated by national rulers, as long as the money for them comes in from the outside and so long as outsiders have been available to pull the country toward rural development. And the advances made in these directions have tended to be slowly starved of funds and attention as soon as the project phase is completed.

Gabon

Television appeared very early in Gabon, in 1963, just four years after the inauguration of radio and three years after independence. In the early 1960s, there were nine French technicians who worked at Radio-Television Gabon, the RTG. They were assisted by five Gabonese staffers. Another eight Gabonese returned from the Studio Ecole where they had undergone broadcast training in Paris. By 1970, there were still five French *coopérants* working with the RTG staff. Later Gabonese producers would continue to be trained in France, at the *Direction de l'action à l'étranger* (DAEC), at the *Organisation de la Radio et la Télévision Française* (ORTF), at the *Institut Nationale de l'audiovisuelle* (INA) and the *Ecole Internationale de Bordeaux* (Bordeaux III). Some have also been trained at the Voice of America, which has included francophone students in its training programs since 1988. Finally, Gabonese broadcasters have also attended regional media training institutions in Africa such as the *Ecole Supérieure de sciences de l'information* at Yaoundé (Cameroon), which takes students from five additional francophone countries: Chad, Central African Republic, Rwanda,[8] Togo, and Gabon.

Color television in Gabon was installed by Thompson CSF, which has enjoyed a near monopoly on the installations of television equipment using the French SECAM system. The color service was inaugurated in 1975, in honor of President Omar Bongo's birthday.

In the early days of television in Gabon, television service was limited to five days a week. Fifty percent of the fare was imported, chiefly from France, and furnished for free by the *Office de Coopération Radiophonique* (OCORA). Other programming came from the United Kingdom, the United States, and West Germany. Local fare consisted of a monthly Gabonese folklore program, for example, *"Bonne Nuit Village d'Afrique"* (Good Night African Village); and weekly classroom games, such as *"Les petits a's"* (The Little As). Other programs treated professions, culture, medicine, or varied entertainment.

Interested in promoting the growth of television, the RTG launched "Chouchou the Cosmonaut" in 1965. Produced in cooperation with the French Cultural Center, the program depicted a fictitious Gabonese astronaut who made Gabon famous as the third country in space exploration. In the early 1970s, an effort was made to produce programs aimed at rural viewers. Two producers, one Gabonese and one French, created *"Où va-tu, Koumba?"* (Where Are You Going, Koumba?), a series which treated problems accompanying rural exodus. Another series dealing with health issues, *"Tant qu'on a la santé"* (While We Have Health), was broadcast at the time. During this period, an effort was made to set up community TV receivers with paid postprogram discussion leaders ("animateurs"). The community receiver project was assisted financially by the U.S. Embassy, the Embassy of China, the Embassy of France, and local rotary clubs. Initially, the listening centers, located mostly in the urban areas, were a big success. Crowds of up to two hundred people would gather to watch the programs, often pushing and shoving to get a better view of the small screen. Eventually, frustrated viewers pillaged the centers, and the project was terminated by the early 1970s (Tudesq, 1992, p. 44).

For a while in the 1970s, Gabon was making steady progress with its locally originated productions. By 1976, it was producing two-thirds of its own broadcasts. But this situation was not to last. Already by 1975, the RTG was spending more than a quarter of its budget on the purchase of foreign programs (Tudesq, 1992, p. 45). And since 1980, Gabonese TV has transmitted mostly entertainment. Indeed, Tudesq argues that as a TV culture develops, educational production diminishes (1992, p. 171).

In 1977, a second TV service, low in power, was established at the presidential palace and could be received throughout Libreville. Gabonese President Omar Bongo and the elite clique in power wanted to increase their own prestige through this new communication medium. To assure the president's control of the media, the national radio and TV services were combined in 1981 with the presidential press office. And as noted in chapter 4, President El Haj Omar Bongo long acted as his own minister of information.

One of the rarities of Gabonese TV is a program entitled *"Dossier de la RTG."* It is a call-in public affairs program which permits the public to phone in anonymously with complaints about social ills and corruption. In one segment, the minister for social security was so embarrassed by the accusations of a caller that he was compelled to leave the studio during a live transmission (Bourgine, 1988, p. 388). Such programs serve to diffuse criticism which might otherwise reflect badly on Bongo himself.

Keenly interested in media, Bongo has sought to make Gabon's capital, Libreville, a center for Bantu culture in the region. In 1981, Africa No. 1, a powerful commercial shortwave radio service, was inaugurated in Gabon. Its signals are received throughout most of Africa. In 1981, the RTG began producing a gala variety program for regional reception. Distributed by satellite under the auspices of the Union of National Radio and Television Organizations in Africa (URTNA), the program brought together African popular artists for the first time. Then in 1986, Bongo began negotiations with CNN. Though Bongo's negotiations with Ted Turner were not fruitful, the head of state continued to pursue his dream of operating his own satellite television service. This has led to the creation of station Télé-Africa, or Africa Numéro 2, which began satellite broadcasting in 1988. The station broadcasts the daily newscasts of La Cinq, a private station in France, two or three films a day, and television serials. Télé-Africa is a private service, owned primarily by members of Bongo's family. It is slated to join forces with Canal Horizon, already operating in Senegal. Canal Horizon, Elf-Gabon, and government parastatals joined together in a commercial venture will supply satellite programming on a pay basis from France and from other African nations which participate in coproductions through Canal Plus Afrique.[9]

Gabon is one of the rare countries in Africa to have financed most of its own TV. The oil boom of the late 1970s, combined with the low population of Gabon, has made this central African nation one of the richest in per capita incomes in Africa. The average income stood at about $2,770 per year in 1989, with most of the wealth being held in the hands of elites living in urban areas.

Since the 1980s, Gabon has broadcast a great deal of entertainment. In 1980, Channel 2 (low-power service) offered 39 percent films, 13 percent television serials, 19.4 percent news, and 13 percent magazine and documentary programs. Channel 1 transmitted 27 percent films, 34 percent television serials, 13 percent news, and 18 percent magazines and documentaries. Another survey, conducted in 1985, showed that 46 percent of the fare was entertainment on Channel 1, and 83.4 percent could be defined as entertainment on Channel 2 (Tchindji, n.d.; as quoted in Tudesq, 1992, p. 145).

Gabon makes liberal use of the services of Canal France Internationale, airing up to 80 percent of the material supplied by the service. It also draws from the broadcast fare of International Television Enterprises, which markets commercially produced material from Great Britain, and from BBC Enterprises, the largest program exporter in the world. Gabonese elites continue to display their taste for entertainment, particularly of a foreign origin. In a survey conducted in 1989, 75 percent of persons owning television also owned VCRs (Tudesq, 1992, p. 257).

Gabon broadcasts almost exclusively in French, although it does offer translations of the daily newscast in Bantou, Miene, Teke, Fang, and Bapanou. There are 60,000 receiver sets in use, about 20 per 1,000 in the population. Eighty percent of the Gabonese territory is reached by television signals.

As is common in so many African countries, media personnel figures were quite high in Gabon in the 1980s. In 1985, there were 154 persons employed by Channel 1, not counting financial, administrative, and support staffers (Tudesq, 1992, pp. 93–94). The pattern of giving jobs to cronies in Gabonese television has been clearly evident.

All three of Gabon's TV channels are commercial. As is typical of television elsewhere in Africa, advertising is largely offered by foreign corporations. The advertisements are placed through Havas Media International, which buys time for these corporations in the Gabonese media (Tudesq, 1992, pp. 191–92). Although the amount spent on television advertising by multinationals is greater than the proportion spent on Gabonese Radio, it is nevertheless small. In 1990, Havas purchased about $200,000 worth of airtime in television. This figure is slightly higher than comparable ones for other francophone countries. Advertising still represents a minimal resource for African media in the 1990s.

Kenya

Television was officially inaugurated in Kenya in 1963, just before independence. At this time, Kenyan television operated under contract by a private consortium of East African, British, Canadian, and American entrepreneurs. The colonial government was anxious to give television an autonomous voice modeled on the British Broadcasting Corporation (Martin, 1988, p. 188). The following year, the new government of Kenya nationalized the Kenya Broadcasting Corporation, which included services in both television and radio. The KBC was placed under the Ministry of Information, Broadcasting, and Tourism.

In the early days of television, 90 percent of the programs came from abroad. In the mid-1970s, Kenya announced that it would produce all of its own programs. By 1983, the percentage of imports had dropped to 59 percent (Martin, 1988, pp. 194–95). It should be noted that a high proportion of all imported programs typically feature entertainment. For Kenya, the entertainment portion of the schedule stood at about 71 percent in a late 1980 survey (Tudesq, 1992, p. 147). As noted above, the pattern of importing primarily entertainment programming is common throughout Africa.

Nearly half of the imports on Kenyan television come from the United

States. Detective and spy programs figure prominently among the fare, and such series as "Dallas," "The Jeffersons," "Roots," "Flintstones' Follies" and the "Little Rascals" have been shown. Nearly one-third of the imports come from Great Britain, which supplies a heavy dose of children's and educational programs. West Germany supplies about nine percent.

Early in Kenya's television history, efforts were also made to provide audiences with locally produced educational material. A number of programs on health and agriculture in Swahili were broadcast to rural areas, and community listening centers were established by USAID and by the Ford Foundation (Tudesq, 1992, p. 33).

During the 1960s and 1970s, the nation was led by the charismatic Jomo Kenyatta. Kenyatta's vice-president, Daniel Arap Moi, became president after Kenyatta's death in 1978. A period of civil unrest following the death of Kenyatta led to insecurity in the country. Kenya was declared a one-party state, under the ruling Kenya African Union (KANU).

Until the late 1980s, there was but one television channel in Kenya. Sixty-five percent of its transmissions were in English and 35 percent were in Swahili. Early in 1989, Kenya once again transferred responsibility for its electronic media services, this time to the KBC, a semiautonomous commercial arrangement, i.e., a parastatal.

The new structure corresponds with World Bank and International Monetary Fund's plans for structural adjustment. These adjustments mandate a reduction in government personnel and public expenditures (Heath, 1992, p. 41). The reform program has been responsible for capping recruitment of government media personnel in Kenya as in numerous other African countries.

Structural adjustment has been precipitated by a need to service national debts in African countries. Thus, the emphasis on commercialization of media has been one designed to "respond to the information needs of investors, and the business community in general" (Heath, 1992, p. 41).

The new organizational structure for Kenyan broadcasting releases the KBC from constraints of the Kenyan national budget, allowing increased flexibility to broadcast authorities to negotiate loans with foreign equipment investors and aid organizations (Heath, 1992, p. 42). The increased autonomy has permitted the KBC to borrow funds for capital investment purposes and to set its own repayment arrangements with Japanese firms for new telecommunication equipment.

The parastatal arrangement also releases the KBC from parliamentary control. The elimination of the oversight role of parliament has weakened the link of the Kenyan public to the Kenyan media. Previously, local members of parliament were able to raise public concerns as regards broadcasting to the appropriate authorities through this mechanism, even within Kenya's one-party system. A parliamentary member who consistently failed to represent his district was not reelected.

The KBC is now governed by a board whose members are appointed by the president. The managing director of the KBC, who has overall responsibility to the board and over the corporation, is also appointed by the president. Thus, the new parastatal arrangement has had the net effect of strengthening the hand of President Moi (Heath, 1992, p. 43).

Television in Kenya has been commercial since its inception. Regulations dictate that commercials must be produced in Kenya and that they must make use of Kenyan talent. In addition to paying for spot announcements, some corporations sponsor entire programs. Advertisers are mostly foreign corporations. While advertisements meet most of the recurrent expenses of radio, they cover only about 25 percent of those of television (Martin, 1988, p. 192). Advertisers are known to be hesitant to place spots in local fare because of its technically sloppy work (Heath, 1990, p. 77).

Production of advertisements is mostly controlled by foreign firms. In 1984, out of 11 advertising agencies, four were branches of international ones, six were local companies with foreign majority shareholders, and only one was entirely Kenyan-owned (Tudesq, 1992, p. 191).

In 1989, Kenya's per capita income stood at $380 per annum. Television set distribution stood at a low 5.4 sets per 1,000. TV signals are limited largely to the territory within a 100-mile radius of Kenya's two major cities, Nairobi and Mombassa, though some parts of Western Kenya are served by a transmitter at Timbora. About 30 percent of the Kenyan territory receives a television signal.

Television programming on the KBC's only channel begins at 5:30 P.M. on weekdays and 4:30 P.M. on weekends. Sign-off is generally at 11:15 P.M. and later on weekends. Kenyan television broadcasts an entertainment program in Swahili, *"Tushauraine"* (Let Us Discuss), a soap opera which shows the problems of daily life in Kenya. It treats such topics as polygamy, intertribal marriage, and conflicts between landlords and tenants. The aim of this program has been to promote family planning, a worthwhile goal for a nation with a population growth rate of 4.1 percent, the highest in the world. Before embarking on this project, the production team spent time in Mexico studying government-sponsored *telenovelas* designed to disseminate a variety of social messages (Booker, 1987, p. 18).

Like that of most other African nations, Kenya's local programming contains a great deal of information about the head of state. Nevertheless, Kenya is moving away from a service skewed in favor of news toward one containing more entertainment. This trend has been apparent since the 1970s (Tudesq, 1992, p. 68).

As is typical of most African countries, news is widely reported to be the most popular television program. (The same is true for radio.) In a 1980 survey, 18 percent said they liked news best. This was the highest percentage achieved for any category of program represented in the survey except for the response "no particular preference." Other categories ranking high included wrestling (11 percent), and sports (4 percent) (Martin, 1988, p. 194).

The Kenyan Television Network, or KTN 62, a pay television service, was installed in 1989. KTN belongs to KTMT, Kenya Times Media Trust, to which the journalism group Kenya Times belongs. Kenya Times is owned by KANU, the ruling party, and the Maxwell newspaper conglomerate based in London (Tudesq, 1992, p. 110).

KTN broadcasts 24 hours a day to an area within a 40-mile radius of Nairobi. The channel offers CNN International, talk shows from CNN, documentaries, sports, MTV Europe, and local programs, including local newscasts. Interestingly, the news is frequently at variance with that reported on the KBC. This was particularly significant as Kenya moved toward multiparty democracy in late 1991 (Heath, 1992, p. 48).

In late 1991, the chairman of the Kenya Times Media Trust announced that neither the KTMT or KANU was a shareholder, and that financing had come from a variety of loans from local banks (Heath, 1992, p. 46). It seemed the chairman was preparing the public for the new investment structure for the KTN.

More recently, KTN has launched a partnership with South Africa's Electronic Media Network or M-Net. South Africa clearly has plans for future investment in the electronic field in the Middle East, the Arabian peninsula, and the vast African continent. Kenya represents an excellent launching point for these ventures. M-Net's involvement may be disastrous for KTN in that it offers an entertainment service with no news. And indeed there has been talk of suspending or at least decreasing KTN's local news services (Heath, 1992, p. 47).

The restructuring of the KBC and the establishment of the KTN seem to have increased Moi's power in Kenya by improving his standing in the international financial community. Meanwhile it has done little to improve local services to the masses. A plan to improve Kenya's radio service and modernize its radio broadcasting facilities, for example, has not materialized (Heath, 1992, p. 48). And KBC radio has had to eliminate some of its vernacular services, a move rendered easier by the elimination of parliamentary oversight provisions for the new broadcasting structure.

The KBC operates a mass communication school, the Kenya Institute of Mass Communication (KIMC). Here KBC (formerly Voice of Kenya) staff and public information officers are trained, engineers as well as production personnel and journalists. The KIMC was begun soon after nationalization of broadcasting in 1964. Its aim was to lessen dependence of Kenya on foreign media training.

The School of Journalism at the University of Nairobi also offers a two-year degree in broadcast journalism. Funds for this venture were provided by UNESCO and the governments of Norway, Denmark, and Austria (Martin, 1988, p. 190). After the educational institutions of Nigeria, Kenyan media-training facilities are considered the best in sub-Saharan Africa, apart from South Africa. For a long time, Kenya operated the only media training schools in East Africa. Later, Malawi and Tanzania added media training institutes, although neither of these has a television service.[10]

Kenya is blessed with a pleasant climate and a modern capital city well equipped with the amenities of modern life. Thus, it serves as the headquarters for numerous international and regional organizations, including some important communications institutions.

Nairobi is the headquarters of the Union of National Radio and Television Organizations in Africa (URTNA). Established by the Organization of African Unity in 1962, the group was intended to facilitate program exchanges between member nations. In 1990, there were 44 members. Owing to financial, technical, and political difficulties, the seat does little more than maintain a catalogue of broadcasts available for exchange.

Nairobi is also the seat of the African Council on Communication Education (ACCE). This organization conducts research, holds seminars, and promotes the development of communication on the African continent. A related institution, the Institute for Communication Development and Research, publishes the *Africa Media Review*, which contains articles on media chiefly from the anglophone countries of Africa.

Nairobi also serves as home base for numerous Western correspondents covering Africa for their news organizations. Among them is the Atlanta-based Cable News Network (CNN), which maintains the only permanently assigned U.S. television correspondent for the American media.

Niger

Television in Niger appeared to present something of a model for a decentralized and nonelitist approach to programming before it fell on especially hard times in the 1990s. Niger television began with the inauguration of an ITV project in 1964. Niger was the first Black African nation to launch a project designed to give children complete instruction through television. Schools were equipped with TV sets controlled by classroom assistants known as *moniteurs*, many of whom had no more than a sixth-grade education. The *moniteurs* were given special courses to help administer the classrooms and guide the children through exercises provided in accompanying manuals. At first, the broadcast reached only 22 schools near the capital, Niamey. The project ultimately expanded to some rural areas of Niger. Solar-powered generators were installed in 1968 (a first for Black Africa) to run TV receiver sets in nonelectrified villages (Tudesq, 1992, p. 79). By the end of the project in 1972, 800 schools were equipped with television (Nwanko, 1974, p. 301).

The *Télé-Niger* project was considered a success by several yardsticks. First, there were no dropouts in the television schools, whereas the traditional schools experienced a 25 percent dropout rate. Second, the television students made remarkable progress in French, as compared to those students in traditional schools. Third, the moniteurs came to love their assignments despite the limits of their training. Unfortunately, there was no funding available to continue the project after 1972 (Nwanko, 1974, p. 301).

Télé-Niger evolved into a national service, Télé-Sahel, in 1979, and with the name came the mandate to serve rural audiences. To this end, television in Niger made serious attempts at nonformal education through regional broadcasting. Télé-Sahel's single channel covers 80 percent of the nation. Until recently, only 30 percent of its broadcasts were in French, including two editions of a daily newscast, which is translated into several vernaculars. Other French programs include *"L'Evenement du mois"* (The Event of the Month), a political program, and *"La Petite Ecole"* (The Little School), which carries cartoons, songs, and games of an educational nature targeted for home viewing by children between the ages of six and eight years. Télé-Sahel has also produced a historical program entitled *"Connaisance de l'Histoire"* (Knowledge of History). Télé-Sahel also carries, in French, news of OAU summit meetings and other French-produced news, as well as documentary reports on regional drought and on the conditions of the Niger River.

Partly because of the threat of Libyan TV to the north and Nigerian TV to the south, Niger has taken seriously its expansion to rural areas. Between 1975 and 1985, it invested 36 billion CFA (about $140 million) to expand its television signal. The technical work was done by Thompson LGT, the primary supplier of French cooperative aid in telecommunication (Tudesq, 1992, p. 182). French government aid no doubt came with a view to Niger's precious supply of uranium (Tudesq, 1992, p. 186). The expansion provided seven transmitting stations and fifteen or so repeater stations. In 1980, Niger also established the *Société Nigérienne de Télévision* (SNTV), a partly private concern responsible for equipping and managing approximately 1,000 communal viewing centers. The government of Niger owns 51 percent of the shares of SNTV, French business interests own 49 percent, and a Nigerian businessman owns one percent (McLellan, 1986, p. 17). By 1991, the number of communal receiving sets was estimated at 1,280, although it was not certain how many were operational (Tudesq, 1992, p. 225). In 1990, there were 50,000 TV receivers in Niger, about 2.4 per thousand (Aoulou, 1988, pp. 408–409).

The government of Niger has been particularly interested in reaching its legions of youth. As is typical of sub-Saharan Africa, the population of Niger is skewed toward the under 15 population age segment. To this end, the government has created *"samarias"* or youth centers in Niamey, each of which is equipped with a television set (McLellan, 1986, p. 17).

Until the 1990s, 70 percent of the TV broadcasts in Niger were carried in national languages: Germa, Hausa, Goumanché, Fulani, Kanuri, Toubou, and Arabic. Every week, *"Détente et sourire"* (Relax and Smile) offered five-minute magazine sketches, some of which were shot on location. Weekly broadcasts included a program on women and development which treated issues of health and nutrition. And *"Arts et métiers"* (Arts and Trades) and *"Caméras au village"* (Cameras in the Village) displayed the work of carpenters, welders, joiners, and other craftsmen. A weekly historical program treated historical events from precolonial times, the colonial era, and the recent past. One innovative program was *"Télé-service,"* which was designed to aid people in making their way through the maze of national bureaucracy, through the mysteries of fertilizer use, or through the use of various patent and prescription drugs (Aoulou, 1988, p. 408).

The content of health programs on Télé-Sahel was controlled entirely by the Ministry of Health (McLellan, 1986, p. 119). Control by the Ministry of Health helped to insure the accuracy of health programs and the coordination of health communication with the other activities and initiatives of that ministry and served to diffuse the potential for turf wars between Ministry of Health personnel and broadcasting organizations.

Among Télé-Sahel's news programs was *"Télé-Débat"* (Tele-Debate), which featured six personalities discussing such topics as the economy or cultural life.

Before launching development series, the *Office de Radiodiffusion Nigérienne* researched quite extensively the educational needs and expectations of the population of Niger. Civil servants, youth groups, village chiefs, and women's organizations were all included in surveys. Such research is very rare in Africa, where producers typically display a "hit or miss" pattern for targeting their audiences. Niger's research was instructive. Producers learned, for example, that the women of Niger were very interested in learning about the problems and progress of women in other Third World countries. Through the research, the producers came to realize that drama is one of the best formats for handling controversial topics such as family planning and sexually transmitted diseases (McLellan, 1986, p. 72).

One of the weaknesses of Télé-Sahel has always been the fact that development series have not been very well planned. Once an idea is agreed upon, producers are given wide-ranging freedom to develop their programs. As a result, their efforts have tended to be somewhat uncoordinated and their programs are often produced haphazardly (McLellan, 1986, p. 72). And because of the poor infrastructure, there has not been much formative evaluation to determine the extent to which the broadcasts are understood. Producers have always looked for feedback from the letters the station receives from viewers (McLellan, 1986, p. 76). This process is quite random and very selective at best, as the illiteracy rate in Niger is 86 percent, which is far higher than the sub-Saharan African average of 51 percent.

Historically, Télé-Sahel has made use of a limited number of *animateurs*, volunteer discussion leaders who organize listening groups, distribute audiovisual material to groups, and manage debates which follow the programs. A few of the centers are equipped with tape recorders that permit the recording of discussions following the broadcasts and thus insure some amount of feedback to the producers based at the Ministry of Rural Development in Niamey (McLellan, 1986, p. 26).

Télé-Sahel also broadcast a program called *"Théâtre populaire"* (Popular Theater), using ordinary peasants as actors, to convey development messages.[11] This program was the most popular program on television. Télé-Sahel also employed traditional music to promote both development and cultural pride.

According to McLellan, the rural listening centers he observed exhibited the same problems that have emerged in other countries with communal viewing groups: noisy crowds of 200 or more persons, including many children, gather in places where television represents the only entertainment for the villagers (1986, pp. 17–19).

According to Tudesq, in countries like Niger where television expansion has progressed less rapidly with more attention to rural audiences, educational programs have remained an important part of the broadcast schedule. In 1989, 24 percent of the broadcasts on Télé-Sahel were educational programs, and 23 percent were cultural (Tudesq, 1992, p. 137). Ghana's programming pattern is similar, with 22.1 percent educational programs, including 6.7 percent devoted specifically to rural listeners gathered in some 200 public viewing centers, some with solar-powered TV sets (Tudesq, 1992, pp. 173, 225).

At the beginning of the 1990s, Télé-Sahel was attempting to avoid excessive program importation, broadcasting only 35 percent imported programming (Tudesq, 1992, p. 154). But an economic crisis hit Télé-Sahel, forcing it to cease local production in 1991, just as an earlier crisis had forced it to abandon the Télé-Niger project. The program director of Télé-Sahel was reported in 1992 to use whatever television material he could obtain from Canal France Internationale, Transtel, and others. And he has requested free material from the United States (Kulakow, 1992, p. 3).

Despite the financial crisis, interest in regional broadcasting remains strong in Niger, and the government is committed to serving rural populations.

In 1992, the *Organisation de Radios et de Télévisions Nationales* (ORTN) was attempting to seek funding to use regional production sites to develop and air videotaped programs on issues of democracy pertinent to the shift toward freely elected government begun after Niger's National Conference. It also sought funding from the United States, the German government, and a variety of nongovernmental organizations to produce *théâtre populaire* on the subjects of democracy, individual rights, the electoral process, and so on (Kulakow, 1992, p. 5). Niger's transition to democracy in early 1993 was smooth, but the economic future of Télé-Sahel remains less certain.[12]

Television in Niger presents a fine example of development dependent upon outside sources. With the end of the Cold War, France's need for uranium has diminished as has the threat of Libyan hegemony in the region. With this turn of events has come a decrease in the aid which made the expansion of Télé-Sahel's services in the 1980s possible. The diminution of outside sources of funding has made Télé-Sahel dependent on inexpensive or free imported programming, and it has caused a decline in the promising rural services it offered during the last decade.

Television signals in Niger cover 80 percent of the sparsely populated territory. There are 2.4 receivers per 1,000 persons, most of them located in public viewing centers. With a per capita income of $290 per annum, the people of Niger can ill afford the purchase of a television set.

Nigeria

Nigeria had the first television station on the African continent, and today it boasts the most extensive service. Nigerian TV began with the inauguration of WNTV in Ibadan in 1959. This commercial venture was established with the assistance of the British firm Overseas Diffusion, Ltd. Soon afterward, in 1960, Nigeria became independent. A second regional television station, the Eastern Nigerian Television (ENTV), began transmission from Enugu that year. In 1962, the Northern Region of Nigeria began broadcasting from Kaduna with the assistance of two private British companies, Grenada and EMI. Thus, all three regions of the newly independent Nigeria had their own TV station, a structure which matched the political organization of the First Republic, a federation of three major regions of Nigeria. The federal government launched a limited television service from Lagos in 1962.

Military rule came to Nigeria in 1966, and it led to a major political reorganization of the country into 12 states. Each state clamored for a TV system of its own. Military Decree 24 of 1977 created the Nigerian Television Authority (NTA) as the only body authorized to broadcast TV signals. By then there were 10 TV stations in Nigeria, and all of them were taken over by the federal government. Several new states were created in the late 1970s. In each of the new states an NTA service was established. By 1978, each of the 19 states had a TV station broadcasting from its state capital.

In 1979, a civilian government returned to power. During the civilian era, states whose governors were not members of the ruling National Party of Nigeria (NPN) began to lobby for the opportunity to create television stations within their areas of jurisdiction. Twelve new state stations (i.e., stations not affiliated with the NTA) were created during this period.

Throughout the history of Nigeria, there has been constant pressure to increase the number of states, as state status is a means through which groups can more easily access federal resources and revenues. By 1990, there were thirty states in Nigeria, plus the new Federal Territory at Abuja, Nigeria's new capital. By this time, there were over 100 broadcasting stations, including 34 television stations. Of these, 22 were operated by the federal governments and 12 by state governments. The federal stations, those of the NTA, broadcast on VHF (very high frequency) signals; state stations use the UHF (ultra high frequency) band.

The NTA has had overall responsibility for all of Nigeria's TV stations since the military government of General Buhari (1984–85). The NTA director general is advised by a board of directors. Both the director general and the board are appointed by the minister of information in consultation with the head of state.

Technical broadcasting matters are the concern of the Ministry of Communication, which issues broadcast licenses. The 1979 Constitution of the Second Republic authorized private individuals to operate radio and television stations, although these provisions were suspended during much of the 1980s.

Estimates vary as to the number of receiving sets existing in the country. Tudesq gives the figure of 8 million (1992, p. 309), the highest figure in Black Africa. Conservatively estimated, this would put the number of sets per 1,000 population at 12.5.

Nigerians are avid consumers of media. *Screen Digest* in 1989 estimated that 16 percent of TV owners also had videocassette recorders (Tudesq, 1992, p. 256). The proportion of VCR owners had dropped somewhat since 1984, when it was estimated at 20 percent of the television-owning public (Tudesq, 1992, p. 259). The decline in VCRs can no doubt be attributed to worsening economic conditions in Nigeria throughout the 1980s.

At the height of the video craze in Nigeria in the early 1980s, videotape sales and rentals were a major business. Not unlike the video fare available elsewhere on the continent, most tapes in Nigeria were and still are illegally copied productions from Western countries. But some of the more popular Nigerian series have also been copied and made available for rent or for sale in the country. As of 1992, video rental was in serious decline due to the overall decline in incomes and the free-fall of the Nigerian naira. Prices for videotape rental had fallen so low (8 naira or about 25 cents a tape) that the video rental business was no longer a profit-making venture. Rental was being used to lure customers into electronics shops in the hopes of selling VCRs or satellite reception dishes to the very rich (Jazza, August 1992, interview).

In the 1990s, a number of entrepreneurs have emerged in the Nigerian media marketplace. Some of these are interested in using conventional TV channels, particularly in the bigger markets. Others are trying to capitalize on the possibility of redistributing international satellite services through cheaper and more convenient MMDS (Multipoint Microwave Distribution System) technology. In the summer of 1992, a number of Nigerian businessmen had established MMDS services without proper licenses. They were distributing international satellite services (CNN, Sky 1, Sky Movies, MTV Europe, Eurosport, Bop-TV [Bophuthatswana], for example) to subscribers, even though no redistribution rights had been obtained from program suppliers. Some suppliers had already appealed to their own governments to pressure the Nigerian Ministry of Communications to regulate the situation (Othman, 1992, interview).

In May 1993, the National Broadcasting Commission (NBC), charged with vetting applications of private broadcasters, announced that 14 licenses had been awarded for conventional over-the-air TV broadcasting and that 11 others had been awarded for satellite redistribution services.

The debates surrounding privatization and license allocation appear to be heated in Nigeria. And a number of turf wars seem to be brewing between potential applicants and their supporters, together with the official government bodies involved in broadcasting and broadcast regulation (*Africa Communications*, September–October 1993, pp. 26–27; *West Africa*, 18–24 April 1994, p. 693; and *West Africa*, 28 February–6 March 1994, p. 357). Likely as not, the changes in Nigerian broadcast structure will be fraught with conflict in the upcoming years.

Quite apart from these latest developments in the private broadcasting sector (which is almost too new to assess), viewers in Nigeria, particularly in the southern half of the country, enjoy multiple public (federal/state-supported) television services. Some areas can pick up four different channels. The north is less well served. Kano benefits from two channels, the state and the federal, while such states as Bauchi and Sokoto have only one channel each, the local NTA affiliate. As of 1988, 70 percent of the Nigerian territory could receive at least one signal.

NTA stations begin transmission at 3:00 P.M. on weekdays, and earlier on weekends. Sign-off is usually around midnight. The timetables of state stations are more varied depending upon their budgets and the importance attached to the service by state authorities. CTV Kano was broadcasting from 8:45 A.M. through 1:00 P.M. and again from 4:45 P.M. through 12:15 A.M. in the summer of 1992. There are some state stations whose transmission hours roughly parallel those of the NTA.

Programming falls into three broad categories: public enlightenment, news and current affairs, and entertainment. The public enlightenment category includes women's programs, children's programs, religious programs, and educational programs. The entertainment programs category subsumes musical productions, comedies, and serious dramas. News and current affairs encompasses national and international news, sports, and documentaries. National news is broadcast on the NTA three times in the evening: at 7:00 (for one-half hour), at 9:00 (for 45 minutes), and at 11:00 (for 15 minutes). The state stations are required to hook up for the 9:00 broadcast. State stations also provide their own local news as do the NTA affiliates. State stations have been allowed to make their own arrangements for purchase of satellite news feeds from CNN. NTA affiliates do not have this luxury, but the network does provide feeds on its national newscasts from CNN International.

National news from the NTA is delivered in flawless English, preferably with an Oxford or a Cambridge accent. National news broadcasters vie with one another to be the most flamboyant in dress. Lavish Yoruba headties are common for the female newscasters; male newscasters dress in national costumes or Western business suits. A typical breakdown for an NTA station reveals that 48 percent of the programming is entertainment, 36 percent is news and current affairs, and 16 percent is public enlightenment (Tudesq, 1992, pp. 111–78).

With the advent of the state stations created during the Second Republic (1979–83), there was a marked overall increase in entertainment. This occurred initially because the new state stations found themselves with a great deal of airtime to fill after they were first launched. Statistics for state and federal stations combined showed that entertainment climbed from 28.8 percent to 57 percent between 1981 and 1984. At the same time, there was an overall decline from 70 percent to 27 percent in the amount of news and current affairs programming provided in Nigeria (Tudesq, 1992, p. 137).

African nations have set a goal of importing no more than 40 percent of their broadcast programming (Tudesq, 1992, p. 143). Nigeria is one of the rare countries which has achieved it. Broadcasting about 61 percent local origination, the country falls short of its own directive which mandates a 70 percent local origination rate (Tudesq, 1992, p. 147).

Proportions of local origination do vary, however, from station to station. In 1981, NTV Ibadan (the old WNTV) broadcast only 15 percent imported programming (Tudesq, 1992, p. 143). Ibadan benefits from a well-developed dramatic tradition among the Yoruba people. But by 1983, the proportion of imports was back up to 31 percent, undoubtedly owing to the loss of production personnel to competing state stations which were proliferating at the time (Tudesq, 1992, p. 148).[13]

Imports in Nigeria come largely from the United States, which supplies on average 54 percent of foreign programming in Nigeria. British fare represents 27 percent of the imported fare (Tudesq, 1992, p. 152). Nigerian TV has aired most of the major American TV series: "Dallas," "Roots," "Charlie's Angels," "The Jeffersons," "Sanford and Son," "Good Times," "Different Strokes," "The Flip Wilson Show," "The Bionic Woman," "Sesame Street," and "Dynasty." British series have included such comedies as "Are You Being Served?" "Doctor in the House," and "Mind Your Language," and such action-adventure series as "The Professionals: MI-5," "Thrillers," "The Saint," "The Avengers," and numerous other detective series.

In 1982, the budget for the NTA (national stations only) was on the order of 100 million naira (about $130 million), about one-third of the budget of the BBC for that same year. Unfortunately, most of that went to pay salaries and running expenses. Only two percent was devoted to program production.

Educational broadcasting has not fared very well in Nigeria. WNTV first introduced educational television in the early days of its service, but its efforts were shortlived. The USAID launched an ETV project, but conflicts soon developed between American project personnel and the British television staffers who operated WNTV along commercial lines, not to mention British teachers who still occupied teaching positions in some of the Nigerian schools (Nwanko, 1974, p. 300). In the 1970s, some states tried rural broadcasting. About 10 receivers were placed in community listening centers in Bendel State, and around 70 were installed in the State of Kaduna. By 1977, there were no programs destined specifically to rural viewers (Tudesq, 1992, p. 30).

In 1978, only 16 percent of the TV broadcasts produced were educational. ETV suffered from a lack of coordination between the television staff and the Ministry of Education. A similar problem existed with the Ministry of Health. The failures encountered in educational TV in Nigeria and in so many other African countries have prompted UNESCO to discontinue its advocacy of ETV projects. Today, UNESCO and other aid-giving organizations advocate small-scale, locally based communication efforts which use radio or videotape.

While Nigeria has not done much in the way of educational programs, it has nevertheless put considerable effort into the development of local popular entertainment. This is especially true of the state stations. Compared with the federal stations, the state stations typically devote more of their budgets to local production. In the mid-1980s, Ogun TV, for example, was devoting 56 percent of its funds to local production (Balogun, 1988, p. 411). And 75 to 90 percent of Kano State Television's programs were locally made in 1992.

Local programs on state stations are for the most part produced in local languages, as the state stations have a special mandate to serve their local constituencies. Such programming tends to be done in one of the "Big Three" Nigerian languages: Hausa, Yoruba, or Ibo, one of which most Nigerians speak, very often in addition to English. Alternatively, stations in the southern half of the country may also use pidgin English in their productions.

All NTA network programs are produced in English in keeping with the "federal character" of the network, though local NTA affiliates often also produce programs in Nigerian languages. This is particularly true in the northern half of the country where Hausa rather than English (or pidgin English) is widely spoken as the *lingua franca* of the region.

Nigeria produces more programs than any other country in Black Africa. Some of its broadcasts are high quality and deserve special mention. "Cock Crow at Dawn" was a series produced in the early 1980s. Shot in Jos, Nigeria, it treated thematically the conflicts between rural and urban Nigerians. The series was sponsored by the Union Bank of Africa, in honor of Nigeria's Green Revolution Campaign, and was designed to stem rural exodus, promote the adoption of modern farming practices, and encourage urban dwellers to return to the soil. Another well-known and well-loved NTA program was "Village Headmaster," which also depicted rural life in a comical way. This program began in the 1970s and was still going strong in the late 1980s.

Other popular programs produced in Nigeria include the comedy *"Alawada"* (produced in Yoruba); the urban soap opera "Mirror in the Sun"; "Masquerade," produced at NTA Enugu (and later raised to a production of the network); and "New Masquerade," produced by the Anambra Broadcasting Service. "Case File," *"Baba Sala,"* and "Play House" were produced by NTA Kaduna. NTA Ibadan produced "My Pikin Friday" and "Jos Play of the Week."

Most of the local productions are comedies, heavily laden with visual humor. But they also contain a good deal of word play characteristic of oral cultural entertainment fare. NTA has also offered a few serious plays. NTV Ibadan does "Play House"; Port Harcourt does "Scope Theatre." But according to one critic, the most serious television drama is done in Benin (Oreh, 1985, pp. 108–109).

One important aspect of these local productions, says one Nigerian author, is their classless quality. Typically, they poke fun at Nigeria's Big Men, permitting Nigerians to laugh at the rich and powerful while secretly identifying with them. Audiences enjoy the local scenes, the typical Nigerian characters depicted, and their characteristically Nigerian style of speaking, often a delightful mixture of pure bombast combined with fractured British expressions and Nigerian pidgin, all blended together with local language terms. These plays seem to provide a genuinely unifying popular cultural force for Nigerians (Oreh, 1985, pp. 108–109).

Nigerian local productions are not without their critics. Local newspaper columnists regularly denounce the poor lighting, bad recording, poor acting and substandard technical coordination which mar many of these productions (Vincent, 1985, pp. 100-107). Others have complained that the dramas contain too much slapstick humor, too much shouting, and too many visual gags (Oreh, 1985, pp. 108-10).

These qualities reflect a larger pattern of indiscipline which characterizes the entire operation of Nigerian television. Equipment, new during the oil boom of the late 1970s, quickly fell into disrepair through lack of maintenance. Lighting technicians were said to regularly blind studio guests, and cameramen often left their posts unattended during live broadcasts (Balogun, 1988, p. 411).

Commenting during the same time period on Nigerian reporters, Mytton noted that few journalists would ever cover stories that demanded patience, time, and money. As a result, Nigerian newspapers, radio, and television stations would vie for the same easy stories, while the more important ones would pass right under their noses (Mytton, 1983, pp. 125-26).

Mytton has aptly described the partisan media situation in Nigeria as one of "fractured pluralism." This was particularly true during the Second Republic. He noted at that time that what one medium in one state would refuse to print or broadcast, another newspaper or station would be happy to circulate (1983, p. 119). Balogun echoes Mytton in her criticism of Nigerian television's "headlong crash into pluralism." She writes that the constant jostling for political power promotes a television service which is wasteful and misses opportunities for program exchange (1988, p. 413). In a related comment concerning program policy, Baya Sanda, general manager of NTV Ibadan, admits that the objectives of Nigerian television have never been clearly articulated: "There has been no planned strategy and programming has been uncoordinated with any other developmental efforts. The various officials have to decide what they want to do with television, identify the problems and allow us to go ahead and deal with them" (quoted in McLellan, 1986, p. 138).

Indiscipline has been a major problem which affects all facets of society. So severe were the problems of public pushing and shoving, failing to form queues, bribery, inattention to work, and absenteeism on the job, that in 1984, the Buhari regime launched a national campaign, the War Against Indiscipline. The WAI was a national attempt to try to root out the causes and manifestations of chaos and disorder typical of Nigerian society. The campaign was as short-lived as the Buhari regime. Considered too austere in his methods for reforming society, Buhari was "retired" and replaced by the Nigerian Military Council with the more genial figure of General Ibrahim Babangida in 1985.

By the mid-1980s, falling oil prices and structural readjustment had forced the country to cut its television budget in half (Balogun, 1988, p. 410). Severe as the economic conditions of the late 1980s and 1990s have been for Nigeria, they may in the long run offer some promise for improvement for some of the chaos which has been characteristic at Nigerian stations. Forced by economic circumstances, Nigeria reduced its television staff from 9,719 in 1985 to 5,200 (Tudesq, 1992, p. 93).

In the 1990s, as economic conditions have failed to improve, the NTA is attempting to decrease affiliate station dependency on the network for revenue. The move toward increased commercialization of government broadcasting services began in 1988 as part of Babangida's own structural adjustment program. At this time, the federal government established through Decree 25 a Technical Committee on Privatisation and Commercialisation (TCPC) (Ibie, 1993, pp. 60–61). Starting in 1989, NTA stations were allowed to charge fixed rates for coverage of news items by nongovernmental groups and individuals. At the same time, moreover, advertising rates began to climb. In 1992, a performance agreement was signed between the TCPC which authorizes the NTA (together with the Federal Radio Corporation of Nigeria and the News Agency of Nigeria) to operate as commercial enterprises. As a result of this new agreement, advertising rates are predicted to undergo constant upward adjustment (Ibie, 1993, p. 65).

The NTA, in effect, is working toward an arrangement where the network will provide funds only for capital investment. According to this plan, salaries and running costs will be borne by the individual stations. Upset with this turn of events, one general manager explained, "When you make your [advertising] target, they increase it the next year" (Abubakar, August 1992, interview). At present, it seems only NTA Lagos 2 is consistently able to meet all of its running costs through self-generated funds (Ibie, 1993, pp. 64–65).

The commercialization of news services does not appear to bode well for the development of a professional corps of journalists in Nigeria. And the trend is being repeated around the continent as public electronic media are forced to comply with structural adjustment programs.

Advertising does offer some promise for supporting Nigeria's extensive television services. Advertising has been well established in Nigeria since 1928 (Tudesq, 1992, p. 190), and more money is spent on television advertising than in any other medium. Nigeria's low per capita income of $250 per annum is deceptive, for Nigeria is a country of enormous contrasts, with one percent of the population controlling 75 percent of the wealth (Lamb, 1985, p. 305). And Nigeria's oil wealth has created a surprising number of millionaires. Nigeria is also Black Africa's wealthiest nation, with a Gross National Product worth more than half of some 45 other Black African nations combined (Lamb, 1985, p. 301). Many advertisers are eager to place advertisements on local drama productions produced in the Nigerian vernaculars.

Nigeria has the most extensive media training operations in Africa, outside of South Africa. First, there are a number of training facilities offered to professionals working in the media. These include those of the Federal Radio Corporation of Nigeria and the Nigerian Union of Journalists, in Lagos, the Institute of Mass Communication Technology (formerly the Nigerian Authority College) in Jos, and the Broadcasting Training Center, Ikeja, Lagos.

Six universities offer bachelor's degree programs in media studies. These include the University of Lagos; the University of Nigeria at Nsukka in Anambra State; the University of Maiduguri in Borno State; Bayero University in Kano State; Anambra State University at Enugu; and the University of Cross River in Akwa-Ibom State. The University of Lagos also offers masters and doctoral programs in mass communication.

Media training is also offered in a number of Nigeria's polytechnics. These include Ogun State Polytechnic, Abeokuta; Ibadan Polytechnic, Oyo State; Institute of Management and Technology, Enugu State; Federal Polytechnic, Bida, Niger State; Auchi Polytechnic, Bendel State; Calabar Polytechnic, Cross River State; Anambra Polytechnic Oko, Anambra State; the Polytechnic of Oguwashi-Uku, Bendel State; the College of Technology, Owerri, Imo State; and the Kaduna Polytechnic, Kaduna State.

The Oral Tradition, Television Production, and the Development of a Television Aesthetic

Orally Based Production Practices

Television training is urgently needed in most of the African states, and television training brings its own special set of pedagogical problems. The operation of a complex technology such as television makes demands on oral peoples not steeped in the stepwise progression of "machine logic." As is the case with management practices, television production in Africa is replete with manifestations of oral thinking styles. Some of what Balogun has described as "indiscipline" is in fact a manifestation of orality superimposed upon the technological demands of the medium. These problems seem quite intractable during media training sessions and merit some examination.

The oral world is an additive one, meaning that story elements in an oral narrative are not planned in advance but are simply added on to narrations as stories progress. Oral bards are oblivious to time and tend to ignore precise chronological markers in their accounts. These narrative stylistics put into sharp explanatory focus numerous practices I have observed in television production in Africa, particularly in Nigeria (Bourgault 1994a).

There is a general lack of time orientation in most areas of broadcast production: programs rarely begin on schedule; production crews rarely arrive on time; program lengths often exceed allotted time slots; and schedules themselves are often replete with errors. There is also a general resistance to the use of scripts, coupled with a tendency to allow programs to run free-form, much like the oral narrative.

Aggregative thinking, that is thinking in clusters or complexes, is also based in oral thinking patterns and can be observed in African media both in the routine production of output and in the values, attitudes, and work orientation of broadcasters. Television (as does radio) demands the simultaneous coordination and control of numerous production components. It also demands a linear or stepwise approach to problem solving. To achieve optimal audio output in a radio or a television studio production, for example, the audio operator must adjust each individual sound source (microphones, music, sound effects, etc.) and then adjust them in combination on the master potentiometer. A voltmeter located on the sound board measures the volume output and indicates when the system is overmodulating.

Audio operators I trained in Nigeria tended to concentrate only on the total sound level, not on the individual contributing components.[14] Thus, when the studio VU meter "peaked," for example, these audio operators would respond by lowering the total sound output rather than searching for the one possibly overmodulating sound source. Thus, they would often allow one excessively loud actor, sound effect, or musical tape to drown out the others.

Camera operators would resort to the same problem-solving style to adjust focus. If the talent in a studio set moved out of focus, camera operators would focus the camera and vary the focal length (i.e., zoom in or out) simultaneously, one operation often canceling out the other. I should mention that none of these behaviors is at all atypical of studio novices in any part of the world. One fully expects students unfamiliar with new technology and studio operations to experience difficulty during an initial phase of operation. What was startling in the Nigerian context was the apparent degree to which students resisted a systematic approach to simple studio tasks once they had been introduced, and once the value of these approaches had been explained. It was noteworthy that these studio staff members, with an education roughly equivalent to seven or eight grades of U.S. education, reacted quite differently to the technical training than did Nigerian university students training in studio techniques. The latter were well able to follow the demands of machine logic once these lessons were presented in studio classes.

Globalistic thinking also appeared in the entire approach to the studio production process in Nigeria. In the training courses I conducted, I established the use of postproduction meetings. Such meetings are typically used in broadcasting for the purposes of crew debriefing. During these sessions, individuals typically discuss the production process they have just undergone. They argue over what went well and what went badly, and they try to analyze the reasons underlying good and poor performances.

I was always surprised at the limited discussion which characterized these meetings, however much I encouraged the students to speak. Whether the program had gone roughly or smoothly, crew members seemed at a loss to explain the reasons. It seemed to me that broadcast students had great difficulty isolating the individual components which contributed to the whole production. Instructors working in these production contexts must be mindful of such limitations when working with broadcast trainees having less than secondary school educations.

Toward the Development of a Television Aesthetic: A Case Study in City TV Drama Production

Katz and Wedell argued in 1977 that Africa was yet to develop its own television aesthetic (pp. 203–207). Some of the technical problems engendered by oral thinking styles no doubt present barriers to this achievement. Broadcasting does, after all, require technical skills which have little resonance in traditional oral societies. As journalist Denis Boyles notes, the average American grows up with some rudimentary knowledge of how to use a pair of pliers, if only to repair poorly made consumer items (1988, p. 160). Africans do not derive much of this sort of technical experience from their backgrounds. Persons imparting technical training to broadcasting staff must pay careful attention to this lacuna, spending extra time with careful attention to stepwise production procedures and problem solving. Such training will be well worth the effort, for once these technical shortcomings have been surmounted, producers can begin to adapt to the media the wealth of creative material provided by African traditional life.

Nigeria's efforts in the production of local drama are noteworthy in this context because they show the beginnings of a television aesthetic in the making. The development of a TV aesthetic is a complicated phenomenon, drawing from technical elements, narrative traditions, managerial procedures, social contexts, and ethical considerations in which the electronic media operate. A short case study on the operations of the Drama Production Unit of City-TV, Kano, Nigeria, is provided below to illustrate the problems surrounding the development of a television aesthetic in sub-Saharan Africa.

CITY-TV, KANO, NIGERIA

CTV Kano City TV is one of several state-operated television stations created during the early 1980s to counterbalance the political and cultural influence of the federal Nigerian Television Authority (NTA), Nigeria's national television network. During the Second Republic, Nigeria was led by President Alhaji Shehu Shagari of the National Party of Nigeria, the NPN. At the time, state governors claiming allegiance to rival parties—the Unity Party of Nigeria (UPN), the Nigerian People's Party (NPP), the People's Redemption Party (PRP), and the Great Nigerian People's Party (GNPP)—clamored for the creation of state-based broadcasting in order to diffuse perceived disproportionate influence of the federal government and the NPN. Out of the political skirmishes which ensued over this question of "states' rights" came CTV and a number of other state television stations.

While all of the state-based stations were established with a mandate to promote local interests and culture (in contrast with the NTA's mandate to reflect Nigeria's national character), CTV embraced its calling with noteworthy enthusiasm. The reasons were both cultural and political. The city of Kano and by extension Kano State are regarded by Nigerians as the cultural homeland of Nigeria's largest ethnic group, the Hausa-Fulani. It was thus fitting that CTV would produce mainly Hausa-oriented programming in the Hausa language. Governor Mallam Abubakar Rimi was clearly interested in maintaining visibility and courting favor with his Hausa-Fulani kinsmen. He thus instituted a policy which mandated that 65 percent of the programming be locally originated, a *de facto* mandate to broadcast primarily in the Hausa language.

This was not only a sound and culturally sensitive programming policy for a primarily Hausa-speaking northern region, it was also politically calculated. One of the governor's chief rivals for the hearts and minds of the people of Kano State was (and still is) the powerful Emir of Kano. Like other traditional rulers, the emir had been stripped of official political power by the Constitution of the Second Republic (1979). But because of Kano's long history (written records which date back to the eighth century A.D.) and the Hausa's very strong traditional culture, many citizens still continued to regard the emir as the primary leader in Kano State, a position long reinforced in northern Nigeria by the British colonial policy of indirect rule. Rimi's rivalry with the emir was well known in Kano, and one of his early attempts at exerting authority over the traditional ruler led to riots by the emir's supporters. The rioters set fire to government buildings, and one of Rimi's important aides died in the blaze. Perhaps coincidentally, it was this aide who had formulated the programming policy for the would-be state station. By creating a popular entertainment medium, Rimi could foster performance traditions less tied to the pageantry and the courtly tradition of the emir's palace, though this was not likely a conscious aim of broadcasting policy.

A major plank of the station's policy was (and still is) to support and foster local culture and to scrupulously avoid programming which would offend the morals of Islamic Hausa culture. Established in 1981, CTV set about creating a fresh entertainment option for the people of the city of Kano. In so doing, it lured away from the NTA's local affiliate, NTA Kano, some of the latter station's better producers and technicians with tempting possibilities of higher salaries, newer facilities, more overseas training, and increased artistic freedom. Within a few years, CTV was producing a heavy dose of local programming, a practice it continues to this day.

Locally produced fare includes news and public affairs; public enlightenment programs incorporating children's programs, women's programs, religious programs, and development programs; and entertainment programs, including dramas and musicals. It is about the drama programs that we shall be concerned in this context.

CTV DRAMA—PROGRAMMING AND PRODUCTION

Each week, CTV produces and airs one new episode of its five different ongoing TV series. These series (locally called dramas) each contain 13 weekly episodes. Any given series may change with each new quarter of the broadcasting year. In summer 1992, two series featured continuing storylines and focused on human relationships. These two, *"Hadarin Kasa"* (Ground Squall) and *"Weeping Heart,"* are reminiscent of Western TV soap operas. The other three, *"Hankaka"* (a Hausa name), *"Sabon Dan Mogori"* (The New Dan Mogori), and *"Kuliya"* (The Local Court), somewhat resemble American situation comedies, with their humorous appeal and weekly plot changes. Four of the dramas were produced in Hausa, the *lingua franca* of northern Nigeria; one was produced in English, the national language of Nigeria. The summer 1992 season's drama production was considered a typical one.

The dramas were shot on ENG equipment, 3/4-inch portable cameras. Those dramas treating rural life were shot out-of-doors, while those treating middle-class issues and concerns used suitable indoor locations. Producers made use of the built-in microphone available on the cameras and rarely provided the actors with separate microphone inputs, oftentimes making for very poor sound quality. The dramas were edited at the station, usually on the day of broadcast.

Acting was handled by part-time actors who pursue this activity as a hobby as well as a means of supplementing their incomes. These actors were paid very modest fees (from about 20 to 200 naira or about $1 to $10) for each episode and were given no residuals. The sums paid are nowhere near enough to support acting as full-time employment. The corps of actors from within the city of Kano was being supplemented by station production personnel who enjoy trying their hand working on-screen as well as off it.

For the most part, the acting was improvised. Actors worked from storylines derived by the producer with his team in preproduction meetings, sometimes with the help of a writer. Only in some of the English dramas was dialogue carefully worked out and scripted. This is because many actors lack natural fluidity in the English language. Actors typically report being completely comfortable with improvisation, and those I spoke to seemed surprised at the very notion of extended rehearsal. In fact these amateurs felt it a mark of their ability and talent that they needed little or no rehearsal.[15]

There are about ten producers who make up the drama production unit. This figure is inexact because many of the producers have multiple duties and responsibilities, serving also as camera operators, sound recorders, and continuity announcers in other units of production. They also act, assistant produce, or serve as crew members, in one another's programs. This creates a very fluid group creative dynamic. Indeed, the producers' room at CTV is often abuzz with producers, actors, technicians, and occasionally visiting members of the public, heatedly discussing stories and plots.

Storylines were created out of the stream of urban gossip which pervades the city of Kano. Producers would transpose these stories to suit their creative needs and didactic purposes and to satisfy the demands of the television medium. Storylines were submitted by other employees at the station and sometimes by outsiders, who are welcomed by the station when they submit ideas for productions. Because of this free interchange of ideas, and because the shows are completed so close to airtime, CTV is easily able to interact with its audience. Some producers have even been known to frequent public viewing centers to eavesdrop on their audiences and to incorporate feedback into developing storylines or future episodes.

CONTENT AND AESTHETICS OF THE "SITUATION COMEDIES"

All three "situation comedies" in production in 1992 revolved around scams or tricksters. These include *"Sabon Dan Mogori," "Kuliya,"* and *"Hankaka."* The first featured a major protagonist who might be considered a lovable rogue, the second centered on a roguish family. The third starred a larger-than-life hero who regularly does battle with rogues.

"Sabon Dan Mogori" appears to be the best known and most popular of the three. Dan Mogori is a wily rural character looking for ways to cheat his neighbors out of money. In one episode he poses as a pseudo-rural travel agent hailing from Saudi Arabia. Dressed in the traditional Saudi head scarf, Dan Mogori meets a stranger in the village who is visiting some of his neighbors. Using a few words of fractured Arabic intermixed with some Hausa and a good deal of gesturing, he convinces the woman that he has long lived in Mecca and can arrange a discount air fare to, and local accommodation in, the Muslim Holy Land. All she needs to do is to provide a deposit on the pilgrimage and she will be well on her way to Islamic fulfillment and heavenly salvation.

Predictably, the woman is convinced and hence turns over a sizable sum of money to Dan Mogori. Both return to their respective lodgings. Dan Mogori and his spouse begin to make elaborate plans as to how they will spend the money. The visitor reveals her encounter to her hosts (her relatives) who are immediately suspicious and begin to inquire about the physical description of this so-called Saudi travel agent. It is not long before they discover that the shifty Dan Mogori is the perpetrator of the deed. They report the crime to the local district head, and Dan Mogori is dragged into the local court. He is found guilty, is given a serious dressing-down for deceiving people especially in the name of Islam, and is made to repay the money.

"*Kuliya*" derives from the name of the local traditional courts or magistrate in Hausaland. The "*Kuliya*" program typically features the swindling antics of Alhaji Buguzum and/or his senior wife, Hajiya. Both are aided in their escapades by elderly and comical senior servants attached to each of the main protagonists.

In one episode, Hajiya is tempted by a trader to purchase a costly necklace. She approaches Alhaji and asks him for the money for this expensive item. He refuses and an argument ensues. He chastises her for quarreling with him, and she feigns contrition while remaining resolute in her lust for the jewelry. With her rascally servant, Namanga, Hajiya hatches a plot to extract money from Alhaji. Hajiya sends Namanga out to the trader to obtain the jewelry, saying the money will come later. The trader promises the servant the customary cut of the profits for the latter's role of middleman in the sale.

The next day Hajiya informs her husband that her younger sister has been in a serious automobile accident. The terrible leg wound the sibling has suffered will require either medical treatment at a costly private hospital or amputation of the limb in a local clinic. Alhaji gives Hajiya the money. She plans to send Namanga out to the trader with money, but forces intervene. Annoyed at the delay in payment, the trader arrives at the Buguzum residence to fetch his money. Hajiya is out, so the trader appeals to the husband for payment. Alhaji knows he has been tricked and hatches a plot with his own servant, Garuje, to force Hajiya to squirm. Later that evening, he asks Hajiya about her sister's health, suggesting they organize a visit to comfort the ailing sister. Hajiya finds a reason why such a trip is unwise at this time, retires to her quarters, and summons her servant. Together they attempt to hatch a counterplot to save themselves. Hajiya sends the servant to find the trader and undo the deal. But the trader is resolute in his demand for cash, saying he has already obtained stock from others on the promise of Hajiya's money. The trader then has her arrested and brought before the *Kuliya*. Alhaji Buguzum pays his spouse's fines in exchange for numerous wifely concessions. And he makes her promise never to demand money for jewels again under pain that he will reveal Hajiya's nasty plot to her junior sister.

"*Hankaka,*" the star and protagonist of the eponymous series, is a hero figure. Hankaka is a retired veteran of World War II who is fond of physical combat and military discipline. An inveterate braggart, he is given to outlandish fabrications regarding his prowess fighting Nazis on the front lines in Germany. Wearing a fifty-year-old frayed British uniform, the larger-than-life Hankaka challenges all who cross him. A typical episode finds Hankaka discussing with a neighbor the case of one foolish night watchman who recently accepted a drugged kola nut from a stranger passing by.[16] Laced with a soporific, the nut put the night watchman to sleep rather than keep him awake. While the watchman slept, the band of thieves collaborating with the kola nut-giver robbed the store the night watchman was hired to guard. Characteristically, Hankaka derides the victim of the deed for his naïveté, boasting that he, the great Hankaka, is too clever and too fearsome to be similarly cheated by wrongdoers.

The scene changes, and Hankaka is alone in his home. A woman comes to his compound saying she is a stranger and is in need of lodging. Hankaka offers her traditional hospitality. Since his wife is out, the woman offers to cook a meal for her host. Hankaka gratefully accepts. The woman retires to the kitchen and prepares the food, adding to it a sleeping potion. After the heavy meal, Hankaka falls fast asleep. While he sleeps, the woman and her accomplices enter his home, strip it of all its possessions, and abscond. Before leaving, they remove Hankaka's uniform and dress him in a woman's wrapper and a very large bra. They add lipstick to his face and turn him over so that his face is turned away from the camera.

Later, Hankaka's wife returns and catches sight of what appears to be a female figure. She starts to rail against Hankaka for cavorting with another woman during her absence. When she begins to kick and abuse the sleeping figure, Hankaka awakens, turns and faces her, and sleepily reveals himself. At that moment, the perpetrators of the deed, including the original scammed night watchman, appear on the scene. They regale in laughter at Hankaka's appearance, reminding Hankaka that he is neither too big nor too frightening to be victimized. Hankaka's arrogance is cured until the next episode!

Aesthetically, these situation comedies are very satisfying. Shot in rural areas, they have authenticity as well as visual charm. Spoken in Hausa, they possess a verbal richness typical of the West African oral tradition. For example, many of the characters of the Hausa dramas bear metaphorical names, epithets which give an insight into their personalities. The situation comedies use a good deal of slapstick humor and visual gags, both of which help, along with predictable outcomes, to mitigate against the muffled sound quality. The casts include many seasoned actors who are comfortable in the idiom and who command a following in Kano after years of acting in theatrical groups or on NTA Kano dramas.

Equally important to their success is the resemblance of these situation comedies to the trickster tales common throughout much of Africa.[17] They differ only in that here the trickster is always punished in the end. It seems that the moral tale, so common among the Hausa, has been superimposed on the trickster tale, an accommodation no doubt engendered by Islamic religion with its strong moral code and its literary tradition.[18]

From observing the producers and actors develop these programs, and from watching audiences react to them, it becomes imminently clear that these situation comedies derive from a performance discourse which is both familiar and comfortable.

CONTENT AND AESTHETICS OF THE "EXTENDED SERIES"

CTV has also been experimenting with another type of drama which I have called the "extended series." Derived from and inspired by the Western soap opera genre, these programs are more difficult to produce because they make demands on continuity not required in the situation comedies. A quick review of the difficulties one such series generated is indicative of the technical leap required of producers as they move from productions derived from simple oral tales to those grounded more firmly in the literary tradition.

A good example of the extended series is "Beyond the Dreams," a 13-part series which focused on the trials and tribulations of a wealthy businessman, Alhaji Rabo, and his family. The program attempted to treat the budding love affair between his daughter, Zara, and her doctor, Rasheed, a social inferior with rural class origins. The program also dealt with Rabo's financial difficulties, problems ultimately solved when he took up farming.

First to be considered were the numerous technical and structural problems which emerged in the course of production. Most of the extended series are shot indoors, necessitating the use of artificial lighting. Typically only one light (a kind of "all-purpose key light") is used, thus creating hard shadows. Walls in modern Nigerian buildings tend to be whitewashed, causing a harsh glare when lights are shone upon them, and forcing the automatic electronic camera iris to "stop down" and underexpose the black faces of the actors. The walls of modern buildings are often made of concrete and floors are made of cement, both creating terrible echoes picked up by microphones. The sound problem is compounded when actors or producers insist on running room air conditioners during shooting. This leads to a general nonintelligibility of program dialogue. And here in these extended series, unlike the situation comedies (which are both gestural and predictable), comprehension of the dialogue is a necessity. Actors too can be a problem. Those capable of acting in English can exhibit a petulance typical of Nigeria's better-educated classes.

Organizational problems became evident in the production of this extended series. "Beyond the Dreams" was initially dependent upon scripts written by a lecturer in mass communications at the local university. Scripts were felt to be necessary because the series was produced in English. Unlike southern Nigerians who are very comfortable with English (at least a Nigerian variant of it), northerners prefer to use Hausa in their day-to-day interactions. It was felt that most actors performing in English would feel they needed to rely on written dialogue.

Halfway through the production of the series, the writer became overburdened with his teaching duties and was unable to continue with the project. The series producer took over the task. Soon afterward, he stopped producing full-blown scripts and resorted to the more common practice of using storylines and allowing the actors to improvise. He felt that his actors were sufficiently comfortable with English to improvise program dialogue.

It was about this time that the advertising department sought and obtained sponsorship from a local agricultural bank. Thus, it was mandated by management that the series turn its attention to the promotion of farming. This switch in theme created a major continuity problem. As if this were not enough, the lead actress in the program was married and forced by her new husband to quit the series.[19] The producer introduced a new female character with a different role to try to sustain romantic interest.

Finally, the planned sequel to the series, one which presumably would have provided closure to some of the ongoing and unfinished subplots, was canceled because of lack of sponsorship and the loss of the original female lead. One producer at CTV nicely summarized the issue of continuity when he remarked, "Nigeria is a place of changes. You just never know what people are going to do next!" (K'Kudu, 14 August 1992, interview).

The extended series, such as "Weeping Heart," *"Hadarin Kasa,"* and "Beyond the Dreams," are series which deal with modern life.[20] Apart from the technical problems encountered in trying to produce these dramas, there are also intractable moral principles which surface rather uneasily in these series. To be aesthetically pleasing, a story should resonate with some kernel of truth, some underlying principle to which the audience can adhere and to which there is widespread if not universal agreement. As we shall see, "Beyond the Dreams" was filled with moral uncertainty, an ambiguity of attitude toward the rich and their manner of acquiring wealth. This ambivalence is characteristic of social mores in Nigeria where recent social/economic upheavals have left the country awash in moral confusion.

"Beyond the Dreams" deals with a middle-class business family whose financial dealings are less than legal and less than ethical. Conflicts arise in the family because the eldest son, Kabiru, a secondary school student, defies his father's request to help out at the family farm. Other points of friction occur in the family over the romantic relationship between daughter Zara and her doctor, Rasheed. Kabiru, in particular, disapproves of the doctor. The young man's social origins, rural and poor, are the main source of Kabiru's disapproval, though his jealous guarding of his father Rabo's wealth is certainly a contributing factor. These issues are only partly explored. At the same time, the young suitor, Rasheed, appears to have access to financial resources well beyond his means. Kabiru charges that Rasheed has stocked his medical clinic with equipment and supplies pilfered from a public hospital. The matter is raised by the youth but is not examined.

The rift between social classes was introduced in the drama, because both the writer and the producer felt strongly about it. But only Kabiru and Rasheed's father were particularly concerned with the matter, and the question was neither adequately treated nor satisfactorily resolved. Kabiru seems mainly concerned with protecting his family's money from a possibly greedy social climber, another issue not developed. Kabiru's own possible selfishness in the matter is never raised. And Rabo's and Kabiru's authoritarian and patriarchal treatment of the daughter Zara is never given critical artistic scrutiny.

Clearly these conflicts are bound up in the mire of moral confusion which has accompanied rapid social and economic change in Nigeria. The transformation to a modern economy has engendered corruption and the breakdown of social mores.[21] How does a business make an honest living when the quickest way to riches is through cronyism at the banks? How does a dedicated medical professional carry out a healing vocation when public hospitals are grossly mismanaged? And how does a doctor from a poor rural family amass the capital and equipment needed to set up an alternative, private clinic, unless he steals from the public till? What traditions can detract the poor from trying to "marry up" in a society where the margins between the haves and the have-nots are so wide? How does a comfortable young man retain his economic position in such an economically precarious world? How does a father accustomed to exerting his will in a strongly patriarchal society keep a daughter from a newly educated generation from trying to exert her own? And how should a girl respond when forced to follow the dictates of her father, rather than those of her own heart?[22]

These are some of the puzzling questions the Hausas of northern Nigeria are asking themselves. The series fails to provide the answers because neither the producer nor the writer have them. They begin the series with little clarity about how it will end, and they are equally unsure of how the moral and social problems they raise should and will resolve themselves. It is clear that the producers of all the programs are straining to find order and create meaning in their socially and ethically turbulent world.

How will solutions for the intractable problems engendered by Nigeria's legendary corruption be solved? How will the social classes resolve their differences? What will be the social consequences of increased visibility and social mobility for women? And what role do CTV dramas play in treating these issues? I would submit that the function of these shows is primarily to reflect on current conditions and to engender a social discussion about the problems which abound in the ever-changing fabric of Hausa society.

To the degree that the situation comedies with their more simple and traditional formats continue to raise clear-cut moral choices, the programs will continue to provide simple, albeit important, moral resolutions, satisfying the urban proletariat and the rural viewers. Meanwhile the extended series will continue to raise morally ambiguous situations, while providing no answers to the moral dilemmas of modern life, all reflective of the day-to-day reality of higher-income groups to whom these series are targeted. And indeed, through all these productions, CTV and its producers will continue to have a hand in reinforcing, resisting, and subverting the prevailing social order.

Meanwhile, what can be done to speed the development of a television aesthetic? First, there are technical irregularities which must be addressed. These include equipment shortages, faulty lighting, poor sound, and unaesthetic sets. These can be remedied through a more coordinated allocation of resources and more technical training. Second, there are production difficulties engendered by the oral mind-set. These include the difficulty managers, producers, scriptwriters, and actors have with conceptualizing a continuous series, the endpoint of which must be known and should be planned in advance. Again, some of these obstacles can be rectified through courses in problem solving, production planning, and improved coordination between management, production, and advertising departments. But the reader must beware of excessive optimism at this juncture. Constant fluctuations in the value of a nation's currency can play havoc with budgets. Budgetary shortfalls can force even well-conceived series into changing their narrative direction.

The third difficulty, the quandary raised by the need for a satisfying moral message in stories about modern life, is the most intractable. The creators of "Beyond the Dreams" and other modern series are caught in the same dilemmas of other Nigerians, fond of deriding the Big Men while secretly wishing to become just like them. Alhaji Rabo is depicted as neither good nor evil. He is, in fact, a very flat and rather boring character, another Nigerian businessman just trying to retain his wealth, his power, his family, and his social position. He encapsulates the dilemma of modern African television, and indeed modern African man. Torn between the past and the present, he can be a mere shell of a person. He lacks the soul and the consciousness, the verve of Africa's traditional characters. Preoccupied with the trappings of modern life, he nevertheless can only imitate them badly. What emerges in the program about him is what often emerges in African TV generally: a hollow-sounding service aimed at elites who have lost their moorings in the modern world.

The evolution of a satisfying television aesthetic will depend upon increased technical training, better managerial coordination, more stable operating budgets, and more universal normative systems regulating the acquisition of wealth, the conduct of public institutions, and the relationships between the "haves" and the "have-nots." Judging from what we have come to know about the elitist and patronage-ridden nature of television, the development of a healthy television aesthetic in Africa will be a long time in the making.

In the meantime, Nigeria's vast television service, Africa's uncontested leader in local production, maintains a focus on entertainment. This is a monument to the missed opportunity to use television in the promotion of positive change. With a concerted effort to coordinate the talent of its many producers and its lively actors, TV could be put to work making dramas about important health, family planning, educational, or agricultural issues where the objectives of the programs could ring with more clarity. The present efforts of Nigerian producers, however laudable, serve mainly to reinforce traditional values in some contexts, and to churn up moral confusion in others.

The confusion no doubt hails from the adoption of a Western program genre or, more generally, a Western model for a television system geared to the provision of entertainment. And the problem is confounded in television systems elsewhere in Africa, specializing in the adulation of political elites. The social confusion engendered by such African television systems with less local production, more imported entertainment, and more political patronage is only more apparent.

6 | Colonial History and Postcolonial Developments of the Press

THIS CHAPTER WILL review the establishment of the press in Black Africa during the colonial period, revealing the ways different policies and approaches of the metropoles toward the colonies affected the print media. It will also examine the role played by economic conditions in shaping the press on different parts of the continent: in anglophone West Africa, East Africa, Central and Southern Africa, and francophone Africa. Phenomena such as development journalism, rural journalism, national news services, and the question of New World Information Order, all press developments in the postindependence era of the 1970s and 1980s, will be explored. Finally, this chapter will briefly trace the decline of the press under authoritarian regimes in the 1970s and 1980s.

Press statistics in Africa over the last fifty-odd years have reflected Africa's political climate. In 1956, just a few years before most nations became independent, Helen Kitchen reported the presence of 100 daily African newspapers. The number of dailies increased during the 1960s, the decade of African independence. The USIA reported 150 dailies in 1966, and Hachten reported 160 in 1969. The 1970s, with its high number of military coups, was a poor decade for African newspaper survival. According to Barton, there were 116 dailies in 1975–76. But by the 1980s, newspapers were again on the upswing. The *World Press Encyclopedia* counted 124 dailies in 1980. And by the end of the 1980s, the press appeared to be bouncing back from its low point in the 1970s. The *UNESCO Statistical Handbook* reported 200 dailies on the African continent in 1988 (figures from Hachten, 1993, p. 5).

In the early 1990s, the African press is flourishing as Africa blossoms with electoral freedoms. How many daily newspapers will remain at the end of the decade will have much to do with the way new governments are able to manage the freedoms of their peoples and the economies of their nations.

The Press in the Colonial Period

Anglophone West Africa

The story of newspapers in sub-Saharan Africa should begin with West Africa in the anglophone countries. The oldest newspaper in Black Africa appears to have been the *Royal Gazette and Sierra Leone Advertiser*, first published in 1801.

The *Royal Gold Coast Gazette* (published first in 1822 in present-day Ghana) was founded by Charles L. Force, a former American slave. In 1820, he arrived in Monrovia (Liberia) with a hand-operated press which had been a gift of the Massachusetts Colonization Society of Boston. He began the *Liberia Herald*, which survived after Force's death a few years later under various editors. Its last editor during the 1860s was the famous writer and scholar Edward W. Blyden, who used the newspaper to propound his pan-Negro philosophy (1857; 1887).

The health of the early press in West Africa has been attributed to three factors: the presence of relatively well educated Negroes returning to West Africa after having lived abroad; the growth of missionary activity stemming from this group and from Europe; and the absence of a white/European settler population in West Africa which might have impeded press growth in West Africa as it did in other regions of the continent (Ainslie, 1966, p. 2).

In 1858, Charles Bannerman, the first truly African editor, produced his *Accra Herald* (later the *West African Herald*) by hand in his own handwriting (Ainslie, 1966, p. 22). The following year African missionaries at Abeokuta (in Nigeria) produced the *Iwe Ihorin* in Yoruba, and later in Yoruba and English.

Early newspapers were used to educate as well as to entertain, and some contained elegant Victorian prose essays (Ainslie, 1966, p. 22), somewhat typical of the European postenlightenment period. But soon the dominant aim of these newspapers was political protest aimed mainly against colonial officials.

The Liberian papers, among those of West Africa, were most concerned with political consciousness raising. This is because they were edited by churchmen strongly influenced by the Negro struggle against slavery in America.

In the 1890s, John Payne Jackson produced the *Lagos Weekly Record*. Born in Liberia, he had gone on to Nigeria to be a trader. In 1891, he began to publish the *Lagos Weekly Record*, which inveighed regularly against the excesses of Sir Frederick Lugard, then governor of Southern Nigeria.

Hachten writes that the British colonial administration "exercised restraint in their treatment of such journalists and usually acted within the bounds of British common law." He adds that "no other area of Africa enjoyed as much comparative press freedom" (Hachten, 1971, pp. 148–49). Ainslie writes that the nineteenth century ended after seeing the establishment of a lively, outspoken political press in all four anglophone territories of West Africa (Sierra Leone, Liberia, Nigeria, and the Gold Coast [now Ghana]) (1966, p. 30). The traditions established in the West African press in the nineteenth century continued with ever more ferocity in the twentieth.

In 1910, the *Nigerian Times* introduced news from Reuters Telegraphic News Service. The *Lagos Daily News*, founded in 1925 by Herbert Macaulay, was the first political party paper and the organ for Macaulay's National Democratic Party.

The 1930s represents an exceptional period of press fertility in West Africa. Accra, Ghana, had two daily newspapers at this time: the *Spectator* begun in 1927 as the *Gold Coast Spectator* and the *West African Times* begun in 1931. Both of these carried international news, and the *Spectator* even had correspondents in Moscow (Ainslie, 1966, p. 32). In Sierra Leone there was the *Sierra Leone Daily Mail* and the *Daily Guardian*.

In 1933, the *Lagos News* was flourishing as was the *Daily Times*. A third daily, the *Daily Service*, started up as the party organ of the Nigerian Youth Movement. Several weeklies were also published by William Coulson Labor, and the *Comet* was published by Duse Mohamed Ali.

During the 1930s, Nmamdi Azikiwe appeared on the journalistic scene. Azikiwe had studied in the United States between 1925 and 1934 and had absorbed American Negro political currents of the 1930s. From his American experiences, he acquired a militant internationalism as a framework within which to view the Nigerian anticolonial struggle. He also acquired a sensational race-conscious style and tone derived from American Negro journalism (Ainslie, 1966, p. 34).

Azikiwe's career as an African journalist got its start when "Zik" became editor of the *African Morning Post* in Accra. In 1937, Azikiwe left Accra and went to Nigeria to found the *West African Pilot*. Recognizing the importance of local papers and failing to achieve national distribution of the *Pilot*, Zik soon created a chain of newspapers. The group was called Zik's Press Ltd. and was the first newspaper chain in West Africa. In 1940, he established the *Eastern Nigerian Guardian* at Port Harcourt. In 1943, he founded the Nigerian Spokesman at Onitsha and the *Southern Nigerian Defender* at Warri.

In 1944, Zik acquired the *Comet* and made it a daily. In 1949, he introduced it to Kano, thereby providing Northern Nigeria with its first daily paper. Each of the three Nigerian regions was thus served by a Zik paper by the end of the 1940s.

Though relatively plentiful in the region, newspapers in the 1940s suffered from lack of facilities, including lack of photographic reproduction capacity; film had to be sent to Europe (the U.K.) for processing. After World War II, West Africa saw the emergence of more newspaper chains. The government of Northern Nigeria established the Gaskiya Corporation, an outgrowth of the Northern Literature Bureau whose aim was to encourage the spread of vernacular languages. The Gaskiya Corporation published the *Nigerian Citizen* and a number of periodicals in the Fulani, Tiv, and Kanuri languages. It also improved its Hausa publication *Gaskiya ta fi Kwabo* through the use of a new press, government money, and block-making facilities.

In 1951, a political party known as the Action Group was formed, and the

Daily Service became its party mouthpiece. The *Service* soon amalgamated with the *Nigerian Tribune* of Ibadan to form the Amalgamated Press of Nigeria. By 1958, the group controlled the Allied Press Ltd., which already had a string of five papers in all three regions of Nigeria. Meanwhile the Zik papers became standard-bearers for the eastern-based National Council of Nigeria and the Cameroons (the NCNC Party).

Thus, by the 1950s Nigeria had a string of papers, one government-run and two run by private capital but also strongly allied to political parties. By 1959, Azikiwe's NCNC controlled ten newspapers in Nigeria. Obafemi Awolowo of the Action Group controlled 14 (Hachten, 1993, p. 16).

Ainslie writes that the development of such a large and diverse press in Nigeria was fostered by the very size of the country and the difficulties of distribution. But she argues that certainly the most important reason was that an African trading/commercial class had developed in Nigeria to a point which allowed the establishment of African-controlled banks. "Newspapers could thus draw on the resources of a bank for capitalization and development loans—and this was true of no other colony in Black Africa" (1966, p. 56).

Into this fertile press climate came foreign press enterprise. In 1947, Cecil King of the British *Daily Mirror* bought the *Nigerian Daily Times* of Lagos. He also purchased the *Gold Coast Daily Graphic*, the *Sunday Mirror* of Accra, and the *Sierra Leone Daily Mail*. Thus, the Mirror Group came to "invade the only economic field dominated by native people" (Ainslie, 1966, p. 56).

Cecil King of the Mirror Group was keen to diversify his empire at home in order to avoid high taxation of the British postwar period. He introduced yet unheard of technical improvements: the first privately owned rotary printing machine in Nigeria, photoengraving, typesetting, and typecasting plants. He also imported skilled foreign journalists and a full-time training officer. He pursued a deliberate policy of Africanization, training reporters, printers, and machine operators.

The Mirror Group also brought numerous innovations to Africa: tabloid page makeup, liberal use of illustrations and photos, human interest stories, short paragraphs and sentences—all of which were highly successful at home among the British working class. The indigenous press found itself out-competed. Circulation grew from 25,000 in 1951 to 120,000 in 1965, the highest in West Africa (Ainslie, 1966, p. 57).

Another British press tycoon, Roy Thompson, produced the *Daily Express*, the *Sunday Express*, and the Yoruba weekly *Iwe Ihorin*. In 1960, Thompson International of Canada became half owner of the Amalgamated Press Group. Allied with Chief Obafemi Awolowo's Action Group, the Group fell into disfavor during Nigeria's First Republic.[1] Financial difficulties forced them to close in 1965 (Ainslie, 1966, p. 67).

Meanwhile, Cecil King's activities in the Gold Coast were relatively short lived. In 1947, N'Krumah and others from the Convention People's Party had started the *Accra Evening News*, a campaigning broadsheet staffed by political hacks rather than journalists. When independence was clearly in the offing, the CPP purchased the Guinea Press, financed by the Industrial Development Corporation and local businesses. N'Krumah's Guinea Press produced the *Ghana Evening News* and the *Ghanaian Times*. By the mid-1960s, there were four papers in Ghana, three controlled by N'Krumah, and one, the *Daily Graphic*, still under the ownership of Cecil King. Kwame N'Krumah, the great idealist and patriot who had inspired so much hope in Africa and so much admiration around the world, had spearheaded the decolonization of Ghana, the first politically independent nation in Africa.

But by 1961, only four years after independence, N'Krumah achieved notoriety for his authoritarian directives against the *Ashanti Pioneer* of Kumasi. N'Krumah demanded the paper's editor submit its copy to his minister of information before printing. The case of prior restraint became internationally known when the Commonwealth Press Union and the International Press Institute rushed to defend the Kumasi newspaper. N'Krumah, the man who had led his country to freedom, seems also to have initiated the decline of the press's freedom in Africa.

Cecil King's *Daily Graphic* never openly opposed the government of Ghana after independence. In 1962, the *Graphic* suggested the government of Ghana buy the paper. An independent trust was set up for this purpose. After the sale, the paper's news coverage declined somewhat. It tended, as did the *Daily Times* of Nigeria, also Mirror-owned, to cover nonpolitical and somewhat liberal news: courtroom dramas and scandals, a practice which would be retained throughout the twentieth century in the West African press. In 1962, N'Krumah's office of the president founded the *Spark*, a Marxist analytical journal speaking out on African affairs. Ainslie describes the editorials in the *Spark*: "Editorials are serious, passionate, and sometimes flamboyant in the best traditions of the rich-phrased West African journalism" (1966, p. 63).

The *Spark* appears to have promoted another trend in African journalism which would be carried out in various parts of the continent: the publication of ideological essays propounding the political rhetoric of the head of state presented with dramatic photographs useful in creating a personality cult around him. The high-toned essays were aimed at the intellectual elite at home and abroad, while the visual elements were aimed at the masses. Sekou Touré of Guinea, Julius Nyerere of Tanzania, and Kenneth Kaunda of Zambia would all commandeer the press of their countries and shape it in similar ways.

Ainslie's comments on the control of Ghana's press in the mid-1960s were a prescient warning of things to come on the African continent in the following decade. Her description of the *Spark* is instructive.

The *Spark* expects to find a considerable proportion of its readership abroad, and derives much of its élan from the fact that it operates within the context of international ideological conflict. But within Ghana, there is no voice of opposition against which the party papers could pit themselves, and to this fact have been attributed many of the weaknesses of the modern press in Ghana: the substitution of abuse for comment, and pictures of Osagyefo [N'Krumah] for news. At their worst, Ghana papers have been known to publish six pictures of the President in a single issue! (Ainslie, 1966, p. 63)

Ainslie goes on charitably to argue that such a propagandist press was necessary for the consolidation of the Ghanaian state, and she points out on a more positive note that the papers "reflect a serious desire to educate and to convince as much as to exhort" (1966, p. 64).

Ainslie also mentions in her 1966 publication that journalistic weaknesses sprang from lack of training and resulted in an insufficient effort by pressmen to examine issues in any depth (p. 64). She also notes a lack of backgrounding in stories. Mytton would echo these comments seventeen years later in his analysis of the Zambian and the Nigerian press (1983, pp. 75, 125).

Ainslie's comments on the one-party state in Ghana also remained predictive, for both Ghana and elsewhere, well into the 1990s:

One problem, however, remains even once the crudities have been eliminated. It is the problem that arises out of the very nature of a one-party press, and it confronts "official" papers anywhere: if public ideological conflict must for any reasons of state, be excluded, how is that dialogue to come about between paper and reader, that makes a newspaper not merely an organ of information from above but a vehicle of comment from below? (1966, p. 64)

By the 1960s, some trends in the West African press were clear. First, there was the use of sophisticated Fleet Street styles, which resulted in flashy looking papers, produced by the Mirror Group and the Thompson Group. Funded from abroad, these papers enjoyed a comparative economic advantage. Second, there was a move toward the indigenization of the press. This process proceeded at full speed, despite deficiencies in training. Third, there were tendencies toward ideological posturing aimed at the national and international elite. This led to the curtailment of press freedom and the use of the press as an instrument for personality cult formation, particularly evident in Ghana.

In addition, the Nigerian press, early on, had acquired characteristics which were to remain with it. These included a lurid popular style, a confusing penchant for partisan overstatement, and a personally abusive tone. Ainslie discussed the Nigerian press in 1966:

If the Ghana Press tends abroad to be derided as monolithic, the Press in Nigeria is admired for its variety. But this too is something of a myth, for the comparative profusion of titles in Nigeria is far less encouraging to any real conflict of ideas than might be expected. With the possible exception of the *Pilot*, which continues to print a high proportion of foreign news, the Nigerian papers are inward looking, preoccupied with local issues, but the confusion of Nigerian political life, where party divisions do not often clearly reflect differences of principle so much as regional and tribal loyalties, or conflicts in personality, tends to produce a journalism of personal and party abuse rather than of political debate. . . . Rather than politics, in fact, the stock in trade of Nigerian journalism is the human interest story culled from the criminal courts or the latest scandal involving a public figure. (1966, pp. 65–66)

To combat the power of the Mirror Group and the Thompson-Amalgamated Press axis, the Nigerian federal government established the Nigerian National Press Ltd., a well-equipped newspaper plant in 1961, which printed the *Morning Post* and the *Sunday Post*. Increase Coker, the *Post*'s editor in the early 1960s, saw the government's participation as somewhat of a compromise. Coker saw his role as separate from government and attempted to make his paper a "vehicle for news, information, and entertainment" rather than an extension of the government (Ainslie, 1966, p. 67).

Ainslie concludes that independence in West Africa actually brought about a diminution of the African-controlled press. Except in Ghana (where the government largely took over the press shortly after independence), foreign-owned presses made it difficult for African papers to compete. She adds ominously that foreign papers retain "a bias toward private economic enterprise and the Western view on international affairs" (Ainslie, 1966, p. 73).

Ainslie saw clearly the economic bind in which the newly independent governments found themselves vis-à-vis the international capitalist information order:

Governments are faced with the dilemma of either excluding foreign press enterprise altogether, and investing vast sums of government money in mass media development, as Ghana has done, or reconciling themselves to the inevitable processes of commercial press development, whereby rich papers gradually devour poor ones; and the small papers are eventually forced out altogether. This process has already taken place in the most highly developed countries of the West. In Africa, it is complicated by the fact that the rich papers are foreign, and the poor ones are indigenous. (1966, p. 73)

Such problems still lie at the heart of the African press as it moves into the twenty-first century.

Southern and Central Africa

In southern Africa and anglophone central Africa, the press was largely a European creation. In 1828, a colonial secretary sanctioned a press law for the Cape Colony based upon the law of England. Press operators had only to deposit 300 pounds plus the equivalent sum in guarantees and then they were free to publish, subject only to libel laws (Ainslie, 1966, p. 40). Although the press in South Africa was already 28 years old, the expansion of press freedom for the colony contributed handsomely to the presses' growth.

The most significant of the southern African papers was the *Cape Argus*, founded in 1857, which would grow into a major newspaper chain expanding northward through South Africa, into Southern and Northern Rhodesia (now respectively Zimbabwe and Zambia). In 1881, Cecil John Rhodes bought controlling interest in the *Cape Argus*. Rhodes, who had already made his fortune in the Kimberley diamond mines, established a conservative approach to matters of political reporting, especially where racial issues were involved. This approach complemented his heavy involvement in the labor-intensive mining industry. Solidly financed, the *Argus* was able to share technological advances with South African readers, including Reuters News Service supplied to South Africa by cable from London by the 1880s.

In the 1890s, Rhodes moved north toward what would become Southern Rhodesia in search of gold. From Queen Victoria, Rhodes obtained a charter to administer the Rhodesian territory where his British South Africa Company had obtained land and mining rights. Rhodes now needed a newspaper to complement his adventures, so he bought the *Mashonaland Herald* and renamed it the *Rhodesian Herald* in 1892. Two years later he established the *Chronicle* at Bulawayo.

Socialistic ideas gained currency in South Africa and elsewhere after World War I and through the 1920s and 1930s. The Argus Group became involved with a venture known as the Bantu Press, formed in 1931 to channel native thoughts away from politics and into safer pursuits. In the 1950s, another mining giant, the Anglo-American Corporation, would join the venture. This new connection with Anglo-American was consistent with Argus' traditional financial base, historically tied through cross-directorships with Central Mines and Rand Mines, two of the biggest mining concerns in South Africa (Ainslie, 1966, p. 74).

The Bantu Press operated a number of newspapers in South Africa and one in Lesotho. In 1944, it expanded northward to Southern Rhodesia with the *Bantu Mirror* published from Salisbury (now Harare) in English, Ndebele, and Lozi and the *African Weekly* in English, Shona, and Chinijanja. These two papers sold in Northern Rhodesia (now Zambia) and Nyasaland (now Malawi) as well.

By 1946, the Bantu Press controlled 11 of the 13 weeklies published in South Africa and Rhodesia. The colonial government subsidized further expansion into Basutoland (now Lesotho), Swaziland, and Bechuanaland (now Botswana), where in all cases, it was felt that demands for self-government must be countered (Ainslie, 1966, p. 52). Editors and staff of most South African papers were Africans, but their work was tightly supervised by white overseers, and editorial control remained firmly with the whites.

In 1965, the Argus Group operated six daily newspapers, two Sunday papers, and a growing periodical press in South Africa. Argus also had a subsidiary, the Rhodesian Printing and Publishing Company, through which it controlled before 1963 every daily newspaper in the Federation of Rhodesia and Nyasaland. After the breakup of the federation,[2] it controlled the two dailies in Southern Rhodesia (through the Thompson organization, Africa Newspapers Ltd.) and published a rival, the *Daily News* in Salisbury, until that paper was banned in 1964. In Southern Rhodesia, the Argus Group ran the *Rhodesia Herald* in Salisbury, the *Chronicle* in Bulawayo, the *Sunday Mail*, and the *Sunday News*. Argus also owned in Northern Rhodesia the *Northern News*, which it eventually sold to Lonrho, the London and Rhodesian Mining Company, in 1964.

The Argus Group was linked with the Central News Agency, which owned a monopoly over newspaper distribution in South Africa. It was closely allied to the South African Press Association, which collected news in the region for participating papers. In 1964, a new news gathering agency was established for Zambia and Southern Rhodesia, the Inter-African News Agency (IANA), which seemed to function essentially to provide by another label, South African stories to Zambian and Southern Rhodesian readers (Ainslie, 1966, p. 77).

Argus control, combined with a strong white settler presence in Southern Rhodesia, kept an opposition press from developing. Apart from a few broadsheets together with the *Central African Mail*, which entered Southern Rhodesia clandestinely from across the Zambezi, there were no papers available in future Zimbabwe to raise native consciousness. For their part, the Argus papers in then Southern Rhodesia in the 1960s championed the status quo by ignoring the national majority. Ainslie remarks on the content of Southern Rhodesia's Argus-owned press in the mid-1960s: "They simply do not report African politics, violent acts, nationalist statements or stories of political arrests, unless they are the subject of court cases, or Government announcement" (Ainslie, 1966, p. 88). The Law and Order (Maintenance) Act passed in 1962 assured a quiescent press. The State of Emergency[3] declared in 1965 eliminated what little press freedom there had been.

In 1951, the Argus Group moved into the business of serving the white settler community of Northern Rhodesia by purchasing the *Northern News* of Ndola on the copperbelt. The *Northern News* had earlier served as the mouthpiece of its owner, Roy Wilensky, who clamored for and became prime minister of the short-lived Federation of Rhodesia and Nyasaland.

In 1960, Alexander Scott, who had previously operated two newspapers, both more liberal than Argus' *Northern News*, established the *African Mail*, a weekly with the financial backing of the London-based *Observer*. Then in 1962, the *African Mail* changed its name to the *Central African Mail*. The *Mail* quickly became an African-oriented paper, campaigning against Wilensky's federation. It was edited by Titus Makupo who later became minister of information after Zambia became independent in 1964. Ainslie notes that the *Mail* "never was an African paper in the sense of being fully African controlled. It continued to bear the clear stamp of liberal British values which it inherited from the *Observer*" (Ainslie, 1966, p. 95).

Shortly after independence the Argus Group sold the *Northern News* to Lonrho. Lonrho had just bought out Heinrich's Brewery, which had briefly operated a daily, the *Zambia Times*, and a weekly, the *Zambia News*. Thus, Lonrho found itself in control of the only two dailies in Zambia and the only weekly.

Lonrho apparently attempted to accomplish what the Argus Group had been unwilling to do: bridge the political gulf between southern African mining interests and the newly independent Zambian government and its reading public. The *Times* under Lonrho continued to share in the news services of the IANA, and this factor contributed to its appropriately schizophrenic approach to news. Influenced by the white-operated news service, the *Times of Zambia* carried a great deal of international news, most of it told from a Western viewpoint. Yet its domestic coverage favored the new Zambian government. When covering points of conflict with its white-controlled neighbors to the south, the paper tried to tread cautiously. But there were incidents when the biases inherent in its Lonrho financial base clearly showed through. This occurred, for instance, when the *Times of Zambia* sided with Southern Rhodesia's white settlers' demand for a unilateral declaration of independence (Ainslie, 1966, p. 97).

The new Zambian government recognized these conflicts of interest and took steps to assure that its own voice would be heard. When the *Central African Mail* underwent financial difficulties in 1965, the government purchased it and transformed it into the *Zambia Mail*. In 1970, it became the *Zambia Daily Mail*. The *Mail* suffered from some of the same ills that plagued many other African papers in the postindependence period. Having clamored for independence, it now lacked a clear ideology to push it forward. It eventually became the government's mouthpiece, especially after 1972, relying rather more heavily than the *Times* on official press releases (Mytton, 1983, p. 74), and it suffered the consequences in advertising and circulation figures. In 1973, the *Zambia Daily Mail* was instructed to become "an instrument in nation building," i.e., to specialize in development journalism (Moore, 1992, p. 46).

During the early 1970s, the *Times of Zambia* and the *Zambia Daily Mail* bore strong influences of their non-African roots. They relied heavily on foreign material, not only for non-African news but also for feature material. The *Sunday Times of Zambia* ran, for example, "cheesecake" pictures of scantily clothed Western women supplied by British feature services. It published European-oriented cultural pieces such as recipes to be prepared in modern English kitchens. Mytton writes that the press in Zambia had broken its ties with the press of South Africa only to forge new ones with the press of Great Britain (1983, p. 75).

When Zambia became a one-party state in 1972, the United National Independence Party (Kaunda's party) took control of the *Times of Zambia*. The government decided to channel most of its financial resources into it. The *Times* retained an outwardly professional look though its content declined due to an excess of party zeal.

East Africa

Like the press in South and Central Africa, the press in East Africa was largely created for its settler population. And the presence of European settlers left a mark on the press of the region for a long time to come.

The first paper was established in the Kenyan coastal city of Mombassa in 1902 by a member of the Asian community, A. M. Jeevanjee. In 1910, it moved upcountry to Nairobi and became known as the *East African Standard*. The *Standard* was and remained a voice for settler demands from the British government, including demands for more soldiers to deal with the "native problem."

In 1930, Jeevanjee was asked by the colonial governor to relocate to Tanganyika (now Tanzania) and to set up a newspaper there. Thus began the *Tanganyika Standard*. Much later, in 1953, he also set up the *Uganda Argus* in Kampala.

After World War II, the Standard Group's papers tried rather timidly to increase circulation and prepare for independence by appealing to nonwhite readers. The names of Africans and Indians began appearing in the letters columns. But the Standard newspapers never really succeeded in being anything but papers for white settlers. Ainslie reports the shock and dismay of many readers when the British government finally announced that Kenya would be independent. The *Standard* had largely ignored the "winds of change" sweeping over Kenya and the British Empire in the 1950s. Not surprisingly, the orientation of the *East African Standard* changed abruptly with independence in 1963.

After independence, African news, rather than accounts of "Lady X's garden party occupied the bulk of news space" (Ainslie, 1966, p. 103). And shortly after independence, links between the *Standard* and the South African Press Association were severed. The newly established Kenya News Agency now provided news directly to the paper. The editorial tone of the *Standard* also shifted. Kenyatta, earlier despised as an evil genius, became the man "to thank for a peaceful transition to independence" (Ainslie, 1966, p. 103). The *Standard*'s staff was almost all white until 1965, and all were British-trained until that time.

The historic rivals of the Standard papers in East Africa were the Nation Group, or the East African Newspapers Ltd. Financing for the Nation Group came from the Aga Khan of the Ismaili Islamic sect. The *Daily Nation* and the *Sunday Nation* began publishing in 1960. In 1962, the group issued the *Taifa Leo* (in Swahili). All three papers were distributed in Tanganyika (now Tanzania) and Uganda. The Aga Khan's publishing interests also spread to Uganda where he published the *Uganda Empya* and the *Taifa Empya*. He also purchased part ownership in *Mwafrika*. The Nation Group brought a new tabloid format and exciting layouts for the first time to East Africa. They used web offset, very new not only in Africa but in the world in the early 1960s.

The Nation papers had the most extensive string of correspondents in all of East Africa. Human interest and spot news tended to predominate, but most of the news was given over to African coverage. Despite their wide appeal, the Nation papers were considered foreign by East African governments. In the early 1960s, all of the Nation's staff was white except for two reporters, one Asian and one African, George Githii. Eventually, Hilary Ng'weno was appointed editor (Ainslie, 1966, p. 106). After 1965, more efforts were made to indigenize the staff. In 1965, George Githii moved from his position as reporter on the *Nation* to that of private secretary to the prime minister and personal assistant to the president.

Engaged in trading, the Indian community was able to amass enough capital in the first half of the twentieth century to have produced a string of papers. The Africans were not. East Africans did not have the economic base to support newspapers. In this way, they were unlike their southern Africa counterparts who were developing into an African urban labor class. And they were also different from their West African counterparts who saw the emergence of an active African trading class within their midst, particularly in Nigeria. The colonial governments in East Africa moreover discouraged indigenous newspaper production. They required the posting of a 500-pound bond before a publication could be launched (Wilcox, 1975, p. 8). Most newspapers targeted to an African readership were supported by missionary efforts or by the colonial governments themselves, the latter starting from the 1950s. In Tanganyika, the government supported an assortment of 20 local papers, plus three Swahili papers in the capital that were all African-run.

Despite the difficulties, an indigenous press did begin helping to crystallize anticolonialist sentiment. Among the most memorable was a newspaper entitled *Muigwithania* (Work and Play), founded in 1925 by Johnstone Kamau. Kamau's publication was the first African-owned paper in East Africa. Later, the editor changed his name to Jomo Kenyatta and established the Kenya

Africa National Union (KANU). Kenyatta championed a string of newspapers, mainly in the Kikuyu language. A number of other editors, many of whom eventually gained positions in the new government, operated vernacular presses. All of these were censored during the Kenyan Emergency except the *Nyanza Times*, run by Oginga Odinga, who later became vice president under Kenyatta. To counter the effects of these papers, the colonial government established the Kenyan Vernacular Press in 1952. European editors working for this press were "instructed to encourage the expression of African opinion, provided it supported the general objectives of the Government!" (Ainslie, 1966, p. 108). Coupled with the creation of this government-controlled press for Africans came the closing of the aforementioned indigenous vernacular presses.

In Uganda, missionaries had spread literacy and had created a vernacular missionary press, particularly among the Baganda. One of these, the *Uganda Eyogera*, agitated for political rights for Africans and became the voice of the Uganda National Congress—the forerunner of the Uganda National Congress (Ainslie, 1966, p. 109).

In Tanzania,[4] the Tanganyika's African National Union (TANU) started *Sauti ya Tanu* in 1957, a paper making moderate and reasoned claims for independence. Though Tanganyika lacked a settler population, the struggle for independence did intensify somewhat by 1959. TANU set up the *National Times* in an attempt to combat foreign domination from the Standard Group, but the effort was short-lived (Ainslie, 1966, p. 111).

Ainslie sums up the state of East Africa's indigenous press at the dawn of independence:

> Thus it is that when independence was won between 1961 and 1963 by each of the East African territories in turn—by Tanganyika in December 1961, Uganda in October 1962, and Kenya and Zanzibar in 1963—such African newspapers as existed were still in no position to compete with either the *Standard* or the *Nation*. TANU, in 1961, ran one printed weekly in Swahili, *Uhuru*, but the only other independent African weekly, Makange's *Mwafrika*, was soon to be forced for financial reasons into partnership with the *Nation*. In Uganda, though the *Uganda Eyogera* survived, *Uganda Empya* had already been taken over by the *Nation* before independence, and in Kenya the *Nyanza Times* stood alone. (Ainslie, 1966 p. 112)

The two major European groups muddled along, caught somewhat between their alliances to the West and the need to serve a new audience. One day before independence was to be declared in Tanganyika, when Nyerere's new cabinet was announced, the *Tanganyika Standard*'s main headline dealt with the fate of British colonial contract holders who would leave the country to the new government (Ainslie, 1966, p. 112).

Already by independence in East Africa, the cost had risen of establishing locally owned newspapers that could compete with the *Standard* and the *Nation*. It was estimated that 10,000 pounds at least were needed to launch a weekly. Only new governments among Black Africans had that kind of capital. The Tanganyikan government was the first to attempt running a newspaper. It decided to turn *Uhuru* into a daily, and it published an English-language companion paper, the *Nationalist*. Like N'Krumah, Nyerere found it necessary and expedient to address the outside world, so TANU established the *Nationalist* in April 1964. Ghanaian James Markham of the *Accra Evening News* was brought in as managing editor. Oddly, there were so few trained African journalists (particularly for editing an English-language paper) that expatriate staff, some former members of the *Tanganyika Standard*, were brought on board. In the mid-1960s, the *Standard* was the best edited of the African-controlled papers. The influence of expatriate editors and the training they imparted on their staff has had a lasting influence on the discourse style and editing quality of the East African papers.

Mytton explains why the Tanzanian government was so interested in newspaper publication, particularly in subsidizing two newspapers, only a third of whose costs could be covered through sales, papers with low circulation, and almost no advertising revenue. First, TANU was interested in "the prestige of the written word" provided by these party-supported papers (Mytton, 1983, p. 93). Tanzania was engaged in a bold new venture and needed to put its case before the outside world, particularly left-leaning governments and political groups likely to be sympathetic to Nyerere's brand of African socialism. Clearly the gulf between the highly literate ideologues of the Nyerere government and Tanzania's masses was already obvious.

Secondly, TANU was interested in a strong *central* paper. In Tanzania, like elsewhere on the continent, the struggle for independence was perceived by indigenous leaders as a unified struggle *against* the colonial masters. There was little interest in fostering decentralized mass communication. Thus, the twenty or so local papers supported by the colonial government died shortly after independence for lack of support from Nyerere's new government. A third reason for heavy investment in a national party paper was the ease of control such a venture offered to elite power holders.

Government efforts in Uganda were less successful than those in Tanzania. One faction paper which emerged in the period was the *People*, a paper allied to the early independent Ugandan government of Milton Obote and supported partly by outside foundations. The paper's contents combined the ponderous elements of a government newspaper with more trivial elements added to give it popular appeal (Ainslie, 1966, p. 117).

Kenya did not establish a party newspaper in the early postcolonial period, though it was the first country in East Africa to place its broadcasting services under state control and to establish a national news agency. Kenyatta was said to understand the value of a free press, a sentiment shared by the elite class of British-trained lawyers and journalists, and members of parliament. As Hachten noted, in 1971, "Under Kenyatta's leadership, . . . the press was beginning to establish itself as a viable institution" (1971, p. 216). A government mouthpiece was not created until the KANU introduced the *Kenya Times* in 1983 in a partnership with the Robert Maxwell Group (*New African*, 1988, p. 40).

During the early independence period, East Africa was burdened or blessed with two well-funded, externally controlled newspaper groups. The groups took a somewhat cautious approach in their reporting of internal politics of Kenya, Tanzania, and Uganda, treating the heads of state with respect and generally eschewing overt criticism of sensitive policy issues. With their greater resources, and with a staff of well-trained reporters and editors, including many Europeans and settlers of British descent, they set a comparatively high standard of newspaper writing and editing on this part of the continent, a complement to their high technical standards. These papers, some printed in English, others in Swahili, circulated quite freely within the region. This was particularly true of the Kenyan papers, which provided tough competition for advertisers and readership for Ugandan and Tanzanian government newspaper ventures.

Francophone Africa

Colonialism in francophone Africa actively discouraged the development of a local press. The government placed a heavy tax on newsprint and printing machinery imported into the colonies. In keeping with the assimilationist policies of French colonialism, newspapers produced in the French metropole always circulated freely. But until the 1930s, only French citizens who were deemed to be in good standing with the government were allowed to publish in the colonies. There was limited action by missionaries in francophone Africa. What little missionary activity there was was largely confined to those countries which had been German colonies before World War I, i.e., Togo and Cameroon.

Those African-based newspapers which did exist served the white settler population. In Senegal, the colony with the largest French population, a significant preindependence press emerged. Senegal had three papers for white settlers and traders before 1900: *Le Réveil du Sénégalais, Le Petit Sénégalais,* and *L'Union Africaine*. The last of these was destined for circulation in France as well as in West Africa.

French government rules notwithstanding, two African-run papers sprang up in the 1920s in Dahomey (now Benin), a country known for its intellectuals.[5] *Le Cri Nègre* and *La Phare du Dahomey* both contributed to the growth of African political consciousness during their time. In the 1930s, Senegalese elected representatives to the French Parliament for the first time. These elections led to the mushrooming of a high number of political broadsheets in Senegal, all of which ceased operation shortly after the election. Their appearance was significant, nevertheless, because they accustomed local people to expect newspapers written by, and for, them. These papers, moreover, sparked political consciousness and the establishment of newspapers in other French colonies. Notable among these was Côte d'Ivoire, where eleven papers are reported to have existed in the 1930s, some of them quite critical of the French administrators and the native chiefs who collaborated with them.

It is worth noting that French policy allowed the growth of indigenous papers during this era while it channeled political activity northward. The French policy of allowing African representation in the French Parliament, begun with Senegal in 1932 and ultimately extended to all interested colonies, anchored the consciousness of African politicians to French political currents. These politicians were the *evolués*, men who had succeeded in becoming Black Frenchmen. Decades later, francophone Africans would still aspire to the linguistic and cultural trappings the term *"evolué"* implies.

The 1930s was also a decade that saw the beginnings of the most powerful commercial newspaper chain in francophone Africa. In Dakar, Senegal, Frenchman Charles de Breteuil established *Paris-Dakar* in 1933. By 1935, it had become a daily. In 1938, de Breteuil added *France-Afrique* in Côte d'Ivoire to his operations. In the 1950s, he would add *La Presse du Guinée*, *L'Echo du Cameroun*, and *Bingo*.

The remaining French colonies of francophone West and Central Africa including what are today Mali, Burkina Faso, Mauritania, Niger, Gabon, Chad, Central African Republic, and the Republic of the Congo had no press whatsoever until World War II, except for limited circulation within their borders of the Senegalese press (Ainslie, 1966, p. 133).

Political consciousness did develop as a result of World War II. Many of francophone Africa's men had fought in Europe or North Africa during the war and were now returning home. Ousmane Sembene's *Le Camp de Thiaroye*, a film detailing French injustice against these former soldiers, sheds light on the growing politicization of African World War II veterans.

In 1946, the new French constitution allowed for representation of French possessions in the French legislative assemblies. That year, the *Reassemblement Democratique Africaine*, francophone Africa's first political party, was formed with separate branches in various francophone colonial territories. But the formation of these parties contributed little to the development of the African press. This was perhaps because the new constitutional structure forced African politicians to form alliances with French political parties. Thus, their energies were directed outward toward France rather than inward toward Africa. Independence from France did not emerge as a serious political issue until 1958, and even then independence currents were already being preempted into the French African community. This would tie the economies of the francophone countries to the French franc and to France.[6]

In the 1950s, two future African leaders were already members of the French Assembly. Leopold Senghor of Senegal and Félix Houphouët-Boigny of Côte d'Ivoire each published party organs, *La Condition Humaine* and *Afrique Noire*, respectively.

Meanwhile, only in Cameroon was there a private press. Papers in that colony included *L'Echo du Cameroon, Dialogue, Le Petit Camerounais,* and *Les Nouvelles du Mungo.* But Cameroon's independent press was short lived. Both postindependence leaders, Ahmadou Ahidjo and Paul Biya, have run highly restrictive regimes. The Cameroonian press has been among the most tightly controlled on the continent (Article 19, 1991, pp. 5–7).

On the whole, the fifteen-year period between World War II and independence, from 1945 to 1960, was not a particularly healthy one for the francophone African press. Some 365 papers appeared and disappeared during this time (Hachten, 1993, p. 19). At independence, granted between 1960 and 1962 to 14 of the French colonies, there were only three dailies, and all three were run by Charles de Breteuil. The de Breteuil papers were by far the most technically sophisticated, containing international news coverage, high-quality photographs, and colorful and varied feature material. They were still, however, basically French newspapers.

At independence, several of the new governments dusted off their party newspapers from the 1950s and created national newspapers, most of them weeklies, at least in the initial years. With little capital in the hands of Africans, only governments could afford to support the press. And these governments had absorbed far less of an ideology of press freedom than their anglophone counterparts. French colonial policy had always been more authoritarian than the British. Moreover, the centripetal forces of French policy, in stark contrast with the more decentralized approach of British governance, reinforced a penchant for centralized information control.

The absence of any French effort to promote literacy in indigenous languages and the relative disinterest in fostering literacy in French to all but a select few was a corollary to Paris-centered governance. Journalistic development was compromised by low levels of literacy in all colonies except Senegal, where French presence dated to the seventeenth century.[7]

The papers that did emerge in the early 1960s—dailies in Mali, Guinea, Togo, and Niger; a weekly in Gabon; and a fortnightly in Central African Republic—were published in French. Even by the mid-1960s, a duplicated bulletin of the *Agence France Presse* (AFP) was the closest thing several countries could offer as a national daily. This was the case in Central African Republic,

Congo, Dahomey (now Benin), Upper Volta (now Burkina Faso), Mauritania, and Chad.

The press was most healthy where the de Breteuil Group had given it a start. The new government of Côte d'Ivoire joined in a partnership with the French *Société Nationale d'Editions Industrielles* (SNEI), bought out *Abidjan-Matin*, and transformed it into *Fraternité Matin*. An Ivorian editor in chief, Laurant Dona-Fologo, was put in charge of its operations.

In Senegal, de Breteuil's *Dakar-Matin* continued as a private paper with a French editor until 1970. At that point, the newspaper's name was changed to *Le Soleil du Sénégal*. The Senegalese government bought 60 percent of the shares of the paper; de Breteuil and SNEI owned the rest.

La Presse du Cameroon remained in Douala (the main commercial city) as the sole daily in the country until 1974 when it was moved to Cameroon's capital, Yaoundé. At this point the paper was renamed the *Cameroon Tribune*, with the government owning 70 percent of the shares, and de Breteuil owning the remaining 30 percent. Despite their relative financial health, all of the de Breteuil papers suffered from a common problem: a failure to significantly indigenize the staff.

The majority of the papers that descended from party organs faced a different set of shortcomings, disadvantages which have plagued them into the 1990s to varying degrees. They did not develop in an information tradition, but rather in a propagandist tradition. Ainslie describes the lacunae this implies:

> Their chief function was one of comment and exhortation. Reporting would normally be limited to party activities, and the speeches of party leaders. Professionalism was the last concern of their editors who were not journalists but politicians. (Ainslie, 1966, p. 137)

There was little space in these papers for the more populist concerns served by such presses as those of Ghana and Nigeria. There were no women's pages or cultural inclusions, no columns reserved for children. Letters to the editors were equally scarce in these government papers. And there was little systematic news collection for the papers as existing news bureaus had been mainly distributing agents for *Agence France Presse*.

Into these various vacuums came the aforementioned French parastatal, *La Société Nationale d'Editions Industrielles*. The company was set up to run printing presses and to train printers and reporters. Another parastatal, *La Société de Financement de Matériel d'Imprimerie*, was set up to assist francophone nations in the purchase of equipment. These state enterprises paved the way for the expansion of the new nationalist francophone African presses that would remain clearly linked to France by means of French technical assistance and subsidized news and feature services. These presses would support and bolster the regimes which were to follow, regimes held up by France and the rest of the Western world for the next 25 years.

Summary

Vast differences in the press had emerged by the end of the colonial period. Southern Africa, including Zambia, and East Africa had a settler press. This press benefited from a technically strong model fostered through financially well-endowed commercial newspapers, made possible through chain ownership, some the products of powerful mining interests. The financial underpinnings of the major papers provided access to news services, Reuters and the South African Press Association, thereby fostering the tradition of an information press. Expatriate management and staff cultivated a tradition of quality writing, editing, and layout. After independence, these papers moved cautiously toward indigenization.

The major commercial presses, both before and after independence, offered only a compromised editorial position and were conservative in their coverage of governmental policies. Overall, since their inception, they have been content with the political status quo, so long as the powers that be allow their newspapers to remain in profit.

In francophone Africa, the press was largely nonexistent or undercapitalized, with the exception of the de Breteuil Group. The francophone countries inherited little in the way of an information press. The party papers favored exhortation and propaganda, and the de Breteuil papers, partially bought out by governments after independence, quickly moved in this direction. There were, moreover, few trained francophone journalists at independence. Journalistic training was undertaken by the SNEI for papers already operating largely under government control.

Anglophone West Africa seemed to have the healthiest press in terms of the freedom of its expression. It had the most experienced African journalists, some of whom had absorbed the British free press tradition in an atmosphere unhampered by settler demands. Some of this freedom veered toward exhortation, partisanship, and a generally undisciplined style of writing, editing, and technical production. Here the West African press suffered from the lack of training in and the absence of models of professionally crafted literate discourse, i.e., a lack of fact-based stories derived from systematic news gathering techniques. The Mirror Group had fostered a technically jazzy style of popular journalism, with scant attention to serious content. Nevertheless it made needed capital available, and this permitted the press to prevail, relatively unhampered by government in Nigeria, Sierra Leone, and initially in Ghana.

Despite differences, the press in all Black African countries had common problems. Internal news gathering remained a major stumbling block, one which was partially rectified through the establishment of national news agencies. Distribution of papers was always difficult due to poor roads and an insufficient number of vehicles plying the interiors of these countries. To this day, only Nigeria has an adequate means of newspaper distribution. Illiteracy has always been a major problem on a continent which today can claim only a 50 percent literacy rate. Illiteracy, particularly among the peoples of the interior, has always kept circulation figures low. The inaccessibility of European-language papers to rural peoples has only further fueled the press' preoccupation with urban, especially elite, issues and governments' wrangling. And vernacular papers have had a patchy history and uneven success. Only in regions where a single vernacular language predominates, such as the northern half of Sudan; parts of Nigeria where large groups are able to read Ibo, Yoruba, or Hausa; or in East Africa where literacy in Swahili is considerable, are the vernacular papers very significant.

In varying degrees, and in various ways, all the nations in Black Africa lacked adequately trained journalists. They lacked technical personnel needed to operate printing facilities; they lacked journalists skilled in gathering and reporting the news; they lacked copy editors skilled in proofreading and layout. And they were seriously bereft of qualified managers, persons able to oversee the technically complicated, "people-oriented," and politically sensitive tasks which are inextricably intertwined in the business of journalism. These various skill, training, and administrative deficits would exacerbate and be exacerbated in and by the awkward economic and political positions in which the newly independent African states would find themselves.

The Press in the Postcolonial Period

Immediately after independence there was a flurry of training activity in the journalism field. Multilateral and bilateral aid organizations, together with foundations and nonprofit groups moved into Africa to assist in journalism training efforts. Groups such as the International Press Institute, the British Council, the Friedrich Naumann Foundation and the Friedrich Ebert Foundation and the United States Information Agency offered a combination of local and overseas courses to train journalists.[8]

The contrast between libertarian journalistic principles imparted by Western trainers and the exigencies of "journalism for nation building" (already apparent in the heady days of early postindependence) caused some disquiet for trainers and trainees alike.[9] African journalists absorbed these contradictions and lived with them, for these were not the only nor the least of the discontinuities in their lives. Meanwhile, free press champions, particularly the United States Information Agency, continued to promote Western press concepts in training courses.

Development Journalism

Much of the foreign initiative in matters concerning the African press in the 1970s and 1980s veered toward the promotion of a kind of operational compromise between "nation building" and "a free and unfettered press." The compromise was known as "development journalism."

Proponents of development journalism took their cues from the early American ideologues (notably Daniel Lerner, Wilbur Schramm, and Everett Rogers) who subscribed to the notion that mass media should be harnessed to the engine of social and economic development. In this view, media becomes a tool for exhorting positive social change by encouraging and promoting development initiatives sponsored by local and foreign governments and international organizations. Thus, the role of the press as government watchdog is overshadowed by its role as public cheerleader for development efforts. Development journalism, then, generally steers clear of politics, preferring to focus instead on health, agriculture, and educational issues.

In theory, a press promoting development should have been free to produce investigative pieces checking the soundness or the relative success or failure of the projects being covered. But this was seldom the case. What emerged instead was what E. J. Rose defined as "sunshine stories," i.e., "there will be a hydro-electric works in five years, new universities in three years, and so on" (quoted in Wilcox, 1975, p. 28). In other words development journalism presented a view of development bereft of pain and difficulty, bereft of conflict and compromise, and bereft of graft and corruption.

Many Western analysts felt the concept of development journalism was another ideological device used by African governments to exert control over their presses (see, for example, Righter, 1978, pp. 15–16; and Hachten, 1987, pp. 30–34).

Rural Journalism

In a related array of development projects, UNESCO became involved in the promotion of rural journalism in Africa. Most of these efforts were tied to the promotion of literacy, usually in a vernacular language.

A rural newspaper effort began in Liberia in 1963; another one began in 1964. Mali launched a paper in 1972, *Kibaru*, in the Bambara language. Rural newspapers tend to be cyclostyled or mimeographed affairs published monthly or bimonthly. Typically, their circulation is in the 1,000–3,000 range.[10] Written in simple language, they focus on development issues: hygiene, agriculture, health, as well as social, cultural, and economic issues and news. Typically, rural newspapers have been printed by ministries of rural development in conjunction with UNESCO. More recently, they have become pet projects among nongovernmental organizations. Ochs reported in 1986 that there were some

53 rural newspapers in Africa (1986, p. 49). According to Boafo, the rural press was circulating in 12 countries at the beginning of this decade (1991, p. 109).

Attempts at rural journalism have until quite recently been just that: attempts. Like the radio *sensibilisation* campaigns sponsored by UNESCO in the 1960s and 1970s, one of the stated aims of these projects besides literacy was the popularization of government policies.

Zambia appears to have had the widest network of rural newspapers. It included six monthlies covering seven different languages. These were published by the Zambian information services and survived throughout most of the 17-year reign of the UNIP Party. By 1990, however, Zambia's rural papers had ceased publication because of cash shortfalls and improper distribution (Moore, 1992, p. 47).

Africa's rural presses have suffered from the age-old problems which present themselves in the "bush." Rural journalism is even less prestigious than urban journalism. Those who work in the medium tend to be especially undereducated and undermotivated. And they are usually poorly trained.

With the flowering of multiparty democracy in the 1990s, rural journalism may be getting a "new lease on life." In some countries, policies of decentralization are being pursued, and, in conjunction with such aims, a rural press may begin to thrive. In 1991, for example, the Rwandan newspaper *Imbaga* was founded by the National Center for Cooperative Training, a center largely supported by Swiss government aid. Along with useful development information, *Imbaga*'s content included generous helpings of material designed to promote self-government and responsible political action in an era of multiparty politics (Kamarera, July 1992, interview).

News Services

The 1960s saw the development of news services in Black Africa. These were typically set up in capital cities to distribute news from the international wire services to the various media which might use them. The initial aim of the national news services was to cut costs, and sometimes to cut stories deemed inappropriate for the national interest. Over the years, national news services began supplying their own contexting or slant to the news coming over the international wires.

Budgetary crises regularly affect the national news services. In 1990, when I visited Uganda, I was told that the country was receiving no international wire services, as Reuters had suspended its service due to nonpayment of arrears. This has occurred quite frequently over the years in Nigeria and many other anglophone countries as well. The francophone countries have been more favored in this regard, as the AFP has usually been available to government media organizations as part of their overall cooperative arrangements with France.

National news services make extensive and regular use of international shortwave radio broadcasts, the BBC being a particular favorite, especially in English-speaking countries. Africa's news services also gather domestic news and submit it to their national headquarters for distribution. A variety of communication techniques are used to gather and transmit stories. Telephones, teletype, telex machines, or computers with satellite linkups are used where available. Sometimes hard copy is carried for distribution by air, motor vehicles, and even motorcycles (Shehu, August 1992, interview).

In some of the smaller countries, news agencies publish government bulletins, circulating them through the national ministries. At various times, these have served as a substitute for a national press. In 1987, for example, Rwanda had no national daily. The *Agence Rwandaise de Presse* published a weekly news bulletin with a circulation of about 1,000 copies. The only other newspaper was *Invaho* in the Kinyarwanda language. The newspaper was a weekly dedicated to development journalism.

New World Information Order

Africans have long been dissatisfied with what they see as a negative or nonflattering image of them projected in the major news agencies of the world. This was behind their cry for a New World Information Order in the late 1970s.

The New World Information Order was the information counterpart of the arguments put forth by Third World nations in the 1970s asking for a New World Economic Order, a cry for a more just distribution of the world's wealth. The New World Information Order debate essentially asked for more even-handed news coverage of Third World societies. In the late 1970s, UNESCO, under the director generalship of Amadou Mahtar M'Bow of Senegal, took up the debate on behalf of Third World nations. The nations charged that the world's news services, especially UPI, AP, Reuters, and AFP, portrayed the Third World only in negative terms, and then only when climactic, ecological, or political crisis affected them. Within the heated political context of the time, the Pan-African News Agency (PANA) was created by the Organization of African Unity (OAU) in 1979. PANA's aims were "to rectify the distorted image of Africa created by the international news agencies and to let the voice of Africa be heard on the international news scene" (Wauthier, 1987, p. 66). PANA was placed under the control of the OAU's Conference of Information Ministers. Its headquarters were established at Dakar, Senegal. As of 1987, 42 of the news agencies of the 51 OAU states were members.

PANA was initially supported by the International Program for the Development of Communication (IPDC), a group established within UNESCO to coordinate aid for communication development. Eventually PANA received contributions from several international organizations and bilateral aid groups. These included the Arab Bank for Development in Africa and the United Nations Development Programme, as well as the governments of France, the United States, and the Soviet Union. National news agencies send their dispatches to PANA's general headquarters, where they are translated into English, French, and Arabic. The news bulletins are then broadcast by short-wave radio or by satellite to member states.

Although the aims of PANA are laudable, the internal policies have been typical of the contradiction which surrounded the NWIO debate. The main sources of information throughout the 1980s came from one-party or military regimes, and PANA's charter originally disallowed its staff members from altering the news bulletins supplied by member states to its headquarters. Thus, PANA has promoted a kind of skewed unity among African governments but has done little or nothing to provide nonofficial groups with an avenue for news distribution or to promote their points of view within Africa. This arrangement is in transition in the 1990s.

Like so many other governmental media organs in sub-Saharan Africa, PANA has recently embarked on a plan for privatization and has announced an investment drive to attract private capital. Sixty percent of the funds are anticipated to come mainly from private African media companies and 15 percent will be supplied by African telecommunication companies. Participating governments will supply the remaining 25 percent.

PANA intends to expand its operations by establishing news bureaus in Paris, London, and New York, as well as 12 bureaus on the African continent (*Africa Communications*, May–June 1993, p. 8). PANA's restructured news service promises to provide livelier and more informative dispatches than in the past.

Press Freedom in the 1970s and 1980s

The history of journalism in the 1970s and 1980s is a history of a continent coming to grips with the contradictions in which it found itself. It is a history of the struggle for the newly independent nations to forge a national consciousness among disparate ethnic groups.

It is a history of elite policy makers who had clamored for independence trying now to shore up the newly found freedoms. It is a history of politicians discovering that political freedom from the colonial masters had been easier to achieve than economic prosperity. It is a history, in fact, of the failure of the nation-state and the modernist paradigm to satisfy the hopes of the African peoples, elites as well as masses, urbanites as well as rural dwellers.

It soon became evident that freedom of expression and freedom of the press were not particularly high on the agenda of the regimes which took power from the colonists. A number of valid explanations have been proffered for this state of affairs, and they bear some reiteration.

First, it has been argued that Africans never inherited a truly free press, the relative liberalism of British colonial press policy in West Africa notwithstanding. The press had been used to a great extent, either directly or indirectly, to foster colonial government aims and interests. Africa inherited controlled legal and administrative information structures and traditions, particularly in the French colonies where restrictions had been the most pronounced (Wilcox, 1975, pp. 12, 31). Second, the governments which wrested power from the colonists had used the press for their own political ends. Cognizant of its power, they were not inclined to unleash an unfettered press on their newly independent populations. Third, African leaders viewed, perhaps conveniently for their own purposes, the history of their struggles for independence as a *national* struggle harnessed out of united *national* energies. Many felt that developing their nations now would require a similar kind of single-mindedness. An excess of press freedom, they believed, would thwart these efforts and therefore could not be tolerated. Fourth, many of the charismatic leaders of the early independence period were so personally involved in the daily creation of their nation's future, that they equated criticism of the state to a personal attack (Wilcox, 1975, p. 29). And fifth, many of the leaders were deeply suspicious of the power of unbridled individuality, the psychological source of the critical posture of the Western journalist. They believed that an emphasis on the promotion of unity was far more in keeping with African traditions. Africans were after all traditionally respectful of authority, and the divisive critic had been customarily viewed as irresponsible and somewhat unsocialized. A free and unbridled press, leaders felt, would be particularly pernicious, unleashing dangerous passions and anarchic political action especially among naive and unschooled masses.

Most of these positions were on the surface reasonable enough, given the enormity and complexity of the mission the elites found before them in forging the new states. Many, it is felt, believed efforts to control the press would be short-lived and that as soon as their people developed economically and socially, the press could be allowed some latitude of operation (Wilcox, 1975, p. 32).

Alas, this did not happen in the 1970s and 1980s. Economic conditions worsened as urban migration without significant industrialization continued unabated. Population growth soared, in many cases negating gains achieved in the social and educational sectors. Concomitantly, governments in Black Africa became more authoritarian in the 1970s and 1980s. And new military strongmen who took over in Congo, Togo, Uganda, Benin, and Mali, to name just a few, were more autocratic than their predecessors. Early leaders who "stayed the course"—in Tanzania, Côte d'Ivoire, Malawi, Zambia, and Cameroon, for example—found ways to tighten their grip over freedom of expression.

Suppressing journalists in Africa has come in a variety of forms. Some of these are legal mechanisms. There are laws against sedition and libel variously defined to shield the head of state, the members of the cabinet, the civil service, and the ruling party from scrutiny. There are laws protecting public morals and others forbidding blasphemy used to suppress opposition views, foreign publications, and minority religions. Some of the legal restrictions, particularly those affecting sedition and libel, date from the colonial period, having never been removed from African legal codes. Others were added after independence. And long-declared States of Emergency may permit periods of lengthy arrest without trial, while packed judiciaries may ensure swift and harsh sentencing without due process.

Legal and bureaucratic procedures control the press. Some states require a newspaper publisher to post expensive bonds before initiating publications. Others require licenses to print. Some require journalists to be licensed, or find other ways of barring certain individuals from the craft. Some governments practice prior restraint, demanding the submission of all copy to government information censors before printing.

Commercial mechanisms control the press as well. Technical equipment for newspaper production may be heavily taxed; access to newsprint may be equally restricted by selective import taxes or government control of paper distribution. Some of these restrictions may appear serendipitous, as in Nigeria, where needed computer equipment for an offending newspaper "goes missing" at the Apapa port, or trucks carrying imported newsprint are hijacked before arriving at their destination.

The system of patronage in most Black African nations has assured collaboration with the authorities. This is most evident, of course, where all newspapers have been government- or party-controlled. In these cases, all staff members are civil servants, so it follows that the professionalism of management and reporters will be molded into contours acceptable to the state. Where the private press operates, newspaper owners tread carefully so as not to lose their licenses, their access to newsprint or equipment, their advertising revenues from government sources, or their distribution rights within the country.

Perhaps the most common form of censorship in African journalism is self-censorship. Mindful of the precarious existence of their newspapers, most editors-in-chief simply treat matters of government reporting with great caution. Overtly or covertly, they pass on the spirit to their staff. The task has not proved very difficult. Some aspects of the oral tradition have in fact, rendered self-censorship quite "natural." This aspect of censorship bears further examination. The following chapter studies the ways in which elements of the preexisting African oral tradition have intermingled with newer oppressive currents to produce the peculiar form of discourse which characterizes much of the African press.

7 | Discourse Style, Oral Tradition, and the Question of Freedom in the Press

MARSHALL MCLUHAN EXHORTS us to see through a culture by attending to the tools for conversation. Using the framework provided in chapter 1, this chapter presents an examination of the discourse style which has characterized the African press, particularly the official press, for the last 20 to 30 years. Those concerned with the future of African media would do well to understand the nature of African journalistic discourse and its diffusion through the mass media.

Following this analysis, the chapter makes concrete suggestions for the improvement in reporting styles based on admittedly Western techniques. It then proceeds to examine briefly the "rhetoric" of resistance to official discourse and advocates searching within the precolonial value system for an alternative approach to social criticism. This position is based on the recognition that a dialectical approach to African press problems is needed to help usher African media into the twenty-first century.

If the legal and administrative climate in Africa during the 1970s and 1980s worked to muffle the press, the discourse style inherited from the oral tradition helped to make legal-procedural irregularities appear quite seamless. Many tendencies derived from the oral tradition help facilitate self-censorship among news persons. This is because, on a normative level, individuals are still bound to the values of plurality and harmony this oral world view implied. The production of critical journalistic postures comes from the ideology of the modern age of literacy and is yet to permeate the consciousness of most journalists in sub-Saharan Africa.

It has been argued that the critical spirit began to emerge in the West during the age of commercial capitalism. Gutenberg, a member of the new burgher class, invented movable type in the Western world, thereby facilitating the rapid and inexpensive reproduction of texts, including the Bible, published for the first time by Gutenberg in the German language. As the printed word became widely available, Westerners could examine, in the solitude of silent reading, the tenets which had been widely held and socially supported through the oral network of tradition since the early days of the Catholic Church.[1]

As literacy spread among the commercial classes of northern Europe in the sixteenth century, Western people came to apprehend the great religious contradiction of the ages. This was made possible through the availability of printed texts, the writings of Martin Luther, John Calvin, and other religious reformers. From the turmoil which resulted as these texts spread through Europe came the Protestant Reformation, "born," as Burke says, "of the printing press" (Burke 1985).

The Reformation was followed by the Age of Enlightenment, in which the ideas of the philosophers were expanded in lengthy treatises whose value was measured in terms of their internal consistency. The Enlightenment is said to have given way to the Age of Scientific Investigation and Discovery, wherein new knowledge is based upon the rigors of scientific testing, and old knowledge is discarded as soon as emerging data show old precepts to be flawed and incomplete. The ability to test new ideas and new facts against previously held wisdom is thought to be fostered by the written word, which provides the reader with the opportunity to examine the writer's words at a safe and impersonal distance (Ong, 1982, p. 15; Goody and Watt, 1991, pp. 48–55). The development of this critical spirit of inquiry, of literacy-based thought, became generalized in society through mass education in the nineteenth century.

This brief historical account encapsulates the development of a literate tradition in the West. It is worth noting that similar historical processes have not occurred in Black Africa. The printed word was introduced during the colonial period on peoples whose social systems were tribal or feudal. Such societies had not evolved communication norms typical of commercial capitalism. They had not, for example, evolved a discourse tradition clearly separating subjective and objective categories (Gouldner 1982). Their communication norms did not call for critical distanced postures typical of literate societies. Their dominant mode of discourse was speech, and the communication norms which these societies used were those of the oral tradition of a folk culture.

Although the press in Black Africa *appears* in printed form, it has inherited little of the reasoned discourse associated with the printed tradition of post-Reformation Europe. Rather, the press in Africa displays "preempirical" stylistics typical of oral discourse. Using examples from the African press, this discussion will illustrate this sometimes astonishing style. And it will attempt to demonstrate that the style, like oral praise poetry, is very useful in creating personality cults in society and is very poor in fostering a critical spirit among its members.

The discussion will be limited to local coverage appearing in the African media because it is mainly the local stories (together with international stories having a local angle) that display these curious stylistics. Materials supplied and left largely unchanged from international wire services or Western-based feature services inevitably display the marks of the more literate traditions of their originators.

The Oral Tradition and the Production of the Discourse of Domination

The stylistics used in much of the Black African press originate from the delivery of the oral tale. By examining the eight traits or oral psychodynamics presented in chapter 1, we will see how easily the African press, through its own culturally fostered inclinations, was harnessed into the production of written "praise songs" for the new states. This occupation took up the lion's share of press energy, crowding out opportunities for developing critical discourse. And the paucity of journalistic training did little to develop a journalistic professionalism.

Empathetic and Participatory Thought

Walter Ong derives his psychodynamic model from a careful and thorough examination of the mode of transmission of the oral narrative. He notes, for example, that the bard, griot, or teller of tales begins his communication by establishing an intimate communication with his audience. He does so by employing a host of rapport-building techniques. Through the use of these stylistic devices, the griot makes himself one with the audience.

An examination of the African press reveals that writers actually employ this technique even in print! Zairian social analyst André Badibanga, who writes on African press and the African personality cult (1979), describes the sycophancy of the press. In so doing, he provides a quote from Côte d'Ivoire's national daily, *Fraternité Matin*, of October 18, 1977. He decries that what passes for journalism in this article is a piece of flowery praise for Houphouët-Boigny, appearing no doubt as part of a holiday commemoration. The reader should note how the writer, through the use of the pronouns "our" and "we," makes himself one with the audience, as he heaps praise upon the president:

> On this blessed day, our prayers rise from our hearts, prayers for you and your family, for all who are dear to you, for yourself, so that we can know that you will be near to us, unequally and totally preoccupied by our continuing improvement and the development of our dear country. [Translation mine] (Cited in Badibanga, 1979, p. 42)

Badibanga notes that this kind of lofty praise is typical of the African press, and anyone who has taken a cursory look at the press in Black Africa would concur.

The tendency of the author to attempt to achieve unity is not just a contrivance, not just a "trick" of the official, exhortatory francophone African papers, although it may be more in evidence in those countries. It can also be identified in relatively unimportant stories carried even in the private and much freer press of Nigeria. In an earlier analysis of the Nigerian press, I found similar tendencies.[2]

A 1984 article by Prince Dimka, for example, "The Need and Guide against Conformism," provided readers with an author who actually changed point of view during the elaboration of his text in order to achieve (presumably) more empathy with them. The article began with a detached formalistic tone, one which expressed general precepts and principles. But about half way through his piece, the author began addressing the audience directly, as if he were addressing them in verbal discourse. He began to write of what "we" do as a society and what "you" boys and girls who are reading this do (cited in Bourgault, 1987, p. 229). It is clear that Dimka had great difficulty distancing himself from his audience. In his piece, he gravitates naturally to the oral discourse style even in print.

The lack of distancing of the journalist from the audience, or in other cases from the subject, makes it difficult or impossible for the reporter to assume a critical, neutral posture in his or her reporting. In effect, the reporter, subject, and audience all form part of the same team, i.e., they are part of a larger whole. Objectivity as it is understood in the Western sense becomes impossible.

Thought Which Is Close to the Human Lifeworld

Ong writes that the oral tradition is "close to the human lifeworld." By this he means that in the oral tradition, events are always understood to have human or spiritual agents which cause them. Lightning strikes a tree because a thunder god is angry, a child dies because his/her mother's jealous co-wife has bewitched the youngster or because an angry spirit has eaten him/her.

Abstractions such as disease or weather do not lend themselves well to narration. Stories need actors who perform actions—gods who send hailstorms; witches who send pestilence; water spirits who cause drownings. In other words, abstractions do not exist in the oral world.[3]

It is in the light of these observations that the tendency to create personality cults becomes clear. African audiences expect active agents to be the perpetrators of human dramas, not causative abstractions contained in legal documents or constitutions. African leaders have a built-in understanding of the thinking of the masses. Thus, they have fashioned themselves into powerful cult figures who appear single-handedly to run their nations. To accomplish this, they have enlisted the help of journalists who themselves are hardly immune to the mindstyles of orality.

Mobutu of Zaire has used the metaphor "Father of the Nation" to personify and personalize his regime. We can now see that it has not been much of a rhetorical leap for Mobutu's machine to suggest that all good things—roads, hospital wings, literacy programs, etc., come from the president. The abstractive quality of administrative machinery providing such services as part of routine governance can easily be overlooked by the largely illiterate or marginally literate of society. Hastings Banda of Malawi takes the metaphor of "Father of the Nation" so far that he has used it as his excuse for remaining single. Since he is the "Father," the logic goes, whom among his children could he marry? (Hove, 1992, p. 24).

While African leaders have gone about personalizing all of their official actions, they have also symbolically embellished their regimes to add to public perceptions of their potency. Cameroonian scholar Achille Mbembe claims that African leaders have created *"un état théologique,"* a theological state. He argues that African leaders have gone so far as to have themselves deified in the discourse concerning them. According to Mbembe, the state in Africa strives to convince all members of society that its actions represent ultimate truth. He references Comi Toulabor's *Le Togo Sous Eyadema* (1986), which shows how Eyadema has legitimated himself through the blending of traditional religious cults and Catholicism.

Mbembe argues that the *"état théologique"* exercises a symbolic hegemony over people and creates a world in which its vision is the only legitimate one. The theological state constitutes itself as the principal of language and myth in society. The state produces consciousness through the various agents, especially the official news media, who put a "spin" on the cultural and symbolic system.

Thus, African rulers have argued for the last 20 to 30 years that the one-party system is "the African way." To this end, they have used traditional maxims (orally based wisdom) to drive home their point. A frequently used proverb in the francophone countries is *"Un même marigot ne peut guère abriter deux caïmans"* (Mbembe, 1988, p. 129). A rough English equivalent would be, "One stream can hardly make two waterfalls." Mbembe says leaders have used this sort of argument and have found their entourage of elites ready to parrot such notions. And Eric Chinje, Work Bank Regional Information Specialist for West Africa, has noted the ready collusion of Africa's journalists (1993, p. 55).

Mbembe also notes that African leaders have coopted ancient African symbols of power. The use of the cane, the leopard skin, or the fly switch constitute signs of an authentic indigenous mode of governing. These symbols suggest visually to the populace that there is a genuine historically based form of African governance. And these things suggest that those who purvey them practice a governance sanctioned by time-honored tradition. By calling up powerful ancient symbols, authoritarian leaders have offered borrowed African authenticity in politics. This has allowed them to tacitly reject Western democratic traditions, parliamentary democracy, and multiple parties (1988, pp. 121–30). Mbembe reminds us that precolonial Africa had a multiplicity of political forms and styles, some authoritarian, but many not so.

In the nonauthoritarian systems, the objects and rituals of social control not only operated to contain and direct the actions of men, but also to redistribute resources, however scarce. They also worked to pacify the forces of nature and to manage the power of darkness and the invisible, all in order to help preserve the life of the individual and the community. Power in these societies included the power of therapy. The final phase of power was to minister and preserve communities against negative forces. The distribution of different power axes within society obliged those wielding force of any kind to negotiate constantly with one another. Thus, power in these societies was very diffuse.

Mbembe describes the polyvalent nature of power in the nonauthoritarian states:

> Brotherhoods, secret societies, castes, and a diversity of other loci of power each controlled, one or a few elements, each within a precise sphere of political existence. The diverse jurisdictions established through different spheres of political existence (the world of the dead, the night and the invisible, water, fire, lightning, rain, harvests) were expected to negotiate with one another and mutually compensate each other. At the same time each balanced out the other in a reciprocal system. [Translation mine] (1988, p. 131)

Power in traditional societies was then suffused through an assemblage of signs which society's members needed to learn to decode and interpret. Wisdom in such systems was the wisdom of a lifetime learning to deconstruct and reabsorb all these codes and reuse them in appropriate contexts.

Aggregative Rather Than Analytic Thought

Ong writes that traditional oral communication is "aggregative," meaning that groups or categories described in traditional oral communications are usually set up in terms or clusters for easy recall (1982, pp. 38–39). Thus, storytellers use aggregative terms such as "brave princes," "ugly witches," and "beautiful maidens" because the clustering of thought makes it easier to remember. Ong makes enlightening references to the modern-day press in this context:

> The clichés in political denunciation in many low technology developing cultures—enemy of the people—capitalist war monger—that strike high literates as mindless are residual formulas of oral thought processes. (1982, p. 38)

The aggregative tendency useful in condemning out groups, aliens, and others has been skillfully used by the African press to blame the economic dilemmas of a particular country on others, especially "imperialists" and "ex-colonial masters."

Congolese communication professor Ludovic Miyouna complained of the excessive use of platitudes and clichés by the Congolese press in the 1980s. He said that this propensity arose from the need of the journalist to adhere to the party line, to frame all reports within the accepted discourse of the overtly Marxist regime governing the nation at the time. The use of well-worn clichés simplified the task of reporting, and it protected the journalist from the risks of using fresh and original phrasing, a writing style which might signal disloyalty among conservative members of the then ruling party, the *Parti Congolais du Travail* (1987, pp. 95–106). There is certainly much truth to this reasoning, and it helps to explain the tedium of the official discourse in the African press. But Miyouna's comments refer not only to the government newspaper and to government-controlled Congolese broadcasting but also to *La Semaine en Afrique*, a well-respected Catholic daily. This suggests that the use of clichés, though sometimes coerced, is not always the result of pressure from the top. Clichés indeed help journalists to mask truth in autocratic regimes, but their use also occurs quite naturally even in less repressive settings.

Aggregative thinking, or the thinking in clusters, makes the use of clichés a regular part of spoken and popular written discourse. A cursory glance through the Nigerian press bears this out. Some of the more popular press clichés include "the suffering masses," "corridors of power," "our men in blue," and "that fateful day" (Bourgault, 1987, pp. 223–24).

My former position as a professor of print and broadcast journalism in Nigeria provided me with many opportunities to discuss the use of clichés in journalism with Nigerian students. Students typically defended the use of clichés, arguing, "But this is the way we speak!" Professional journalists were surprised and puzzled when told that journalism texts (Western ones, the only ones available) condemned the use of clichés. Most practicing journalists felt that these clichés were a useful way to present information. To prove otherwise, I once asked a group of journalists in a news-writing seminar to produce, individually on paper, the definition of the common press cliché "a friend in need." Out of fifteen seminar participants nearly half as many different definitions were produced (Media Development Consultants. Seminar in Newswriting for NTA News Personnel. Kano, Nigeria. January 1983).

Clichés obviously form a natural part of spoken speech patterns and are particularly prevalent in societies with a high degree of orality. Their use has been fostered in discourse style by regimes intent on controlling information as has been the case in the Congo. But this use in Nigeria revealed tendencies far less officially imposed. For Nigerian journalism, with its popular writing style, its long Africanized reporter corps, and its relatively free content, abounds in clichés. The very popularity of expressions suggests they have great resonance within the culture. I would submit that in oral cultures, cliché-ridden writing comes naturally to mind and appears completely normal to the reader.

Agonistically Toned Thought

Related to aggregative thinking is thinking which is agonistically toned. Agonistically toned communication is combative in its reporting of out groups. It should be recalled that oral narratives situate actors in a struggle between opponents who are described in these stories with opposing sets of descriptive (aggregative) complexes.

Agonistically toned reporting is often used to describe the actions of foreign powers on local citizens. Painful effects of structural adjustment on ordinary citizens in African countries have been reported in highly agonistic ways. This technique conveniently deflects the blame for economic mismanagement away from local elites and onto the evil forces of the West. This is an entirely expected response on the part of local authorities and therefore makes for a somewhat poor illustration of agnostic thinking. A better example of the thinking in operation can be examined in the light of domestic occurrences. Though the official press in many African countries often tends to ignore local uprisings (Ellis, 1989, pp. 323-25), the Nigerian press has sometimes been more inclusive. This occurred, for example, in the wake of the Maitatsine Uprisings in the northern city of Kano in December 1980.

Mallam Muhammadu Marwa, popularly known as Maitatsine, was a cult leader of Cameroonian origin. In late 1980, he assembled a group of at least 3,000 Nigerian followers in Kano, arming them with explosives and firearms. Maitatsine's group took over the Yan Awoki section of Kano's ancient walled city, occupying the homes of many of its residents. The cult was finally routed by the Nigerian army who overpowered them with mortar, rocket, machine-gun, and automatic weapon fire. A government inquest followed the incident.

For several weeks, the Nigerian press reported the proceedings of the inquest. Despite the extensive coverage of the proceedings by most of the Nigerian press, the vast majority of stories were reported from the government's point of view. The inquest focused on the following kinds of questions: Who had given Maitatsine permission to enter the Old City? How had he come to occupy such a large area? Where had he obtained his weapons? What/who was Maitatsine's source of funding? (Clarke, 1987, p. 111). Given the millennarian and seditious nature of the confrontation, it is not surprising that the press of Nigeria carried no interviews with followers, former followers, or sympathizers. But what was perhaps surprising to outsiders was the absence of think pieces or editorials speculating on the social sources of the attractiveness of Maitatsine's message.[4]

Instead, the Maitatsine incident was consistently painted in agonistic terms. Maitatsine was repeatedly depicted in the press as an *outsider*, one who had used evil powers, false logic, and false prophecy to lead "good" Nigerian Muslims astray and to disturb the peace of the *good* people of Kano. This was in fact the official view generated by the inquest (Clarke, 1987, p. 111).

It might be argued that the social significance of such a story was too hot for the press to handle. Journalists must certainly have feared deviation from the official line on such a sensitive issue. But this is, in fact, exactly my point.

The development of such a line of inquiry does not come easily in orally tinged societies. An analytical, self-critical posture, has been little fostered regarding domestic issues. Even in Nigeria where freedom of the press was (then) legally guaranteed by the constitution,[5] where the press has largely been considered as free as anywhere, this press has mainly been free to exhort, to chant, to root for a team and against another foe—all with blatant disregard for or disinterest in the facts (Mytton, 1983, p. 125).

As Hachten notes, "even the adherents of the Nigerian press argue that it stresses advocacy and opinion more than information" (1993, p. 43). Thus, when reading the Nigerian press one has the sense of pursuing a series of wildly partisan accounts. It is only by consulting a range of newspapers or listening to an array of Nigerian news broadcasts (each differently controlled) that one may hope to gain a complete rendition of any given news item (Mytton, 1983, p. 119).

Agonistic accounts have appeared in great profusion in recent years in the controlled African presses in treatments of the newly emerging opposition. The following is an account of the Movement for Multiparty Democracy which appeared in the election edition, October 31, 1991, of the UNIP (Kaunda-controlled) *Eagle Express* just before the elections which ended Kaunda's reign in Zambia:

> Another truth about MMD is that they have nothing to offer apart from condemning UNIP and one party state. If by a miracle they form the next government, they will spend one term lying and insulting UNIP since they graduated with diplomas and degrees in these fields. So what can one expect from a bunch of mandrake dealers, ex-coup plotters, power hungry elements, dictators, tribalists, fake lay preachers, corrupt and disgruntled misfits. (Cited in Maja-Pearce, 1992a, p. 58)

According to Walter Ong, "the other side of agonistic name calling or vituperation in oral or residually oral culture is praise singing." It is known both in Africa and in the residual "oral Western rhetorical tradition stretching from classical antiquity through the 18th century" (1982, p. 45).

Praise singing is alive and well in the popular culture of Africa. As Ruth Finnegan notes, "even university lecturers who entertain in their homes are not above hiring praise-singers to 'panegyricize' hosts and guests" (1970, p. 54). Nigerian scholar Emmanuel Obeichina reminds us that orally based patterns of thought persist in Africa even among modern literates (1975, pp. 26–27).[6]

A number of francophone African media analysts actually use the term "griotage" to describe the kind of fulsome praise singing which regularly appears in the African press. Among such analysts include the already cited André Badibanga (1979, p. 41), Francis K'patindé (1991, p. 12), and Theophile Vittin (1991, p. 52). And W. A. E. Skurnik makes reference to the practice of praise singing in African media when he remarks that "some reporters complain that too many of their confreres are something less than the modern version of griots, less because a griot was able to influence his employer" (1986, p. 157). One need only to turn to the African press to find ready examples.

The Christmas issue of *La Nouvelle Marché*, the official Togolese weekly, provides us with this panegyric jewel in its lead story, "At Home the President Eyadema Attended Midnight Mass." The story quotes at length from the sermon of Monseigneur Dosseh-Anyron—itself a piece of fulsome praise, not so much for the Christ Child, but for the chief dignitary who graced the religious service with his presence. Dosseh-Anyron is quoted at length:

> Your only presence, here, Mister President of the Republic, at this Christmas Eucharist, which you love to celebrate in the midst of your brothers each year with your assiduousness, your devoted involvement, never distracted from the issues of the country, is as much testimony as it is an argument, a veritable lesson. [Translation mine] (*La Nouvelle Marché*, December 27, 1982, p. 3)

As bizarre as this sort of journalism may seem, it is not unlike the traditional praise poetry supplied in chapter 1 of this volume and analyzed by Okpewho. He reminds us that this genre functioned, in its oral form, to instill group pride. And Achille Mbembe reminds us that "officialdom and the people share many references in common, not the least of which is a certain conception of the aesthetics and the stylistics of power" (1992, p. 13).

Redundant and Copious Thought

In his analysis of the dialectics of power in Zaire, Michael Schatzberg notes that political elites who are tied to the system of patronage "often justify political directions and policies on the grounds that they will be good for the larger national family" (Schatzberg, 1988, p. 72). It is thus clear that they have internalized the symbols and the rhetoric of Mobutu as "Father of the Nation."

These symbols are repeated over and over again in the daily press. Schatzberg quotes from the front page, October 24, 1975, of *Elima*, a state-supported newspaper:

Citizen Mobutu Sese Seko, in his capacity as father of the large Zairian family, profoundly touched by the fatal accident provoked by a falling tree in the enclosure of the Ecole officielle de la Gare, which resulted in the death of one pupil, and three seriously wounded, has just sympathized with the misfortune of the stricken families by giving them Z. 2,250. (Quoted in Schatzberg, 1988, p. 71)

This kind of report, whose emphasis is not on the tragedy of ordinary victims but on the benevolence of the head of state, is repeated daily, over and over again in the African press.

It might be argued that *Elima* is an official newspaper and that such slavish repetition is therefore mandated in the oppressive nation of Zaire. But an examination of the Nigerian press suggests that redundancy also occurs quite naturally in that country's journalistic discourse, even though it is not strictly required.

Ong argues that oral traditions favor copiousness and repetition because audiences cannot "back-loop" or reread should they become distracted and miss portions of the oral narrative. Speakers must repeat points several times to ensure that audiences have taken in the message (1982, pp. 39–41). André Badibanga argues that the repetition of stock phrases tends to inure readers into the realities they are being presented, i.e., to lull them into internalizing a set of beliefs by crowding out other possibilities, other points of view. Information thus takes on a ritualistic or chant-like quality and leads to collective catharsis (1979, p. 41). Nowhere was this more apparent in Nigeria than at political rallies that marked the preelection season in the spring and summer of 1983. At these gatherings, politicians would shout slogan after political slogan in seemingly endless repetition (Bourgault, 1987, p. 224).

The Nigerian news media's coverage of lengthy and copious speeches has been noted in chapters 3 and 5. In this connection it might be added that speeches covering the same subject by persons in different localities are normally each given separate write-ups by any given newspaper, within the same week, or even sometimes within the same day. This is especially common during graduation season when commencement speakers typically exhort youthful audiences to be virtuous. It would be unthinkable in Nigeria to find a story which begins, "In five separate prize-giving ceremonies, keynote speakers asked graduates to uphold the values of the nation," because each speaker, however minor his or her title, expects to have the full text of his or her speech, redundancies and clichés notwithstanding, to be fully reported in the press.

As Mbembe notes, people in the postcolony have absorbed the epistemology of grandeur and excess "to the point where they reproduce it themselves in all minor circumstances of daily life" (1992, p. 23). Mbembe argues that lacking its own natural comfort, "the popular world borrows the whole ideological repertoire of officialdom along with its idioms and forms" (1992, p.

14). Thus, the speech-giver in Nigeria expects his or her discourse to be reproduced in a state-supported or national newspaper just as the president's orations are reproduced in the *New Nigerian* or the *Daily Times*.[7]

In the foreign-owned press, such as Kenya's *Nation* or *Standard*, such excessive redundancies are much less apparent. These papers were founded after all in an information tradition and have a heritage of providing more real news. Yet such papers do give coverage to speeches and do exhibit similar exhortatory tendencies, though articles covering such events tend to be shorter, focusing more on key points. Such a report, for example, appeared on page 5 of the *Standard* of Monday, March 2, 1987. It begins with this lead: "Kenyans have been told to nurture the peace and stability prevailing in the country today to ensure continued economic growth."

Despite their relative lack of redundancy, the Kenyan newspapers are guilty of paying excessive homage to authority. As the above-quoted story continues, the patronage debt of the speaker (and by association the Kenya News Agency who filed the story, and that of the *Standard* which printed it) becomes clear:

> Speaking in Malo South, Nakuru District, the Managing Director of the Kenya Post and Telecommunications Corporation, Mr. Kipng'eno arap Ng'eny, said Kenya enjoyed unprecedented tranquillity because of the wise leadership of President Moi.

And soon the paternalistic exhortations of this style of speech become apparent as the article continues: "He urged the *wananchi* (common people) to maintain peace.—He told parents to take education of their children seriously by providing physical facilities in schools." Soon the evidence of insidious webs of patronage characteristic of authoritarian states emerges: "Mr. Ng'eny donated Shs. 30,200 while a member of Parliament for the area, Mr. John Njenga Mungai, gave Shs. 2,000." And soon the agonistic elements also emerge: "Mr. Mungai told the gathering not to be swayed by the hostile propaganda being waged against Kenya by disgruntled elements who had lost their direction." The ritualistic elements of such a speech-story are abundantly clear.

Another type of report riddled with ritualistic redundancy is the coverage of "transfer of office" ceremonies which punctuate bureaucratic time in patronage-laden African administrations where government transfers are common. Such events are described with a relentless relish for the symbolic trappings of power. They are replete with tedious enumerations of all educational achievements of the new officers, together with all official and honorary titles. Mbembe quotes from an account provided on page 3 of the *Cameroon Tribune*, April 19, 1989, on the installation of Mr. Pokossy Ndoumbe as head of the borough of Douala.

> Mr. Pokossy Ndoumbe first saw the light of day on August 21, 1932 at Bonamikengue, Akwa. He attended the main school in Akwa, obtaining his

certificate in 1947. Then he left for France. He passed his first courses without difficulty at the Jules Ferry school in Coulonniers. He passed the baccalaureate in experimental sciences in 1954 at the Michelet high school in Vannes. He was drawn to pharmaceutical studies in Paris, and he diligently attended the Faculty of Pharmacy in Paris, where he obtained his diploma in 1959. During his final years at the University, he worked as an intern at the Emile Roux Hospital in Brevannes before returning to his native country in January 1960. (Quoted in Mbembe, 1992, p. 25)

What is always most astonishing for the outsider reading these accounts, incidentally, is the absence or near absence of any mention of the work responsibilities and duties of office these new assignments entail. At best, such information will be conveyed in platitudinous statements by the new official, fatuously citing his intention to carry out his obligations for the betterment of the nation.

The outside reader is left to assume that little work will be accomplished by this new officeholder, an assumption quickly borne out by a visit to any number of overstaffed Black African bureaucracies. Meanwhile, the press, by its own omissions, does little to suggest that there is, or should be, a job of work connected to a given civil servant posting.

The truth of the matter, of course, is that so many of these positions are positions of pure patronage designated primarily by the head of state to extend his power and to "maintain an intimate and proximate relationship with the ruled" (Mbembe, 1992, p. 15). They may include party officials, police (certainly the chief of police), soldiers, administrators and officials, couriers, and militiamen. The appointment of a pharmacist, M. Pokossy Ndoumbe, as borough chief, seems peculiar. The outsider may indeed wonder in which way a knowledge of pharmaceutical sciences could contribute to Cameroonian administration! The redundant enumeration of his qualifications together with those of all new officeholders will numb the Cameroonian public and keep them, elite politicians hope, from raising the same critical questions.

Conservative or Traditionalist Thought

Ong remarks that "Oral societies must invest great energy in saying over and over again what has been learned arduously over the ages." He argues that this "establishes a highly traditionalist or conservative set of mind that with good reason inhibits intellectual experimentation" (1982, p. 41). This accounts in part for the strong approbations of various African governments against seemingly minor criticisms which may appear in print or even in public discourse.

Suppression of free expression has been taken to the point of silliness in Malawi. A lecturer who discussed the reproductive capacity of old men was detained without trial as this was deemed disrespectful to the aged life president Kamuzu (Hastings) Banda![8] And in that same country a lawyer was arrested for criticizing Malawi's dress code, which prohibits women from wearing trousers (Carver, 1992, p. 14).

In Kenya, one man was charged with possessing seditious material because he wore a t-shirt bearing a V-sign and other inscriptions suggesting 1990 was the year of victory for multiparties. Iredi Kanampio was arrested for remarks he made suggesting similarities between the Moi regime and the Romanian regime of Ceausescu (Imanyara, 1992, p. 21).

After President Samuel Doe of Liberia issued a directive calling all civil servants to arrive promptly at work at the start of official business hours, one broadcast announcer took it upon himself to report that media personnel on shift work would be exempt from this rule. The television journalist who announced the exception was suspended without pay for one month for showing "disrespect" to the head of state (Davis, 1988, interview).

The conservative mind-set engendered by the oral tradition encourages a mode of thinking which leaves little tolerance for complex exceptional cases. These are perceived by the leaders as simple cases of insubordination and officially redefined as such for the populace. In this way, the blind authority of the state is reinforced.

Conservative and traditionalist thought is also evident in less controlled presses such as those of Nigeria. A think piece by Apollos Bitrus entitled "Why Women's Liberation Was Unpopular" (*Sunday Standard*, January 3, 1982), for example, is a classic piece of conservative and traditional oral thought presented in a semianalytical writing style. In this article, Bitrus follows a fairly common practice of the Nigerian press of "borrowing" pieces from the Western (usually British) press. In this case, he takes verbatim a report discussing the results of a comparative study conducted in 23 countries on the acquisition of gender role attitudes and behavior. The study shows that by the age of five, most children in a majority of countries have absorbed the expected sex role concepts of their respective cultures. To this report Bitrus adds his own beginning and ending. At the outset he claims his article will answer "the million dollar question: 'Are women under bondage'?" He seems unaware that these research reports could not, in any case, serve to answer directly his rhetorical query.

Though Bitrus does not clearly state it, he apparently concludes that since sex stereotyped perceptions exist around the world they must represent the natural order of events. Quite obviously he has missed the point of these studies, which focus on the *acquisition* of cultural attitudes rather than their validity (in any case, nontestable) in the cosmic order.

At any rate, these issues are quite beside the point. The crux of his "argument" can be found in his last two paragraphs. Here he simply repeats that women do not need to be liberated because they are not:

In the Nigerian situation, a lot of historical, social researchers [*sic*] conducted, indicated that the [*sic*] women's place is in the home. Right from childhood, children (male and female) are taught to keep the roles associated with their sexes. For example, a boy cannot be taught how to cook in the kitchen, except after his seemday [*sic*] education he may be interested in catering studies as a profession.

To this "argument," he adds a more revealing "proof" that the social position of women in Nigeria represents the "natural" order of things:

The Nigerian Constitution which is the only document which would have declared nil [*sic*] and void the role of women as mothers in our homes only provides for equality in terms of voting and contesting elections. (*Sunday Standard*, January 3, 1982, p. 11)

Apparently he means that since the constitution did not release women from childbearing and domestic duties, they should not aspire to full social equality. It does not occur to the author that such a nullification is unprecedented in society. But far more importantly, it does not occur to him to see the constitution (which provides for full citizenship rights as regards voting and office holding) as a new model of thinking or a new code for society. Rather, he interprets this new document in terms of a preconstitutional *Weltanschauung*. Bitrus displays conservative thought typical of orally based thinking.

Additive Rather Than Subordinative Thought

Ong isolates another important characteristic of the oral mind-set: the tendency to speak "additively rather than subordinatively." This characteristic is related to the propensity of the oral bard to use the conjunction "and" rather than such subordinative words as "then," "while," "when," "because," etc. The use of the word "and" facilitates the delivery of the oral narrative. It allows the bard to add elements to his story as he calls them up from memory or as the audience shouts them out for him. The bard is less likely to use subordinate conjunctions because what follows such words must be planned in advance by the teller of the tale. The use of subordinatives leaves less room for forgetting and less room for audience participation.

Stories from the Nigerian press often reveal additive tendencies borrowed, no doubt, from the oral tradition. The *Sunday Herald* of July 8, 1984, for example, ran a third-page story with the following headline: "Give Children Choice of Religion." The "lead" (as indicated by boldface type) reads, "Parents have been charged to pass to their children whatever religion of their choice" [*sic*].

A reading of the entire story reveals the piece in fact to be a report of events (actually speeches) delivered at the "prize-giving" (graduation) ceremony. The issue of religious choice is no more than one of many of the points made in a series of three speeches. Clearly the story follows neither the inverted pyramid style nor the standard Western literary narrative style. Rather it begins in the words Horace used to describe the style of the epic poets of preliterate Greece, *in medias res*, i.e., in the middle of things (Ong, 1982, p. 142).

Indeed, it is common to find elements added at the ends of stories in the Nigerian press which seem only tangentially connected with the main subject. The absence of backgrounder stories or summaries to bring the reader up to date is equally noticeable in much of the African press. There seems to be a built-in assumption that the reader is closely following unfolding events and therefore does not need such assistance. This may be because the journalist perceives himself to be writing for (or perhaps more aptly "speaking to") a small group of elites intimately linked through gossip networks within the ministries, or the journalist may expect the readers' companions to fill in the appropriate details omitted from the story, as newspaper reading (as does most of African life) occurs in group settings and serves as a source for lively group interaction.[9] An additive style of writing, whether intentional or not, provides the reader the opportunity to incorporate his or her own comments into the story for the audience. Thus, like most traditional African interchange, it is dialogical in its approach to reality and essentially incomplete until the audience participates in its deconstruction and reconstruction.[10]

Situational Rather Than Abstract Thought

Literate styles of narration stress the logical and chronological order of a story. They create their own context within the text and are thus rooted to it. This has the net effect of grounding the stories in historical time. Oral stories are focused outward on the audience. The bard selects elements from the audience and immediate setting and weaves them into the story. Audience members usually offer details, providing assistance to the teller of the tale. Thus, the tale acquires both an immediacy and a timelessness. Stories are simultaneously rooted in the past and presented for the here and now.

André Badibanga's analysis of official discourse in the African press stresses that journalists use the present active tense (even for past events), both to heighten the drama of a reported event and to distance the reader from a critical perspective which might be engendered through the use of the past composite tense.[11] Thus, the story recounting that "the minister of health today leaves Maradi for Zinder" (Niger), for example, implies that the journalist was present (though he/she may not have been) and that he/she is providing the reader an "eyewitness account" of the event.[12] This rendering affords the reader a kind of vicarious participation in this ritualistic ministerial visit, while distracting him or her from asking what the minister, in fact, *accomplished* in Maradi. The use of the present active tense thus encourages the reader to be swept up in unfolding pageantry of these visits to rural areas (Badibanga, 1979, p. 41). The propensities of journalists to eschew background stories, follow-up stories, or summative accounts (avoidance itself resulting from an orally based thinking style) assures that embarrassing questions will not be asked by the public later on.

Timeliness has never been an important factor in local journalism in Africa. Where the time element is not finessed for the dramatic purposes heretofore suggested by Badibanga, it is ignored for other reasons, some of which are admittedly technical. The slow pace of life in Africa combined with the inadequacy of telecommunication infrastructures on the continent render Western standards of timelines quite inappropriate and unworkable. But very often timeliness is disregarded along with other demands of precision, because news is expected to carry out a didactic function. Thus, it is not unusual to read, in the African press, accounts of events which occurred days, weeks, and even months earlier.

L. John Martin's analysis of the Black African press sheds some light on this news value:

> Timeliness here, as in most African intercourse, is of secondary importance. Neither the interest nor the usefulness of a story diminishes with time. Accuracy is a frill and often a detriment since events that are used as object lessons to make or illustrate a point lose their didactic potency if they must conform to fact in all their details. Objectivity is seen as a red herring with which Western media attempt to arrogate truth to their viewpoints. Importance and size, other Western criteria of newsworthiness, are relative. Only proximity holds the kind of importance it has in the West except more so. African media are highly parochial in their interest. (1983, p. 194)

Indeed, the emphasis on parochial considerations provides yet another example of situational thinking typical of oral societies.

Homeostatic Thought

The final mind-set typical of oral societies is homeostatic thinking. Ong provides the following elaboration: "Oral societies live very much in the present which keeps itself in equilibrium or homeostasis by sloughing off memories which no longer have present relevance" (1982, p. 46). Goody and Watt use the term "structural amnesia" to describe homeostatic thought (1991, p. 49). The tendency toward homeostasis or "structural amnesia" may explain how it is possible for a journalist in the pay of one government to wake up one morning to find his original employer toppled and a new government demanding he lambaste the former in print. This happened, for example, to journalists at *Sidwaya*, Burkina Faso's daily newspaper, which was full of praise for Thomas Sankara until a coup on October 15, 1987, toppled him. On October 16, all government-owned media branded the late president as a villain (Niyii, 1988, p. 35)!

In all parts of the world reality is socially constructed and socially upheld, but where writing has permeated the social structure, codes, rules, and laws are rendered more permanent, because they have been fixed by the written form. Eventually, the average citizen internalizes, at least partially, these written codes: the Bill of Rights, the Magna Carta, the Ten Commandments, and the various verses and passages from the Bible or the Quran. All these written documents achieve an existence independent of their framers, anchoring many individuals and society in compliance with the codes they offer and tempting others to their outright defiance.

The very mode and degree to which individuals have differentially internalized abstract principles into their core personalities helps to differentiate one personality type from another. Both within the development of an individual and within society, literacy fosters individuality by promoting quiet contemplation of abstract principles and allowing for selective application of socially held principles (Luria, 1976, pp. 15, 55, 150; Goody and Watt, 1991, pp. 52–54).

In oral societies, where literacy is less pronounced, individuality is less marked and the group mind is more evident. Positions are far more ephemeral, because they are held outside the individual, i.e., they are supported by situational group norms rather than being deeply internalized. Time and time again in media courses I have taught in Africa, I have asked an individual what he or she thinks or why he or she has written a particular story, only to be answered with a group-oriented reply, e.g., "We Liberians think this, or we Swazis think that" (Bourgault, 1993, p. 80). The presence of group mind promotes homeostatic thought, fostered by an ahistorical rhetorical discourse, not based upon written codes or records but on what is happening *now*, what people are doing and saying *today*.

Political praxis in African societies is hardly based on written principles enshrined into law. The very large number of coups which have occurred on the continent is testimony enough to that fact, as is the regular contravening of written law by patronage ridden judiciaries.

The homeostatic tendency revealed in the press (especially after shifts in governments) certainly comes in part from coercion from the top. But it also comes from the bottom, i.e., from deep within the peoples themselves. Mbembe writes metaphorically that "dictators go to sleep at night lulled by roars of adulation and support only to wake up the next morning to find their golden calves smashed and their tablets of law overturned!" (1992, p. 15). He says this is because the postcolonial state has fragmented people's identities. I would argue rather along with Victor Turner that identities have always been polyvalent in traditional Africa, that the demands of social roles and social etiquette required a person to act out a multiplicity of situationally and inter-actionally determined behaviors. Turner's prescient analysis of traditional African life argues that it constituted an unending series of dramatic engagements:

> In the simpler, pre-industrial societies acting a role and employing a status was so much a part of everyday life that the ritual playing of a role even if it was different from that played in mundane life, was the same kind as the one played as son, daughter, headman, shaman, mother, chief, or queen sister. (1982, p. 115)

The homeostatic mind-set, described by Ong, represents the tendency of group-oriented persons to adjust to new realities by donning new postures or roles appropriate to a new political situation. This is performed with relative ease because old positions have not been deeply internalized into core person-alities by abstractive analysis.

An article on the 100-day-old Buhari regime, in the *Sunday Triumph* of Kano, Nigeria (April 8, 1984, p. 7), admirably illustrates the move toward ho-meostasis by authors Iredi Obazee and Abubakar Tanimu. In "Journey So Far Encouraging," the authors begin by roundly defaming the Shagari civilian re-gime, which held power only a few months earlier and which was reelected for a second term less than a year before the article was written. The agonistic tone the authors use in defaming the Shagari government is noteworthy:

> This [Buhari regime] is a regime which inherited a savagely depleted treas-ury, a badly depressed and disenchanted populace. A populace whose yearn-ings have been led to root which the ladder removed beneath [*sic*] after their feet. A hapless and helpless populace who seemed to have been literally sen-tenced to endless penury and starvation. Many of them seemed to have re-signed to fate to await death by installment.

In general, it seems fair to say that the populace favored the Buhari coup of 1983. It seems an overstatement, however, to suggest that the populace was "sentenced to endless penury and starvation." The Shagari government had, in fact, resisted devaluation of the Nigerian currency and other harsh economic measures demanded by the IMF in its loan-granting negotiations.[13] It must be added that many Nigerians view the Shagari regime (1979–83) as one of great prosperity for their country (a consequence, albeit, less of Shagari's managerial acumen than of OPEC petroleum price increases).

Obazee and Tanimu proceed in their analysis to attribute the success of a local government project to the Buhari regime. They note that "group farm-ing, a do-it-myself program has saved the [Hadeja Local] council 200 percent." Given the pace of life in Nigeria and the intransigence of its crippling bureauc-racy, it is difficult to imagine that any program, particularly one destined for a rural area, could not only be conceived but also implemented in only 100 days! The "do-it-myself program" to which they refer was in fact a project of the government of Olusagun Obasanjo, who acceded power to Shehu Shagari in 1979! But such inconvenient details are merely swept aside by these authors in their quest to ally themselves with the new team in power. With a lack of historical memory, such homeostatic writing is possible. And this kind of gravitation toward homeostasis has been equally apparent in more recent shifts in political power in Africa in the 1990s.

Zambia's *Daily Mail*, taken over by the Kaunda government and the UNIP Party in 1975, strongly supported its candidate until he was defeated at the polls on October 31, 1991. Nevertheless the *Mail*'s November 1, 1991, issue reported the results of the election with a piece entitled "Chiluba Takes Over." The homeostatic quality of the article is noteworthy:

> Charismatic leader of the Movement for Multiparty Democracy (MMD), Mr. Frederick Chiluba was yesterday sworn in as Zambia's second Republican President at the Lusaka High Court . . .
> President Chiluba's ascendancy to office follows the landslide victory which his party gained over former President Kaunda and his United National Independence Party which has ruled the country for 27 years . . .
> The new President immediately pledged to honor MMD's manifesto and vowed never to allow his leadership to fall prey to what he termed "hypocrisy; dictatorship, and self-deceit." (Quoted in Maja-Pearce, 1992a, p. 59)

Writing about Zambia's press for the *Index on Censorship*, Adewale Maja-Pearce comments on the stand taken by the *Daily Mail*:

> This was all very well and accurate enough in terms of the speech Chiluba gave, but the *Mail* itself has been a staunch supporter of the one-party state which promoted the hypocrisy, dictatorship, and self-deceit that it was now, and shamelessly, happy enough to report. On the evidence of the article, the *Mail* will presumably have little difficulty switching its allegiance to the new power brokers. (Quoted in Maja-Pearce, 1992a, p. 61)

Discussion and Suggestions

An opinion press, one to which advocacy comes naturally, derives from an orally based culture—one where there is little distancing between the reporter, the subject, and the audience. A didactic press emerges quite comfortably in a society with a traditionalist and homeostatic world view and an additive and redundant discourse style. And indeed, objectivity is a near impossibility to those whose thinking is close to the human lifeworld, situational, aggregative, and agonistically toned.

One-party regimes have manipulated the press in Africa, skillfully bending the styles of oral discourse to suit their purposes. In so doing, they have stymied efforts toward the development of a more rational discourse useful in the exchange of views between those who govern and those who are governed. If a free press standard is to develop and be retained, the manipulated discourse style which has shaped the thinking of the masses for the last three decades will need serious adjustment.

Short-term cosmetic improvements, I think, could be made in the African press through increased training of journalists. Again, training needs to be given in the development of critical-thinking skills, so that journalists can develop the habit of presenting information, logically ordered. Typically, journalists have not been trained in this way. Most of them have learned their craft on the job. They have proceeded by imitation, learning from the sycophantic and exhortatory news-writing styles of their elders, many of whom copied the techniques of preindependence political news sheets.

One useful approach in training journalists is to begin by asking them to report on common, ordinary, nonpolitical events occurring in their milieu. They may be asked to describe the birth of a farm animal, the maintenance of a neighborhood water pump, or the cultivation of a certain crop. Practice with providing systematic, step-wise accounts of ordinary events will help provide journalists with necessary narrative building blocks they may not possess. Once journalists have mastered these elementary skills, they can be asked to proceed to more complex tasks: describing how bills are passed in legislatures or providing accounts on the effects of given government directives on various sectors of society.

Journalists should be presented with samples of logically derived discourse, quality news reporting, literary essays, even clearly written instruction manuals. These should be carefully analyzed in their rhetorical detail, to show how these accounts have been structured to convey information. Afterwards, news persons can proceed to adapt their own stories to make them better conform to a systematic style of information presentation. Journalists could then begin to remove empty laudatory phrases, replacing these with accounts of actual events which have occurred.

More work needs to be done in the area of training for interviewing. First, journalists must be trained in interview preparation. They must learn to formulate in their own minds the purpose of an interview; they must learn the importance of structuring questions to elicit clear responses and to insure coverage of key points. They must learn the importance of preinterview research, reporter preparation, and source cultivation. Too much training has taken place on the job with hurried senior reporters inviting junior reporters to come along on an interview assignment to learn the technique. Background preparation for the interview (if any) may easily be missed by the young journalist through such a haphazard "hands on" approach.

I believe journalists must start with "practice interviews" in familiar territory with sympathetic subjects. Once they have mastered the techniques of deriving useful information from subjects, they may graduate to more complex topics and more recalcitrant interviewees.

These are just a small sampling of some of the journalist training techniques I have found useful in the course of my work with African news personnel. But they represent a kind of "top-down" approach to the tackling of a Black African press steeped in an oral tradition, one which has encouraged personality cults around Africa's "Big Men."[14]

But better training for journalists cannot be the sole answer for Africa's press problems. Increased training will do little unless the current shifting winds in Black Africa move to broader economic and political enfranchisement of the rural and urban masses. Without this necessary integration, the masses will continue to deride the tenets of the official press and to find ways to undermine its message. This too has occurred over the postcolonial period, unbeknownst, at least, to outside observers.

Popular Response to Official Discourse

Responses to the manipulation by officialdom are many and merit some attention. This area of study has been little researched, particularly outside of francophone Africa (Geschiere, 1988, pp. 35–36). From a potentially vast area of explication, this subsection will briefly treat only three forms of popular resistance to the "praise singing" media. These will include the phenomena of parallel discourse, *radio trottoir*, and witchcraft.

Parallel discourse is described by a number of francophone scholars as the means through which Black African masses deform, through deconstruction and reconstruction, the praises they are forced to sing and perform. Comi Toulabor (1981), for example, discusses this process at length, elaborating on the rhetorical shifts created by the masses as they participate in forced political chanting known in Togo as *"animation."*[15]

Typically, *animation* is expected of all able-bodied people during official visits to rural areas by federal government officials, particularly by the head of state himself. On such occasions, dancing troupes, often clad in clothing bearing an imprint of the president's photograph, gather to perform for the occasion. Led by a government *animateur*, one often posted in the village, the people are exhorted to shout slogans and sing songs glorifying the nation, the party, and the president.

Toulabor describes the particular capacity of the Eve language (a near *lingua franca* in Togo and the tongue in which much of this *animation* takes place) for creative manipulation by recalcitrant subjects:

> Eve, like other Negro-African languages, is a tonal language, one which uses homophones; and which does not hesitate to use neologisms or onomato-

poeia to identify objects in its environment. These linguistic traits encourage subtle word play, shifting meanings, and insinuations which for the most part are incomprehensible to those who speak the language imperfectly. [Translation mine] (1981, p. 58)

Toulabor's analysis, largely linguistic, describes the way in which official party propaganda is transformed by the masses into party mockery, often replete with sexual references and scatological humor. Mbembe's analysis draws heavily from Toulabor:

When Togolese were called upon to shout the party slogans they would travesty the metaphors meant to glorify state power. With a simple change of intonation, the same metaphor could take on several meanings. Thus under the cover of official slogans, people sang about the "enormous" and "rigid" presidential phallus of how it remains in this position, and of its contact with "vaginal fluids." . . . The poaching of meanings can go much farther. For example, the Togolese party acronym, RPT, was identified with "the sound of faecal matter dropping into a septic tank," or the "sound of a fart emitted by quivering buttocks which can only smell disgusting." (Mbembe, 1992, pp. 7–8)

Mbembe (1992) finds similar popular meaning shifts in Cameroon, as did Dubuch in his study of Burkinabe political rhetoric during the Sankara (1983–87) era (1985, pp. 44–53).

Clearly, there is a vast area of research to be conducted on the nature of resistance, both social and verbal, to the suffocating political discourse of the African postcolonial state of the 1970s and 1980s. Though communication studies have tended to ignore it, the subject is slowly emerging in anglophone circles particularly within the disciplines of anthropology and religious studies.[16]

A second important mode of communication, long overlooked by mass media scholars in Africa, is the phenomenon known as the *radio trottoir*, perhaps best translated into English as "pavement radio" (Ellis, 1989, p. 321). Anyone who has lived for a time in Africa knows that African urban areas are constantly abuzz with rumor. Pavement radio indeed refers to the circulation of lively news through nonofficial oral channels of interpersonal communication which penetrate African cities. The stories which circulate typically treat topics of interest that the official press ignores or covers scantily in coded language. Thus, *radio trottoir* is underground news, an alternative to the official press, which is tedious, censored, uninformative, and often unintelligible.

The sources of pavement radio are numerous, for everyone is a potential contributor to this free and uncontrolled "medium." Some of the rumors circulating through *radio trottoir* also no doubt begin through foreign shortwave broadcasts, only partially understood. And knowledgeable sources of news and gossip are particularly sought out.

Stephen Ellis, editor of the newsletter *Africa Confidential*, expands upon this point:

> The most believable purveyors of information [for pavement radio] are likely to be those whose jobs give them some access either to top level gossip, such as government drivers, servants, or hairdressers, or people with wide social or geographical contacts, such as market sellers and long distance lorry drivers. (1989, p. 322)

Ellis also comments on the content of *radio trottoir*: "Pavement radio has certain favorite topics of discussion. It thrives on scandal in the sense of malicious news, and rarely has anything good to say about any prominent persons or politician" (1989, p. 322).

Like language itself, the subjects of pavement radio are often metaphoric or allusive. *Radio trottoir* is replete with stories about witchcraft and other strange phenomena. To outsiders, such tales seem highly irrational because they can be understood only within a "backgrounded" context, supplied by knowledge of African myth, folklore, and oral history. The purveyors of *radio trottoir* often transpose folkloric stories to account for modern events, trying to interpret news about the government and elites within their own cultural framework (Nkanga, 1992, p. 4). David Williams, in his *Malawi: The Politics of Despair*, describes a series of rumors about corpses found being drained of blood. The story was said to have derived from an old myth, now transposed to explain the flow of Malawiian manpower to the South African mines (1978, pp. 252–53).

These functional explanations of *radio trottoir* stories make good sense to outsiders once they appreciate the allusive power of African language and African oral tradition. Anthropologist Victor Turner might explain the easy transformations in popular news accounts partly with the same rationale he uses to explain transformations occurring through the ritual process: the objective (the realm of day-to-day reality) and the subjective (the realm of possibility) in African social life are far closer than they are in the West (1982, p. 115).

The phenomenon of pavement radio can be the bane of African journalists. Instructed to check sources and pursue leads springing from these rumors, news persons soon discover sources are evanescent. The sources of these stories are both everywhere and nowhere. Everyone knows about a given rumor but no one knows from where it came!

In some places, journalists do try to grapple with the phenomenon. In both Zaire and Central African Republic, reporters asked me how to best handle stories about witchcraft and other rumors circulating in the *quartiers populaires* (USIA Seminar for Journalists. Bangui and Kinshasa. May–June 1990).[17]

The transposition of stories, like the transposition of language (described by Toulabor, Dubuch, and Mbembe), renders social criticism possible if not permissible. In the late 1980s, the Liberian press was replete with stories of "dragons," "heartmen," witches, and other beings or objects associated with the extratemporal world.[18] When I inquired among journalists about these phenomena, I was told that in the absence of a free press, witchcraft stories are substituted for real news because these stories are popular among the people, and they help to boost sales. At the time, the double sense of this reply escaped me.

Geschiere describes the operation and function of sorcery among the Maka in southeast Cameroon. His work suggests that sorcery operates within both modern and traditional contexts in Black Africa as a social "leveler." He observes that the application of extratemporal powers outside their village context (in cities, for example), is often excessive because it is not balanced through socially sanctioned counterforces emanating from pluralistic village power nexus:

> Of old, sorcery (*djambe*) has been the obvious idiom to explain power relations and to canalize social inequality. No wonder this idiom is equally applied to the new forms of inequality that seem to violate the old restrictions. The powers of *djambe* have a strong levelling tendency and are therefore a convenient form of expression for popular modes of reaction against the state elite and its new riches. (1988, p. 43)

Geschiere's research cites numerous examples of *evolués* who reject village life because they fear "being eaten by witches" (1988, p. 49). Indeed, he notes: "The refrain that 'the villagers spoil everything by their sorcery' recurs time and time again among civil servants" (1988, p. 49).

Power in traditional societies was diffuse, and one of the many levelers of power was witchcraft:

> Even within the village, the elders' authority was circumscribed by strong levelling tendencies—the ever present threat of group fission, the idiom of sorcery, and an egalitarian ideology emphasizing personal autonomy for each man. No wonder the imposition of colonial state authority involved enormous problems. (Geschiere, 1988, p. 41)

Stories about witchcraft pepper much of the African press, particularly the private popular presses of West Africa. Generally freer and more populist in their appeal, these presses have served some of the functions carried out by the *radio trottoir* in the francophone countries where the press has generally been more controlled and where there were few, if any, private presses.[19] To what extent these stories represent a veiled critique of governments is difficult to determine without more critical analysis by folklorists, anthropologists, and literary scholars well steeped within the traditions of their countries. French scholar C. Dubuch recommends such studies of the African press to native African scholars:

> The site of double speak; of veiled illusion, of suggestive attacks, of which the meaning is accessible only to those steeped in the history of the country, constitutes a very revealing area of study for those who possess the keys for doing so. [Translation mine] (1985, p. 47)

The Black African masses at the bottom of society, far from being passive, have evolved their own means to resist oppressive discourse heaped upon them from the top. It is clear that earlier, more traditional societies employed a host of their own leveling techniques so as to mitigate the concentration of forces and to deconstruct social power. In which ways can we look to African tradition for sources of critical posturing? To what extent can a new generation of journalists use the techniques of the past for their present professions? Again, this question has been understudied. I offer only a few meager and tentative suggestions.

Griots, although employed as praise singers, were permitted to criticize their patrons provided the criticism bore the weight of group norms and values. Typically, they used humor and indirection in their critiques. Watremez notes that "the local griot tradition, which gives limited right to poke fun within the tribal kinship system, has also encouraged the growth of the satirical press" (1992, p. 35). A related phenomenon, "cousinage of jest" "allows members of the same tribe to criticize one another through poking fun" (Ouedraogo, 1992, p. 35). Burkinabe sociologist Moussa Ouedraogo recommends that the new satirical press in Africa should make more use of this tradition. A spate of satirical journals are now on sale in francophone Africa: in Cameroon, Mali, Senegal, Burkina Faso, Côte d'Ivoire, Gabon, Rwanda, and the Comores. Perhaps they are drawing from traditional Africa's acceptance of humor in criticism.

What is clear is that media personnel must begin to look deeper into their egalitarian roots to derive more populist-based genres for challenging authority. Given the diversity of these roots, it seems likely that a plurality of media voices and media forms will be necessary to satisfy multiple demands.

8 | The Flowering of Democracy and the Press in the 1990s

THIS CHAPTER WILL examine the latest shifts in press currents which have been characteristic of the 1990s. It will review the conditions surrounding the flowering of multiparty politics in Africa and will then consider their relationship with the African press. The chapter will also examine in more detail the state of the press in Zambia, the first anglophone country in recent years to have undergone successful multiparty elections. It will identify both signs of progress and signals of alarm regarding Zambia's press future. In so doing, it will consider, in general terms, the future of Black African newspapers.

The reader is cautioned at this juncture that changes are occurring so rapidly in the Black African media during this decade that events documented one month are likely to be out of date the next. The developments detailed here represent Africa at the time of the final manuscript preparation in the spring of 1994.

Developments in Politics, Economics, and Communications

A noticeable shift has taken place in the African media in the 1990s, particularly in the press. Whereas broadcasting is still largely under government control, print journalism has been able to respond rapidly to political changes in Africa.

In the 1990s, journalists have moved from defending the compromised press of their countries to disavowing it. They now display the desire Mbembe predicted. They are moving to "smash the golden calves of dictators and overturn the tablets of law" which have kept the press in bondage (1992, p. 15). The response on the part of the press is in part the latest version of "homeostatic thinking" discussed in the last chapter. Journalists are adjusting to a new single world order where Western values of democracy and respect for human rights are gaining currency.

These changes are healthy for the continent and its peoples. Positive shifts are coming from both within and outside the continent, a phenomenon of a globalized world order of instantaneous communication. The fall of the Berlin wall in the spring of 1989 put an end to the Cold War model of world politics, a model which propped up Africa's single party authoritarian regimes in the 1970s and 1980s, however embarrassing they were at times to their patrons (*Africa Report*, September–October, 1991, pp. 5–6).

Meanwhile, new communication technologies have speeded up the access Africans have had to fast-breaking events in other parts of the world. Satellite TV reception dishes, emerging on the African market in the late 1980s, brought the news of the fall of the Soviet empire to Africa. Particularly resonant was the dramatic footage of Ceausescu's death before a firing squad made up of his own militia. (Mobutu was said to have been particularly disturbed by this turn of events.) And the visual effect of Eastern Europeans removing statues of Lenin from city squares had enormous symbolic impact. As Samuel Decalo argues, "Africans could clearly see that their own country's departures from democratic standards closely parallel defects exposed in Eastern Europe" (1992, p. 14). The freeing of Nelson Mandela in February 1990, coupled with the prospect of eventual reform in South Africa, had ripple effects on the continent, as did the independence of Namibia the following month.

As the last decade of the twentieth century began, a senior French official suggested in *Le Monde* that France should begin to disengage itself from its former colonies which had become "the conservatory of the ills of humanity" (cited in Decalo, 1992, p. 19). In the ensuing months, the French foreign minister quietly put francophone African countries on notice. Continued assistance would henceforth be tied to progress in human rights and a general relaxation of authoritarian abuses. The French shift in policy was highly significant because France's activity in Africa had been particularly visible and direct. As Decalo notes, "Fiscally sustaining one-third of the African states to the point of annually balancing the budgets of many, France has not hesitated to make and unmake governments by direct military intervention" (1992, p. 19). Other bilateral and multilateral donors echoed the position around the continent. This news was widely reported on Radio France International, and other international shortwave broadcasting services (Vittin, 1991, p. 55). Local civil rights groups, many alive and well because of thirty years of monitoring activity by such international groups as Amnesty International, were given new impetus. With the world aid community now at last on their side, these groups could finally pursue reformist agendas with a vengeance. Quiet diplomatic pressure on African governments has forced the vast majority of Black African regimes to begin an overhaul of their political systems and establish timetables for multiparty elections.

Not to be discounted in the power shifts in Africa is the role of new communication technology. As in Eastern Europe, the growing number of fax machines and computer-based networks in the hands of private individuals, of companies, and of nongovernmental organizations has facilitated linkages with the outside world while eroding monolithic information control within.

These new technologies have helped nascent democratic groups to establish and maintain contact with a myriad of human rights organizations and other parties interested in the democratic process in Africa (Chinje, 1993, pp. 52–53).

Some of the North American civil-rights groups actively engaged in networking and social justice and solidarity work include: Africa Faith and Justice Network (Washington, D.C.); Africa Resource Center (Oakland, Calif.); American Committee on Africa and Africa Fund (New York); American Friends Service Committee, Southern Africa Program (Philadelphia); and the Inter-Church Coalition on Africa (Toronto). And some African-based groups include: Council for the Development of Economic and Social Research in Africa (Dakar); African Commission on Health and Human Rights (Brazzaville); African Bar Association (Nairobi); the African Institute for Economic Development and Planning (Dakar); and the Monitoring and Defense of Press Freedom Branch of the West African Union of Journalists (Dakar).[1]

A new generation of African patriots is using new communication technologies to maintain contact with civic groups within and outside the continent. The Benin Commission on Human Rights, for example, has sent telexes to Togolese President Eyadema, condemning his actions, and the Beninese group used the telex to maintain contact with the Malian League of Human Rights during unrest in Mali in 1991 (Novicki, 1991a, p. 41).

In the more liberal climate which has preceded elections, a veritable mushrooming of the press has occurred. In tiny Rwanda, for example, more than 60 newspapers have sprung up since 1991 as President Habyarimana announced his intention to move the country to multiparty democracy. After years of muffled expression in Rwanda, many would-be journalists have not waited for new press laws to be enacted which might protect them.[2] They have simply gone ahead and begun to publish. This pattern has been repeated in a number of countries, where a spate of new newspapers—many of them wildly partisan and vitriolic in their criticism of the present (or previous) regime—have emerged. So eager have been political writers to have their say that they have used their own funds to get out their news sheets. Throughout the continent, newspapers have sprung up overnight, in some cases, only to publish for a few issues and then to die, starved of funds.

Internal factors within Africa itself have contributed to the shift in attitudes of the public when a number of African countries became bankrupt, a result of internal mismanagement, crippling debt burden, and the lack of further capital from Western loan facilities. In order to receive additional loans needed to keep their economies afloat, they were forced to take the harsh medicine prescribed by the World Bank and the International Monetary Fund. Loan-mandated economic liberalization policies led to the end of subsidies for food staples and increased channeling of agricultural production into export crops. The former change was particularly hard on the urban masses, and the latter had its most serious repercussions among the peasants.

But IMF/World Bank restructuring has also meant massive layoffs and firings among the civil servants, the better-educated sector of the population, whose favor had been especially curried through the patronage system. Cut off from the pocketbooks of the regimes who had nurtured them, this group was now widely disaffected and ready to criticize those still in power.

Throughout the 1980s, the African populace at large experienced increased penury. Their sheer misery and dissatisfaction have given them the courage by the 1990s to organize demonstrations against their governments. In some cases, widespread popular discontent with existing regimes has inhibited local militia (often owed months of "back pay") from taking brutal measures against protesters. This occurred, for example, in Kenya on November 16, 1991, during a public rally for multiparty elections, when hundreds of armed police and security agents massed for the demonstration did not shoot into the crowds as they had during a similar demonstration one and a half years earlier (Press, 1992, pp. 39–40).

In Benin after a bankrupt treasury caused months of strikes, dictator Mathieu Kérékou acceded to the holding of a national conference in early 1990.[3] Unable to manage the conference as he had expected, he came out of it powerless. Delegates at the conference named Nicéphore Soglo, a former World Bank official, interim prime minister. When elections were held one year later, Kérékou surprised the Beninese populace by running for office. He was soundly defeated, and Soglo emerged as the winner. News of Benin's national conference was carried by international radio, notably *Radio France Internationale*, and led to massive shake-ups in the capitals of francophone Africa. Opposition groups in Cameroon, Côte d'Ivoire, Central African Republic, and Guinea soon demanded their own national conferences (Vittin, 1991, p. 55).

The political situation in African countries is changing daily and is being carefully monitored by a number of human rights groups. Among them is the Carter Center at Emory University in Atlanta, which biannually publishes *Africa Demos*, a progress report on African electoral reform. In August 1992, it reported that 30 African regimes were in political transition. The center rated the strength of the commitment of these regimes to democracy. Those rated as having a "strong" commitment included Angola, Congo, Gabon, and Nigeria.[4] Fourteen countries were rated as having a "moderate" commitment,[5] including Burkina Faso, Cameroon, Côte d'Ivoire, Eritrea,[6] Ethiopia, Guinea-Bissau, Lesotho, Madagascar, Mauritania, Mozambique, Niger, Seychelles, Tanzania, and Uganda. At the time, there were 11 countries rated as "ambiguous" in their commitment.[7] Holders of this rating included Burundi, Central African Republic, Chad, Comores Islands, Equatorial Guinea, Guinea, Kenya, Rwanda, Sierra Leone, Togo, and Zaire.

In some cases, the Carter Center's predictions have been overly optimistic. Cameroon, for example, did hold elections during the last quarter of 1992. Standing President Paul Biya won with four percentage points more than his nearest opponent. But the election procedure in Cameroon was reported by international observers as having been skewed in favor of incumbent Biya (Geekie, 1993, pp. 62–63).

Zaire's "ambiguous" rating is well deserved. Mobutu agreed to multiparty elections in April 1990 but allowed so many parties to form, according to *World Monitor* reporter Robert Press, that the "political landscape became confusing" (February 1992, p. 41). When the public demanded a national conference with the authority of a constituent assembly, Mobutu acceded but asserted its role would be only advisory. In early autumn 1991, he expanded the powers of the assembly and then tried to rig the meeting by hand-picking conferees. Public outcry ensued, giving way to massive demonstrations which left hundreds dead. In the aftermath, Mobutu agreed to nominate a prime minister, Etienne Tshisekedi wa Malumba, with whom he would share power. One week later, Mobutu had discarded Tshisekedi. Shortly thereafter, a second prime minister, Bernadin Mongul Diaka, was named. Diaka lasted only a month and was replaced by Nguza Karl-I-Bond.

In January 1992, the national conference reopened. In the interim, on December 4, 1991, Mobutu's seven-year term of office had expired. Nguza closed the conference and more public protests and killings followed. International and domestic pressure once more forced the reopening of the conference, this time in late March 1992. Among other issues conference members implicated Mobutu and the CIA in the killings of Zairian independence hero Patrice Lumumba in 1961.

Mobutu continued to claim that only he had the right to name a prime minister. On June 20, 1992, Mobutu announced to the world media, "It is I who convened the conference, it is I who created it; it is I who organized it." Using his old Mobutuist rhetoric, he indicated that he had suspended the previous two conferences "each time there was an attempt for things to get out of hand, like a good head of family" (cited in wa Mutua, 1992, p. 55).

According to a 1992 Africa Watch report, "Mobutu's efforts to sabotage the conference included a pilgrimage to the Vatican, bribes to conference members, and a public campaign to redirect the work of the conference" (cited in wa Mutua, 1992, pp. 55–56).

As of May 1993, Mobutu had appointed five prime ministers (wa Mutua, 1993, pp. 53–55). In June 1993, Zaire was a country divided by two factions vying for power. Mobutu led one group, and Tshisekedi, the prime minister appointed by the national conference, clearly headed the opposition, the *Union pour la démocratie et le progrés sociale* (UDPS). The Tshisekedi group is allied with the *Haut Conseil de la République*, a legislative organ which came out of the national conference, a conference whose acts Mobutu has long refused to ratify. Mobutu, rejecting Tshisekedi, meanwhile nominated his own prime minister, Faustin Birindwa. At Mobutu's behest, Birindwa was busy in 1993 reviving the old parliament, a body dissolved by the national conference (wa Mutua, May–June 1993, p. 55). Anicet Mobe, of the Paris-based periodical *Afrique-Asie*, suggested in August 1993 that Zaire was in a permanent coup d'état (p. 21).

In 1994, Mobutu spent much of his time attempting to divide the opposition while Tshisekedi tried to keep it united. The latter organized mass strikes and civil disobedience against the Mobutu government.

Meanwhile, Zaire's economy was on its knees. In 1993, Zaire had an inflation rate of 8,319 percent, the highest of any country in the world since World War II, a notoriety duly recorded in the 1993 *Guinness Book of World Records*.

By April 1994, Mobutu seemed resigned to some sort of power-sharing arrangement between himself and his chief rival. His latest solution to the long impasse in Zairian politics was an arrangement which would appoint with Tshisekedi's consent, an interim prime minister, one who would lead the country toward (eventual) presidential elections. As of late April 1994, Tshisekedi had not agreed to the plan.

The comments of *West Africa* correspondent George Ola Davies on the political situation in Zaire were noteworthy:

> This is not the first plan that has been proposed to take Zaire out of its international isolation and economic strangulation. What it has, which the others did not, is [*sic*] components which show respect for the opposition by the highest authority. This might well do the trick, if and only if, Tshisekedi does not consider the plan a gimmick that will in the near future sideline him from the mainstream of Zaire's politics. (Davies, 1994, p. 647)

Besides the nations with political systems in transition, the 1992 *Africa Demos* provided four other classifications for the regimes in Black Africa. These include "authoritarian regimes," "directed democracies," regimes with "contested sovereignty," and "democratic regimes."

The "authoritarian regimes" are defined by the Carter Center as having a "system with highly restricted opportunities for political mobilization," where "power is exercised by a leader or small group not formally accountable to an electorate." Authoritarian regimes are defined as having "no effective constitutional limits to the exercise of political power" (*Africa Demos*, 1992, p. 15).

Authoritarian regimes included in the Carter Center classification were Djibouti, Malawi, Sudan, and Swaziland. Also listed was the "directed democracy" of Zimbabwe. A "directed democracy" was defined as "a system in which formal institutions and practices of constitutional democracy are present, but in practice, the extensive powers of the ruler, party, or regime severely limit contestation by individuals, organized groups, legislative assemblies, and the judiciary" (*Africa Demos*, 1992, p. 15). The center also identified three countries with "contested sovereignty." These were countries engaged in civil war, including Liberia, Somalia, and Western Sahara.

Finally, ten Black African countries were listed as "democratic." These were Benin, Botswana, Cape Verde, the Gambia, Mauritius, Mali, Namibia, São Tomé and Príncipe, Senegal, and Zambia. Three of these, Botswana, the Gambia, and Mauritius, have long been considered democratic,[8] Senegal has been recognized as such since the early 1980s,[9] and Namibia had recently gained independence from South Africa. The other four—São Tomé and Príncipe, Mali, Benin, and Zambia—successfully held multiparty elections in the early 1990s.

The Carter Center's next monitoring report, published in February 1993, showed some progress and some back-pedaling on the question of democratic reform. Gabon, Ghana, and Nigeria were now rated only as "moderate" in their commitment to democracy. This represented a fall from their previously "strong" rating. Angola had moved to the "ambiguous" category, a decline from its earlier "strong" position. Only Congo, among those previously listed as "strongly committed to democracy," had improved its rating. It was listed by February 1993 as "democratic," the result, no doubt, of presidential elections held in August 1992. Congo was the only new country to fall in the "democratic" classification in the February 1993 rating.

Four of the countries in the "moderate" category had improved within their category scores: Kenya, Mozambique, Niger, and Seychelles. Djibouti had also improved its standing, moving from the "authoritarian" classification to the "ambiguous" category. Within the "ambiguous" category, Sierra Leone had improved its rating, which suggests that some small progress was being made toward democratic reform.

Since the February 1993 report, at least two of the authoritarian nations have experienced a thaw in their positions. Djibouti held elections in the spring of 1993, and Malawi held a referendum on the one-party state in June 1993. This resulted from mounting pressure internally but more importantly from the suspension of aid from major donor governments including Germany, the United Kingdom, and the United States.

In early 1993, a United Nations team visited Malawi to advise on referendum preparations. The team recommended the establishment of impartial rules governing access to the media and the creation of statutes allowing free public assembly. Despite the stated intention to help the referendum, President Banda repeatedly denied access to the airwaves for multiparty campaigners, and the new independent newspaper, the *Michuru Sun*, was often denied printing facilities at the parastatal which prints Malawi's government daily.

Despite these setbacks, the Malawi referendum was successfully held in June 1993. Banda's one-party state was roundly defeated. By the end of June 1993, Banda had granted amnesty to all political exiles from Malawi, inviting them to return home to take up the task of forming a transition government until multiparty elections could be held (BBC Report, June 22, 1993). The date of May 17, 1994, was later set for Malawi's first multiparty election. Opposition leader Bakili Muluzi of the United Democratic Front won a victory against Hastings Banda and his Malawi Congress Party (BBC Report, May 19, 1994). Banda's long and repressive rule had been in place just a few weeks shy of 30 years.

In the wake of political changes rapidly emerging in Malawi, 12 newly licensed independent newspapers had been established as of September 1993. Publishers nevertheless faced threats, questioning, and even arrest by authorities still accustomed to operating according to the old rules of Malawi, where "citizens have been afraid to even say the president's name aloud since the 1960s" (Kelso, 1993, pp. 52–53).

The Malawi parliament passed a series of reforms in November 1993 amending the sedition provisions of the penal code and many other laws restricting freedom of expression. Nevertheless, in early 1994, the Censorship Act remained in force, and consequently thousands of books, records, and films were still banned. And the Preservation of Public Security Act still in place permitted the government to ban newspapers and detain journalists for up to five years (Carver, 1994, p. 58). Nevertheless, as the May 1994 election loomed ever closer in Malawi, a vigorous and critical press was said by *Africa Report* to be "freely available on the streets of Lilongwe and Blantyre," and that "even the Malawi Broadcasting Corporation [was] moving somewhat haltingly with the times" (Carver, 1994, p. 58).

It is clear that the newly emergent newspapers of Africa have been in the forefront of political change. The task they have taken on has been fraught with danger. In 1991, the Committee to Protect Journalists, a group which researches and protests violations of press freedom, documented more violations in Africa than in any other region of the world. The group published the following account of press abuses: "[There were] 30 African countries, in which 91 journalists were subject to short or long term detentions, 46 were prosecuted, 19 publications were banned, and 71 issues of publications were confiscated" (Brice, 1992, p. 50). And these figures were far from inclusive as "wars, coups, or attempted coups in Chad, Somalia, and Togo, for example, made it difficult for the Committee to Protect Journalists to gather information" (Brice, 1992, p. 50).

Today's journalistic scene in Africa is a complex one indeed. In some countries, press control has tightened in the wake of the announcement of multiparty elections. In Côte d'Ivoire, for example, independent newspapers began to flourish in 1990 when opposition parties were legalized. But in 1991, a new press law was passed. It authorized suspension or seizure of publications for those who disparage the head of state, give away national secrets, or deride the nation (Brice, 1992, p. 51). Meanwhile Houphouët-Boigny was reelected in elections held in October 1991, elections said to have been marked by wide-spread fraud (McColm, 1991, p. 10). In Uganda, in 1992, President Yoweri Museveni was said to be examining a new press law which would have a chilling effect on free expression (Brice, 1992, p. 51). And in 1994, the Committee to Protect Journalists, citing Nigeria and Zaire as two examples, pointed out that some countries gearing up for elections had increasingly cracked down on the opposition press (*West Africa*, 4–10 April 1994, p. 601). See above and chapter 7, note 5.

The fate of the press in the so-called democratic regimes seems equally precarious. In Benin, only a year after the installation of democratically elected Nicéphore Soglo, the new regime attempted to reimpose censorship. The editor in chief of Radio Benin, Clement Houenontin, was dismissed for "siding with trade unionists and the opposition." He was given the consolation prize of heading FM radio's entertainment department but told to clear any opposition communiqué with the government (Chabi, 1992, p. 36). Other violations in Benin include the transfer from news to the production department of a journalist who reported, on a Beninese TV broadcast, the results of an independent survey on public confidence in the new government. Meanwhile, the Soglo government in 1992 created the Department of Propaganda, charged with the supervision of public relations and the promotion of government policies (Chabi, 1992, p. 36). By 1994, Soglo's critics were calling on the Beninese president to put an end to the use of the state media houses for the cult of personality (*West Africa*, 24–30 January 1994, p. 132).

Index on Censorship reports that despite President Soglo's often repeated wish to grant complete freedom to the press, some ministers continue more or less openly to bring pressure to bear on journalists (Chabi, 1992, p. 37). This pressure is particularly strong among journalists in the electronic media and the official press who fear losing their jobs (Novicki, 1991b, p. 45).

A related tendency which mitigates against fact-based news gathering and reporting techniques is an avowed cultural preference for partisan journalism. In a seminar I conducted in Cotonou in March 1992, journalists told me they enjoyed reading the opinions of their colleagues. They argued that the function of the press, at least in Benin, was "to delight the reader with well-argued opinions," preferably in high-quality French prose. Journalists averred they favored this "francophone" style of press more than that of their anglophone neighbors (USIA, American Partners Lecture Tour, March 1992, Cotonou).

In Tanzania, in 1992, one month after recommending multiparty politics for the country, the government was attempting to devise new ways of managing the free flow of information by empowering the Tanzanian director of information to assume the controlling role previously held by *Shihata*, the party newspaper (Maja-Pearce, 1992b, p. 72).

The Press and Newly Emerged Democracy: The Case of Zambia

In the 1970s, Zambia's press fell under heavy government control. The government purchased the *Daily Mail* and charged it with building the nation. The *Mail* was under the control of the parastatal National Media Corporation (NAMECO). Then in 1975, the Zambian government announced the takeover from Lonrho of the *Times of Zambia*, and in 1983, it had acquired all of the shares. By 1989, the *Times* also fell under complete control of NAMECO. As noted earlier, the Zambian government also published a number of vernacular newspapers until funds ran out in the late 1980s.

The only credible opposition to Zambia's single party, UNIP, was the *National Mirror*, founded in 1972 by an interdenominational organization of Christian churches. The paper published fortnightly and "uncovered scandals, corruption, and allowed access to any group, including the government wishing to express views" (Moore, 1992, p. 47). All radio and television in Zambia was government-controlled, run as a semicommercial parastatal owned by the Zambia Industrial Mining Corporation (ZIMCO).

During the years of single-party rule, repression was the order of the day. Adewale Maja-Pearce describes the state of Zambia after one-party rule was declared in 1972: "Kaunda attempted to justify his own brand of tyranny by a species of sophistry in which the imprisonment of his political opponents was understood as part and parcel of the philosophy of Humanism" (1992a, p. 58). A national emergency was declared in 1976, facilitating the suppression of the voices of opposition. The Preservation of Public Security Act permitted detention without trial.

Economic conditions steadily worsened in the 1980s as copper prices continued to fall. In the late 1980s, when Kaunda was strapped for cash, he accepted an IMF loan with unpleasant economic strings attached. In 1989, the government devalued the Zambian currency by 60 percent and then increased the price of maize meal (the national staple) and fuel. This move resulted in food riots and looting in many towns on the Copperbelt (Article 19, 1991, p. 66).

In May 1990, Kaunda announced there would be a referendum on multiparty democracy but warned that without single-party rule the country would slip into economic and political chaos. In June 1990, food prices climbed once again and more riots followed. Twenty-three persons were killed in the clashes. At the University of Zambia, students protesting the government were attacked by armed troops and the university was closed for the third time in six months. During the course of the protests, however, a small band of soldiers took over the national radio stations and declared the overthrow of President Kaunda (Article 19, 1991, p. 64). Though the overthrow claim was false, the actions of the soldiers gave fresh impetus to the Movement for Multiparty Democracy, an ever-growing anti-UNIP force which already included labor, students, and professionals.

In October 1990, Kaunda's party agreed to hold multiparty elections in 1991 with the proviso that Kaunda would be the sole presidential candidate. Afterwards, the police prevented the Movement for Multiparty Democracy from assembling in Lusaka (Article 19, 1991, p. 64).

By December 1990, with internal and external pressure building, Kaunda agreed to lift the 1972 ban on political parties. And he agreed to presidential multiparty elections! In March 1991, the Movement for Multiparty Democracy was registered as a political party and Frederick Chiluba was elected as its president.

Soon afterwards, a group of Zambian businessmen launched the *Weekly Post*. Apart from the *National Mirror*, it was the first independent newspaper in Zambia in twenty years. Interestingly, it was owned by a consortium of twenty-five shareholders including members of UNIP and the new MMD. No single individual could own more than 15 percent of the shares (Maja-Pearce, 1992a, p. 62).

The editor-in-chief at the *Post* was Robinson Makayi, a former *Times of Zambia* editor who was detained without trial for six months after having revealed Zambia's ties with South Africa in supporting the UNITA party in the Angolan civil war.[10] After being fired, Makayi had left Zambia and gone to work for the UN Commission for Namibia, helping to organize the media of the Southwest Africa People's Organization (SWAPO), Namibia's major liberation group. Makayi returned from Namibia in March 1991, eager to become involved in the emerging democratic process in Zambia (Ham, 1991, p. 71).

The *Weekly Post* was launched in July 1991. It tried to be impartial in its news coverage, but it had a difficult time shedding its anti-UNIP bias, so strong was the anti-UNIP sentiment in the country. The government, for its part, attempted to prevent the *Post* from publication by asking the parastatal Printpak, which produces Zambia's papers (except the *Daily Mail*), not to print the new independent weekly. Printpak's general manager, Henry Chipewo, resisted the pressure and the *Post* began to flourish, selling up to 60,000 copies per issue (Maja-Pearce, 1992a, p. 62).

In July 1991, a new constitution was written for the Third Republic. Then the government began to waver and back-pedal on its election promise. The opposition called upon impartial international observers to monitor the upcoming Zambian election. Meanwhile, Zambians began forming their own election monitoring group. The Zambia Independent Monitoring Team (ZIMT) was created in July 1991, staffed by lawyers, bankers, and other professionals.

In September, another group, the Zambia Election Monitoring Coordinating Committee (ZEMCC), was established. An umbrella organization, the ZEMCC included the Christian Church Monitoring Group, the Law Association of Zambia, the National Women's Lobbying Group, the Press Association of Zambia, the University of Zambia Students Union, and other nongovernmental organizations (Novicki, 1992, p. 16).

Belatedly, President Kaunda issued the invitation to foreign monitoring teams he had earlier resisted. The Carter Center together with the National Democratic Institute of International Affairs set up a Zambia voting observation team to advise local officials on the conduct of free and fair elections, thereby serving to demonstrate international support for the electoral process.

Forced by the pressure of events to grant concessions, Kaunda did so begrudgingly. Meanwhile his supporters in UNIP worked to undermine democratic advances. When the international observation team arrived, the *Times of Zambia* ran an advertisement denouncing the team members as part of a "big imperialist plot" with an "assignment to facilitate the removal of the UNIP government and replace it with a puppet one" (Novicki, 1992, p. 17).

The weeks and months before the election were tense. Two newspapers suddenly appeared: the *Eagle Express*, an obvious UNIP broadsheet, and the *Daily Express*, a propaganda sheet for the MMD (Maja-Pearce, 1992a, pp. 58–59). Both newspapers hurled accusations back and forth at respective political enemies and their supporters.

In the streets, it was open season for political thuggery, particularly among UNIP supporters. Maja-Pearce describes what he saw just before the Zambian election:

> More disturbing was the behavior of the party stalwarts, the otherwise unemployable hustlers recruited from the streets of Lusaka, whose vigilance in rooting out suspected members of the opposition was exceeded only by the brutality with which they dealt with them. Suddenly there would be a commotion, a helpless figure would be dragged from somewhere in the crowd, and six men were to be seen kicking him from one end of the ground to the other while the Great Humanist heaped personal abuse on individual members of the opposition and the police stood idly by. (1992a, p. 59)

In this atmosphere, the MMD feared it would be unable to gain access to the government-controlled media and that their political advertisements would not be run. To remedy this problem, the Press Association of Zambia (PAZA) won a high court injunction which forced temporary suspension of top civil servant post holders at the Zambia National Broadcasting Corporation and the *Times of Zambia* (Novicki, 1992, p. 15). The Supreme Court later reversed the injunction just before the elections.

During the earlier part of the campaign, monitoring groups found that the ZNBC did provide some balance in their coverage of the two sides. But by mid-September, with the election looming nearer, the ZNBC began to favor the UNIP. And for a time, the ZNBC *did* refuse to air MMD campaign spots until a court injunction forced them to do so. This was not, however, until *after* a judge had revoked this injunction and the MMD had compromised with the media by editing MMD commercials to soften their attacks on the government (Bjornlund, Bratton, and Gibson, 1992, pp. 419–20).

Surprisingly, after all this, the election took place in a peaceful atmosphere. Voters lined up in the 110 degree Fahrenheit heat and waited for hours to cast their ballots. Some had walked for miles to participate for the first time ever in this process (Novicki, 1992, p. 17).

The ballots were counted, and the international observation team was pleased to confirm the results. Frederick Chiluba of the MMD had won a landslide victory. International confirmation facilitated a rapid transition of power to the new political group (Novicki, 1992, p. 17).

Kaunda, to his credit, gracefully conceded defeat to the MMD. He clutched his characteristic white handkerchief and said apologetically to his supporters, "I tried to do my very best. We must accept the verdict of the Zambian people. This is the nature of multiparty elections. You win some and you lose some" (Novicki, 1992, p. 14).

Frederick Chiluba and the Movement for Multiparty Democracy had managed to win the first successful transition from a one-party to a multiparty state in all of anglophone Africa. But with the victory came staggering problems. Chiluba's new government inherited an international debt of over seven billion dollars, one of the largest per capita debts on the continent (Ham, 1992, p. 19).

The severe economic problems of Zambia have dulled the shine of Chiluba's achievement. Liberalization of the economy has put more products on the shelves but less money in the pockets of the people who would buy these goods. Freedom of expression has given way to increased industrial action, and there were more than 50 strikes during the first year of Chiluba's new government. There is already evidence of corruption among ministers of the new government (Ham, 1992, p. 19; Wunsch, Bratton, and Kareithi, 1992, p. 5).

After the election, Bwendo Mulenga, the managing editor of the *Times of Zambia*, and Stephen Moyo, the director of the Zambia National Broadcasting Corporation, were permanently removed from their posts (Ham, 1992, p. 19). The move was popular among journalists, who always resented the two figures because they were academics rather than trained journalists.

Frederick Chiluba appears to be committed enough to press freedom. He has promised that the press shall "never be stifled again." Still, the *New African* noted in March 1992 that "some of his cabinet colleagues do not agree with Chiluba" (Nyakutemba, 1992, p. 9). And a report produced for the democracy and governance unit of USAID's Africa bureau reveals deep-seated problems in Zambia's body politic.[11] Some of these problems reside deep within the psyches of the populace:

> Zambians are grievously under-informed about the new multiparty political system. Years of dependency on the patronage system maintained for 17 years under Kaunda and his UNIP party engendered deeply ingrained habits of deference to authority. (Wunsch, Bratton, and Kareithi, 1992, p. 6)

Nor do Zambians have much knowledge of the rights and responsibilities of citizenship, the written paraphernalia of democracy, the constitution, the various electoral codes, or legal procedures and processes. Rural dwellers and women, the most illiterate groups in the population, are particularly ignorant of their rights. And although the free and fair elections in Zambia were hailed as a milestone in African democracy, turnout was only about 45 percent, a reflection of practical problems—incomplete registration forms and difficulties with transport in rural areas, combined with the political alienation of ordinary people.

The habits of patronage seem deeply entrenched in the population, evidenced by "mass defections of voters and junior party officials from UNIP to the MMD" during 1992. Observers wonder whether the Chiluba government will be able to offer a political system based more on merit and the rule of law and less on cronyism (Wunsch, Bratton, and Kareithi, 1992, p. 7).

But Zambia does hold a certain promise. It is one of the most urbanized countries in Black Africa, with about 60 percent of the population living in cities. It also benefits from a literacy rate of about 76 percent, among the highest in sub-Saharan Africa.[12]

The news media is still uncertain of its role in the emerging democracy. Unlike the press under UNIP which sometimes attacked cabinet ministers, but never President Kaunda and his policies of "humanism," some elements of the new press attack Chiluba. And many members of the public are disquieted by this.

Meanwhile the character of the press has not altered overnight. Wunsch, Bratton, and Kareithi report echoes of the comments made by Mytton in 1983:

> Zambian journalists are generally poorly educated, poorly trained, and poorly paid compared to other professionals in the country. Fewer than one out of ten have a college degree. They have little motivation, suffer from low self-esteem, and enjoy a poor public image, fostered under the previous government, and continued under the new administration. (1992, pp. 10–11)

Journalism training facilities available in Zambia are also largely regarded as poorly equipped and poorly staffed (Wunsch, Bratton, and Kareithi, 1992, p. 11).[13]

The Kaunda regime worked consistently in Zambia to muzzle the press, and to inhibit its development. Wunsch, Bratton, and Kareithi describe this underdeveloped press legacy as it presents itself in the journalists themselves:

> Individually, most journalists strongly appreciate the need to provide a counter view to that of the government. Efforts to do so with their limited skills, however, tend to merely perpetuate some of the popular myths and misconceptions espoused in the past by opponents of political and economic reform. (1992, p. 10)

In other words, it is difficult for journalists to carve out for themselves an independent and distanced posture. Steeped in the oral tradition, the writing of Zambian journalists tends to be agonistic, aligning itself with one camp or another. As Wunsch, Bratton, and Kareithi note, "The media have a tendency of equating news with advocacy" (1992, p. 25).

The verdict seems to be divided on the press in Zambia. In March 1992, *New African* called the *Daily Mail* and *Sunday Express* "fiercely independent" (Nyakutemba, p. 9). Wunsch, Bratton, and Kareithi, in June that year, noted that these papers could hardly be considered more than "mouthpieces" for the MMD (1992, p. 10).

New African also glorified in the Press Association of Zambia's rejection of the new government's attempt to revive the idea of a press council, a proposal originally introduced in the heat of the New World Information Order debate. The *New African* lauded the PAZA for agreeing to work instead on a bill to set up its own press monitoring group, one which would help to ensure standards of credibility for journalists (Nyakutemba, 1992, p. 9). But Wunsch, Bratton, and Kareithi blasted the PAZA for assisting in the drafting of this legislation, calling it a "ruse to enact a law empowering the government to license journalists and regulate their conduct" (1992, p. 25). The bill presented to the new government contained no provision guaranteeing freedom of information as the PAZA had originally promised its members. On this subject, the USAID consultants comment ominously: "Some of the drafters of the bill have since been appointed to senior information management posts by the government" (1992, p. 25). Indeed, the notion of the press as the Fourth Estate in Zambia seems illusory at best.

As of June 1992, there were still only two printing presses in the country: Printpak Limited, which prints the *Times of Zambia*, and the Zambian Printing Company, which prints the *Daily Mail*. The lack of independent printing facilities has put a damper on more extensive development of the independent press for the time being. To date, there have been no new independent newspapers since the MMD took power. The *Mirror* and the *Weekly Post* still publish, both attempting to retain a distanced stand on political issues; the *Daily Mail* and its weekly supplement, the *Financial Mail*, initially scheduled for privatization by the MMD, were still in government hands in mid-1994.

Meanwhile, the MMD has begun reviving the rural press, tabloid papers which served as Kaunda's mouthpieces until the funds ran out at the end of the 1980s. There is considerable evidence that the new MMD government will use these papers as megaphones for their own policies (Wunsch, Bratton, and Kareithi, 1992, p. 12).

The MMD inherited a controlled structure for the media. The two mainstream daily papers, the *Times of Zambia* and the *Daily Mail*, were operated through the National Media Corporation (NAMECO), as was the Zambia National Broadcasting Corporation. The media were controlled through the office of the president, who appointed the newspapers' editors and the heads of radio and television. During the election campaign, the MMD pledged to privatize these media as a matter of urgency. But government media have already come to serve a public relations function for the Chiluba government, and the MMD in 1994 seemed disinclined to sell them off (Mwiinga, 1994, p. 60). The Zambia News Agency is a department within the Ministry of Information. Requests to decrease its gatekeeper function by allowing news organs to receive items directly from foreign news agencies, a move favored by the PAZA, had received no response from the government as of March 1992 (Nyakutemba, 1992, p. 10).

The press is threatened by legal statutes in Zambia as it is in so many other Black African states. In Zambia and elsewhere, enforcement of censorship laws has been relaxed for the time being. But they have not been expunged from the law codes. In Zambia, it is still a criminal offense to ridicule the head of state. Zambia's libel laws, considered among the most rigid of any in the world, do not recognize truth as a defense in libel cases. Many other statutes inhibit freedom of expression through the regulation of sedition, public morality, public order, and state security.

The *Index on Censorship* during 1992 reported numerous complaints about repression in the new regime. A Muslim radio program was banned on the grounds that Zambia is a predominantly Christian country. Certain television musicals were banned for their alleged immorality (May, 1992, p. 41). The culprit behind such actions appears to be the Reverend Stan Kristofor, a fundamentalist Christian, who is Chiluba's information minister (Nyakutemba, 1992, p. 9).

Although the new government intends to retain the ZNBC as a government service, it also plans to open the airwaves to private broadcasting. The new stations will be allowed to compete with the ZNBC, now once more subsidized by the government.[14] In June 1992, a telecommunications subcommittee was drafting new legislative proposals for the private electronic media. The legislation in preparation appeared highly restrictive: curbs on ownership by certain religious and political groups were suggested, as was the banning of some political and religious messages. A proscription on criticism of Zambia's foreign allies was even proposed! (Wunsch, Bratton, and Kareithi, 1992, p. 26).

Wunsch, Bratton, and Kareithi conclude that the strongest form of press control in Zambia is still the government's ownership of media institutions. Government ownership makes it all too easy to slip into the familiar and comfortable pattern of self-censorship, with the eye of the journalist on job security and possibly an eventual professional promotion (1992, p. 25).

These are the habits engendered by one-party rule and the system of patronage which maintained it. And the tendency toward sycophancy, also characteristic of systems of patronage, seems alive and well among Chiluba supporters. The independent-minded *Weekly Post* issue of October 29–31 reported as much just before the elections:

> But Chiluba has already found himself surrounded by many people who are little more than professional praise singers and they are looking for jobs if the MMD forms a government. They already call him "Your Excellency," some (quite senior people) even get down on their knees to talk to him. It is the kind of thing Kaunda has been used to for decades. (Quoted in Maja-Pearce, 1992a, p. 63)

When Adewale Maja-Pearce composed the article on Zambia for the *Index*, he pondered the future of the *Weekly Post*. A few months later, the USAID Democratic Initiatives team reported the arrest and subsequent questioning of the *Post*'s editor in conjunction with an article critical of Chiluba published by the paper (Wunsch, Bratton, and Kareithi, 1992, p. 24). On the issue, the team made a prescient comment: "The willingness of the new government to invoke [the law against ridiculing the head of state] has raised serious doubts about the government's commitment to scrapping or amending such laws" (1992, p. 25).

Observers were right to be leery about the new Zambian government's commitment to democracy. On March 4, 1993, President Chiluba declared a State of Emergency. Apparently the 17-month-old MMD government had acted out of alarm against an article printed in the state-run *Times of Zambia*. The article contained excerpts from a document called the Zero Option plan. The plan itself was apparently penned by high-ranking members of the opposition (the UNIP long headed by Kenneth Kaunda). The plan called upon Zambians to engage in civil disobedience, strikes, riots, and crime—all of this in an effort to dismantle the power of the MMD government.

In conjunction with the Emergency declaration, 14 members of the UNIP were arrested and detained without trial. Thus, by mid-1993, Chiluba found himself embroiled in contradictions of his own making. He declared that the fundamental freedoms of Zambians would be protected during the Emergency period, though the very purpose of such a declaration is to deny these rights.

Interestingly, Chiluba has allowed the Zambian media to cover the Emergency in full detail. UNIP and other opposition groups have protested the Emergency, and the Law Association of Zambia has criticized the government for its lethargy in revamping legal codes. These and other charges against the government have appeared in the Zambian press. Longtime Zambia observer Melinda Ham suggests that "all this criticism demonstrates the beginnings of a vibrant civic society. But the Emergency has also demonstrated how fragile Zambia's democracy is" (Ham, 1993, p. 16).

In 1994, it is yet unclear whether Zambia's experiment in transition to democracy will succeed or fail. Peter Kareithi, himself an exiled Kenyan journalist, has commented on the state of the African press during the transition period of the 1990s:

> African leaders are practicing managed change so that they can control the agenda of [political] reformation. Africans can never go back to treating their presidents like demigods. This does not mean that there is freedom for journalists. It means that journalists will be writing things that they were never able to write before but at greater risk. (Quoted in Brice, 1992, p. 51)

Kareithi's forecast came true again in 1993, when the office of the *Weekly Post* was twice stormed by cadres of the ruling party and a box carrying copies of the newspaper was later hijacked (Mwiinga, 1994, p. 60).

An uncertain future clearly looms over the press in Africa. Multipartyism and its cousin press freedom are tottering in Zambia. There are some ominous signs for the press on the continent's horizon. First, the press, the populace, and the new officials are unused to the new found freedoms. Many journalists have responded to their new liberties by producing a proliferation of opportunistic newspapers laying themselves wide open for the charge of unprofessional conduct. Cyclostyled broadsheets replete with dangerous lies, unfair comments, and unbalanced reports have emerged in almost all countries where the enforcement of press laws has been relaxed. Second, in other places, the privatization of the press in conditions of scarcity has only fueled the tendency to produce journalism for a fee. Third, the severity of the economic crisis inherited by new regimes, coupled with the need to enforce harsh economic measures, only further fuels popular discontent. In such an atmosphere the tendency to repress information (already in evidence in Benin and Zambia) can easily be heightened.

In francophone Africa, an opinion press has long been the model, and some journalists are even resistant to an information press. And anglophone West Africans lean to a more garrulous and popular variant of the opinion press, a wildly partisan style of journalism. The experience in Zambia seems to suggest that after the first dramatic blush with democracy, the players—politicians and civil servants, journalists, and the people—all tend to return to their ingrained habits. New regimes retain the old repressive laws if such laws suit their purposes. Elites merely switch camps to curry favor and enjoy the spoils of the new group in power.

Privatization of the electronic media holds some promise for the promotion of pluralism, but observers are cautious in their optimism. Wunsch, Bratton, and Kareithi report, for example, that Zambia is inviting inquiries from investors interested in establishing private radio and television in the country. To date, most of the interest has come from outsiders, mainly South Africans, and U.S.-based financial sources. As of June 1992, only two Zambian parties were among those showing interest in establishing private broadcasting ventures. And all inquiries to the Zambian government were for FM radio in urban areas (Wunsch, Bratton, and Kareithi, 1992, p. 26). Privatization of the Zambian airwaves could easily lead to a greater emphasis on entertainment and dependency on outside capital. Whether privatization will also lead to increased domestic freedom of expression will depend upon many factors, including the yet to be established framework of broadcast programming and news control, together with the relative dominance of commercial considerations.

I believe it is important to look to history for models of the development of pluralist perspectives. In the West, press freedom gradually grew with the rise of a new bourgeois class whose growth was promoted through increased mercantile activity. This growth increased with advances in shipping and related commercial activities associated with the development of new markets in the East Indies and the New World. The study of the flowering of press freedom in Europe is the study of the decline of monarchical regimes and their control over access to resources. In short, new markets brought together new ideas and newly capitalized groups who emerged from under the yoke of European feudal rulers. New capital, moreover, was available in the mercantile age because Europeans were able to wrest surplus value from raw materials and commercial ventures outside of Europe, one of the most profitable having been the slave trade (Amin, 1990, p. 137).

Press freedom in Africa will flower only if new sources of finance can be harnessed in a new economic order, i.e., if the management of capital can be wrested away from the all-controlling powers of centralized government on the one hand and from foreign-dominated government or multinational sources on the other. And as yet, there is little evidence that many newly elected African governments will be willing to give up their new found financial advantages. To be sure, parastatals are being rapidly sold off. But in Zambia, as elsewhere, there is widespread fear that the sale of public corporations will not be conducted in an equitable or transparent manner (Wunsch, Bratton, and Kareithi, 1992, p. 4). Indeed, there is clear evidence that MMD cabinet ministers and other well-connected elites in Zambia will use undue influence to once again carve out disproportionate shares of the national cake (Mwiinga, 1994, pp. 58–59). And as yet, there is little evidence that the economic liberalization policies demanded by external government funders and international banks will do little more than increase the dependency of Africa on the international capitalistic system.

Samir Amin maintains that Africa must return to its agrarian roots, find its center and feed itself, and rebuild its economic foundation through a revolution in agriculture (1990, pp. 8–9). He believes this action can emerge from a "polycentric" world order. This polyvalent mode of world social organization would extend and diversify the ties between Africa and the outside world (1990, pp. 228–34).

Such a view requires that where formerly only linkages for trade existed, there should now be bonds of solidarity created to connect other issues—the environment, human rights, and labor demands. Such ties should involve noncommercial, nonprofit groups—women's organizations, development associations, and sister city alliances. Through these linkages, a plurality of voices can resound with increasing strength. It is hoped that such a pluralistic social network will offer an alternative to the centralizing paradigm of "modernity." For the modern mode of world organization has wrought great havoc on the African continent in the nineteenth and twentieth centuries.

9 | Modernization, Development, and the Communitarian Social Agenda

THIS BOOK HAS made only passing reference to social information theory. This chapter will now take up some of these important theoretical threads in an attempt to tie social information theory more closely to the African media situation and its prospects for the future. In so doing, it will review theories of "modernism," in preparation for a proposal to adopt a radical postmodern paradigm as a solution to Africa's current dilemma.

The Modernity Model

The creation of nation-states in Africa represents a wholesale experiment in the imposition of the modernity model (Davidson 1992). The colonization of Africa was a social and economic process tied to the imperial order and represented a new wave of capitalist expansion of the dominant European powers of the late nineteenth century. The bequeathing of the status of the nation-state on the African colonies in the 1960s was an historical event resulting from changes in the world economic order, changes brought about by World War II and the contracting power of these European states, especially Great Britain and France. By the time this occurred, an African elite class had established close ties with Europe. These linkages—economic, political, educational, and cultural—rendered implicit the adoption by African political elites of the Western European mode of social and political organization, the nation-state, and its economic support system, industrial capitalism.[1] And for the last 30 years, Africa has had to live with the political and economic inheritance it was bequeathed. These two components are the cornerstones of the modern social system.

Two overarching legacies acquired by the African mass media at independence are worth repeating. The first has been the need to foster and promote nationalism or national consciousness. As we have seen, efforts in this direction have taken up the greater part of the media's energy and efforts. We have also observed that the exigencies of nationalism have fostered tightly controlled and highly centralized media systems. Central control has been aided and abetted by a system of political patronage through which rewards for service to the federal government have been distributed among those closest to the focal points of political power. These persons/groups have comprised an elite class of Black Africans, a group with modern Western educations, a class whose economic survival is tied to continued social and economic interchange with the modern industrialized world.

Until quite recently (the late 1980s and early 1990s), the elite class in Africa has been largely content to share the spoils of the patronage system and to parrot the value of the modernity model for their countries. But the modern social order in Black Africa has largely disenfranchised a good three-quarters of Black Africa's population, namely the rural masses and most of the urban proletariat.

Political patronage and its operation by alienated elite classes can be looked upon as the sociostructural aspect of the postcolonial African social system. They are, in the words of Clifford Geertz, the "causal-functional" mechanisms of social organization. Geertz reminds us that another mechanism exists in the ordering of societies. This is the "logico-meaningful" level of social functioning, the means through which beliefs are sustained and social norms are upheld (Geertz, 1973, p. 145). On this level, most Africans participate and share in a precolonial culture, described in this volume as an oral culture.

Africans, even the highly urbanized elite, still retain a good deal of the beliefs and values fostered by the precolonial *Weltanschauung*. This world view, organized on the basis of kinship and still tied to rural areas, has served to humanize African society, including the mass media systems.

Geertz posits that strain in social systems is caused by a mismatch (in his terminology, a lack of integration) between causal-functional modes of social organization and its logico-meaningful structures. He notes that because of the phenomenon some have called "cultural lag," there is always some strain, some incongruity and tension, between these components of a social system. These irregularities are the source of social change in social systems (1973, p. 145). It is at moments of intense strain that the most dramatic social change occurs.

The ideology of folk society, like any "ideology"[2] is subject to misuse and manipulation. It can be applied out of context and skillfully used to mask irregularities in society. As Geertz notes, ideology provides a "symbolic outlet for emotional disturbances generated by social disequilibrium" (1973, p. 204). Under the guise of promoting a unified national polity, the oral tradition has supported and bolstered corrupt systems of political patronage. In the postcolonial era the vehicle or channel of this ideology has been primarily the African mass media. In promoting patronage, the media have manipulated the symbols and misapplied the values of precolonial Africa in their bid for national unity. In the process they have become the griots or praise singers of the modern political order which has governed Africa for the last thirty years.

The second exigency thrust upon Africa and its media through colonial contact has been the need to promote "modernization." Since independence, economists, among others, have invited Africa to partake in the prosperity of the industrialized world by adopting a course of "development." Development implied industrialization, a process which was seen as the cornerstone of the Western world's astonishing ascent to preeminence in world affairs and its unparalleled ability to provide its citizens with material well-being.

The path to development for Africa (and indeed for all of the developing world) was conceived at first as a mechanical series of steps Africa could take in order to resemble the West in its political and economic behavior (Servaes, 1991, p. 54). This has meant that Africa's people must be enjoined to adopt economic and social practices which would bring them into the modern world of monied economies. The market economy would foster industrialization, industrialization would foster economic growth, economic growth would bring about a more "rational" society, and rational society would support representative democracy.

The order in which these events were projected to occur depended largely upon the scholarly discipline of the theorist advocating this development. But theorists were quite consistent in their belief that traditional Africa had little or nothing to contribute to this new quest for modernity. Indeed they believed that precolonial Africa, its social organization, its mode of production, and its systems of beliefs were counterproductive to the quest for modernity. Africans were believed to be clannish, present-tense oriented, superstitious, and ill-adapted to change. They were capable of loyalty only to their own kin; they produced only what they consumed; they quaked before powerful forces of good and evil; they clung excessively to tradition (Malamah-Thomas, 1987, p. 61). Theorists felt all of these beliefs and attitudes and the behaviors they engendered must be expunged. There was a need to reconstitute African peoples for the modern world. The mass media were enlisted in this program of development for Africa.

We have seen that under the guise of promoting development, African governments rushed in and established or extended mass media systems. And under the guise of promoting development, UNESCO, bilateral aid organizations, together with private investors in some cases, assisted African governments in their efforts. But we have also observed that structural distortions in African society created conditions through which the elites benefited disproportionately from this aid in communication, in development, and in development communication.[3] We have further seen that elites have often exhibited deep ambivalence about development projects and they have been hesitant to embrace efforts to extend uncontrolled communication into rural areas. Recognizing the potential of these activities to awaken the masses, elites have often served to slow the pace of development in rural areas and to redirect its aims and messages.

Over the years, the technique of "doing development" and its corollary communication component have undergone their own evolution. Thus, "development communication" has changed along with them.

Mass Media and Development

The theory and practice of promoting development began with a globalistic assumption about the media's power to promote positive change in Third World countries (Lerner 1958; Schramm 1964). Vague and naive, it implied that the very introduction of media would lead to development (West and Fair, 1993, p. 92). The assumptions of the 1950s and 1960s soon proved to be wanting. Gradually they made way for evolution of more focused theories.[4]

By the early 1970s, communication experts began to use the "diffusion of innovations" approach to development. This diffusionist perspective recommended the use of scientifically designed procedures to trace the flow of messages promoting the adoption of specific modern ideas or practices through society. It was largely concerned with the cognitive stages through which a target individual passes before adopting a course of action. The perspective assumed that messages concerning development must perforce emanate from the top of society (the social planners and the development agencies) and that its targets were individuals rather than groups. "Diffusion of innovations" was both sensitive to the salience of messages for audience targets and to the effects of communication channels or communication contexts within which the communication operated (Rogers 1962).

A related approach to development communication was that propounded by the school of "social marketing." Social marketing was derived from advertising techniques perfected in the United States. Its use has been harnessed in promoting discrete observable and measurable behaviors, such as the use of oral rehydration therapy or children's inoculation services. Social marketing stresses the importance of audience research, campaign and project monitoring, and message pretesting among individual message targets.

Both social marketing and diffusionist approaches have enjoyed considerable success within their own terms. Yet they can be faulted for their failure to better engage "targets" in their own development. This is because their approach to development is "top-down" and assumes that change agents, experts, elites, and outsiders are in possession of the solutions to the problems of African villagers.

The use of the individual as a target of communication is an added problem implied through these strategies. The community-based lifestyle of villag-

ers soon becomes evident to researchers who have difficulty isolating rural villagers to complete interview schedules in the service of Western-designed projects (Obeng-Quaidoo, 1985b and 1987). It is also apparent to instructors
teaching research techniques to would-be social marketers (Bourgault 1989).
The difficulties experienced in the research process underlie a broader problem
of individual orientation in project design. Development aimed at individuals
has often resulted in improvement of the standard of living of only the wealthiest, the most Westernized of the targets. It has therefore exacerbated the social
inequality it is ostensibly designed to mitigate (Beltran, 1976, p. 21). Today
many scholars caution developers to attend to the disparate distribution of
power in society (Riley, 1990, p. 302). To stem the tide of uneven development,
Esman and Uphoff, for example, advocate channeling development through
traditional rural *groups*: age-graders, female choruses, and traditional warrior
associations (1984, p. 240).

In the mid to late 1980s, the thrust in development communication shifted
once again to small-scale projects where developers worked closely with small
communities, from the ground up, helping villagers to craft projects of their
own design. The communication component of these projects stresses interaction among villagers and change agents, increasingly urging dialogue in the
change processes. Many of today's development communication projects ask
villagers themselves to create communication for change through active participation in broadcast efforts. Such projects have included Kenya's Homa Bay
radio station (Mills and Kangawa, 1983, p. 20); Ghana's *Wonsuom* clubs
(Obeng-Quaidoo, 1988, pp. 77–94); Zimbabwe's FAMWZ/Radio 4 project
for women's rural development (Moyo, 1990, p. 1920); and, until recently, Liberia's Rural Communication Network (see chapter 4). Initiatives such as
these engage villagers in fund-raising activities, in site construction, in advisory board service, in broadcast production/delivery, in program feedback dia-
logues, and even in the staging of village-based development dramas.

What has occurred in development circles at the planning level has been
a redefinition of development. Planners have understood that macroeconomic
measures of "progress" mask societal inequality and detract attention from
a host of pressing social and educational needs.[5] They have come to see that
growth in the Gross National Product for a given country, for example, rarely
implies improvement in the quality of life for a substantial number of its people. Thus, planners have gradually come to define development in terms other
than economic. With growing sensitivity to human needs, development agents
increasingly reject "top-down" development, preferring projects which initiate
from the people themselves. Proponents of development have seen that rural
folk must be more than simple "targets" of initiatives; rather, they must be the
driving force in these efforts. In theoretical terms, the *transportation* view of
communication, wherein messages are sent through space from a "source" to

a "receiver," has been replaced with a *ritual* view of communication, wherein messages are shared in time by persons within a social grouping (McQuail, 1987, pp. 44–45).

Planners have come to see that development is first and foremost a process of "conscientization," wherein people take stock of their situation and devise as a *group* the steps needed to improve the conditions of their lives.[6] These processes are seen as profoundly "empowering," enabling the most disenfranchised individuals and groups to take control over their own lives and engage in collective action designed to maximize social well-being for the local community. It is noteworthy that such activities are often at variance with the overt or covert designs of their national governments. In conjunction with these shifts of emphasis in development has come a gradual sense of disquiet, in sociological circles worldwide, with the entire project of "modernity" (Giddens 1990).

Modernity's Failure

In the West, dissatisfaction of ordinary citizens with the effects of hyper-individualism, a by-product of modern life, has been building for some time. People appear to recognize that the materialist values and consumerist lifestyles they have wrought have brought about a sense of purposeless and a feeling of personal and political alienation (Bellah 1985). A major social phenomenon of the late twentieth century, for example, is the move by younger Americans to small towns. In these communities they hope to rediscover tradition and find meaning and quality of life through the celebration of group values. The quest for meaning through social interconnectedness is said to represent an antidote to the excesses of modern life. This trend is one of the obvious indicators of the new social world order presently emerging.

Theorists have noted that the modernity model is wanting for Africa, just as it is for other parts of the world, for the by-products of modern life, with its never-ending cycle of industrial production and consumption, have been ecological devastation, economic dualism, unlivable cities, high crime rates, and industrial diseases.

In the Western democracies, modern civil society has operated to a greater or lesser degree to rectify some of these imbalances and defects, thereby mitigating for its own people a portion of modernity's most nefarious by-products. Some of this Western governmental activity has further added to the misery of Third World polities. Western environmental regulation, to cite one example, promotes the export of polluting industries abroad; and Western trade negotiation, to mention another, shores up the buying power of Western consumers to the detriment of Third World producers.

The effects of modernity thus have had dual negative effects on Third

World people. Modernity has lured the political and social elites of the developing world into compliance with the modern system, thereby inhibiting the growth of the very institutions which might offer some protection for Third World masses. Meanwhile industrialized societies have exported some of the more pernicious by-products of the modern world. It used to be assumed that the positive trade-offs of modernization would be worth the drawbacks in most countries. Today, theorists disagree on the matter. What is clear, however, is that the modernity model for Africa has been utterly disappointing.

The modicum of industrialization on the African continent, for example, has extracted a very high price. With industrialization has come urbanization, but hardly the formation of a comfortable working class. A combination of low wages paid to workers and other distortions in the African economies has led to the ghettoization of African cities. Urbanization in Africa preceded industrialization in many cases and has occurred with or without the significant growth of industry. The burgeoning state bureaucracies, themselves creations of the modernist enterprise, have served as magnets for would-be urban dwellers, luring them away from unrewarding, undervalued agricultural production with the hope of a better life.

A Look at Foreign Aid

The motives behind foreign aid are mixed, and foreign aid policy is often still very much tied to the Western model of development (Korten, 1990, p. 144). Nevertheless, an evolution in thinking and project design has been occurring upward, from the field where development is conducted, to the centers of power in the Western metropoles where policy is formulated.

Conscious of the distortions within African societies, many development organizations (themselves beneficiaries of these same distortions on a global level) are attempting to circumvent existing African governmental and social structures, in order to deliver aid directly to the "people." So-called grass roots projects have had mixed success in aiding the neediest. Their ability to function well at this level depends upon a nexus of factors. These include, among others: the source of funding of development projects; the overt and covert aims of projects; the strength of project design; the attractiveness of project operations; the personalities and talents of expatriate and local operatives; and the extent of their commitment to empowering local people in the face of government resistance and elite intransigency.

One example of a grass roots project is the Liberian Rural Communications Network. The driving philosophy of that project was essentially decentralist, as were many of its practices and projects. As someone who worked closely with the LRCN project, I am comfortable in asserting that the techniques employed therein were rooted in a genuine interest in village-level participation and empowerment. These techniques included the broadcast of programs in local languages by local producers; the pretesting of programs together with the solicitation of audience feedback by field assistants; the collection, preservation, and transmission of traditional cultural material; and the incorporation of target support through the use of volunteers producers, local advisory boards, and community-based fund-raising activities. But the LRCN project suffered from the contradictions inherent in all large-scale government-to-government aid projects. The political positioning of such projects often compromises their best intentions. However decentralist they may be in their design and their outreach, such undertakings have powerful centripetal forces. In the end, these projects serve to reinforce the national government of the country in which they are sited. This is particularly counterproductive when the regime they help to bolster is less than benign. Such was the case with the Liberian government of Samuel Doe (1980–90), a major abuser of human rights in Africa (Tarr, 1993, pp. 74–75).

The Liberian Rural Communications Network was only one of many projects supported by the U.S. government in Liberia during the Doe era. There were other projects with equally good aims and with similarly sound operating procedures, each promoting decentralized development and local empowerment. These included the Improved Efficiency in Learning and the Primary Education Projects, which fostered learner-based teaching methods (Thiagarajan, 1993, p. 3), the Control of Childhood Communicable Disease Project, which promoted and funded mobile vaccination clinics in local communities, and the Revolving Drug Fund, which provided credit needed by local clinics to maintain a stock of frequently used pharmaceuticals. But there were aid operations of a more sinister nature, notably the training and equipping of Doe's military forces by the U.S. Defense Military Attaché (Clough, 1992, pp. 89–95).

It is useful to examine how good projects can come to support bad leaders. The momentum of Washington or any other Western government is rarely (if ever) synchronized with events occurring in Africa. A case in point is again the LRCN project, whose initial planning began in 1977 (Institute for International Research, 1989, p. 3). While USAID officers and interested sectors in Liberia were busy planning a locally responsive, grass roots radio network, the government of William Tolbert fell, and the ruthless Samuel Doe came to replace him.[7] Already by then the course was set. The United States had spent two years preparing the implementation of this project and was eager to normalize relations with the new government and proceed with business.[8] A pattern of patronage had long governed relations between the United States and its client state, Liberia. This no doubt contributed to the rush to normalize relations with Doe (Liebenow, 1987, pp. 145–47; Bourgault, 1994b).

Based upon the lessons of Liberia (together with other U.S. aid debacles in

Africa, notably in Zaire and in Somalia),[9] some observers have been tempted to call for a moratorium on all government-to-government aid, or at least all U.S. government aid in Africa.

Do the "mixed motives" of government foreign aid or their structural inflexibility suggest that all government aid should be abandoned? It must be recognized that foreign aid has its own lobby within home governments and its own national momentum. The professionalization of foreign aid suggests that foreign aid is not in any case likely to disappear.[10]

Moreover, as Jan Knippers Black argues in *Development in Theory and Practice*, many projects are able to find a way around the less than altruistic aid motivations of Western governments:

> It is quite common for agents in the field or even agency directors, to have motives very different from those of the governments they are presumed to represent. Even USAID, which has been drawn into U.S. efforts in several countries to destabilize democratic governments, is a multifaceted agency with as many motives as it has officers, field agents, and contractees. Along with projects undoubtedly designed to propagandize, divide or pacify, it also funds many projects having the potential of promoting *desarrolo* [self-generated development] as opposed to *desarrollismo* [top-down development]. And even those which are launched as *desarrollismo* may eventually be turned inside out by their intended beneficiaries. Paul Fritz, deputy director of AID-Ecuador in 1982, said that the agency's most effective programs happen by serendipity—through informal contacts and response to "targets of opportunity," which have nothing to do with what Washington happens to be pushing. (1991, p. 189)

And, as we have seen, the work of development has churned up its own contradictions and produced its own rather healthy evolution.

Recommending the abolition of all U.S. bilateral aid to Africa and elsewhere is an extreme position to take in the light of obvious positive advances which have come from some of the projects. It is far more reasonable to argue as does Clough that America and other industrialized nations should adopt a policy of doing "no harm" in Africa. Enshrined in this "no harm" policy would be four cardinal principles: (1) providing no weapons and no military aid for any of Africa's government or opposition movements; (2) supporting no government that does not guarantee basic civil liberties, including freedom of speech, free association and due process of law; (3) providing no funds for African political parties or candidates; and (4) channeling at least 50 percent of bilateral aid through nongovernmental organizations (Clough, 1992, pp. 117–18).

To throw all U.S. or other bilateral funding out would be sheer folly, given the potential and the size of these funds. Nevertheless, there are alternative ways to better channel government funds.

I have repeatedly referred to the LRCN project because it throws up so many of the difficulties and the contradictions which have been inherent in development. It was a large-scale, capital-intensive, government-to-government project that involved elites and government bureaucracies.[11]

Because of these structural conditions, the LRCN project suffered from the same problems which have beset many previous efforts in development communication. In chapters 4 and 5, we saw that UNESCO and private investors rushed into Africa just after independence and promoted the installation of the first generation of mass communication systems. Politics and cost came to dictate the content of these systems. And the African mass media became, in the main, exhortatory mouthpieces who substituted redundant government bulletins for information and who transmitted cheap, imported advertiser-supported entertainment fare for diversion. This mix of programming satisfied the interests of both politicians and investors, providing the former with a podium and the latter with a return on investment.

We saw that UNESCO promoted literacy campaigns in rural areas using radio throughout the 1960s. But the governments were far more interested in using these radio literacy campaigns to engage in *sensibilisation*, political sensitizing of the rural peoples. Television was harnessed to promote education in Côte d'Ivoire and elsewhere, but gradually such educational systems imploded in their own contradictions.

And we have noted that most of the large-scale communication for development efforts (together with many of the smaller ones) have floundered, through lack of funds or government commitment, and have slowly died of strangulation once the project planners and the aid-givers have gone. Patronage-ridden administrations supported by and beholden to elites are unable or unwilling to support projects targeted at rural groups, those largely disenfranchised from the political process.

If repeated failure of communication in Africa to foster the intended development has led to an evolution in development strategies, this evolution owes part of its genesis to "development's" sharpest critics.

Dependency Theory

It was long before the 1980s that objections were raised to the modernization paradigm heretofore described. As early as the late 1950s, Latin American scholar P. Baran proposed the social theory of *dependency*. Baran argued that modernization schemes for the Third World required imported technologies. This in itself created technological and financial dependence on the West. He observed, moreover, that the social structure in most Third World countries kept the demand for goods limited to a small group of upper-middle-class consumers. This fostered economic dualism. Drawing from Marxism, Baran and the proponents of dependency theory argued that the international division of labor was the most significant obstacle to widespread development. The proponents of this theory, often known in the literature as *dependistas*, argued that Third World nations should try to detach themselves from dependence on the West. But Third World economies (including those of Africa) were already tied to the modern world. Forsaking Western capitalist masters, in practice, merely meant adopting social Eastern ones. Thus, Julius Nyerere of Tanzania established close links with the Peoples' Republic of China; Sekou Touré of Guinea and Mengistu Haile-Mariam of Ethiopia became tied with the Soviet Union and the Eastern Bloc.

The communication component of the dependency paradigm has become known as *media imperialism* or *cultural imperialism*. Within this theoretical framework, scholars focus their analyses on the structures of ownership of the technology of communication. Here it is argued that since communication technologies—satellite services, telecommunication and computer hardware, etc.—are all owned by the major industrial giants, the purchase or use of these technologies by developing nations further cements dependency (Schiller 1969; Sussman and Lent 1991). These scholars argue further that communication hardware ultimately spreads the demand for software, chiefly entertainment fare whose production is again dominated by interlocking corporate Western and Japanese giants. The media imperialism school notes, moreover, that mass communication leads to the demand for more consumer goods, thereby spreading consumerist/capitalist values around the globe (Mattelart, Delcourt, and Mattelart 1984; Schiller 1989).

Most proponents of cultural imperialism adhere to the principles of *hegemony theory*, which argues that capitalist mass media influence world consciousness so that the world economic order seems "natural." The media deflect any attempts to alter the status quo by transforming and trivializing social movements, turning these efforts into entertaining fare or into commercial announcements (Becker, Hedebro, and Paldan 1986).[12] Through their hegemonic power, the rich industrialized nations are said to dominate world consciousness, promoting values and behaviors congenial to the prosperity of the capitalistic system (Marcuse 1964). Meanwhile, the capitalistic system continues to extract labor and/or raw materials from the periphery states (the Third World). Under capitalism, these materials are turned into manufactured products which are then resold to developing countries at considerable profit. This system keeps the peripheral states in perpetual impoverishment and contributes to the further enrichment of the core states of the West.[13]

Indeed, the last 30 years have seen a massive transfer of wealth from the poor to the rich nations. In 1960, the wealthiest 20 percent of the world's countries had incomes 30 times larger than the poorest 20 percent. By 1990, the richest 20 percent were accruing 60 times the income of their poor nation counterparts (UNDP, 1992, p. 1). Per capita income in the poorest region of the world, sub-Saharan Africa, dropped from $560 in 1980 to $450 (in 1980 dollars) in 1988. During the same period, per capita income in the industrialized countries increased from $11,000 to $13,000 (Cook, 1989, p. 3; cited in Black, 1991, p. 7).

Africa's dismal debit sheet, with its negative balance of payments, suggests that the continent's economic plight has reached crisis proportions. And since 1983, the IMF has drained $3 billion out of Africa in debt servicing (Brittain, 1993, p. 7)! While the World Bank is predicting growth rates of 4.7 percent for the developing world, the figures specific to Africa are far less promising. Economic growth is expected to rise during the 1990s from between only 2.0 to 3.7 percent, all of which will be counteracted by Africa's high average population growth rate of 3 percent (Tolba, 1992, p. 178). And the number of Africa's poor could well increase from 200 million to 300 million, nearly 45 percent of the projected population by the year 2000 (World Bank 1993; cited in Brummer, 1993, p. 21).

Unlike certain other states, notably the Pacific Rim nations and some Latin American countries where economic growth rates are predicted to reach a high of 7 percent (Brummer, 1993, p. 21), no African nation seems poised to move away from its peripheral position within the world economic order. Samir Amin comments that the differences between some of the more prosperous developing countries and Africa contain a warning we would do well to heed:

> If in Asia and Latin America, the margin of adjustment to world development is still broad enough to contain the expectation (or illusion) of bourgeois national crystallization, in Africa and the Arab world, there is almost no such scope. More than elsewhere there is a stark alternative: going forward quickly to a national and popular plan or perishing (sometimes in a literal sense through famine). (1990, p. 207)

Samir Amin's *Maldevelopment*, from which the above quotation is taken, documents the supreme failure of the modernization model in Africa. So severe was the plight of Africa, he observed, writing just before the end of the Cold War, that his advocacy of a new world order resounded like a plea: "The only remaining hope is for wisdom. Acceptance of a plurality of productive systems, political visions, and cultures requires reconstitution within a *polycentric* [emphasis mine], regionalized perspective" (1990, p. 223).

Recent advances in social and communication theory amplify Amin's notion of polycentrism, advocating models of communitarian social organization. Calls for a new world social order are coming from a plurality of voices. We have seen that Marxist-inspired thinking critiqued the modernity model, recommending disengagement from the Western capitalist system. Since the end of the Cold War the African nations who depended upon the Eastern bloc, hardly more successful, are scrambling to reinvent themselves. We have noted that Africanists such as Samir Amin have clearly outlined the failure of the model in Africa. And we have observed that development communication, originally implemented top-down and originally favoring national markets, industry and technology, is now evolving toward a more participatory model favoring small-scale, sustainable improvements in people's lives. And we have remarked on the West's own disquiet with what Giddens calls "the project of modernity" (1990).

Toward a New World Order

Recent advances in social and communication theory amplify Amin's notion of polycentrism, proposing models of "communitarian" social organization. If the key concept of modern social organization was *progress*, the key concept of communitarian social theory is *interdependence*. Communitarians such as Leslie Sklair, Majid Tehranian, Johan Galtung, E. F. Schumacher, Ivan Illich, Jürgen Habermas, just to name a few, note that modern industrialization has given way to the information society. And the information society with its highly centralizing communication and information technologies has fostered a new era of global *interdependence*.

Sociologists note that satellite communications have been used mainly to promote communication between elites, the collection of military and commercial information, and the global transmission of entertainment (Sklair, 1991, p. 146). But Tehranian informs us that information technologies have always shown a Janus face—they have served centralizing as well as devolutionary trends, unifying as well as disintegrating forces, and homogenizing as well as pluralizing values (1990, p. 65).

Global communication technology allows businesses to better gather information to exploit new markets, but it also permits groups concerned with protecting these resources to link up with distant allies to stem this resource exploitation. Multinationals use data transmission facilities to transmit financial information supporting their activity, but a whole new generation of Third World cooperatives use computerized mail and direct marketing to sell "rainforest friendly products" and crafts produced by self-help groups to eager world consumers.[14]

The information society, indeed information technologies, as Tehranian observes, all have their own centralizing and decentralist tendencies. For every data bank containing psychographic profiles of targets for commercial industrial goods, there springs another data bank bearing a list of potential supporters of communitarian principles: human/animal rights advocates, environmental protectors, women's advocates, free-speech proponents, and so on.

In the wake of the global information order has come the increased production of knowledge. The information generated not only keeps us abreast of the latest threats to the market but also the latest onslaughts to the environment. With the globalization of the world's social system has come a heightened awareness of the fragility of the planet. The ability to wage wars of massive destruction, enhanced by sophisticated computer-assisted weaponry and global surveillance systems, has also made requisite the need to contain weaponry through dialogue. The ability to locate, through surveillance computers, tracks of rainforest accessible for hardwood harvesting has also brought with it the painful realization of the rainforest's rapid disappearance.

A by-product of the information society has been the formation of numerous interest groups, groups of individuals who share common interests and perspectives. Elise Boulding writes that the idea of globe-spanning associations, scarcely a century old, is one of the most striking phenomena of the twentieth century. It is based on the "new-old" precept that humankind has common interests. Writing in 1988, Boulding reported the existence of 18,000 nongovernmental organizations worldwide (1988, p. 35).[15]

Most of these groups are nonprofit organizations. Michael Clough, Senior Fellow for Africa, Council on Foreign Relations, calls the collectivity of American nongovernmental organizations "America's Third Sector" (1992, p. 119). The name is appropriate as the United States is particularly blessed with nonprofit organizations. Peter Drucker calls the nonprofit sector "the fastest growing part of American society" (1989, p. 196). Clough notes that in 1989 the *World Almanac* listed 21,911 U.S.-based nonprofit organizations alone (1992, p. 71). Michael O'Neill points out that the yearly budget of the American nonprofit sector is greater than the annual budget of all but seven nations in the world (1990, pp. 1–2).

Today these groups link with international counterparts through computer networks, facsimile machines, telex systems, and, in some places, interactive cable television. The global information technologies make cross-national group alliances possible in a way hardly imagined 20 years ago.

Bridging the Gap: A Handbook to Linking Citizens of the First and Third Worlds lists more than 200 American-based organizations actively involved with Third World issues and peoples (Benjamin and Freedman 1989). Many of these—Habitat for Humanity, Oxfam, US-South Africa Sister Community Project, Grassroots International, International Voluntary Service, Plenty USA, Physicians for Human Rights, and so on—are actively engaged in projects and linkages in Africa.

Boulding argues that international nongovernmental organizations (INGOs) have been in the forefront of political change lobbying for constructive foreign policy of nation-states. The YWCA, for example, has established peace sites in over 70 countries, operating peace education centers and nuclear free zones.

Similar groups, such as Rotary International, have promoted scholarly exchanges, thereby assisting in education for world citizenship (1988, p. 39). INGOs produce thousands of newsletters calling for local grass roots and national lobbying efforts over such global concerns as peace and environmental protection, human rights, and free speech.

In the information arena, an array of new groups such as the Institut Panos, Article 19, the Index on Censorship, the Committee to Protect Journalists, and the Women's Institute for Freedom of the Press have recently been formed. They have joined the ranks of older press organizations such as the Commonwealth Press Association, the International Press Institute, and the Investigative Reporters and Editors. Such groups band together to protect journalists, i.e., to raise legal fees needed to defend prosecuted journalists and to lobby governments who detain journalists without trial.

Telecommunication linkages make it possible for these groups to maintain contact with local press groups in Africa, rapidly circulating information about the latest harassment of journalists and quickly mobilizing voices to pressure governments. These linkages permit heretofore silent voices in Africa and elsewhere to be heard.

New human rights groups, such as Africa Watch, Asia Watch, and Liberia Watch liaise with such older groups as Amnesty International and also link up with local human rights groups and empower them to demand change. The role of local democracy movements in Zambia, Benin, and Mali has been a key component in the movements for multiparty democracy.

While many INGOs are new, some of them represent an earlier genre of the nonprofit organization, the religiously affiliated philanthropic group. Church groups have long been recognized as some of the most cost-effective distributors of foreign aid. In many places, church groups have been able to bypass entrenched elites with their projects, relying instead on the efforts of highly committed, idealistically driven indigenes.

In the 1980s, INGOs collected several billion dollars, funds which were matched and augmented by many government aid agencies. By 1983, INGOs controlled one tenth of all bilateral assistance (Staudt, 1991, p. 183).

The U.S. government, slow to respond to famine in Ethiopia, ultimately provided food aid through relief channels set up by more than 40 private voluntary organizations. Michael Clough describes the important role played by INGOs in Ethiopia:

> When in the crisis, aid began to flow into the country, private agencies such as CARE, Lutheran World Services, and World Vision and their local counterparts assumed responsibility for transporting and distributing relief supplies. Without the private voluntary organizations (PVOs) and the local infrastructure they helped to build, Washington would not have been able to

respond effectively to the famine crisis. Just as important, while the U.S. government strictly limited its operations to the provision of emergency relief, private groups set up programs to address long-term needs. Because of the efforts of the PVOs, thousands of Ethiopians were employed and trained, thus enhancing the country's human infrastructure. (1992, p. 107)

Catholic Relief Services promoted self-reliance in Ethiopia. It now has 130 relief workers, all but two of whom are Ethiopian. And according to Clough, international relief efforts in that country did not help Ethiopian President Mengistu Haile Mariam to survive as some U.S. government officials had feared. The world focus on famine in Ethiopia, largely brought about by INGO relief efforts, embarrassed Mengistu and his supporters and led to his demise (Clough, 1992, p. 107). Meanwhile, through INGO training, the Tigrean People's Liberation Front and the Eritrean People's Liberation Front established viable networks of relief assistance. The strength of the Eritrean group was superbly manifest in the near total turnout and the all but unanimous (99.8 percent) "yes" vote in the 1993 referendum for Eritrean independence (Jouandet, 1993, p. 13). Even more astonishing was the fact that Eritrean referenda were conducted outside the Horn of Africa, in cities to which Eritreans had fled. In these centers the turnout was also near total, an indication of the strength of the EPLF movement and its ability to foster worldwide linkages (Sheckler, 1993, personal communication). The 30-year struggle of the organization has given the group a chance to reshape the aims of their society. And the new government of Eritrea has a host of plans for the continuance of grass roots development and the empowering of women's groups (Jouandet, 1993, p. 13).

The training of local operatives is an important part of the work of the INGOs. In 1986, David Korten described the development of an INGO in terms of stages or generations. In the first stage, INGOs are concerned primarily with emergency relief assistance. In the second, they move to "small-scale, self-reliant local development," strengthening the mechanisms to help people meet their own needs. In the third, they progress toward "sustainable systems development," working to change policy at the local and national level (Korten 1986). Korten's newer work has added a fourth generation which aims to foster "people-centered development" on a global scale. This means the work of INGOs must proceed through "people power" to reinvent the social, political, and economic arrangement at the root of the disparities between the north (the industrialized nations) and the south (the developing nations) (Korten, 1990, p. 124). This means chipping away at the modernity model itself.

Voluntary organizations are rapidly increasing in the Third World, including Africa. Alan Durning has estimated that in 1984 there were over 16,000 local women's groups operating in Kenya. By 1988, this figure stood at 25,000.

A similar explosion of grass roots activity has taken place in Zimbabwe after the 1980 transfer to African rule (Durning, 1989, p. 71). And in the Sahelian region, there is a unique African peasant self-help network known as 6–5. Entirely run by farmers, it stretches across nine countries, includes 3,500 active farmer groups, and involves 200,000 persons (Pradervand, 1990, p. xiv).

Because of the efficiency of voluntary organizations and their success in penetrating the "grass roots," Clough advises the U.S. government to adopt a policy of channeling at least 50 percent of its foreign aid through NGOs (1992, p. 118). He also recommends that 10 percent of U.S. aid funds be set aside to help build and strengthen America's third sector linkages with Africa (1992, p. 120). Sociologist Jan Knippers Black also recommends these avenues for aid. And to insure the course of democracy, she further argues that the Western powers should cease to hold responsible the peoples of the Third World for debts incurred by leaders not of their own choosing (1991, p. 196). These approaches, combined with Clough's other recommendations against arming African governments, against supporting African political candidates, and against assisting human rights/free speech abusers, are sensible bilateral aid policies for a potential new communitarian world order.

Elise Boulding suggests that voluntary organizations originating in the Southern Hemisphere provide the nations of the Northern Hemisphere the opportunity to learn new perspectives. This is because southern-based organizations tend to be small and resource poor, relying on community involvement and "people power." Their focus tends to be holistic, incorporating environmental concerns, community development, peace and nonviolence, all suffused with spiritual values (Boulding, 1988, p. 40).

Malaysia is the headquarters for a Third World consumers cooperative which stresses peace and ecology among its central themes. Latin America is blessed with a string of peace and human rights networks stressing local activity and consciousness raising.[16] The Council on Indigenous Peoples, originated in the developing world, has branches on all continents. It works to promote traditional crafts, healing, and community organization. But one of the most remarkable southern NGOs is the Sardovaya Shramadana International Movement.

The Sardovaya Shramadana International Movement

The Sardovaya movement is a self-help organization which originated in 1958 in Sri Lanka with three camps and 97 participants. It was founded by A. T. Ariyaratne, himself inspired by Vinoba Bhave, Ghandi's spiritual successor in India. *Sardovaya* means "awakening" and *shramadana* translates roughly into "labor sharing." Based on Buddhist precepts, the movement was designed to promote moral awakening of communities through the development of self-help programs rooted in the ethos of indigenous culture (Dissanayake, 1991, p. 328).

Sardovayans seek to conceptualize development not solely in terms of per capita income but within the broader definition of community growth and the fulfillment of the human personality. The founder elaborates on the need for growth in both human and spiritual dimensions.

Majid Tehranian explains the core precepts of the Sardovaya movement:

> Sardovaya philosophy begins with Buddha's Four Noble Truths: a) that there is human suffering (*dukkha*) in the world; b) that this suffering is caused by human craving (*tanha*) and greed (*lobbha*); c) that this craving and suffering can indeed cease; and 4) that there is a Middle Path to follow for human enlightenment and happiness. This Middle Path or the Noble Eightfold Path consists of Right Understanding, Right Intention, Right Speech, Right Action, Right Livelihood, Right Effort, Right Mindfulness, and Right Concentration. This philosophy has been transformed by the Sardovaya movement into a theory of development born out by its own practices. (Tehranian, 1990, p. 229)

Sardovaya was initially inspired by church-sponsored youth work camps set up for reconstruction in postwar Europe.[17] Ariyaratne set out to reformulate this model of community participation, readapting it to Sinhalese culture.[18] In its early phase, Sardovaya was primarily a youth movement attracting privileged high school students and young teachers to assist the people in "destitute outcast villages." Volunteers helped villagers to meet basic survival needs such as obtaining water for irrigation and household use. By the late 1960s, Ariyaratne had advanced the scope of work of the organization to encompass broader self-help aims. He launched the Hundred Villages Development Scheme in 1968, thereby promoting integrated self-development. By the late 1970s, the movement had spread to 2,000 villages. In its third phase, begun in 1978, the movement was advancing toward a plan for national development. This strategy incorporated the principle of "no poverty, no affluence." Its cardinal principle was one advocating harmony between national development and the ethos of village life (Tehranian, 1990, p. 229).

Clearly the movement is growing. By 1985, Sardovaya was active in over 7,000 villages, touching the lives of over 2.5 million people. Ariyaratne's aim for the early 1990s was to reach seven million people, about half the population of Sri Lanka (Ariyaratne, 1986, p. 108). Sardovaya's network has now expanded outside Sri Lanka. The movement has an international headquarters in Geneva (Boulding, 1988, p. 40). The Sardovaya Shramadana movement appears to have followed the NGO evolutionary model described by David Korten.

What makes Sardovaya an important model for communitarian social organization is its approach to five basic principles: ecology, nonviolence, social responsibility, participatory democracy, and dialogical communication. Ecological sensitivity is in fact enshrined in the Buddhist philosophy which sees all life as circular and believes all life, including the life of human beings, continues to evolve from one form into another. As Tehranian notes, "from this perspective, ecological protection is no longer a matter of expedient policy, it is a cosmic duty" (1990, p. 232).

In the area of nonviolence, Sardovaya relies again on the teachings of the lord Buddha: "He who, seeking his own happiness, inflicts pain through punishments on beings who are yearning for happiness, does not obtain happiness after death" (quoted in Tehranian, 1990, p. 232). Principles of social responsibility and participatory democracy are enshrined in the work the movement does and in the manner in which they carry out their projects. As noted, the name *Shramadana* means "labor sharing." In the initial stage, a Sardovaya volunteer is invited to a village to help start programs. Acting in the role of facilitator, the Sardovaya worker helps villagers to identify their needs and establish their projects. Sardovayans are careful to exclude no group from participation. Children, youth, mothers, farmers, elders, middle-aged men, etc., are all enjoined to become active in the work.

The volunteer assists local groups in forming their own local Sardovaya movements. These new groups then generate their own leaders. Eventually the new leaders will provide a counterforce to the power of feudal village landowners. In this way, Sardovaya serves as the basis for a new social structure.

Ultimately local groups are incorporated into Village Awakening Councils who hold legal status and design their own development programs. National and regional Sardovaya groups liaise with these local groups providing legal aid, library services, immunization and nutrition programs, and other assistance more easily organized from Sri Lanka's capital, Colombo. The National Council also maintains contact with German, Dutch, and American aid organizations keen on supporting the movement (Tehranian, 1990, pp. 234–35).

Dialogical communication is enshrined in the Buddhist precept of "pleasant speech." Pleasant speech requires dialogue, listening, and sharing ideas in the promotion of unity, dignity, and equality. Sardovayans are careful to avoid pejorative language reflecting class or gender bias as these would conflict with the Buddhist concept of harmony (Tehranian, 1990, p. 233).

The Sardovaya movement has been phenomenally successful, and Western development agencies are proud and pleased to be associated with its efforts.[19] Macy cites one Dutch-sponsored study which showed that Sardovaya camps generated in revenues far more than the initial investment. In one year, Sardovayans paved three times as much roadway as did the Sri Lanka government with a budget only 9 percent as large (1983, p. 43)!

One of the most important contributions of this movement to global consciousness is the notion of incorporating ethical principles into the process of development. Buddhist ethics are deeply concerned with the maintenance of social harmony. A discussion of religious values also now forms an important part of the discourse on the concept of world sustainability. Environmental advocate Robert Prescott-Allen, for example, advocates a new planetary vision which incorporates principles of democracy, ecology, and moral faith (1992, pp. 126–38).

Environmental consciousness, community-based action, peace, harmony, equality, and nonviolence are among the major concerns of NGOs initiated in the West. These aims are increasingly nourished by global ethical philosophy now emerging (Rockefeller and Elder, 1992, p. 10).

Sociologists who study the phenomena of globalization recognize that global scarcity, environmental degradation, personal and political alienation, economic dualism, and the threat of violence are concerns of such magnitude that they have brought the world to a crisis point in the late modern age. Self-help and nongovernmental associations have come in to address problems the modern participatory democracies are unable or unwilling to solve. And the activity of these groups has forced governments to shift policies. This occurred, for example, with the Reagan policy toward Ethiopia and the Reagan-Bush policy toward South Africa in the 1980s (Clough, 1992, pp. 101–16).[20]

The pressure of the so-called special interest groups, decried by politicians in the United States, is said to cause "gridlock." Both the Bush and the Clinton administrations have been particularly plagued by the phenomenon. This gridlock is symptomatic of the larger decline in the modernist paradigm. Unable to obtain desired action through representative democracy, groups have taken to grass roots organization, fund raising, and lobbying across party lines (Dye and Zeigler, 1989, p. 186). The mix of cross-cutting interests and demands makes legislative platforms unstable, inconsistent, and difficult to pass. At the same time, the modern system increasingly experiences crisis, for as we have seen, the marketplace has created its own contradictions. In its search for profits, the capitalist system has awakened new constituencies. These groups are now aware that they have been left out of the international consumerist order. Disgruntled masses in the First World took their complaints to the street, rioting in Los Angeles in the summer of 1992. In Lagos, Nigeria, "copy-cat" demonstrations broke out after Nigerians saw L. A. riot footage through the Cable News Network feeds (Narag, personal communication, August 1992). In Germany, disgruntled Easterners take out their wrath on migrant workers who remind them of their own peripheral economic positions vis-à-vis their wealthier West German cousins.

Everywhere in the Western world there seems to be the same crisis in industrial capitalism, a crisis raised by problems the nation-state seems ill-equipped to solve. Sociologist Leslie Sklair says the source of the modern crisis is the ideology of consumerism, the religion of the modern age. He theorizes optimistically that the Second and the Third Worlds will learn from the West's mistakes and adopt a different social course, one which he calls a "Third Way."

> It is not unreasonable for the poor, as well as the rich, to want the best of all worlds. This being so, it is reasonable to assume that people in the Second and Third Worlds might think twice before choosing the global capitalist project. A more likely preference, but perhaps not in the short run, is a Third Way, combining some of the efficiencies of the market, forms of private enterprise in peripheral areas of the economy, and commitment to the rule of law that have developed under capitalism, with some of the welfare structures, restrictions on the abuse of private economic power, and the commitment to grass roots democracy that have developed in some socialist societies, even where the national polity is quite undemocratic. There is a growing band of people who believe that some form of market can be created and will be efficient without being exploitative. (Sklair, 1991, pp. 237–38)

Other sociologists of a similar mind-set speculate on the organizing principles of a new world order yet to emerge. Amidst their speculation is also a good deal of exhortation.

Sklair notes that his "Third Way" might well have a great deal in common with democratic feminist socialism. And when he speaks of democracy, he is referring to participatory, grass roots democracy. When he mentions feminism, he is speaking of universal self-fulfillment and equality enshrined in feminist philosophy, particularly eco-feminism.[21] When he refers to socialism, he is alluding to classless society and the end of economic dualism (1991, pp. 235–39).

For Tehranian, the new social system envisioned is one he calls "Communitarian Democracy." The principles of communitarian democracy are those which have already been highlighted in the discussion of the Sardovaya Shramadana movement. They include ecological sensitivity, nonviolence, social responsibility, participatory democracy, and communication based on dialogue.

Anthony Giddens proposes a social system which he calls "Utopian Realism." It is a vision which creates models of a better social system "which are limited neither to the sphere of the nation-state nor to only one of the institutional dimensions of modernity." It is a system which recognizes the importance of "emancipatory politics" which "needs to be linked with a life politics or a politics of self-actualization." It is allied with movements we have already described: workers' cooperatives, peace movements, free speech movements, ecological movements, and feminism (Giddens, 1990, pp. 156–59).

Near the end of Giddens's 1990 work *The Consequences of Modernity*, which outlines his vision, the author poses an important rhetorical question for which he supplies a useful answer:

> Why should we assume that world events will move in the direction outlined by these various utopian considerations? Clearly we can make no such as-

sumptions, although all discussions which propose such futures, including this one, can by their very nature make some impact. (1990, p. 171)

It is with this encouragement that we turn our attention back to the African media.

Communitarian Models for African Media

The social and economic organization imposed upon Africa, the modernity model which has given preeminence to the nation-state mode of political organization and which has supported industrial expansion, is now in crisis. Globalization of the industrial world and its communication systems are both the cause and the effect of this crisis. Globalization, a late-twentieth-century outgrowth of industrialization, thus presages industrialism's decline.

The crisis in modernity has been fueled by economic and social practices, notably industrial expansion supported within the framework of the nation-state, developments whose origins are at least 500 years old.[22] The alternative vision of this system has been offered by twentieth-century developments, notably the proliferation of international nongovernmental organizations, groups which use "big communication technologies" (satellites, data banks, etc.) to tie together common-interest collectivities. A significant healthy trend is the growth of groups founded in the Southern Hemisphere, assemblages of persons promoting communitarian politics, grass roots awareness, feminist consciousness of peace and equality, and environmental stewardship, all within an ethical or religious framework. African groups have also participated in this process, many in connection with the flowering of democracy movements.[23]

Throughout this volume, I have exhorted the value of media operations at the grass roots level. In chapter 4 on African radio broadcasting, for example, I lauded the operations of rural radio in Liberia. In chapter 5, treating African television broadcasting, I exhorted the value of grass roots television production in Niger. Throughout the discussions on development communication, however, I have pointed out the near universal second-class status of development vis-à-vis the needs of the States and the interests of the elites. Nevertheless, the work of the NGOs and their efforts at "empowerment" continue to evolve, however rapacious are the politicians in their efforts to control development activities, however pressing are the elites in their demand for the spoils of these projects.

Nongovernmental organizations use "big media technologies" to maintain contact with the West and to raise funds. But at the grass roots level, they are increasingly incorporating the "small media" in their activities. Newsletters have already been mentioned as an example of small media. Other small electronic media are helping to promote dialogue and horizontal communication between persons and groups.

The new thrust in development is a focus on "interactivity." Interactivity implies nonhierarchical, dialogical communication and grass roots participation in development. As we have seen, the recognition of the importance of interactivity grew from repeated failures in development, failures attributed in part to the "top-down" character of development initiatives and messages.

Interactivity as a cardinal organizing principle in development communication allows people to participate in their own efforts for improving the quality of their lives. It raises their consciousness and allows them to develop themselves in conjunction with their communities.

Interactive media facilitate these dialogical processes because they can be locally programmed, locally managed, and locally utilized to meet immediate local needs. A review of a few noteworthy projects will serve to illustrate these points.

KARATE KIDS PROJECT—EAST AND WEST AFRICA

The Karate Kids project, for example, uses the principles of interactive learning through small media to teach children about the dangers of sexually transmitted disease. The project is the brainchild of the INGO Street Kids International. This organization, together with the National Board of Canada and the World Health Organization, produced a 21-minute cartoon targeted to Third World street children. The cartoon reveals the perils street children face, highlighting the dangers from hunger and sexual exploitation by adults. It sensitively portrays a child who is lured by a rich man into his big car and made to perform sex acts. The child later falls ill and dies of AIDS. The tape appeals to the ethics of group loyalty among street kids while bolstering their sense of self-worth. The videotape warns children of the dangers of AIDS and recommends avoidance of sex until they are older and have a faithful partner. It suggests condom use if sex cannot be avoided.

The Karate Kids tape is shown to small groups of Third World street children from video vans equipped with videocassette recorders. The tape is designed to be followed by a discussion conducted by a sensitive local youth worker comfortable with the subject. Repeated use of the tape shows that its use "breaks the ice" on sensitive sexual issues and helps to elicit questions and promote dialogue between and among the facilitator and the children. Street Kids International recommends facilitators stop the tape as the need arises to generate discussion. Facilitators are encouraged to ask the children such questions as "What do you think will happen next?"; "What does the man in the big car want in exchange for the gifts he is giving?"; "Do such things happen in this neighborhood?"; and "What will you do if such a person comes to you?" Through these techniques, children can mentally rehearse dangerous situations and their responses to them before they occur.

"Karate Kids" has been used successfully throughout the Third World. For use in Africa, it has been translated into Fulani, Wolof, Moore, Bambara, and Kiswahili (Lowery, 1993, pp. 12–13). The relative low cost of VCR technology has revolutionized the work of development communicators wishing to use visual information and visual story-telling techniques to impart lessons. It is user friendly and adapts easily to small settings conducive to group discussion.

RADIO LISTENING CLUBS—ZIMBABWE

In 1985, the Federation of African Media Women of Zimbabwe (FAMWZ) established itself as a nonprofit, nongovernmental organization. The goal of FAMWZ was to "conscientize women through education and to spread information to women on their importance in developing rural and urban areas" (Moyo, 1990, p. 17).

FAMWZ decided to use Radio 4, Zimbabwe's rural radio service, to develop programs aimed at poor women. First they met with representatives of the Zimbabwe National Broadcasting Corporation to enlist their cooperation. Then FAMWZ linked up with the Association of Women's Clubs which runs 20,000 women's organizations in Zimbabwe in order to obtain help and guidance. Next, FAMWZ approached UNESCO and the Friedrich Ebert Foundation for funds.

The group chose three rural areas as target sites for project activities and held meetings with local women in an effort to determine women's needs. The local women agreed to an idea of forming Radio Listening Clubs. Because so few had access to private radio, village women felt that clubs would indeed be needed to provide them access to broadcasts specially designed for them and to permit them to hear other general radio fare.

Since the project began in 1985, 45 Radio Listening Clubs have been established. The listening clubs function as a forum for women's concerns and problems, providing feedback to the Radio Listening Club program.

The deliberations of the clubs are recorded on audiocassette and taken to collection points where a Radio Listening Club program coordinator listens to the tapes and arranges appropriate responses. These responses typically include information the community needs to solve its problems. The coordinator then packages the RLC inputs and his or her own recordings and produces a half-hour program aired in three Zimbabwean languages (Moyo, 1990, p. 19).

The RLC project has been effective in calling attention to the problem of impure water in 12 villages in the Zimbabwean region of Mhondoro. Through a series of programs, together with subsequent linkages and interventions, the project obtained a water test in these areas from the Ministry of Water Development. The test showed that the water in the region exceeded safe levels of iron and magnesium.

Having called attention to the problem, the Mhondoro Radio Listening

Clubs served as the hub of increased networking activities. At the behest of the clubs, the Ministry of Energy and Water Resources was contacted to determine what interventions it might make. Then the local health minister became involved in the problem, suggesting water filtration on an RLC program as a temporary measure. Next, the Zimbabwean Red Cross was asked to form local chapters in the affected areas so that they could benefit from Red Cross assistance. Then, the Zimbabwean Red Cross set aside needed funds for the construction of new boreholes for the villages. Finally, the project sought out the assistance of INGOs for help in digging new wells. The services of World Vision International and the Catholic Development Commission were thus enlisted. Moyo concludes that the project "has made it possible for some people to realize that they can be involved in identifying their own problems and use the radio to communicate them to policy makers" (1990, p. 20).

WONSUOM CLUBS—GHANA

Engaged in a UNESCO-sponsored rural broadcasting and newspaper project, the faculty of the School of Communication at Legon University, Ghana, discovered that one of the most significant achievements of the undertaking was actually a project offshoot: the formation of *Wonsuom* Clubs. These clubs are self-help organizations working to build such amenities as day-care centers, clinics, and latrines.

Ghanaian scholar Isaac Obeng-Quaidoo stresses the self-generated quality of the *Wonsuom* Clubs:

> The *Wonsuom* Clubs are neither radio listening nor newspaper reading Clubs. They are not the same as the Radio Farm Forums which operated in Ghana and a UNESCO report revealed in 1964–65. The *Wonsuom* Clubs are self-initiated and self-motivated organizations which have sprung up in the Project towns and villages to undertake self-help projects in those areas. When individuals hear on the radio or read in the *Wonsuom* [rural newspaper] how certain towns and villages are undertaking certain self-help or communal projects, then they decide to come together to do likewise. (1988a, p. 82)

As a complement to their practical activity, the *Wonsuom* Clubs also entertain communities. Obeng-Quaidoo notes that their performances often surpass those of Ghana television. And he adds, "they are versatile in proverbs, can perform concerts, and sing songs with developmental messages" (1988b, p. 66).

"SMALL SYSTEMS" VIDEO TECHNOLOGY—UNIVERSITY OF MALAWI, ZOMBA

Small systems video recording technology made possible the transformation of a "white elephant" audiovisual center at the Chancellor College campus of the University of Malawi at Zomba. Originally equipped in the 1970s with expensive U-matic video technology destined for use in teacher training, the center quickly fell into disuse.

In 1988, the center was reequipped with VHS equipment and enjoined to produce video materials for outside organizations. Students have since used the equipment to document their views and to produce cultural programs. The Fine Arts and Performing Arts Department of the college, for example, has used small format video to record village drama on forestry issues. And a program on aquaculture and the rural African farmer was produced at the center for an international conference on fish farming.

By serving NGOs and other agencies for negotiated fees, the audiovisual center at Zomba is beginning to approach self-sufficiency. Meanwhile, students at the teacher training college learn valuable lessons in grass roots education (McCurry, 1991, pp. 8–9).

While none of these applications is revolutionary, each project described here demonstrates the role of "small systems media" in the ongoing evolution of development and in the empowerment of rural people. This is a process of promoting self-help and dialogue, an evolution occurring in conjunction with the growth of NGOs, local, national, and international organizations, all linking together to solve human problems and to satisfy human needs. There are hundreds of projects like these all over Africa.

The new emphasis on interactivity in communications has spawned a growing interest in traditional culture within the Third World, including Africa.

African Traditional Culture Revitalized

Advocates of the "culturalist" paradigm for development have argued in favor of harnessing traditional culture in the service of development rather than discarding these forms as backward. Frank Ugboajah, the key proponent of this position, extolled the value of Africa's rich cultural and performance tradition. He noted that songs, dance, dramas, drumming, storytelling, and proverbs are all powerful modes of communication useful in spreading information (1985, pp. 165–75).

Ugboajah has influenced a whole new generation of African media scholars. The interest in working at the grass roots level and using traditional modes of communication has uncovered other potentials which promise to revitalize traditional communication and to give them increased respectability. Isaac Obeng-Quaidoo is one African media scholar whose development and research techniques have been significantly influenced by Ugboajah's concept of "oramedia" (1985b; 1987; 1988a; 1988b).

The very positive role of folk traditions in African group activity is well known to scholars of the oral medium. Ethnomusicologist Ruth Stone notes that for many Africans "singing and playing moves them to do unusual things, calms them if they are overwrought, stirs them to dance if they are apathetic" (1986, p. 246). François Bebey observes that, far from being an art form used only for special rituals and festive celebrations, "music is a driving force that animates the life of the entire community" (1975, p. 8).

Finnegan's collection of oral art lists songs for every occasion: harvest songs, hunting songs, planting songs, building songs, war songs, canoeing songs, drinking songs, initiation songs, marriage songs, love songs, worship songs, praise songs, lullabies, and funeral dirges. These all make up only a short list of the music and poetry used commonly in every day activity (Finnegan 1970).

In African musical life there is constant improvisation. Postal workers hand-cancel letters to a definite identifiable cadence; women thump mortars in tandem producing complex pleasant rhythms; taxi drivers blare out rhythmic car horn greeting as they careen past one another. Indeed, as Bebey notes, "music is clearly an integral part of the life of every African individual from the moment of his birth" (1975, p. 8).

Stone discusses the relationship of music to social life in most African circles: "To be an adult means learning to perform with some degree of proficiency in song and dance. Music is not just something special, but something social and to be a social being is to know something about performance" (1986, p. 241).

Chernoff argues that music is both a metaphor for African communal life and a means for negotiating social tension:

> Africans rely on music to build a context for community action, and analogously, many aspects of their community life reflect their musical sensibility. Knowing what we do about artistic realization in musical events, we should be better able to appreciate the way that, in Africa, the power of community comes from the dramatic coordination and even ritualized opposition of distinct personalities. . . . On the broadest level, the African musical sensibility offers a highly sophisticated example of a tendency frequently seen in traditional African political and economic institutions, a tendency toward situating multiple conflicting and opposing forces into a process of mediated and balanced communication. (1979, p. 162)

Those who would criticize the cultural school, suggesting it is but a slicker version of top-down communication (Fair and West, 1993, pp. 93–94), have failed to fully appreciate the dialogical nature of African art forms.

AFRICAN POPULAR THEATER

Village participatory theater in Africa takes the harmonious dynamism of African folk traditions a further step. It builds upon the use of song, dance, and mime and incorporates these forms into the staging of popular theater or village-based drama.

The popular theater movement has been conceived as a highly dialogic form of communication for empowerment. In a special 1988 issue of *Media Development* entitled "Popular Theater for Change," for example, the introductory editorial states the framework in which this art form can be viewed:

> Communication, like social change and political emancipation hinges on another concept crucial to both: participation. Neither social transformation nor genuine communication are possible without the active participation of people who wish to interact with each other. (Quoted in Morrison, 1991, p. 30)

Popular theater typically begins with facilitators who come from outside the community. They team up with local residents and the local drama group, if available,[24] to identify grievances and problems experienced in the village. In the course of these interactions, different opinions emerge from the people regarding the source and solutions to problems (West and Fair, 1993, p. 103).

Armed with this information, the troupe and other interested persons go about creating a performance. Typically the plays produced are highly improvisational, characterized by incomplete plots into which audience members are invited to assume roles and propose solutions to the dilemmas facing the characters.

After the play has been performed, audience members, dramatists (who are often one and the same), and facilitators are invited to meet together to discuss the issues raised by the performance and to try to devise solutions. Often the first play leads to a second and a third, as villagers continue to grapple with the problems churned up in the performative process.

At the grass roots level, the plays work to empower the voiceless by allowing them to voice grievances in a nonthreatening manner (Morrison, 1989, p. 13). Village drama has been used successfully in Burkina Faso to tackle the sensitive issue of family planning. Women who assume roles in these plays are able to express problems of unequal gender relations which are at the very heart of family planning issues. The plays use metaphor to distance audiences from their immediate situation and to see their problems from a new perspective (Hearn, 1976–77, p. 150), and the adoption of roles by players helps them to build empathy with their village colleagues.

The genre promotes change in villages without destroying the fabric of the village social system (Wang and Dissanayake, 1982, pp. 3–8). And it allows both individuals and the group to try out, i.e., to "role play," active solutions to their difficulties. The therapeutic value of "role playing" as a problem-solving tool is well known in Western psychological therapeutic circles.

All of these benefits are steps to "conscientization," a term used by Paulo Freire, to refer to "the process of learning to perceive contradictory social, political, and economic realities that engender opposition against which action must be taken" (Freire, 1974, p. 15; cited in Ukpokodu, 1992, p. 29).

The degree to which groups tackle political issues head on may vary according to circumstances. The level of "conscientization" and "empowerment" generated by these productions depends to some extent on the facilitators. If they arrive in the villages armed with fixed agendas and predetermined themes and storylines (as can sometimes be the case),[25] the performances will be far less revolutionary than the proponents, notably, Freire (1974), Boal (1979), and Desai (1990), envision.

Just as is the case with folk media, government elites may try to co-opt village-based drama or popular theater seeking to thrust their designs on the masses. But as I have argued with regard to folk media, the open and interactive forms of these genres do not lend themselves well to top-down communication. At the very least, villagers will alter top-down communication through their performance to suit their situation, just as Chernoff suggests, or they will devise forms to resist it.[26]

Meanwhile, the very popularity of this genre among INGOs and bilateral assistance agencies suggests their growing appreciation for dialogical communication. Groups such as DANICOM, Dutch Aid, USAID, and numerous INGOs are all supporting this approach to development. This is suggestive of a broader move toward communitarian social organizations marking the late twentieth century.

Popular theater for development has been used in numerous countries in Africa. These include Nigeria, Sierra Leone, Liberia, Zimbabwe, Botswana, Malawi, Cameroon, Zambia, and Kenya (Desai, 1990, pp. 67–76).

A more openly political theater group, the Kamiriithu Theatre Experiment, organized by Kenyan writer Ngugi wa Thiong'o, was harassed by the Kenyan government. According to Ngugi, this was because it promoted "the kind of awareness, this conscientization of erstwhile carefree people, that the government vehemently opposed" (Ngugi, 1986, p. 60). But the Kenyan group spawned other less politicized groups, who operate openly as cultural troupes in Kenya, and other more political groups, who exist in the underground (Ukpokodu, 1992, p. 34).

Other popular theater groups have chosen a more cautious path, couching their designs for empowerment in language and themes less threatening to the establishment. Hansel Eyoh, the coordinator of a theater for development project in Cameroon, addresses the need to "tread softly" in political matters when using this genre:

> While the popular theater need not become so marginalized as to dissipate its efforts, its radicalization ought to be done in such a way as to ascertain its survival, rather than exposing it to repression. (Eyoh, 1984, n.p.; quoted in Ukpokodu, 1992, p. 38)

Theater for development is providing a needed impetus for drama groups which have often operated on the fringes of society. The widespread use of their organizing and performing talents and their growing popularity will ultimately provide them increased exposure in the mass media. In Liberia, for example, the LRCN project experimented with village-based *radio* drama (Bourgault 1991).

The Nigerian Television Authority, Enugu, in collaboration with Johns Hopkins University Popular Communication Services, produced family planning drama segments inserted into its TV variety program "In a Lighter Mood" (Singhal and Rogers, 1989, p. 41). Nigerian television programs a great deal of locally originated material. It has long benefited from the services of popular theatrical groups, groups which express the ethos and concerns of Nigeria's rural and urban proletariat. Far from rejecting Africa's oral tradition, these groups reintegrate it into the social fabric, using it in new mass mediated forms.

THE ORAL TRADITION REVISITED

Oral discourse, like any communication technology, displays a Janus face. Like any mode of communication, it can be harnessed in socially positive and socially negative ways.

Throughout this volume, I have sought to demonstrate that Africa's oral tradition is not conducive to individualistic critical postures, which are of major importance in the modern era. I have also shown how Africa's rural-based oral tradition was expropriated and cleverly harnessed by Africa's Westernized educated elites, in the promotion of personality cults around Africa's Big Men. The manipulation of the oral tradition has served for a time to mystify the masses and to inure them into an acceptance of autocratic regimes.

I have tried to demonstrate how the values of the oral tradition, i.e., the values of balance, harmony, and plurality, engender efforts toward social stability and pluralistic negotiation in human interaction and world outlook. I have also attempted to demonstrate the strain inherent in the application of the orally based normative system (which evolved in the premodern world) to the circumstances existing in the modern world imposed by the colonial and postcolonial situation.

Geertz reminds us that inherent strains between the political-social structures and the normative ones in social operation eventually lead to social change. This is because humans strive to live in a world "to which [they] can attribute some significance" (1973, p. 169). Geertz's formulations suggest to me that positive change in Africa is in the making.

The world is now linked through international nongovernmental organizations seeking meaning through a new kind of global interactivity. These groups have given impetus to thousands of local NGOs on the continent of Africa. The work of NGOs, locally, nationally, and internationally, is promoting grass roots, nonviolent, socially responsible, ecologically sensitive, personally empowering, democratic, dialogical, and humanistic forms of communication in Africa. This is communication suited to a communitarian world order.

Within this decade and throughout the next century, it will be the task of the African mass media to incorporate these forms of communication into their regular offerings. Locally based NGOs are poised to lobby to this end, demanding their voices be heard, their activities and projects be covered, and their creative efforts be aired. New private electronic media must be enjoined to share in these undertakings in their attempts to fill airtime.

Meanwhile, the suggestions I have proffered for the African media within this volume are all concrete steps which these media may take at the present time and within their present circumstances. The suggested changes will help to mitigate, in the short term, some of the nefarious effects and contradictions which the nation-state model and the modernity paradigm have imposed upon African government media.

Although the present decade is fraught with perils for Africa, the prospects for the next century appear brighter. Africa's precolonial, community-based values of harmony, plurality, and balance are well suited to a steady state communitarian world order toward which the planet must inevitably move or face perdition. This notion alone is the basis for hope for the continent and the empowerment of its people. During the next century, Africa will need to gather its human resources to spread its social models of plurality and harmony over the planet.

Notes

1. The Precolonial Legacy

1. The countries included in Black Africa are the following: Angola, Benin, Botswana, Burkina Faso, Burundi, Cameroon, Cape Verde Islands, Central African Republic, Chad, Comoro Islands, Congo, Côte d'Ivoire, Djibouti, Equatorial Guinea, Ethiopia, Gabon, the Gambia, Ghana, Guinea, Guinea-Bissau, Kenya, Lesotho, Liberia, Malagasy Republic, Malawi, Mali, Mauritania, Mauritius, Mozambique, Namibia, Niger, Nigeria, Rwanda, São Tomé and Príncipe, Senegal, Seychelles, Sierra Leone, Somalia, Sudan, Swaziland, Tanzania, Togo, Uganda, Western Sahara, Zaire, Zambia, and Zimbabwe. Eritrea, the newest African country, became a sovereign nation in 1993.

2. Existing African countries which were colonies solely of Great Britain include: Botswana, the Gambia, Ghana, Kenya, Lesotho, Malawi, Nigeria, Sierra Leone, Swaziland, Uganda, Zambia, and Zimbabwe. Existing African countries which were colonies solely of France include: Benin, Burkina Faso, Central African Republic, Chad, Comoro Islands, Congo, Côte d'Ivoire, Djibouti, Gabon, Guinea, Malagasy Republic, Mali, Mauritania, Niger, and Senegal. Existing African countries which were solely colonies of Portugal include: Angola, Cape Verde Islands, Guinea-Bissau, Mozambique, and São Tomé and Príncipe. The only existing African country which was solely the colony of Spain is Equatorial Guinea. Spanish Sahara, whose sovereignty is at present contested, and which nominally is under the control of Morocco, was once a Spanish colony. The only existing African country which was solely the colony of Belgium is Zaire, and the only existing African country which was solely the colony of Italy is Eritrea.

A number of African countries came under the domination of more than one colonial power at different times in their histories. Others have separate regions which were dominated by different powers. Burundi, at first a German colony, later came under Belgian colonial control. Cameroon, initially a German colony, later came under French and British domination. Mauritius, originally colonized by Dutch and French settlers, later came under the colonial rule of Great Britain. Namibia, originally a German colony, later came under the rule of the Republic of South Africa. Rwanda, originally a German colony, later came under Belgian colonial rule. Seychelles, originally colonized by French settlers, later came under British colonial rule. Somalia was colonized by two powers: the northern region by Italy; the southern region by Great Britain. Sudan was first a colony of Egypt and later of Great Britain. Togo, originally a colony of Germany, later came under French and British colonial rule.

3. For purposes of clarity, this work provides mainly a contrast between the primary orality of the preliterate African world and the print-based culture ushered in by the Gutenberg Revolution. It has been widely recognized that the electronic media, particularly television, have introduced yet a new technologically-based culture and consciousness. Drawing on the work of Marshall McLuhan and others, Walter Ong introduced the concept of "sec-

ondary orality" to explain the phenomenon. Ong defined secondary orality in the following way:

> The new orality has striking resemblances to the old in its participatory mystique, its fostering of a communal sense, its concentration on the present moment, and even its use of formulas. But it is essentially a more deliberate and self-conscious orality, based permanently on the use of writing and print, which are essential for the manufacture and operation of the equipment and for the use of it as well. (1982, p. 196)

For a more complete discussion of secondary orality, see Farrell 1991; Silverstone 1991; and Postman 1985.

2. The Colonial Legacy

1. George Ayittey sees the modern African caste system (which he calls a "quasi-apartheid system") in terms of a two-class structure, one which divides citizens into elites, which make up five percent of the population, and peasants, which make up the other 95 percent of the public. Ayittey identifies the elite as containing five subgroups. The first four consist respectively of professional politicians, intelligentsia, the military, bureaucrats, and chairmen of public corporations. For Ayittey, the fifth and lowest level of elites includes urban workers and secondary school and university students (1992, p. 117). Because of increasing urbanization bereft of industrialization, urban wages for labor are on the decline as urban workers face increasing competition from the rising tide of new urban migrants. For this reason, I have chosen to divide African social classes into three categories: the elites, represented by Ayittey's first four groups of elites plus students and better paid workers; the urban proletariat, representing unemployed or underemployed urban workers; and rural peasants.

2. John Gay, a former professor of social science in Liberia, and an American, has written fictional biographies of Kpelle (Liberian) twins who undergo the trauma of kin/village separation for purposes of Western education. See John Gay's *Red Dust on the Green Leaves* (1973) and *The Brightening Shadow* (1980).

3. Goody and Watt note that even for Westerners, formal education sets up discontinuities between primary social values learned at home and secondary social values learned at school (1991, pp. 50–51).

3. Broadcast Management

1. The Liberian Rural Communications Network was a radio network devoted to the production and dissemination of development messages. It was established in the West African nation in cooperation with the United States Agency for International Development. The network broadcast on three rural-based stations from 1986 through 1990 when its operations were interrupted by events surrounding the Liberian Civil War. The LRCN project is discussed in detail in chapter 4.

2. *Doing Business in Africa* by Chudi Ukpabi (1990) provides some useful guidelines to cultural norms operating within business and professional environments in sub-Saharan Africa.

3. A floor manager is positioned in the television studio and is linked to the television control room with headsets. The television director issues commands from the control room over these headsets to the floor manager, who uses hand signals to convey needed information to studio technical personnel and talent (actors). Hand signals are a necessary means of communication during videotaping or live-on-air production, as audible commands would be picked up on studio microphones.

4. Voltmeters, also known as VU meters, are volume unit meters, i.e., audio meters indicating the volume level of sound.

5. See also Bourgault, 1993, pp. 83–84; and Bourgault, 1989, pp. 85–86.

4. Radio Broadcasting

1. The British policy of indirect rule, elaborated largely by Sir Frederick (later Lord) Lugard, one of the British representatives of British imperial expansion in Africa, was designed to use existing African chieftains and kings to govern Africa under the overlordship of the British Crown. The British colonies were seen as protectorates of the crown, and the subjects were not expected to ever become part of Great Britain. See von Albertini, 1971, pp. 279–307.

2. French imperial policy was organized under a system of direct rule whereby the French government superimposed its own governmental structures on its colonies and envisioned, theoretically, the assimilation of colonial peoples into the motherland. See von Albertini, 1971, pp. 279–307.

3. Waldemar A. Nielson notes: "For France, the colonies were not mere appendages loosely related to the metropole; they had been incorporated into a tight trade and monetary system, built into the life of France itself. To cut them loose even partially meant therefore the risk of trauma to both severed parts, France as well as the former colonies" (1969, p. 93).

Independence arrangements worked out with all former colonies except Guinea (who voted "no" on the referendum of the Constitution of 1958) were, according to Nielson, "so formidably complex and interrelated . . . that no single element could be understood without reference to the whole" (1969, p. 99). There were umbrella arrangements for cooperation in economic, financial, trade, aid, and monetary matters, and military cooperation. Perhaps the most visible was the institution of the Franc Zone in francophone West and Central Africa, a policy which tied African currencies to the French franc and provided considerable guarantees on the liquidities of central banks of the former French colonies. See Nielson, 1969, pp. 76–127. In early 1994, the French government announced that the CFA franc would be devalued. This announcement is widely believed to signal the demise of France's "special relationship" with its former colonies.

4. For an analysis of political developments in sub-Saharan Africa in the 1990s, see chapter 8 in this volume.

5. Lack of animation by radio personnel is of course compounded by the fact that broadcasters are rarely using their mother tongue on air.

6. The CIERRO is a center operated under the auspices of *l'Union des radios et télévisions nationales d'Afrique* (URTNA).

7. The *Union des radios et télévisions nationales d'Afrique* was established by the Organization of African Unity in 1962 with the purpose of facilitating the exchange of broadcast programs in Africa. The URTNA is based in Nairobi, Kenya.

8. Liberia's civil war, begun at the end of 1989, led to the capture of all three stations by Charles Taylor's forces. In September 1993, only the central headquarters of the project remained. It was producing a limited amount of development broadcasting for transmission on the Liberian Broadcasting System.

9. Upcountry audiences had been served in vernacular languages by ELWA (Eternal Love Winning Africa), a Christian evangelical station founded by the Sudan Interior Mission in 1954. The service broadcast in English and several local languages within Liberia and operated an external service aimed at West, Central, and North Africa together with the Middle East. Some of ELWA's transmitters damaged by the ongoing civil war, were under repair in 1993.

10. The initial training period for producers required a two-year stay in Monrovia. No women were allowed to leave their families for this length of time. Later in the project, some women came forth to work as volunteers at the local stations. They helped to meet important needs in women's and children's programming.

Though a Mandingo service was not initially offered through ELRZ, Zwedru, the Mandingo community of Grand Gedeh County sponsored their own program.

11. They were quick to point out "creeping Americanisms" in the vernacular delivery of the young and somewhat urbanized producers.

12. In reality, these revenues represented less than five percent of the LRCN's total operating budget.

13. In places where there is no telephone service, broadcasting often serves the function of a private message system.

14. For a discussion of this training, see Bourgault 1989.

15. Oral Rehydration Solution is recommended by the World Health Organization and other international agencies working in the field of public health. The solution is given to diarrhetic infants and children and is intended to replace water, salts, and minerals drained from the body through fluid loss. The Oral Rehydration Therapy recipe used in Liberia included the following ingredients: one coca-cola bottle full of clean water, five bottle caps full of sugar, one pinch of salt, and the juice from one-half grapefruit or one whole orange.

16. For a more extensive treatment of the village-based drama endeavor, see Bourgault 1991.

17. See "Final Report of the Evaluation of the Liberian Rural Communication Network," a report to the Institute for International Research, prepared by Applied Communication Technology of Menlo Park, Calif., by Dennis Foote, Judith McDevitt, and Diana Cassady with an introduction by Michael Laflin (December 1988). The report can be found in the Institute for International Research, "Final Report of the Rural Information Systems Project," a report to the United States Agency for International Development (Arlington, Va.: Institute for International Research, March 1989).

It is worth noting that despite tremendous gains in knowledge and awareness of development issues and an increased use of radio by Liberian audiences, there was little evidence of behavior change after one year of broadcasting. The lack of evidence of behavior change did not surprise social scientists familiar with the complex processes involved in social and behavioral changes.

18. For a critical analysis of the LRCN project, see Bourgault 1994b.

5. Television Broadcasting

1. Both official and unofficial charges leveled by stations or news personnel for covering events open the floodgates of news media to the possibility of corruption. *Publi-reportage* has long been a problem in Africa, where financial resources are at a minimum. Increasingly, stations in Africa are being forced by structural adjustment plans to commercialize parts of their services. In Nigeria, for example, President Babangida introduced the commercialization of news services in 1989. All events covered by network news, except for federal government matters, are subject to coverage fees.

2. Between 1981 and 1983, I conducted training sessions for a variety of Nigerian news personnel, including reporters from NTA and FRCN affiliates and journalists from the *New Nigerian* newspaper. Analyses of some of these experiences are covered in Bourgault 1987; Bourgault 1989; Bourgault 1993; and Bourgault 1994a.

3. Chernoff points out that laughter is often used in the African context to show

amusement with the contradictions and discontinuity of a situation. He describes how African bar girls giggle when they attempt to dance with American or European partners, not to mock them, but simply in response to the difficulties imposed by non-African dancers whose action is neither synchronized with the music nor with the movements of their partners (1979, p. 147).

4. Côte d'Ivoire's late President Félix Houphouët-Boigny had constructed in his native village of Yamoussoukro, the Basilica of Our Lady of Peace. The edifice holds the distinction of being the tallest church in Christendom, standing about 100 feet higher than Saint Peter's in Rome. It cost the Ivorian nation over $200 million.

5. Lenglet notes that major evaluation studies conducted for the *Télé-Scolaire* project by the Laboratory for Experimental Pedagogy in Liège, Belgium, did not include scientific comparisons between televised and non-televised schools. Nevertheless, it was well known by educational experts working within the feedback unit of the project that pupils from rural schools served by television out-performed those in similar areas not served by television, in the subjects of French language arts. The reason was quite simple. The broadcasts provided a higher standard of French than could be expected from rural teachers. Comparisons between urban televised and non-televised schools were more problematic, confounded by variables of teacher and pupil social/economic class together with issues of accessibility of other educational resources.

6. Côte d'Ivoire authorized one private TV service which went on the air in 1992 (USIA, 1992, p. 1).

7. The SOFIRAD, the *Société financière de Radiodiffusion*, under the direction of Hervé Bourges, created *Images Sud-Nord* to provide a means through which African film and television producers can distribute their work to European television services.

8. Rwandan students have attended the *Ecole Supérieure des Sciences et Techniques* (ESSTI) at Yaoundé, Cameroon, in anticipation of their future television service. Moreover, the Rwandan students also benefit from training in radio provided by the center.

9. Canal Plus Afrique is a subscriber-based satellite service owned by private interests in Gabon, Tunisia, and Senegal, together with French private interests of Canal Plus and the French government-owned SOFIRAD.

10. In 1993, Tanzania announced plans to establish Tanzania Television (TT) as a public corporation (*Africa Communications*, November–December 1993, p. 30).

11. The role of village-based drama for development is discussed more extensively in chapter 9. See also Morrison 1989; Morrison 1991; Desai 1990; and Ukpokodu 1992.

12. On February 27, 1993, Mahame Ousmane was elected president of Niger. He was supported by the Alliance of Forces of Change, a coalition of nine opposition groups.

13. Some state stations established during the Shagari regime (1979–83) tended to attract employees away from local NTA affiliates. The promise of higher salaries, newer equipment, increased opportunities for training abroad, and in some cases more producer and reporter autonomy encouraged NTA personnel to leave the network for work in the new state-operated stations.

14. I conducted a series of training workshops for television production personnel at NTA stations between 1981 and 1983. The stations included were NTA Kano, NTA Jos, NTA Bauchi, and NTA Maiduguri.

15. Comfort with improvisation has been noted in Boal 1979; Fabian 1990; and Bourgault 1991. Turner provides an explanation for this phenomenon, noting that traditional African social life represents for individuals an ongoing assumption of social roles (1982, p. 15).

16. The gift of a kola nut is a sign of friendship and social solidarity in West Africa.

Kola nuts are often shared before a discussion takes place or a ritual is performed. Giving a kola nut before robbing a man represents a nasty violation of social and moral ethics.

17. For an analysis of the structure of the trickster tale, see Haring, 1972, p. 165.

18. See Haring 1972 on trickster tales. See also Hiskett 1975; Yahaya 1981; Dabia 1981; and Kofoworola 1981 on Islamic poetry. See Fiombo and Speciale 1992 on moral tales in Hausa culture.

19. Married Hausa women are generally not allowed by their spouses to perform as actresses.

20. "Weeping Heart" and *"Hadarin Kasa"* were both in production at the time this research was conducted in 1992. "Beyond the Dreams" had been produced a few years earlier. I analyzed the older series because all 13 episodes were available in the CTV library, while the other two were incomplete. See Bourgault 1992b.

21. Corruption in Nigeria has been extensively treated in Ungar, 1989, pp. 121–61; and Harden, 1990, pp. 271–307.

22. The difficulty with the presentation of the women's point of view stems in part from the lack of women drama producers, itself a manifestation of the separation of male and female social worlds. For a discussion of this issue in African cinema, see Petty, 1992, pp. 29–30.

6. Colonial History and Postcolonial Developments of the Press

1. Nigeria became independent by an act of the British Parliament on October 1, 1960. Azikiwe (himself of the Eastern Region) was installed as governor general of the federation which represented the three regions of Nigeria: the Northern Region, the Western Region, and the Eastern Region. Sir Abubakar Tafewa Balewa (of the Northern Region) was prime minister serving as head of a democratically elected parliament. During the first three years after independence, the federal government represented a coalition of the Northern People's Congress (NPC) and the Eastern-based National Council of Nigeria and the Cameroons (NCNC). Denied a strong role in the federal government, Awolowo's Western-based Action Group squabbled internally. See Metz, 1992, pp. 48–50.

2. The Nyasaland protectorate (now Malawi) was joined in 1953 with Northern and Southern Rhodesia (now respectively Zambia and Zimbabwe) to form the Federation of Rhodesia and Nyasaland. The federation faced extreme internal opposition and was dissolved at the end of 1963 as the three partners prepared to claim their independence. Malawi and Zambia obtained their independence in 1964, while the struggle for self-rule in Zimbabwe, protracted and bitter, continued until 1980. See note 3, below.

3. Present-day Zimbabwe, known in colonial times as Southern Rhodesia, was initially developed and administered by the British South Africa Company. In 1923, the British government granted Southern Rhodesia internal self-government, with power vested in the hands of the white minority. In 1953, Southern Rhodesia became part of the Federation of Rhodesia and Nyasaland. The Federation broke up in 1963. Meanwhile, in 1961, the British government had attempted to create a new constitution for Southern Rhodesia, one which gave increased powers of self-government to the colony, and one which attempted to guarantee certain rights, such as limited parliamentary representation to the Black majority. The move failed as the majority continued to clamor for full political equality. In 1965, the Southern Rhodesian government under Prime Minister Ian Smith issued a Unilateral Declaration of Independence, designed to make Southern Rhodesia an independent state, one which would maintain white minority political control. Unrest followed, and Smith declared a State of Emergency. Black majority rule finally came to Zimbabwe in 1980 after years of guerrilla war.

4. The Republic of Tanganyika was established from the British East African colony of Tanganyika in 1961. It amalgamated with the People's Republic of Zanzibar (independent in 1963) to form the United Republic of Tanzania in 1964.

5. The presence of an elite educated class finds its origins in the establishment by Portuguese slavers of fortified castle towns on the gold coast in the seventeenth century. From the trade in commodities and slaves, there emerged in these coastal towns a small group of entrepreneurial families who mixed and intermarried with resident Europeans. These mulatto communities organized European-style education for their own kin, inviting churchmen to teach them even before the pioneering missionary efforts on the coast in the 1820s and 1830s. (See Gifford and Weiskel, 1971, p. 679.) Because education had become widespread in Dahomey earlier than in other French colonies, it became a center for training francophone Africa's clerical and administrative personnel during the colonial and postcolonial period (Andreski, 1968, p. 156).

6. After World War II, France reorganized and drafted a new Constitution for the Fourth Republic that included a series of steps intended to strengthen and make more equitable the various components of the French empire without dissolving it. Economic and social reforms were planned, including increased medical services and better positions for natives in administrative services. Politically, the colonies and protectorates were represented in constituent assemblies wherein 63 of the 600 seats were reserved for them. The reorganization of the French government after the war thus led to a general upsurge in political activity among Black African statesmen who formed important alliances with the French Communist and Socialist parties active in the National Assembly of the Fourth Republic. But the French empire was quickly unraveling in the 1950s. France had been forced to give up its mandate in Syria and Lebanon in 1946. In Vietnam, rebel forces defeated the French at Dien Bien Phu in 1954. By the mid-1950s, nationalist rebellion had broken out in armed struggle in Algeria. The Algerian conflict created a crisis in government in France and stalled the reforms promised to the remaining colonies. A group of sub-Saharan African leaders under the direction of Félix Houphouët-Boigny came up with the idea of a French African Community. In 1958, Charles de Gaulle prepared a new constitution for a Fifth French Republic. Members of the colonies were enjoined to vote on the new constitution. They were given a choice of continued association with France through the French African Community or opting for complete independence. De Gaulle made it clear that rejection of the Community option would mean an end to economic assistance. All of the French African colonies except Guinea voted "yes" to the referendum. See Nielson, 1969, pp. 82–127. See also chapter 4, note 3.

7. Senegal came under French influence in the seventeenth century when French mercantile interests promoted the establishment of trading posts at the mouth of the Senegal River and on the island of Saint Louis. See Fage, 1969, pp. 70–72.

8. Media training was also provided by groups from Eastern Europe, the Czech Press Institute, TASS, and the Press Institute of Hungary, for example.

9. See Barton, 1969, pp. 10, 33–54, 73–75.

10. *Kibaru* is an exception here, having reached a peak circulation of 22,000 in 1983. See Karikari, 1993, pp. 64, 66.

7. Discourse Style, Oral Tradition, and the Question of Freedom in the Press

1. Although the Catholic Church retains a great body of written doctrine and history dating from the early days of the Church, this written material was not accessible to the masses until well after the Reformation. Earlier literacy was limited to monks and priests and eventually to some members of the noble classes in the late middle ages. Catholic com-

mon folk depended for religious knowledge on the oral tradition, i.e., church sermons and stories of the saints, and on illustrations and carvings transmitted through gothic architecture. See Burke, 1991, pp. 67–68.

2. In 1985, I produced an analysis of the Nigerian press which focused on the oral tendencies I had observed in Nigerian newspapers over the four-year period (1980–84) during which I lived in Nigeria. The examples I used were derived from a collection of about 30 newspapers in my possession at the time. See Bourgault 1987.

3. Despite many years of working with African media practitioners in urban settings in 14 different countries, I did not arrive at an appreciation of the power of the underlying rural *Weltanschauung* until I conducted ethnographic research in a rural Liberian village. See Bourgault 1992a. The differences in thinking styles between literate and nonliterate societies have been codified in Lee 1959 and Whorf 1956.

4. The lack of exploration by Nigerian journalists of wider issues surrounding the Maitatsine riots was reminiscent, in some ways, of the press' handling of an abortion bill introduced into the Nigerian legislature in the early 1980s. Abortion-related reporting became a subject for discussion in seminars I conducted with reporters from the *New Nigerian* newspaper and with television reporters from NTA Kaduna in 1982. I remarked that I had observed no provision by any reporter of a full account of the contents or even the essence of the abortion bill. I indicated my surprise that all of the coverage appearing in the news roundly condemned the bill and its sponsor in the name of Islam and Christianity, yet little reference to scripture was provided therein. Reporters duly informed me that abortion was contrary to religion and therefore no exposé on the bill was necessary. Nevertheless, no single reporter present could cite the relevant scriptural passage which allegedly condemned abortion, and no one had bothered to search through scripture in the preparation of articles they had prepared condemning the proposed legislation. The pieces they had written or broadcast, moreover, were cast as news and not as editorials. One perceptive reporter noted that to expose the bill in its legislative detail would be tantamount to suggesting agreement with its contents. Other reporters concurred with this position. Clearly a distanced, critical, and analytical posture was beyond the reportorial habits of this group or the expectations of their readers. I would argue that similar analytical pieces on the Maitatsine uprising were eschewed by the Nigerian press for similar reasons.

5. The constitution of the Second Republic of Nigeria (1979–83) guaranteed that "every persons [*sic*] shall be entitled to establish and operate any medium for the dissemination of ideas and opinions" (quoted in Edeani, 1985, p. 45). Similar provisions were codified in the constitution of the Third Republic, which was to become law with the resumption of civilian rule scheduled for 1993. But Babangida manipulated the transition to democracy, canceling the result of the June 1993 election, claiming irregularities in the election victory of Social Democratic Party (SDP) contender Chief Moshood Abiola. In August 1993, Babangida appointed civilian Ernest Shoenkan to head a caretaker government. In November 1993, General Sani Abacha took over the reins of power in Nigeria, and once again the military was back in charge. Abacha intends to call a constitutional conference to determine appropriate forms of governance for Nigeria (Adams, 1994, pp. 47–49).

6. Orality persists among literates, according to Obeichina, because they never completely lose touch with their oral culture. The oral culture is predominant in rural areas where the vast majority of the population lives and where literacy is the exception rather than the rule. Villages and towns remain complementary, with town dwellers living or visiting part of the time in villages, and villagers living or visiting from time to time in towns. Goody and Watt remind us that oral culture persists even in highly literate societies, though it operates at the inward and individual level of privately held values and beliefs (1991, p. 55). Obeichina notes further that values are particularly resistant to cultural change (1975, p. 27).

7. The *New Nigerian*, published in Kaduna, is owned by the federal government of Nigeria. The *Daily Times*, published in Lagos, is 60 percent privately owned and 40 percent government-owned. The pronouncements of the head of state appear regularly (if not daily) in these papers. But they also appear with great frequency in the rest of the Nigerian press, including the state-owned and the private papers.

8. The age of Hastings Banda is an official secret. In 1992, Banda's age was estimated to be between 90 and 95.

9. In many parts of the developing world where literacy is low, newspapers are read aloud by literates to groups of nonliterates.

10. I am indebted to Philip Graham for this insight. Graham lived and worked at fiction writing in an Ivorian village while his anthropologist spouse, Alma Gottlieb, conducted field work. See Gottlieb and Graham, 1993, pp. 162–67.

11. Goody and Watt note that the introduction of writing in ancient Greece "brought about an awareness of two things: of the past as different from the present, and of the inherent inconsistencies in the picture of life as it was inherited by the individual from the cultural tradition in its recorded form" (1991, p. 49).

12. The analogy between the "situational" style of writing in the laudatory African press and that of electronic news gathering techniques evident in the "Eyewitness News" style of reporting should not be missed. "Eyewitness News" provides U.S. audiences with the same sense of participating vicariously in news-making dramas, and it similarly diverts the literary reflex of asking *why* an event has occurred. McLuhan 1991, Ong 1982, Goody and Watt 1991 and many others would suggest the U.S. example is one of "secondary orality."

13. President Babangida was later forced to introduce harsher economic reforms in Nigeria. See Harden, 1990, p. 293.

14. For a fuller account of training issues in African media, see Bourgault 1989 and Bourgault 1994a.

15. A session of *animation* might loosely be described as a political rally or celebration, designed by central government representatives or party officials who enjoin rural and urban masses to participate in group praise singing and dancing on behalf of the head of state. For a description of such events in Togo, see Packer, 1988, pp. 107–17.

16. See, for example, David Lan's *Guns and Rain*, 1985.

17. In discussions about reporter accuracy and credibility, journalists in both Kinshasa and Bangui raised questions on how to treat popular rumors in the written press.

18. "Dragons" are described in popular Liberian culture as long black tube-like talismans or charms imbued with evil power. It is said that dragons are planted in the homes of unsuspecting victims by evildoers intent on causing harm. Heartmen are persons who kill victims in order to obtain body parts (usually hearts) either for sale to others or for their own use. The human body parts are said to be used in the preparation of magical potions used to illicitly acquire power. Liberian popular cosmology is populated with many different types of witches. They are said to belong to a range of secret, illicit societies. Members are said to fly to meeting places in the dead of night to perform evil deeds. Ordinary persons who are not members of such groups may consort with members to arrange for the misfortune of their enemies.

19. This is not meant to suggest that no gossip networks operate in anglophone countries, but only that the popular style of reporting common in the West African anglophone presses serves part of the same functions as *radio trottoir* in the francophone countries.

8. The Flowering of Democracy and the Press in the 1990s

1. See also *Africa: A Directory of Resources*, compiled and edited by Thomas P. Fenton and Mary J. Heffron (Maryknoll, N.Y.: Orbis, 1987).

2. At the time of the final preparation of this volume, Rwanda was embroiled in a bloody ethnic conflict, ushered in, in part, by the death of its President Juvenal Habyarimana and that of neighboring Burundi President Cyprien Ntaryamera, when their plane was shot down by unidentified armed men (*West Africa*, 18–24 April 1994, p. 684).

3. A national conference is a sociopolitical instrument used primarily in francophone African countries to assemble all groups peacefully in order to hold discussions on the overhaul of central governments. *Africa Report* has described national conferences as "surrogate democratic mechanisms constructed in the absence of real democratic institutions—an amalgam of legislative, judicial, and executive authority designed to unseat regimes by questioning their legitimacy and raising issues of accountability" ("National Conference: Out with the Old Leaders," September–October 1991, p. 5).

4. A "strong commitment" to democracy was defined as one in which "the government is solidly committed to the creation of a more democratic political system. The strength of commitment is demonstrated by substantive incorporation of democratic processes, by devolution of power and gradual or wholesale abandonment of party monopolies" (*Africa Demos*, August 1992, p. 15).

5. A "moderate commitment" to democracy was defined as one in which "formal commitments to a democratic transition are accompanied by only measured, cautious, and preliminary steps toward institutionalization or pluralism. Promises reflect a sense of democratic purpose, but deeds are not yet commensurate with pledges" (*Africa Demos*, August 1992, p. 15).

6. Eritrea was then a province of Ethiopia. It held a referendum in April 1993 and won its independence. See Biles, 1993, pp. 13–19.

7. An "ambiguous commitment" to democracy was defined as one in which the "ruling elite's commitment to democracy is at best precarious, at worst a ruse, and at most times unclear. On the one hand, stated commitments are often suspended due to the exigencies of the moment. On the other hand, the construction of elaborate democratic structures suggests little more than political maneuvering" (*Africa Demos*, August 1992, p. 15).

8. Botswana, the former British protectorate of Bechuanaland in southern Africa, achieved independence in 1966 and has enjoyed parliamentary democracy since that year. The Gambia, a West African microstate, achieved its independence from Great Britain in 1965. Initially a parliamentary-style democracy, Gambia changed to a republican form of government following a referendum in 1970. Four successive elections have returned the original president to power. Mauritius achieved independence from Great Britain in 1968. Apart from three separate States of Emergency (in 1970, in 1971, and in 1978), the Indian Ocean island nation has enjoyed a stable parliamentary democracy.

9. Senegal, a former French colony in the Sahelian region of West Africa, achieved independence in 1960. Senegal established a presidential system of government with Leopold Senghor as president. As early as the late 1970s, Senghor began experimenting with multiparty democracy. Senghor allowed some but not all of his staunchest opponents to contest his party's leadership in parliamentary elections. The Senegalese people are justly proud of having practiced "multiparty" elections before it was "imposed" upon them by the West. They are also proud of their first president, poet-statesman Senghor, who in 1980, was the first president in sub-Saharan Africa to relinquish power voluntarily and turn it over to a successor.

10. Led by Jonas Savimbi, the UNITA (National Movement for the Total Liberation of Angola) Party has been backed intermittently by the United States and more consistently by South Africa. Since Angola's independence from Portugal in 1975, Savimbi has waged civil war against the Marxist government of Agostino Neto and his successor José Eduardo dos Santos, both of the MPLA (Popular Movement for the Liberation of Angola) Party. Attempts

to broker a peace in Angola in the 1990s have proved unsatisfactory, largely due to the ambitions of Savimbi.

11. The Africa bureau's democracy and governance unit of the United States Agency for International Development is specifically charged with promoting democratic reform on the African continent.

12. The relatively high rate of Zambian literacy should favor popular acceptance of the abstract nature of representative democratic processes.

13. Media training facilities in Zambia include the following four programs. First, the Evelyn Hone College in Lusaka offers a three-year diploma course in journalism and takes about 24 students per year. The African Literature Center in Kitwe offers a one-year diploma program, serving about 20 students annually. The University of Zambia in Lusaka recently created a bachelor's degree program in communication in which roughly 30 students were enrolled in 1992. Finally, the Zambian Institute of Mass Communication (ZAMCOM) in Lusaka maintains a semicontinuous program of in-service training consisting of one- to six-week courses for working reporters.

14. Government subsidies for the broadcast media were suspended just prior to the elections in 1991 after members of the MMD complained of the danger of pro-UNIP bias from government-subsidized electronic media.

9. Modernization, Development, and the Communitarian Social Agenda

1. Although some Black African states chose the socialist model of development (for example, Guinea under Sekou Touré and Tanzania under Julius Nyerere), these states experienced similar internal contradictions. The socialist states were victims of the same dominant world economic order and were forced to adopt similar courses of economic action to generate capital: industrialization, modernization, and dependence on outside sources of revenue. For these reasons, Davidson calls them "rhetorically socialist states." Under such governments, more control of economic processes and policy was vested in governmental structures (also controlled by a parasitic elite class) than in the allegedly private hands of elites operating in the capitalist countries (see Davidson, 1992, pp. 233–42).

2. The term "ideology" as applied to precolonial African polities might be considered problematic for some because the term has usually been applied to philosophical systems articulated in written treatises. To the degree that most African societies were preliterate, their ideologies were not articulated in this way. Nevertheless, a host of methods have been devised in the field of anthropology to piece together "working ideologies" from preliterate polities from cosmologies. See, for example, Karp and Bird 1987 and Arens and Karp 1989.

3. Development communication is regarded by some theorists as the information component of other projects in development. Today, most developers argue that communication should be an integral component of all efforts aimed at social change. This interactive approach to communications is one which I share. Therefore, future references to either development or communication will imply the other.

4. In 1970, a group of communication scholars met at the East-West Center to examine the progress or the lack thereof brought about in development through communication. Their book, *Communication and Change: The Last Ten Years and the Next*, edited by Wilbur Schramm and Daniel Lerner (1976) documents the many failures and disappointments of the optimistic decade of the 1960s.

5. In the 1990s, the United Nations has spearheaded a number of efforts to begin describing human progress in terms other than in Gross National Product figures. In 1990, the United Nations Development Programme began publishing the *Human Development Report*. This first *Human Development Report* defined human development as "the process of

enabling people to have wider choices." In this context, the *Report* also designed a new measure for socioeconomic progress, the human development index, or HDI. The HDI combines measures of life expectancy, adult literacy, and income in an innovative way in order to produce a yardstick more comprehensive than GNP alone as a measure of a country's progress. The 1991 *Human Development Report* added a Human Freedom Index, and the 1992 *Human Development Report* examined, among other considerations, disparities in the distribution of wealth within countries of the world and between regions of the world. See UNDP's *Human Development Report*, 1992, pp. 1–11.

6. Some theorists, notably, Paulo Freire (1974), who coined the term "conscientization," have seen the process in highly political terms. Freire notes that the first aim of conscientization for the peasant is the recognition of the social conditions that oppress him or her.

7. William Tolbert's regime (1971–80) was also heavily steeped in patronage. But Tolbert was regarded by many as a decent man, and his record on human rights was far better than that of his successor Samuel Doe.

8. The U.S. policy toward the Doe regime is covered extensively in Clough, 1992, pp. 56, and 89–95; and Harden, 1990, pp. 238–48.

9. Clough, 1992, pp. 76–100, provides a grim account of U.S. policy toward its African client states: Zaire, Liberia, Somalia, and Sudan (under Numieri).

10. Dennis Boyles, in *African Lives: White Lies, Tropical Truth, Darkest Gossip, and Rumblings of Rumor*, 1988, pp. 103–40, provides, for example, a disheartening description of the growing professionalization and bureaucratization of famine relief.

11. David Korten, a former USAID operative, arrived at similar dismal predictions for large-scale government-to-government aid. See his preface in *Getting to the 21st Century*, 1990, especially pp. xi–xii.

12. Films that depict the Vietnam War as a personal struggle for American G.I.s—*Platoon* or *Born on the Fourth of July*, for example, or more especially, those which depict American heroes Chuck Norris or Sylvester Stallone fighting anonymous Asian enemies—tend to mask the significant social struggle of the Vietnamese people in that protracted conflict. Advertisements which reduce women's social struggle for equal pay and equal rights to the choosing of appropriate "career clothing" or "sports bras" is another example of how the media co-opts and trivializes movements for social change.

13. See Immanuel Wallerstein's elaboration of "core-periphery theory" in *The Modern World System*, 1974.

14. There is a wide range of these groups marketing such products in the United States. Pueblo to People, for example, is a nonprofit organization founded in 1979. It markets handicrafts from 85 cooperatives and production groups in Guatemala, El Salvador, and Mexico. Another group is Marketplace: Handiwork of India, a nonprofit organization committed to increasing employment opportunities for women and handicapped persons in Bombay. Marketplace sells clothing and handicrafts produced by SHARE (Support the Handicapped Rehabilitation Effort), a cooperative umbrella organization which works with cooperatives each employing 30 to 50 women artisans. Yet another organization, Cultural Survival, engages in resource management programs to aid native peoples to manage natural resources. It also operates Cultural Survival Enterprises, which aids in creating markets for products native communities can collect in a sustainable manner. CSE helped originate Rainforest Crunch, which uses Brazil nuts harvested from the Amazonian rain forest. There is also Oxfam America, which markets the handicrafts of small-scale producers working in remote sections of some of the world's poorest countries. Oxfam America also maintains projects to help indigenous people gain deeds to their traditional lands, to prevent illegal resource ex-

traction from traditional lands, and to develop sustainable land management schemes reflective of traditional wisdom.

15. Boulding's figures were taken from the 1985–86 *Yearbook of International Organizations.*

16. The Latin American organizations have mushroomed under the influence of Paulo Freire and his followers.

17. Many nongovernmental organizations were initially set up during the post–World War II era with the intention of rebuilding Europe. See Korten, 1990, p. 116.

18. Despite Sardovaya's Sinhalese Buddhist origins, the movement's leaders have tried to keep the organization as ecumenical as possible. Sardovaya incorporates prayers and rituals from Christian, Hindu, and Muslim practice. See Tehranian, 1990, p. 231.

19. Eighty percent of Sardovaya's funds come from Dutch, German, and American agencies. See Tehranian, 1990, pp. 234–35.

20. The Reagan administration was forced to commit food aid to Marxist Ethiopia after Americans saw footage of starving Ethiopians on their TV screens in the mid-1980s. Intense pressure from interest groups in the United States also resulted in the abandonment by the Bush administration of its policy toward South Africa of "constructive engagement." The shift in the U.S. position helped bring about the end of apartheid in South Africa. See Clough, 1992, pp. 101–109.

21. "Eco-feminism" takes the position that the root causes of gender disequilibrium are also the source of class oppression and over-exploitation and degradation of the natural world. See Ruether 1983.

22. The period of mercantile capitalism of the sixteenth century is said to have given rise to the nation-state and to the scientific method. The scientific method had a penchant for objectification of things and people.

23. Multiparty movements have flourished, in large measure, through the work of grass roots organizations. Multiparty democracy is far closer to participatory democracy than is the one-party state.

24. Organized drama groups tend to be available in villages with more Western contact. Other more traditional entertainment groups may also be used. In Liberia, for example, the LRCN's experiments with village-based drama for radio used only one organized village drama troupe. In the two other villages, traditional entertainment/ritual groups were used. See Brooke, 1989, pp. 6, 9–10; Bourgault, 1991, pp. 67–68.

25. See, for example, Kidd, 1983, pp. 33–42; Etherton, 1988, pp. 2–4.

26. Comi Toulabor 1981 describes the way government-sponsored *animation* is ridiculed in the performance process. See also Toulabor 1986, especially chapter 8.

References Cited

Abubakar, Bello. General Manager, Nigerian Television Authority, Kano, Nigeria. 1992. Interview by author, August, Kano, Nigeria. Unpublished notes.

Adams, Paul. 1994. "Nigeria: The Army Calls the Tune." *Africa Report* (January–February): 47–49.

Africa Communications. 1992. "BBC World Television Service Extends to Africa." (July–August): 21.

Africa Communications. 1993. "Afcom '93: Broadcasting Report." (November–December): 28–31.

Africa Communications. 1993. "Deutsche Welle TV Embarks on Satellite Broadcasting: Signal Covers Africa." (May–June): 20–21.

Africa Communications. 1993. "Nigeria's Broadcasting Commission Announces Licenses." (September–October): 26–27.

Africa Communications. 1993. "PANA Agency on the Road to Revival." (May–June): 8.

Africa Communications. 1993. "Uganda Licenses First Private Radio Station." (May–June): 8.

Africa Demos. 1992. "Phases of Transition to Democracy." 2 (August): 15.

Africa Demos. 1993. "Milestones." 3 (July–August): 17–18.

Africa Demos. 1993. "Phases of Transition to Democracy." 3 (February): 19.

Africa Report. 1991. "National Conferences: Out with the Old Leaders." (September–October): 5–6.

Africa Report. 1991. "Update in the News." (September–October): 5–6.

Africa Report. 1994. "Gabon's President Wins Contested Election." (January–February): 8–9.

Ainslie, Rosalynde. 1966. *The Press in Africa: Communications Past and Present.* London: Gollancz.

von Albertini, Rudolf. 1971. *Decolonization: The Administration and Future of the Colonies, 1916–1960.* Trans. Francisca Garvie. Garden City, N.Y.: Doubleday.

Aliyu, Auwalu. 1982. "Television Programming in Nigeria: A Study of NTA Bauchi." Senior thesis, Department of Mass Communication, Bayero University, Kano, Nigeria. Unpublished paper.

Amakyi, Richard. 1988. "Community FM Radio in Ghana." *Combroad* 79 (June): 15–17.

Amin, Samir. 1990. *Maldevelopment.* London: Zed.

Amupala, Johannes Ndeshihala. 1989. *Developmental Radio Broadcasting in Namibia and Tanzania: A Comparative Study.* Tampere, Finland: University of Tampere, Department of Journalism and Mass Communication.

Andreski, Stanislav. 1968. *The African Predicament.* London: Michael Joseph.

Ansah, Paul. 1979. "Problems of Localizing Radio in Ghana." *Gazette* 25 (1): 1–16.

Aoulou, Yves. 1988. "Ghana." In *Les Télévisions du Monde. Télérama,* no. 48, Special Edition, 389–90. Paris: Télérama-Cerf-Corlet.

Aoulou, Yves. 1988. "Niger." In *Les Télévisions du Monde. Télérama,* no. 48, Special Edition, 408–409. Paris: Télérama-Cerf-Corlet.

d'Arcier, Bernard Faivre. 1978. "Politique Culturelle." Technical report conducted under the direction of UNESCO, Paris. Series no. FMR/CC/78/126. Unpublished paper.

Arens, W., and Ivan Karp, eds. 1989. *Creativity of Power: Cosmology and Action in African Societies.* Washington: Smithsonian Institution Press.

Ariyaratne, A. T. 1986. "Learning in Sardovaya." In *Learning and Development: A Global Perspective,* ed. Alan Thomas and Edward W. Ploman, 108–24. Toronto: Ontario Institute for Studies in Education.

Article 19. 1991. *Information, Freedom, and Censorship.* World Report. Chicago: American Library Association.

Ayittey, George B. N. 1992. *Africa Betrayed.* New York: St. Martin's.

d'Azevedo, Warren L., ed. 1975. *The Traditional Artist in African Societies.* Bloomington: Indiana University Press.

Badibanga, André. 1979. "La Presse Africaine et le culte de la personalité." *Revue Française d'Etudes Politiques Africaines* (March): 40–57.

Bagilishya, Chantal. 1988. "Les Télévisions d'Afrique noire francophone." In *Les Télévisions du Monde. Télérama,* no. 48, Special Edition, 70–75. Paris: Télérama-Cerf-Corlet.

Balandier, Georges. 1976. *Ambiguous Africa: Cultures in Collision.* Trans. Helen Weaver. New York: Discuss Books, Avon.

Balogun, Françoise. 1988. "Nigeria." In *Les Télévisions du Monde. Télérama,* no. 48, Special Edition, 410–13. Paris: Télérama-Cerf-Corlet.

Barton, Frank. 1969. *African Assignment: The Story of IPI's Six Year Training Programme in Tropical Africa.* Zurich: International Press Institute.

Bebey, François. 1975. *African Music: A People's Art.* Trans. Josephine Bennett. Westport, Conn.: Lawrence Hill.

Becker, Jorg, Goran Hedebro, and Leena Paldan, eds. 1986. *Communication and Domination.* Norwood, N.J.: Ablex.

Bejot, Jean-Pierre. 1993. "L'émancipation des médias." *Jeune Afrique Economie,* Special Supplement on Burkina Faso, no. 168 (June): 90–91.

Bellah, Robert. 1985. *Habits of the Heart: Individualism and Commitment in American Life.* New York: Harper and Row.

Bellman, Beryl L. 1984. *The Language of Secrecy: Symbols and Metaphors in Poro Ritual.* New Brunswick, N.J.: Rutgers University Press.

Beltran, Luis Ramiro. 1976. "Alien Premises, Objects, and Methods in Latin American Research." In *Communication and Development: Critical Perspectives,* ed. Everett Rogers, 15–42. Beverly Hills: Sage.

Benjamin, Medea, and Andrea Freedman. 1989. *Bridging the Global Gap: A Handbook Linking Citizens of the First and Third Worlds.* Cabin John, Md.: Seven Locks.

Bessi, Mouelle. "Communauté urbaine de Douala: Place à M. Pokossy Ndoumbe." *Cameroon Tribune* (Douala and Yaoundé), 19 April 1989, 3.

Biebuyck, D., and K. C. Mateene. 1969. *The Mwindo Epic from the Banyanga.* Berkeley: University of California Press.

Biles, Peter. 1993. "Eritrea: Birth of a Nation." *Africa Report* (July–August): 13–19.

Bitrus, Apollos. 1982. "Why Women's Liberation Was Unpopular." *Sunday Standard* (Jos, Nigeria), 3 January, 11.

Bjornlund, Eric, Michael Bratton, and Clark Gibson. 1992. "Observing Multiparty Elections in Africa: Lessons from Zambia." *African Affairs* 91: 405–31.

Black, Jan Knippers. 1991. *Development in Theory and Practice: Bridging the Gap.* Boulder, Colo.: Westview.

Blyden, Edward. 1857. *A Vindication of the Negro Race: Being a Brief Examination of the Arguments in Favour of African Inferiority.* With an Introduction by Rev. Alexander Crummel. Monrovia, Liberia: Killian.

Blyden, Edward. 1887. *Christianity, Islam, and the Negro Race.* London: Whittingham.

Boafo, S. T. Kwame. 1991. "Communication Technology and Dependent Development in Sub-Saharan Africa." In *Transnational Communications: Wiring the Third World*, ed. Gerald Sussman and John Lent, 103–24. Newbury Park, Calif.: Sage.

Boal, Angusto. 1979. *Theater of the Oppressed.* Trans. Charles and Maria-Odilia Lead McBride. New York: Urizen Books.

Booker, Maria. 1987. "Un Soap opéra Kenyan." *Libération* (Paris), 19 July, 18.

Boulding, Elise. 1988. *Building a Global Civic Culture: Education for an Interdependent World.* New York: Teacher College Press: Teachers College, Columbia University.

Bourgault, Louise M. 1987. "The Oral Tradition in the Nigerian Press." *World Communication* 16 (2): 211–35.

Bourgault, Louise. 1988–89. Unpublished field notes. Ethnographic study of a Gola-Kpelle Village, Liberia.

Bourgault, Louise M. 1989. "Training Researchers for Development Communication in Africa." *World Communication* 18 (1): 73–92.

Bourgault, Louise M. 1991. "Village Based Drama for Development in Africa." *Journal of Development Communication* 2, 2 (December): 49–73.

Bourgault, Louise M. 1992a. "Talking to People in the Oral Tradition: Ethnographic Research for Development Communication." *International Communication Bulletin* 27, 3–4 (Fall): 19–24.

Bourgault, Louise. 1992b. "TV Drama in Hausaland: The Search for a New Aesthetic and a New Ethic." Paper presented to the 11th annual SSISS/SAGP Conference. New York. October. Unpublished paper.

Bourgault, Louise M. 1993. "Press Freedom in Africa: A Cultural Analysis." *Journal of Communication Inquiry* 17, 2 (Summer): 69–92.

Bourgault, Louise M. 1994a. "Training African Media Personnel: Some Psychocultural Considerations." *Africana Journal* 16: 51–65.

Bourgault, Louise M. 1994b. "The Liberian Rural Communications Network: A Study in the Contradictions of Development Communication." *Journal of Development Communication* 5, 2 (June): 57–71.

Bourgault, Louise M. 1995. "Nigeria." In *The International World of Electronic Media*, ed. Lynne Gross. New York: McGraw-Hill (in press).

Bourgine, Caroline. 1988. "Gabon." In *Les Télévisions du Monde. Télérama*, no. 48, Special Edition, 387–89. Paris: Télérama-Cerf-Corlet.

Boyles, Denis. 1988. *African Lives: White Lies, Tropical Truth, Darkest Gossip, and*

Rumblings of Rumor—From Chinese Gorden to Beryl Markham, and Beyond. New York: Weidenfeld and Nicolson.

Bretton, Henry. 1973. *Power and Politics in Africa.* Chicago: Aldine.

Brice, Kim. 1992. "Muzzling the Media." *Africa Report* (July–August): 50–51.

British Broadcasting Corporation, News Bulletin. 1993. World Service, 22 June. Radio Broadcast.

British Broadcasting Corporation, News Bulletin. 1994. World Service, 19 May. Radio Broadcast.

Brittain, Victoria. 1993. "Oxfam Plea for Africa." *Guardian Weekly* (Manchester), 9 May, 7.

Brooke, Pamela. 1989. "Adapting Village Drama to Radio." A report presented to the Institute for International Research. Monrovia, Liberia. March. Unpublished paper.

Brummer, Alex. 1993. "Africa Facing Deeper Gloom." *Guardian Weekly* (Manchester), 25 April, 21.

Bruner, Edward. 1986. "Experience and Its Expressions." In *The Anthropology of Experience*, ed. Victor Turner and Edward Bruner, 3–29. Urbana: University of Illinois Press.

Burke, James. 1985. *Printing Transforms Knowledge*, vol. 4 of 10-part series "The Day the Universe Changed." Produced by the British Broadcasting Corporation. 60 min. Videotape.

Burke, James. 1991. "Communication in the Middle Ages." In *Communication in History: Technology, Culture, and Society*, ed. David Crowley and Paul Heyer, 67–77. New York: Longman.

Carver, Richard. 1992. "A Licence to Kill." *Index on Censorship* (May): 14–17.

Carver, Richard. 1994. "Malawi: The Army Factor." *Africa Report* (January–February): 56–58.

Chabi, Maurice. 1992. "Benin: Growing Pains." *Index on Censorship* (July): 36–37.

Chernoff, John Miller. 1979. *African Rhythm and African Sensibility: Aesthetics and Social Action in African Musical Idioms.* Chicago: University of Chicago Press.

Chinje, Eric. 1993. "The Media in Emerging African Democracies: Power Politics and the Role of the Press." *The Fletcher Forum* 17 (Winter): 49–65.

Clarke, Peter. 1987. "The Maitatsene Movement in Northern Nigeria in Historical and Current Perspective." In *New Religious Movements in Nigeria*, ed. Rosalind I. J. Hackett, 161–78. Lewiston, N.Y.: Edwin Mellen.

Clifford, James, and George Marcus, eds. 1986. *Writing Culture: The Poetics and Politics of Ethnography.* Berkeley: University of California Press.

Clough, Michael. 1992. *Free at Last?: U.S. Policy toward Africa and the End of the Cold War.* New York: Council on Foreign Relations Press.

Conateh, Swaebou J. S. 1974. "The Gambia." In *Broadcasting in Africa: A Continental Survey of Radio and Television*, ed. Sydney Head, 96–101. Philadelphia: Temple University Press.

Cook, Clive. 1989. "The Third World: Survey." *The Economist*, Special Section (23 September): 3.

Cruise-O'Brien, Rita. 1985. "Broadcast Professionalism in Senegal." In *Mass Media, Culture, and Society in West Africa*, ed. Frank Ugboajah, 187–99. Munich: Hans Zell.

Dabia, Habib Ahmed. 1981. "The Case of Dan Maraya Jos: A Hausa Poet." In *Oral*

Poetry in Nigeria, ed. Uchegbulam N. Abalogu, Garba Ashiwaju, and Regina Amadi-Tshiwala, 209–29. Lagos, Nigeria. *Nigeria Magazine*, published in conjunction with UNESCO, Paris.

Daddah, Turkia Ould. 1988. "Bringing the Public Administrations and the Populations Closer Together: Problems and Methods in Socio-Cultural Contexts in Africa." In *Participative Administration and Endogenous Development*, ed. Huynh Cao Tri, 101–32. Brussels: International Institute of Administrative Sciences and Paris: UNESCO.

Davidson, Basil. 1992. *The Black Man's Burden: Africa and the Curse of the Nation State*. New York: Times Books.

Davies, Desmond. 1994. "BBC's First in Africa." *West Africa* (18–24 April): 679–81.

Davies, George Ola. 1994. "Zaire: Ending the Stalemate." *West Africa* (11–17 April): 647.

Davis, St. Jerome. Chief of Development Services, Liberian Rural Communications Network, Monrovia, Liberia. 1988. Interview by author, October, Monrovia, Liberia. Unpublished notes.

Decalo, Samuel. 1992. "The Process, Prospects and Constraints of Democratization in Africa." *African Affairs* 91: 7–35.

Desai, Gurav. 1990. "Theater as Praxis: Discursive Strategies in African Popular Theater." *African Studies Review* 33 (April): 65–92.

de Sola Pool, Ithiel. 1963. "Mass Media and Politics in the Modernization Process." In *Communications and Political Development*, ed. Lucian Pye, 234–53. Princeton: Princeton University Press.

Dimka, Prince. 1984. "The Need to Guide against Conformism." *Nigeria Voice*, 6 July, 2.

Dissanayake, Wimal. 1991. "Ethics, Development, and Communication: A Buddhist Approach." In *Communication in Development*, ed. Fred L. Casmir, 319–37. Norwood, N.J.: Ablex.

Domatob, Jerry. 1991. "Serious Problems Face Media Education in Sub-Saharan Africa." *Media Development* 38 (1): 31–34.

Drucker, Peter. 1989. *New Realities*. New York: Harper Collins.

Dubuch, C. 1985. "Langage de pouvoir, pouvoir du langage." *Politique Africaine* 20: 44–55.

Durning, Alan. 1989. "People, Power, and Development." *Foreign Policy* 76 (Fall): 66–82.

Dye, Thomas, and Harmon Zeigler. 1989. *American Politics in the Media Age*. 3rd ed. Pacific Grove, Calif.: Brooks/Cole.

Eagle Express. 1991. "Zambia Don't Be Tempted." *Eagle Express* (Lusaka, Zambia), 31 October.

Economou, Persephone, Michelle Gittelman, and Mulatu Wubneh. 1993. "Europe 1992 and Foreign Direct Investment in Africa." In *Europe and Africa: The New Phase*, ed. I. William Zartman, 95–119. Boulder: Lynne Rienner.

Edeani, David Omazo. 1985. "Press Ownership and Control in Nigeria." In *Mass Communication, Culture, and Society in West Africa*, ed. Frank Okwu Ugboajah, 44–62. Munich: Hans Zell.

Elima. (Kinshasa, Zaire). 1975. 24 October, 1.

Elliott, Philip, and Peter Golding. 1979. *Making the News*. London: Longman, 1979.

Ellis, Stephen. 1989. "Turning to Pavement Radio." *African Affairs* 88 (July): 321–30.

Esman, Milton J., and Norman T. Uphoff. 1984. *Local Organizations: Intermediaries in Rural Development*. Ithaca: Cornell University Press.

Etherton, Michael. 1988. "Popular Theater for Change: From Literacy to Oracy." *Media Development* 35 (3): 2–4.

Eyoh, Hansel. 1984. "Trends in African Theatre: The Popular Theatre Approach." Paper presented at the International African Oral Literature Association Conference. Budapest. Unpublished paper.

Fabian, Johannes. 1990. *Power and Performance: Ethnographic Explorations through Proverbial Wisdom in Theater Shown in Shaba, Zaire*. Madison: University of Wisconsin Press.

Fage, J. D. 1969. *A History of West Africa: An Introductory Survey*. 4th ed. Cambridge: Cambridge University Press.

Fanon, Frantz. 1967. *Black Skin, White Masks*. Trans. Charles Lam Markmann. New York: Grove.

Faringer, Gunilla. 1991. *Press Freedom in Africa*. New York: Praeger.

Farrell, Thomas. 1991. "Secondary Orality and Consciousness Today." In *Media, Consciousness, and Culture*, ed. Bruce Gronbeck, Thomas Farrell, and Paul Soukup, 194–209. Newbury Park, Calif.: Sage.

Fenton, Thomas, and Mary J. Heffron, eds. 1987. *Africa: A Directory of Resources*. New York: Orbis.

Fernandez, James. 1975. "The Exposition and Imposition of Order: Artistic Expression in Fang Culture." In *The Traditional Artist in African Societies*, ed. Warren L. d'Azevedo, 194–220. Bloomington: Indiana University Press.

Fernandez, James. 1984. Foreword to *The Language of Secrecy: Symbols and Metaphors in Poro Ritual*, by Beryl L. Bellman. New Brunswick: Rutgers University Press.

Finnegan, Ruth. 1970. *Oral Poetry in Africa*. Oxford: Clarendon.

Fiombo, Angelo, and Allesandra Speciale. 1992. "At First Sight." *Ecrans d'Afrique* (Paris) (Second Quarter): 22–23.

Fortes, M., and E. E. Evans-Pritchard, eds. 1940. *African Political Systems*. London: Oxford University Press.

Fortner, Robert. 1993. *International Communication: History, Conflict, and Control of the Global Metropolis*. Belmont, Calif.: Wadsworth.

Fraenkel, Peter. 1959. *Wayaleshi Radio in Central Africa*. London: Weidenfeld and Nicolson.

Freire, Paulo. 1974. *Pedagogy of the Oppressed*. Trans. Myra Bergman Ramos. New York: Seabury.

Galtung, Johan. 1992. *Global Glasnost: Toward a New World Information and Communication Order?* Cresskill, N.J.: Hampton.

Gardinier, David E. 1982. "Decolonization in French, Belgian, and Portuguese Africa: A Bibliographical Essay." In *The Transfer of Power in Africa: Decolonization 1940–1960*, ed. Prosser Gifford and William Roger Louis, 515–66. New Haven: Yale University Press.

Gay, John. 1973. *Red Dust on the Green Leaves*. With the editorial advice of John Kellemu. Yarmouth, Maine: Intercultural.

Gay, John. 1980. *The Brightening Shadow*. With the editorial advice of John Kellemu. Chicago: Intercultural.

Geekie, Russell. 1993. "Interview with Ni John Fru." *Africa Report* (March–April): 62–63.

Geertz, Clifford. 1973. *The Interpretation of Cultures*. New York: Basic Books.

Geschiere, Peter. 1988. "Sorcery and the State: Popular Modes of Action among the Maka of Southeast Cameroon." *Critique of Anthropology* 8 (1): 35–63.

Gibbons, R. Arnold. 1974. "Francophone West and Equatorial Africa." In *Broadcasting in Africa: A Continental Survey of Radio and Television*, ed. Sydney Head, 107–24. Philadelphia. Temple University Press.

Giddens, Anthony. 1990. *The Consequences of Modernity*. Stanford: Stanford University Press.

Gifford, Prosser, and Timothy C. Weiskel. 1971. "African Education in a Colonial Context: French and British Styles." In *France and Britain in Africa*, ed. Prosser Gifford and William Roger Louis, 663–711. New Haven: Yale University Press.

Goody, Jack. 1968. "Restricted Literacy in Northern Ghana." In *Literacy in Traditional Societies*, ed. Jack Goody, 199–264. Cambridge: Cambridge University Press.

Goody, Jack, ed. 1968. *Literacy in Traditional Societies*. Cambridge: Cambridge University Press.

Goody, Jack, and Ian Watt. 1968. "The Consequences of Literacy." In *Literacy in Traditional Societies*, ed. Jack Goody, 27–68. Cambridge: Cambridge University Press.

Goody, Jack, and Ian Watt. 1991. "The Consequences of Literacy." In *Communication in History: Technology, Culture, and Society*, ed. David Crowley and Paul Heyer, 48–56. New York: Longman.

Gottlieb, Alma, and Philip Graham. 1993. *Parallel Worlds: An Anthropologist and a Writer Encounter Africa*. New York: Crown.

Gouldner, Alvin. 1982. *The Dialectic of Ideology and Technology: The Origins, Grammar, and Future of Ideology*. New York: Oxford University Press.

Habermas, Jürgen. 1983. *A Theory of Communicative Action*, 3 vols. Boston: Beacon.

Hachten, William. 1971. *Muffled Drums: The News Media in Africa*. Ames: Iowa State University Press.

Hachten, William. 1987. *The World News Prism: Changing Media, Clashing Ideologies*. 2nd ed. Ames: Iowa State University Press.

Hachten, William. 1993. *The Growth of Media in the Third World: African Failures, Asian Successes*. Ames: Iowa State University Press.

Ham, Melinda. 1991. "Post-Independence Zambia." *Africa Report* (September–October): 68–71.

Ham, Melinda. 1992. "Zambia: A New Page." *Africa Report* (January–February): 19–20.

Ham, Melinda. 1993. "Zambia: History Repeats Itself." *Africa Report* (May–June): 13–16.

Harden, Blaine. 1990. *Africa: Dispatches from a Fragile Continent*. Boston: Houghton Mifflin.

Haring, Lee. 1972. "A Characteristic African Folktale Pattern." In *African Folklore*, ed. Richard M. Dorson, 165–79. Garden City, N.Y.: Doubleday.

Head, Sydney. 1974. "An Agenda for Further Study." In *Broadcasting in Africa: A Continental Survey*, ed. Sydney Head, 347–74. Philadelphia: Temple University Press.

Head, Sydney. 1974. "Broadcasting and Commerce." In *Broadcasting in Africa: A Con-*

tinental Survey of Radio and Television, ed. Sydney Head, 336–42. Philadelphia: Temple University Press.

Head, Sydney. 1974. "Research." In *Broadcasting in Africa: A Continental Survey of Radio and Television*, ed. Sydney Head, 320–35. Philadelphia: Temple University Press.

Head, Sydney. 1985. *World Broadcasting Systems: A Comparative Analysis*. Belmont, Calif.: Wadsworth.

Hearn, Francis. 1976–77. "Toward a Critical Theory of Play." *Telos* 30: 145–60.

Heath, Carla. 1986. "Politics of Broadcasting in Kenya—Community Radio Suffers." *Media Development* 33 (2): 10–14.

Heath, Carla. 1990. "Private Sector Participation in Public Service Broadcasting: The Case of Kenya." In *Current Issues in International Communication*, ed. L. John Martin and Ray Eldon Hiebert, 74–81. White Plains, N.Y.: Longman.

Heath, Carla. 1992. "Structural Changes in Kenya's Broadcasting System: A Manifestation of Presidential Authoritarianism." *Gazette* 37: 37–51.

Hiskett, Mervyn. 1975. *A History of Hausa Islamic Verse*. London: School of Oriental and African Studies.

Houphouët-Boigny, Félix. 1980. *Propos Sur La Culture: Excerpts from Speeches, 1959–1980*. Abidjan, Côte d'Ivoire: Editions CEDA.

Hove, Chenjerai. 1992. "Zimbabwe in Tatters." *Index on Censorship* (April): 24–25.

Ibie, Nosa Owens. 1993. "The Commercialization of the Mass Media in Nigeria: The Challenge of Social Responsibility." *Journal of Development Communication* 4, 1 (June): 60–68.

Illich, Ivan. 1971. *Deschooling Society*. Harmondsworth: Penguin.

Imanyara, Gitobu. 1992. "Kenya: Indecent Exposure." *Index on Censorship* (April): 21–22.

Index on Censorship. 1992. "Index." *Index on Censorship* (May): 34–41.

Innes, Gordon, ed. 1974. *Sunjata: Three Mandinka Versions*. London: School of Oriental and African Studies.

Institute for International Research. 1989. Final Report of the Rural Information Systems Project, Liberia. Prepared for USAID/Liberia. Arlington, Va.: Institute for International Research. March. Unpublished paper.

Jaumain, Yves, and Belco Tamboura. 1992. "Beware of Bats in the Radio Belfry." *Index on Censorship* (November): 39.

Jazza, Joseph. Proprietor, Excellence Video-Electronics, Kano, Nigeria. 1992. Interview by author, August, Kano, Nigeria. Unpublished notes.

Jones, Eldred, Eustace Palmer, and Marjorie Jones, eds. 1992. *Orature in African Literature Today*. Trenton: Africa World Press.

Jouandet, Nicholas. 1993. "La Volonté d'indépendance." *Afrique/Asie* (Paris) (June): 13.

Justice, J. 1986. *Policies, Plans, and People: Culture and Health Development in Nepal*. Berkeley: University of California Press.

Kamarera, Gaspard. Editor, *Imbaga*, Kigali, Rwanda. 1992. Interview by author, July, Kigali, Rwanda. Unpublished notes.

Kane, Cheikh Hamidou. 1969. *Ambiguous Adventure*. Trans. Katherine Woods. New York: Collier.

Karikari, Kwame. 1993. "Africa: The Press and Democracy." *Race and Class* 34 (3): 55–66.

Karp, Ivan, and Charles Bird, eds. 1987. *Explorations in African Systems of Thought.* Washington, D.C.: Smithsonian Institution Press.

Katz, Elihu, and George Wedell. 1977. *Broadcasting in the Third World: Promise and Performance.* Cambridge: Harvard University Press.

Kelso, B. J. 1993. "Malawi: Banda the Democrat?" *Africa Report* (September–October): 50–53.

Kidd, Ross. 1988. "Didactic Theater." *Media in Education and Development* (March): 33–42.

Kinner, Joseph. 1988. "Nigeria." In *International Handbook of Broadcasting Systems,* ed. Philip T. Rosen, 225–35. New York: Greenwood.

Kirk-Greene, A. H. M. 1982. "A Historiographical Perspective on the Transfer of Power in British Colonial Africa: A Bibliographical Essay." In *The Transfer of Power in Africa: Decolonization 1940–1960,* ed. Prosser Gifford and William Roger Louis, 567–602. New Haven: Yale University Press.

Kitchen, Helen. 1956. *The Press in Africa.* Washington, D.C.: Ruth Sloane Associates.

K'Kudu, Ali. Producer, CTV Kano, Nigeria. 1992. Interview by author, August, Kano, Nigeria. Unpublished notes.

Kofoworola, Ziky O. 1981. "The Hausa Example." In *Oral Poetry in Nigeria,* ed. Uchegbulam N. Abalogu, Garba Ashiwaju, and Regina Amadi-Tshiwala, 290–308. Lagos, Nigeria: *Nigeria Magazine,* published in conjunction with UNESCO, Paris.

Kolade, Chris. 1974. "Nigeria." In *Broadcasting in Africa: A Continental Survey of Radio and Television,* ed. Sydney Head, 78–87. Philadelphia: Temple University Press.

Korten, David C. 1986. *Micro-Policy Reform: The Role of Private Development Agencies.* Washington, D.C.: National Association of Schools of Public Affairs and Administration. Working Paper 12. [Also published in *World Development,* Special Supplement, 1987.]

Korten, David C. 1990. *Getting to the 21st Century: Voluntary Action and the Global Agenda.* West Hartford: Kumarian.

Kouassi, Edmond Kwam, and John White. 1993. "The Impact of Reduced European Security Roles in African Relations." In *Europe and Africa: The New Phase,* ed. I. William Zartman, 27–40. Boulder: Lynne Rienner.

Kpatindé, Francis. 1991. "La Presse privée enfin à la 'une.' " *Jeune Afrique* 1570 (30 January–5 February): 12–15.

Kuhne, Winrich. 1993. "Looking South after the End of the Cold War." In *Europe and Africa: The New Phase,* ed. I. William Zartman, 17–26. Boulder: Lynne Rienner.

Kulakow, Allan. 1992. "The Mass Media and Democratization in Niger." Paper submitted to the Ambassador of the United States in Niger, the Director, USAID; and the Public Affairs Officer, United States Information Service. Burlington, Vt.: Associates in Rural Development. February. Unpublished paper.

Kweekeh, Florida. Project Director, Liberian Rural Communications Network, Monrovia, Liberia. 1988. Interview by author, September, Monrovia, Liberia. Unpublished notes.

Laké, René. 1993. "The Emergence of Pluralism in West African Radio Broadcasting." Paper presented at the Institute for Advanced Study and Research in the African Humanities. Northwestern University, Evanston, Ill. April. Unpublished paper.

Lamb, David. 1985. *The Africans.* New York: Vintage.

Lan, David. 1985. *Guns and Rain: Guerrillas and Spirit Mediums in Zimbabwe.* London: James Currey.

Land, Mitchell. 1991. "The Ivorian State and Cultural Imperialism through Television." Paper presented to the Association of Education in Journalism. Boston. August. Unpublished paper.

Lee, Dorothy D. 1959. "Codifications of Reality: Lineal and Nonlineal." In *Freedom and Culture*, ed. Dorothy D. Lee, 105–20. Englewood Cliffs, N.J.: 1971.

Lenglet, Frans. 1985. "Educational Television in Ivory Coast." In *Mass Communication, Culture and Society in West Africa*, ed. Frank Ugboajah, 153–64. Munich: Hans Zell.

Lerner, Daniel. 1958. *The Passing of Traditional Society*. Glencoe, Ill.: Free Press.

LeVine, Robert A. 1971. "Dreams and Deeds: Achievement Motivation in Nigeria." In *Nigeria: Modernization and the Politics of Communicalism*, ed. Robert Melson and Howard Wolpe, 170–214. East Lansing: Michigan State University Press.

Liebenow, Gus. 1987. *Liberia: The Quest for Democracy*. Bloomington: Indiana University Press.

Lord, A. B. 1960. *The Singer of Tales*. Cambridge: Harvard University Press.

Lowery, Christopher. 1993. "Breaking the Ice: The Karate Kids Mixed Media Package." *Development Communication Report* 81 (2): 12–13.

Luria, A. R. 1976. *Cognitive Development: Its Cultural and Social Foundations*. Trans. M. Lopez-Morillas and L. Solotaroff. Cambridge: Harvard University Press.

Macy, J. 1983. *Dharma and Development: Religion as a Resource in the Sarvodaya Self-Help Movement*. West Hartford: Kumarian.

Maja-Pearce, Adewale. 1992a. "The Press in Central and Southern Africa." *Index on Censorship* (April): 42–73.

Maja-Pearce, Adewale. 1992b. "The Press in East Africa." *Index on Censorship* (July): 51–73.

Maja-Pearce, Adewale. 1993. "The Popular Front for the Liberation of 20 Million Ecus." *Index on Censorship* (April): 2.

Malamah-Thomas, D. H. 1987. "Community Theatre with and by the People: The Sierra Leone Experience." *Convergence* 20 (1): 59–68.

Marcuse, Herbert. 1964. *One-dimensional Man: Studies in the Ideology of Advanced Industrial Society*. Boston: Beacon.

Martin, L. John. 1983. "Africa." In *Global Journalism: A Survey of the World's Mass Media*, ed. John C. Merrill. Ist ed., 190–248. New York: Longman.

Martin, L. John. 1988. "Kenya." In *International Handbook of Broadcasting Systems*, ed. Philip T. Rosen, 198–99. New York: Greenwood.

Martin, L. John. 1991. "Africa." In *Global Journalism: A Survey of International Communication*, ed. John C. Merrill. 2nd ed., 155–204. New York: Longman, 1991.

Mattelart, Armand, Xavier Delcourt, and Michelle Mattelart. 1984. *International Image Markets: In Search of an Alternative Perspective*. Trans. David Buxton. London: Comedia.

Mbachu, Dilue. 1992. "Owners and Censors." *Index on Censorship* (February): 28–29.

Mbembe, Achille. 1988. *Afriques Indociles: Christianisme, pouvoir et état en société postcoloniale*. Paris: Editions Karthala.

Mbembe, Achille. 1992. "The Banality of Power and the Aesthetics of Vulgarity in the Postcolony." Trans. Janet Roitman. *Public Culture* 4, 2 (Spring): 1–30.

Mbiti, John. 1971. *African Religions and Philosophy*. New York: Praeger.

McColm, R. Bruce. 1991. "The Comparative Survey of Freedom: 1991, the Democratic Movement." *Freedom Review* 22 (1): 5–12.

McCurry, David S. 1991. "Harnessing a White Elephant." *Development Communication Report* 73 (2): 8–9.

McGregor, Douglas. 1960. *The Human Side of Enterprise*. New York: McGraw-Hill.

McLellan, Iain. 1986. *Television and Development: The African Experience*. Ottawa: International Development Research Center.

McLuhan, Marshall. 1991. "Understanding Radio." In *Communication in History: Technology, Culture, and Society*, ed. David Crowley and Paul Heyer, 207–13. New York: Longman.

McQuail, Denis. 1987. *Mass Communication Theory: An Introduction*. Newbury Park, Calif.: Sage.

Media Development. 1988. "Editorial: The Real Play Starts Where the Actors Leave Off." *Media Development* 35 (3): 1.

Media Development Consultants. 1983. Seminar in Newswriting for Nigerian Television Authority News Personnel, Kano, Nigeria. January.

Merrill, John. 1971. "The Role of the Mass Media in National Development: An Open Question for Speculation." *Gazette* 17, 4 (December): 236–42.

Metz, Helen Chapin, ed. 1992. *Nigeria: A Country Study*. 5th ed. Library of Congress. Federal Research Division. Washington, D.C.: U.S. Department of the Army.

Mills, Jack, and James Kangawa. 1983. "Community Radio in Kenya." *Combroad* (September): 20–22.

Miyouna, Ludovic. 1987. "Text and Context in Information Production." *Africa Media Review* 1 (3): 95–106.

Mobe, Anicet. 1993. "Zaire: Coup d'Etat Permanent." *Afrique-Asie* (Paris) (July–August): 21.

Moore, Robert C. 1992. *The Political Reality of Freedom of the Press in Zambia*. Lanham, Md.: University Press of America.

Morris, H. F. 1964. *The Heroic Recitations of the Bahima of Ankole*. Oxford: Clarendon.

Morrison, Joy. 1989. "Fatouma, the Baby Machine: A Case Study of the Use of Forum Theater in a Family Planning Campaign in Burkina Faso." Paper presented at the 32nd Annual Meeting of the African Studies Association. Atlanta. November. Unpublished paper.

Morrison, Joy. 1991. "Forum Theater in West Africa: An Alternative Medium for Information Exchange." *Research in African Literatures* 22 (Fall): 29–40.

Moyo, Mavis. 1990. "Development through Radio: The Zimbabwe Experience." In *Communication Processes: Alternative Channels and Strategies for Development Support*, ed. S. T. Kwame Boafo and Nancy George, 16–20. Ottawa: International Research Development Council.

Mudimbe, Valentine. 1988. *The Invention of Africa: Gnosis, Philosophy, and the Order of Knowledge*. Bloomington: Indiana University Press.

wa Mutua, Makau. 1992. "The Last Chapter." *Africa Report* (September–October): 50–51.

wa Mutua, Makau. 1993. "Zaire: Permanent Anarchy?" *Africa Report* (May–June): 53–55.

Mwiinga, Jowie. 1994. "Zambia: Chill for Chiluba." *Africa Report* (March–April): 58–60.

Mytton, Graham. 1983. *Mass Communication in Africa*. London: Edward Arnold.

Narag, Jasmer Singh. General Manager, Media Development Consultants, Kano, Nigeria. 1992. Personal communication with author, August, Kano, Nigeria. Unpublished notes.

New African. 1988. "Publish and Survive. (Part I: African Press Survey)." *New African* (May): 35-42.

Ngabirano, Devoté. 1993. " 'Ni Nde?': A Case Study of Radio Soap Operas in Burundi." Paper presented at the Institute for Advanced Study and Research in the African Humanities. Northwestern University, Evanston, Ill. April. Unpublished paper.

Ngugi wa Thiong'o. 1986. *Decolonising the Mind.* London: James Currey and Nairobi: Heinemann.

Nielson, Waldemar A. 1969. *The Great Powers and Africa.* New York: Praeger. Published for the Council on Foreign Relations.

Niyii, Abali. 1988. "African Press Survey: Publish and Survive." *New African* (May): 35-36.

Nkanga, Dieudonné Mbala. 1992. "Radio-Trottoir in Central Africa." *Passages: A Chronicle of the Humanities* 4: 4-5, 8.

La Nouvelle Marché. 1982. "A Lomé Le President Eyadema a assisté à la Messe de Minuit." *La Nouvelle Marché* (Lomé, Togo), 27 December, 1, 3.

Novicki, Margaret. 1991a. "A Human Rights Lodestar." *Africa Report* (May-June): 41-42.

Novicki, Margaret. 1991b. "Interview with Monsignor Isidore de Souza: Building a New Benin." *Africa Report* (May-June): 43-45.

Novicki, Margaret. 1992. "Zambia: A Lesson in Democracy." *Africa Report* (January-February): 13-17.

Nwanko, Robert. 1974. "Educational Uses of Broadcasting." In *Broadcasting in Africa: A Continental Survey of Radio and Television*, ed. Sydney Head, 292-302. Philadelphia: Temple University Press.

Nwosu, Ikechukwu. 1985. "Communication Realities in Nigeria." *Final Report of the ACCE/UNESCO/ISS Regional Planning Seminar on Communication Policy and Planning for Development*, ed. I. E. Nwosu, 45-57. Nairobi, Kenya: African Council on Communications Education.

Nyakutemba, Elias. 1992. "Zambia's Press Defends Its Freedom." *New African* (March): 9-10.

Nyamnjoh, Francis B. 1988. "Broadcasting in Francophone Africa: Crusading for French Culture?" *Gazette* 42: 81-92.

Obazee, Iredi, and Abubakar Tanimu. 1984. "A Journey So Far Encouraging." *Sunday Triumph* (Kano, Nigeria), 8 April, 7.

Obeichina, Emmanuel. 1975. *Communication Tradition, and Society in the West African Novel.* Cambridge: Cambridge University Press.

Obeng-Quaidoo, Isaac. 1985a. "Media Habits of Ghanaian Youth." In *Mass Communication, Culture, and Society in West Africa*, ed. Frank Ugboajah, 237-49. Munich: Hans Zell.

Obeng-Quaidoo, Isaac. 1985b. "Culture and Communication Research Methodologies." *Gazette* 36 (2): 109-20.

Obeng-Quaidoo, Isaac. 1987. "New Development Oriented Models of Communication Research: The Case of Focus Group Research." In *Communicatio Socialis Yearbook*, 115-25. Indore, India: Sat Prachar.

Obeng-Quaidoo, Isaac. 1988a. "Communication and the Organization of Rural People for Change: The Case of the *Wonsuom* Project," 77-94. In *Communicatio Socialis Yearbook*. Indore, India: Sat Prachar.

Obeng-Quaidoo, Isaac. 1988b. "Assessment of the Experience in the Production of

Messages and Programmes for Rural Communication Systems: The Case of the *Wonsuom* Project in Ghana." *Gazette* 42, 53–67.

Ochs, Martin. 1986. *The African Press*. Cairo: American University in Cairo Press.

Ogundele, Wole. 1992. "Orality versus Literacy in Mazisi Kunene's Emperor Shaka the Great." In *Orature in African Literature Today*, ed. Eldred Jones, Eustace Palmer, and Marjorie Jones, 9–23. Trenton: Africa World.

Okpewho, Isidore. 1992. *African Oral Literature: Backgrounds, Character, and Continuity*. Bloomington: Indiana University Press.

Okpewho, Isidore, ed. 1985. *The Heritage of African Poetry*. London: Longman.

O'Neill, Michael. 1990. *The Third America*. San Francisco: Jossey-Bass.

Ong, Walter. 1982. *Orality and Literacy: The Technologizing of the Word*. London: Methuen.

Oreh, O. O. 1985. "Masquerade and Other Plays on Nigerian Television." In *Mass Communication, Culture and Society in West Africa*, ed. Frank Ugboajah, 108–12. Munich: Hans Zell.

Othman, Farouk. General Manager, City TV Kano, Nigeria. 1992. Interview by author, August, Kano, Nigeria. Unpublished notes.

Ouedraogo, Moussa. 1992. "Jokers in the Blood." *Index on Censorship* (October): 35.

Packer, George. 1988. *The Village of Waiting*. New York: Vintage.

Peebles, Dana. 1984. "Changing the Status of Women in Development." *CUSO Journal: Women in Development*. Special Edition, 9–13.

Petty, Sheila. 1992. "African Cinema and (Re)Education: Using Recent African Films." *Issue: A Journal of Opinion* 20 (2): 26–30.

Postman, Neil. 1985. *Amusing Ourselves to Death: Public Discourse in the Age of Show Business*. New York: Penguin.

Pradervand, Pierre. 1990. *Listening to Africa: Developing Africa from the Grassroots*. New York: Praeger.

Prescott-Allen, Robert C. 1992. "Caring for the World." In *Spirit and Nature: Why the Environment Is a Religious Issue*, ed. Steven C. Rockefeller and John C. Elder, 125–38. Boston: Beacon.

Press, Robert. 1992. "Africa's Turn." *World Monitor*, February, 36–43.

Pye, Lucian, ed. 1963. *Communications and Political Development*. Princeton: Princeton University Press.

Quaal, Ward, and James A. Brown. 1976. *Broadcast Management: Radio, Television*. 2nd ed. New York: Hastings House.

Rahnema, Majid. 1992. "Poverty." In *The Development Dictionary*, ed. Wolfgang Sachs, 158–76. London: Zed.

Real, Michael. 1985. "Broadcast Music in Nigeria and Liberia: A Comparative Note." In *Mass Communication, Culture, and Society in West Africa*, ed. Frank Ugboajah, 95–99. Munich: Hans Zell.

Reed, David. 1992. *Structural Adjustment and the Environment*. Boulder: Westview.

Riddell, Roger. 1993. "Aid Performance and Prospects." In *Europe and Africa: The New Phase*, ed. I. William Zartman, 139–58. Boulder: Lynne Rienner.

Riesman, Paul. 1986. "The Person and the Life Cycle in African Social Life and Thought." *African Studies Review* 29 (2): 71–138.

Righter, Rosemary. 1978. *Whose News? Politics, the Press and the Third World*. New York: Times Books.

Riley, Marie. 1990. "Indigenous Resources in Africa: Unexplored Communication Potential." *Howard Journal of Communication* 2 (Summer): 301–14.

Robertson, E. H. 1974. "Christian Broadcasting in and to Africa." In *Broadcasting in Africa: A Continental Survey of Radio and Television*, ed. Sydney Head, 204–11. Philadelphia: Temple University Press.

Rockefeller, Steven C., and John C. Elder, eds. 1992. *Spirit and Nature: Why the Environment Is a Religious Issue*. Boston: Beacon.

Rodney, Walter. 1972. *How Europe Underdeveloped Africa*. London: Bogle L'Ouverture.

Rogers, Everett. 1962. *The Diffusion of Innovations*. New York: Free Press.

Rose, E. J. 1962. "Problems of the Press in Africa. A Report by the International Press Institute." Munster University, Munster, Germany.

Royle, David. 1986. *Assignment Africa*. Press and Public Project, Inc. 58 min. Videotape.

Rubin, Leslie, and Brian Weinstein. 1974. *Introduction to African Politics: A Continental Approach*. New York: Praeger.

Ruether, Rosemary R. 1983. *Sexism and God Talk: Toward a Feminist Theology*. Boston: Beacon.

Ruijter, Jose M. 1989. "State and Media in Africa: A Quarrelsome though Faithful Marriage." *Gazette* 44: 57–69.

Saitoti, Tepilit Ole. 1986. *The Worlds of a Maasai Warrior: An Autobiography*. Berkeley: University of California Press.

Sbert, José Maria. 1992. "Progress." In *The Development Dictionary*, ed. Wolfgang Sachs, 192–205. London: Zed.

Scarrit, James R. 1971. "Elite Values, Ideology, and Power in Post-Independence Zambia." *African Studies Review* 14 (1): 31–59.

Schatzberg, Michael. 1988. *The Dialectics of Oppression in Zaire*. Bloomington: Indiana University Press.

Schiller, Herbert. 1969. *Mass Communication and American Empire*. New York: Augustus M. Kelley.

Schiller, Herbert. 1989. *Culture Inc.: The Corporate Takeover of Public Expression*. Oxford: Oxford University Press.

Schiller, Herbert. 1992. *Mass Communications and American Empire*. 2nd ed. Boulder: Westview.

Schramm, Wilbur. 1964. *Mass Media and National Development*. Stanford: Stanford University Press.

Schramm, Wilbur, and Daniel Lerner, eds. 1976. *Communication and Change: The Last Ten Years and the Next*. Honolulu: University of Hawaii Press.

Schumacher, E. F. 1973. *Small Is Beautiful: Economics as if People Mattered*. New York: Harper and Row.

Scotton, James. 1974. "Training in Africa." In *Broadcasting in Africa: A Continental Survey of Radio and Television*, ed. Sydney Head, 281–85. Philadelphia: Temple University Press.

Servaes, Jan. 1991. "Toward a New Perspective for Communication and Development." In *Communication in Development*, ed. Fred Casmir, 51–86. Norwood, N.J.: Ablex.

Sheckler, Annette. Eritrean Referendum Election Monitor, Program Officer, African American Institute, Washington, D.C. 1993. Personal communication with author, June, Brazzaville, Congo. Unpublished notes.

Shehu, Garba. Editor-in-Chief, *The Triumph*, Kano, Nigeria. 1992. Interview by author, August, Kano, Nigeria. Unpublished notes.

Sieber, Roy, and Roslyn Walker. 1987. *African Art in the Cycle of Life*. Washington, D.C.: Smithsonian Institution Press.

Silverstone, Roger. 1991. "Television, Rhetoric, and the Return of the Unconscious in Secondary Oral Culture." In *Media: Consciousness, and Culture*, ed. Bruce Gronbeck, Thomas Farrell, and Paul Soukup, 147–59. Newbury Park, Calif.: Sage.

Singhal, Arvind, and Everett Rogers. 1989. "Educating through Television." *Populi* 16 (2): 38–47.

Sklair, Leslie. 1991. *Sociology of the Global System*. Baltimore: Johns Hopkins University Press.

Skurnik, W. A. E. 1986. "Press Freedom in Africa: From Pessimism to Optimism." In *Democracy and Pluralism in Africa*, ed. Dov Ronen, 145–64. Boulder: Lynne Rienner.

Smitherman, Geneva. 1977. *Talkin and Testifyin: The Language of Black America*. Detroit: Wayne State University Press.

Smythe, Hugh, and Mabel Smythe. 1960. *The New Nigerian Elite*. Stanford: Stanford University Press.

The Standard. "Stability the Key." 1987. *The Standard* (Nairobi, Kenya), 2 March, 5.

Staudt, Kathleen. 1991. *Managing Development: State, Society, and International Contexts*. Newbury Park, Calif.: Sage.

Stengers, Jean. 1982. "Precipitous Decolonization: The Case of the Belgian Congo." In *The Transfer of Power in Africa: Decolonization 1940-1960*, ed. Prosser Gifford and William Roger Louis, 305–37. New Haven: Yale University Press.

Stone, Ruth. 1986. "African Music Performed." In *Africa*, ed. Phyllis M. Martin and Patrick O'Meara, 233–48. 2nd ed. Bloomington: Indiana University Press.

Sunday Herald. 1984. "Give Children Choice of Religion." *Sunday Herald* (Illorin, Nigeria), 8 July, 3.

Sussman, Gerald, and John Lent, eds. 1991. *Transnational Communications: Wiring Up the Third World*. Newbury Park, Calif.: Sage.

Tarr, S. Byron. 1993. "The ECOMOG Initiative in Liberia: A Liberian Perspective." *Issue: A Journal of Opinion* 21 (1–2): 74–83.

Taylor, 'Shola. 1992. RASCOM: Pooling Resources Together. Towards an Integrated African Telecommunications Network. Speech delivered at AFCOM '92; first U.S.-Africa Communications Conference. Recorded in Afcom '93. Washington, D.C. AFCOM International.

Tchindji, Pierre Paul. n.d. "L'Utilisation des productions audiovisuelles étrangères par des organismes de télévision d'Afrique francophone: Sénégal, Côte d'Ivoire, Burkina Faso, Gabon." Doctoral thesis, University of Paris II.

Tehranian, Majid. 1980. "The Curse of Modernity: The Dialectics of Modernization and Communication." *International Social Science Journal* 32 (2): 247–61.

Tehranian, Majid. 1990. *Technologies of Power: Information Technologies and Democratic Prospects*. Norwood, N.J.: Ablex.

Tempels, Placide. 1959. *Bantu Philosophy*. Trans. A. Rubbens. Paris: Présence Africaine.

Theobald, Robin. 1990. *Corruption, Development, and Underdevelopment*. Durham: Duke University Press.

Thiagarajan, Sivasailam. 1993. "People-Based Interactive Instruction." *Development Communication Report* 81, 1–4.

Tolba, Mustafa K. 1992. *Saving Our Planet*. London: Chapman and Hall.

Toulabor, Comi. 1981. "Jeu de mots, jeu de vilains." *Politique Africaine* 3: 55–71.

Toulabor, Comi. 1986. *Le Togo Sous Eyadema*. Paris: Karthala.

Tudesq, André-Jean. 1991. "Nouvelles Technologies de la communication et dépendance renforcée de l'Afrique Noire." *Mondes en Développement* (Paris) 19 (73): 81–95.

Tudesq, André-Jean. 1992. *L'Afrique Noire et ses Télévisions*. Paris: Anthropos/INA.

Tudesq, André-Jean. 1983. *La Radio en Afrique Noire*. Paris: Editions A. Pédone.

Tunstall, Jeremy. 1977. *The Media Are American*. New York: Columbia University Press.

Turner, Victor. 1982. *From Ritual to Theatre*. New York: Performing Arts Journal Publications.

Uche, Luke Uka. 1986. "The Youth and Music Culture: A Nigerian Case Study." *Gazette* 37: 63–78.

Ugboajah, Frank, ed. 1985. *Mass Communication, Culture, and Society in West Africa*. Munich: Hans Zell.

Ukpabi, Chudi. 1990. *Doing Business in Africa: Myths and Realities*. Amsterdam: Royal Tropical Institute.

Ukpokodu, I. Peter. 1992. "Plays, Possession and Rock-and-Roll: Political Theatre in Africa." *The Drama Review* (Winter): 28–53.

UNESCO. 1961. *Mass Media in Developing Countries*. Reports and Papers on Mass Communication, N. 33. Paris: UNESCO.

UNESCO. 1989. *World Communication Report*. Paris: UNESCO.

Ungar, Sanford. 1989. *Africa: The People and Politics of an Emerging Continent*. 3rd rev. ed. New York: Simon and Schuster.

United Nations Development Programme. 1992. *Human Development Report*. New York: Oxford University Press.

United States Agency for International Development. 1987. Training Course for Research Methods for Development Communications. Mbabane, Swaziland. July–August.

United States Agency for International Development. 1992. Project Paper Preparation. U.S. Democratic Initiatives Project, Kigali, Rwanda. July.

United States Information Agency. 1987. American Partners Lecture Tour. Antananarivo, Madagascar; Kigali, Rwanda; Dar es Salaam, Tanzania; and N'djamena, Chad. February–March.

United States Information Agency. 1990. American Partners Lecture Tour. Bangui, Central African Republic; Kinshasa and Lubumbashi, Zaire; and Kampala, Uganda. May–June.

United States Information Agency. 1992. American Partners Lecture Tour. Cotonou, Benin; and Kaduna, Illorin, Ibadan, Kano, and Lagos, Nigeria. February–March.

United States Information Agency. 1992. American Partners Lecture Tour. Round-table Discussion for Women Journalists on Women in Nigerian Politics. Lagos, Nigeria. March.

United States Information Agency. 1992. "Media Research Memorandum." Washington, D.C. October. Unpublished paper.

Unoma, Ray. 1993. "The Regional African Satellite Communications Project: A Status Report." *Africa Communications* (May–June): 12–13, 17.

Vansina, Jan. 1982. "Mwasi's Trials." *Daedalus* 111: 49–70.

Varis, Tapio. 1985. *Etudes et Documents d'Information.* Reports and Papers on Mass Communication, N. 100. Paris: UNESCO.

Vincent, Theo. 1985. "Television Drama in Nigeria: A Critical Assessment." In *Mass Media Culture and Society in West Africa,* ed. Frank Ugboajah, 100–107. Munich: Hans Zell.

Vittin, Theophile. 1991. "L'Ecoute des radios étrangères en Afrique Noire." *Mondes en développement* (Paris), 19 (73): 45–56.

Wallerstein, Immanuel. 1974. *The Modern World System.* New York: Academic.

Wang, Georgette, and Wimal Dissanayake. 1982. "The Study of Indigenous Communication Systems in Development: Phasing-Out or Phasing In?" *Media Asia* 9 (1): 3–8.

Waterman, Christopher. 1990. *Juju: A Social History and Ethnography of an African Popular Music.* Chicago: University of Chicago Press.

Watremez, Emmanuel. 1992. "The Satirical Press in Francophone Africa." *Index on Censorship* (November): 34–36.

Wauthier, Claude. 1987. "PANA: The Voice of Africa." *Africa Report* (March–April): 65–67.

Weekly Post (Lusaka, Zambia). 1991. 29–30 October.

West, Harvey G., and Jo Ellen Fair. 1993. "Development Communication and Popular Resistance in Africa: An Examination of the Struggle over Tradition and Modernity through Media." *African Studies Review* 36 (1): 91–114.

West Africa. 1994. "Benin: Anti-Corruption Move." (24–30 January): 132.

West Africa. 1994. "Carnage in Rwanda." (18–24 April): 684–85.

West Africa. 1994. "Journalists under Attack." (4–10 April): 601.

West Africa. 1994. "NITEL for Probe." (28 February–6 March): 357.

West Africa. 1994. "TV Station Illegal." (18–24 April): 693.

White-Halbert, Dorinda. 1994. "GAMTEL: The Gambia's Newest Broadcaster?" *Africa Communications* (March–April): 43.

Whorf, Benjamin Lee. 1956. *Language, Thought, and Reality: Selected Writings of Benjamin Lee Whorf,* ed. John B. Carroll. New York: Wiley.

Wilcox, Dennis. 1975. *Mass Media in Black Africa: Philosophy and Control.* New York: Praeger.

Williams, David. 1978. *Malawi: The Politics of Despair.* Ithaca: Cornell University Press.

Wiseman, John. 1991. "Democratic Resurgence in Black Africa." *Contemporary Review* 259 (June): 7–13.

World Bank. 1993. *Global Economic Prospects and the Developing Countries.* Washington, D.C.: World Bank.

Wright, Bonnie. 1989. "The Power of Articulation." In *Creativity of Power: Cosmology and Action in African Societies,* ed. W. Arens and Ivan Karp, 39–59. Washington, D.C.: Smithsonian Institution Press.

Wright, Richard. 1966. *Black Boy.* New York: Harper and Row.

Wunsch, James, Michael Bratton, and Peter Kareithi. 1992. "Democracy and Governance in Zambia: An Assessment and Proposed Strategy." Prepared for USAID/Zambia. Burlington, Vt.: Associates in Rural Development. June. Unpublished paper.

Yahaya, Ibrahim Yaro. 1981. "The Hausa Poet." In *Oral Poetry in Nigeria,* ed. Uchegbulam N. Abalogu, Garba Ashiwaju, and Regina Amadi-Tshiwala, 139–56. Lagos, Nigeria: *Nigeria Magazine*, published in conjunction with UNESCO, Paris.

Yearbook of International Organizations. 1985–86. 2 vols. London: Saur.

Yeboah-Afari, Ajoa. 1988. "Liberating the Airwaves." *West Africa* 11 (July): 1284.

Zambia Daily Mail. 1991. "Chiluba Takes Over." *Zambia Daily Mail* (Lusaka), 3 November, 1.

Index

LOUISE M. BOURGAULT is Professor of Mass Communication at Northern Michigan University, Marquette. She has been involved in media development in Africa for the last twenty years and has worked in fourteen African countries, serving with the United Nations, the USIA, and the United States Agency for International Development. She has published numerous scholarly articles on African mass media and other topics.